D1083996

SAVING THE LIGHT AT CHARTRES

How the Great Cathedral and Its Stained-Glass
Treasures Were Rescued during World War II

VICTOR A. POLLAK

STACKPOLE
BOOKS

Guilford, Connecticut

Published by Stackpole Books
An imprint of The Rowman & Littlefield Publishing Group, Inc.
4501 Forbes Blvd., Ste. 200
Lanham, MD 20706
www.rowman.com

Distributed by NATIONAL BOOK NETWORK
800-462-6420

Maps created by Mary Lee Eggart

British Library Cataloguing in Publication Information available

Library of Congress Cataloging-in-Publication Data available
Names: Pollak, Victor A., 1948– author.
Title: Saving the light at Chartres : how the great cathedral and its
    stained-glass treasures were rescued during World War II / Victor A.
    Pollak.
Description: Guilford, Connecticut : Stackpole Books, [2020] | Includes
    bibliographical references and index. | Summary: "The cathedral at
    Chartres survived World War II thanks to the efforts of French citizens
    and an unrecognized American officer. In a book written in the spirit of
    The Monuments Men, Victor Pollak describes the efforts to save Chartres
    Cathedral"— Provided by publisher.
Identifiers: LCCN 2019038528 (print) | LCCN 2019038529 (ebook) | ISBN
    9780811739016 (cloth) | ISBN 9780811768979 (epub)
Subjects: LCSH: Stained glass windows—France—Chartres. | Cathédrale de
    Chartres. | Art treasures in war—France—Chartres—History—20th
    century. | Cultural property—Protection—France—Chartres—History—20th
    century. | Griffith, Welborn Barton, 1901–1944.
Classification: LCC NK5349.C5 P65 2020 (print) | LCC NK5349.C5 (ebook) |
    DDC 748.50944/51240904—dc23
LC record available at https://lccn.loc.gov/2019038528
LC ebook record available at https://lccn.loc.gov/2019038529

For Elizabeth Russell Pollak

Contents

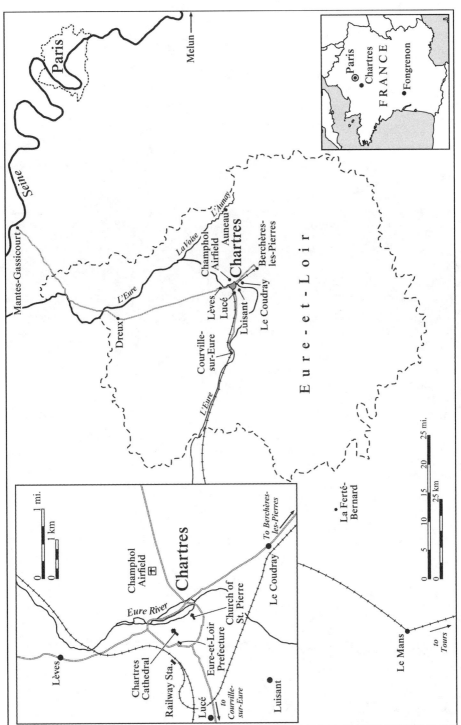

Chartres and Vicinity

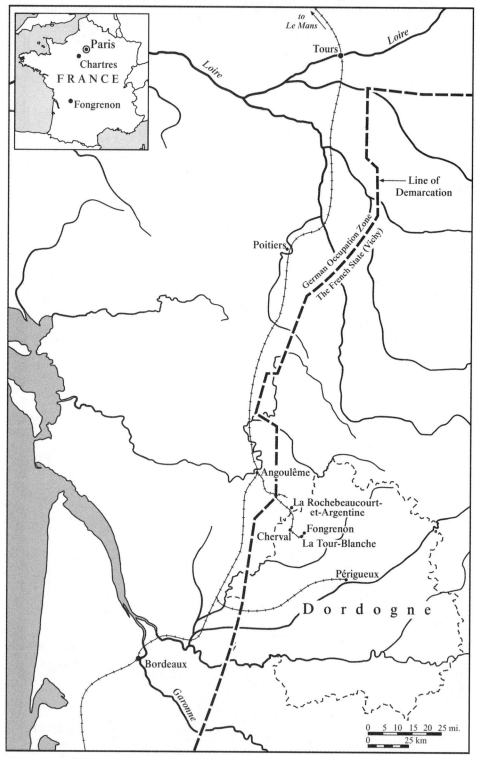

Western Dordogne and Fongrenon Castle (Château de Fongrenon)

PREFACE

In May 2013, my wife and I drove a good portion of the route of what would be that year's Tour de France, its hundredth running, taking a path through a countryside abundant with landmarks of historical significance to the race, to France, and to the world: Nice, Marseilles, Ax 3 Domaines, Saint-Malo, Mont-Saint-Michel, Lyon, Mont Ventoux, Alpe d'Huez, and of course the fabled cobbles of the Champs-Élysées in Paris. There was so much to see in this beautiful country, so many treasures like the Bayeux Tapestry, châteaus and vineyards and mountains and cathedrals—all of them jewels to our eyes—but something in Paris struck me as particularly poignant: I remember standing inside Sainte-Chapelle in Paris, with its medieval stained-glass windows that transformed daylight into lilac. We were bathed in majesty and from this feeling coming to a profound understanding: a cultural monument—a cathedral, a statue, a bicycle race—is a jewel for the world to keep and to cherish for as long as humans live on this earth.

A year later, I was in my living room watching a CNN newscast when crackles of an explosion resounded from my TV. A stone building erupted in the Iraqi desert from a bomb blast deep in the ground, sending a shock wave of black-gray dust and smoke over a dry field. Cannonballs of sandstone fragmented in all directions. The voice-over reporter spoke: "More than three thousand years of history obliterated in seconds. This video was released by ISIS. CNN cannot independently verify its authenticity, but it purports to show the radicals destroying Nimrud, one of the most important archaeological sites in Iraq."

In the video, I saw a bearded youth wielding a sledgehammer and smashing it into a stone wall covered with relief carvings. Pieces fell to the floor. He struck again and shoved it off the wall. It crashed onto the stone floor and scattered fist-sized chunks and dust.

Another man on a ladder swung a hammer and severed a white plaster sculpture from a wall. It was a man's face, flat and round, with prominent forehead, Roman hair, and dark holes for eyes, which looked straight forward, almost smiling. When the blow struck, the eyes looked down despondently, while the face ripped loose and crashed to the ground, breaking into chips and dust.

Again, the voice-over: "These are remnants of the ancient Assyrian civilization. Nimrud used to be its capital. They've stood since the thirteenth-century BC and survived many wars but were destroyed by the militants—probably in less than a day."

ISIS had posted this video within weeks of the destruction.

The following year, in the public square under the ancient Arch of Triumph in Palmyra, in Syria, built in the second millennium BC, ISIS publicly beheaded Khaled al-Asaad, a university professor and Palmyra's general manager for museums. He had spent his life preserving antiquities. "His crime," according to a Syrian official, "was refusing to pledge allegiance to ISIS and refusing . . . to reveal the location of archaeological treasures and two chests of gold" that ISIS thought were in the city.

ISIS claimed that it destroyed the antiquities out of religious duty, but its real motivation was purely financial and hypocritical: "looting archaeological sites to support its thriving illegal trade in antiquities." When I saw the CNN video, a sense of loss and anger welled up inside me. Elise Blackwell wrote, "It is a tragedy when human gifts that have survived across generations are disrespected for any reason short of basic survival. To loot artifacts for spending money—or to allow that to happen—is a violation of history."

Around the same time, I'd also been listening to some lectures about great cathedrals, including Saint-Denis, Notre-Dame de Paris, Reims and Rouen Cathedrals, and Notre-Dame de Chartres. In World War II, the lecturer noted, Chartres' stained-glass windows had been removed and hidden in the countryside to protect them from war damage.

I was amazed. I wondered how a project of such magnitude could be accomplished. I imagined scores of French workers in 1939, under threat of German invasion, working through the night—hoisting cranes, scaffolding, cables, and packing cases from trucks into the cathedral, and then craftsmen dismantling and removing thousands of glass pieces to be packed and transported. Where did they hide them? Who planned the project, and who did the work?

Unconnected in space and loosely connected in time, these three experiences are how this book started.

Over the years, I'd heard of cultural monuments and artworks under attack during World War II. Yet hearing of Chartres in the wake of seeing that ISIS video propelled me to learn more about what's been done in the past to protect cultural treasures. How have people prepared to avoid such destruction and looting?

Chartres' 176 windows are the largest collection of twelfth- and thirteenth-century stained glass in one place on Earth, consisting of twenty-seven thousand square feet of glass. Many individual windows are more than a dozen feet wide and twenty feet tall and have as many as fifty panels. The collection comprises 5,500 panels.

But among the thousands of books written about the nine-hundred-year-old Chartres Cathedral—and the many about its windows—none describes this story of the windows' removal during the war.

What better demonstration of reverence for the distinctly human achievement the windows represent than to dismantle, pack, and transport them to secret locations to protect them? That task, I later learned, had also been accomplished in World War I at Chartres Cathedral, another chapter in the nine-hundred-year story of the windows' survival through religious wars, fires, and revolutions.

I set out to learn enough about stained glass and about Chartres to appreciate the difficulty and risks of the task—not even imagining that much of the work was done as German bombs fell around Chartres and ground forces approached.

During my research, I came across multiple blog references to a career American Army colonel, Welborn Barton Griffith Jr., from rural Quanah in north Texas, who was the headquarters operations officer—the number-three man—in the Twentieth Corps in Patton's Third Army in 1944. Twentieth Corps was one of what one might call the "A Teams" in the Army. Its job was to wait and come ashore at Utah Beach three weeks after D-Day to break out of the beachheads and chase the Germans across France and toward Berlin until ordered elsewhere. And Chartres was its first sizable, challenging battle after the breakout. Scattered German units had been ordered to reassemble and resupply at Chartres to resume the fight—and they did, overseen by virtue of the commanding 360-degree view from the twin four-hundred-foot towers of Chartres Cathedral, over the wheat fields that surrounded Chartres.

Those blog references to Griffith echoed strangely similar language that credited him with having "questioned" an order for Allied forces to shell and destroy the cathedral and having "volunteered" to "go behind enemy lines" to personally inspect the cathedral and determine whether the Germans were using it as an observation post to direct artillery fire on Allied forces. The blogs went on to say that Griffith found that the towers were "not so being used by the Germans . . . and [that he] managed to call off any further Allied firing" on the cathedral.

They said he then headed to the commune of Lèves northeast of Chartres, where he directed a tank "toward enemy forces [that] he had located and [he] was killed in action."

The common source I found for those many blog posts was the Army's 1944 citation that awarded the Distinguished Service Cross to Griffith posthumously. What it didn't mention was that Griffith had chosen to ride outside on the rear of the tank. He was killed by intense enemy machine-gun, rifle, and rocket-launcher fire, his body to be found that afternoon on the street by villagers with his empty rifle in one hand and empty pistol in the other. The next day the corps retrieved his body and buried him in a simple funeral in a nearby field.

To this day, the French honor Griffith annually in Chartres and in Lèves as the man who saved the cathedral. Yet nothing centered around his story has been published.

So the story of Chartres Cathedral and its windows and the story of Colonel Griffith are separate but intertwined narratives.

I have set out to explore the colonel's background and role in the corps to understand his motivations. It seems that simply calling him a hero is inadequate. But the further I've dug, the more questions have arisen.

My challenge has been not just to seek the truth but also to spot where truth can't be determined. During my work on this book, I have traveled several times to Paris and in 2015 twice to Chartres, and I have twice visited the cathedral, searched archives, retrieved project documents and more from Chartres and Paris, and visited Colonel Griffith's hometown, Quanah, Texas, and have been astounded by what I have found. I've interviewed Griffith's daughter in Florida and his nephew—a retired US Army lieutenant general—and also Eugene G. Schulz, a surviving GI in Milwaukee who worked as Griff's clerk-typist during the war for more than a year up to the time Griff died, and I've corresponded with two other of Griff's grandnephews and the surviving husband of one of his nieces, who provided me with family photos, letters, and other documents; I've also reconstructed Griff's military career, his Army personnel file having been destroyed in a fire at the National Archives in Saint Louis in the 1970s. From those interviews, Army combat records, and an unpublished diary written by a Father Douin—a French priest who, to his surprise, encountered Griff as Griff was inspecting the cathedral during the battle—I have uncovered more questions.

Despite all my research, there are times when I've had to use my imagination to depict aspects of both stories.

Why had Griffith left his desk to take up a frontline combat role for the first time? Why had he gone to the cathedral himself rather than order military intelligence to do so? Why had he assumed command of the tank column? And why had he exposed himself to danger by riding on the back of the tank? He seems to have been driven by something. Unanswerable questions leave ambiguity and mystery in his story.

He was consumed by a personal drive to take command—not just to lead but also to exercise his full talents, and for a once-in-a-lifetime purpose. He had a clear path for promotion to the rank of general within a month; yet, by risking his life, perhaps he needlessly chose not to take it. He was a fierce competitor, respected and valued by his superiors, revered by his peers and subordinates. He wanted something, and he discovered something big was at stake. His daughter described him as "very serious" and told me he would have been annoyed to be called a hero.

I've spent several years trying to know and understand Griffith. While his saving of the cathedral was honorable, he was not a saint. In author Tilar Mazzeo's words, making him a saint in the telling of his story would "dishonor . . . the true complexity and difficulty of [his] very human choices." Like most of us, he was flawed and conflicted.

Did Griffith have a public purpose, or was he driven by private vanity or ambition?

I have come to appreciate that it is important to save historic monuments. It is important because monuments are our means to symbolize ancestors, civilizations, and ideas that teach many of us who we are, the foundation whence we have come.

Forces of the universe have conjoined—by natural selection or higher power—to create the human mind, heart, and emotions. Humans have capacity to be aware—of themselves, other humans, other life forms, and surroundings. We can think and feel emotion, and we discern joy and have capacity to harness emotions into campaigns larger than ourselves.

Churches are venues in which individuals' core life events occur, through which they garner memories. For entire parishes, communities, and nations, churches host rituals that spawn similar remembrances on a communal scale.

Historic French cathedrals reveal art and history apart from religion. As buildings owned by the state, they represent the nation's patrimony, symbolizing France's political essence.

We must save monuments because without them evildoers can distort and fabricate, and impose savagery. Nazis destroyed monuments in conquered countries to eliminate symbols of culture, like Poland's statues of Chopin. ISIS and others do so today.

Chartres Cathedral has meaning to millions. Hundreds of thousands depend on it as their vessel for negotiating life's passages, and the French economy has depended every year on money from millions of visitors and pilgrims.

The tale of the World War II rescue of the Chartres windows has its roots in the French Revolution, which decimated many cathedrals. As a result, Chartres Cathedral—like most others in France—became a state-owned historic monument. The French have since developed leading methods for protection of monuments, which were invented because they had to be. The modern phase of this tale began in World War I, with the theretofore-unthinkable 1914 German artillery bombardment of the city of Reims and its cathedral (France's Westminster Abbey). The attack destroyed Reims Cathedral and most of its stained-glass windows. Then, as the war dragged on, a string of deadly accidental explosions surrounding Paris led at long last to the first precarious protective actions at Chartres.

During the war, General Eisenhower declared that historic monuments symbolize to the world all we are fighting for and ordered that when destruction is unnecessary and can't be justified, commanders must preserve them through exercise of restraint and discipline.

Apart from Griffith's story, the story of the rescue of the Chartres windows revolves around four central characters, two of whom—Jean Zay and Jean Moulin—are among the most famous of French Resistance martyrs. The others are compelling in other ways.

But without volunteer assistance and financing that was provided by local Chartres citizens—and, probably also, the last-minute strains and sweat and grit of refugee volunteer workers—the windows wouldn't have been saved from danger and later would have been destroyed during the battles.

At Chartres, ordinary people took responsibility for saving these symbols. A group of dedicated men and women felt compelled to protect their cathedral. Most were French. Griffith was an American whom we remember for choosing to join their cause during battle and by risking his life to prevent needless destruction, and in the process perhaps he learned who he was. Griff's bravery saved the cathedral, and his drive to press his column forward through Lèves contributed to the corps' success in cutting off the enemy at the Seine and liberating Paris—even allowing for the day they stopped the war to bury him.

As I was completing this book, the April 2019 fire at Notre-Dame de Paris erupted. Frightening video reminded the world that even elaborate precautions don't relieve us of the need to vigilantly gauge how historic monuments would hold up against all perils. Notre-Dame de Paris is the preeminent cultural and religious landmark—the romantic symbol—of France, the landmark against which all others in France are compared. Professor Peter Sahlins, who grew up near Paris, describes it as "the focal point of Parisian life in ways that surpass religion." The 2019 tragedy at the Paris cathedral suddenly shined the spotlight of relevance on this story of how Chartres Cathedral and its windows were rescued during World War II.

Prologue—Reims, a Burning Symbol of Hope for Preservationists

On September 4, 1914, after he had finished his monthly First Friday Mass at the cathedral, Monseigneur Maurice Landrieux—archpriest of Reims for the previous two years and a cardinal for twenty-five before that—was walking near the cathedral. He was tall, with broad shoulders and a round face with a large forehead and dark hair, and his generous smile revealed strength and invited confidence. Most Reims citizens were outdoors that morning, because the fighting had ceased—for the moment. Landrieux would have seen and greeted locals—a shopkeeper minding his store, a nun heading to her convent, a civil servant nearing city hall, a child holding her mother's hand.

This was barely twenty days since the German armies had thrust into France at the start of World War I, and the French, in retreat, had declared their northeastern city of Reims an open city. Its hundred thousand residents expected the invading Germans to simply march in to occupy the city, and this had come to pass: an advance German Saxon Guard unit had arrived at Reims's gates and taken city hall for the night, while French forces had continued their retreat southwest of the city. The Germans' next moves, however, were not what the citizenry expected.

Normally Landrieux's walk around town helped him maintain pastoral contact with the citizens, but now it served a more complex purpose: to observe the Germans and assess their intentions. The city's crown jewel was its cathedral, the largest in France, which could seat three thousand for Mass, with another thousand standing. Germans entering the city were assembling around the cathedral and the nearby city hall to collect orders from commanders. A line of German cars and caissons clamored into the cobblestone courtyards and plazas, followed by horsemen, infantry, and artillery. The masses of men and equipment rattled, screeched, and yelled, but their ruckus was generally peaceful. The prevailing concerns of the townspeople, Landrieux knew, were how soon and how adamantly German command would force the people to accept officers for billeting in their homes and how severe the German requisitions would be for food and supplies.

Landrieux heard a strange detonation. Then he heard a second and a third. At first, he was not greatly concerned about the explosion, thinking the Germans were blowing up bridges or celebrating the anniversary of their victory in the last war. But as he walked a few blocks east of the cathedral, the distant whistling sounds and booming in the air startled him when a shell splinter fell at his feet. He knew then what it meant: the Germans were bombarding the city.

He headed back to the cathedral. On the way, ten shells whistled over his head. He arrived to see the west side of the cathedral covered in a cloud of smoke and dust and could barely make out the outline of the Palace of Justice adjacent to the cathedral on the north side. Explosions continued near the cathedral's entrance and surrounding houses. Stone trim under a cathedral porch fell from the coping. He circled the cathedral, finding his assistant, Abbé Andrieux, with a church employee, Mr. Huilleret, taking refuge in the clock tower staircase.

Mr. Rouné, a civil defenseman, ran up to the cathedral, carrying from city hall a bed sheet nailed to a Turk's head broom. He and Andrieux climbed the cathedral's north tower, raised the top stairway door off its axis to get to the top, and flaunted the sheet as a flag in the brisk wind. But the cannonade stormed on. Dust rose to the roof. They heard the echoes of glass from the cathedral's windows crashing onto the floors of the naves. Jets of smoke and dust in the town marked places hit by shells, including several houses. Fires broke out in the surrounding quarter.

It was not only Landrieux and his fellow citizens of Reims who were astonished by the bombardment. Two German officers couldn't believe they were being bombarded by their own guns. So they sent a car with two German soldiers and a city employee in the direction of the firing to get it to stop. Those soldiers found that batteries of a different German unit—the Imperial German Army, Prussian guards—not the Saxon

Guard, were firing from Les Mesneux, more than four miles southwest of Reims. The Prussians claimed that they hadn't known the Saxon Guard was in the city and that the shelling was a mistake.

By 10:30 that morning, another churchman joined Landrieux to inspect for damage. He was forty-year-old Abbé Rémi Thinot, master of the chapel. The cathedral seemed to tremble, and its structure magnified the intensity of the explosion like the shell of a mammoth bass viol. They found no points of explosion inside but did locate damage to cathedral sculptures outside. A shell had hit the street on the north side, gouging a ditch that had filled with water by the time they'd reached it. Landrieux dipped his hand in the water to find it still warm from hot metal fragments. Splinters had splashed across the high arches of the buttresses. A shell had hit the cathedral at the north crossbar of the transept and dislodged large masonry. In the clock tower staircase, a violent gust of air pushed Abbé Andrieux and his companions to their knees.

Even if the Germans had tried to miss the cathedral on September 4, their intention changed within a week. The next day, the Germans requisitioned from the town tons of meat, vegetables, bread, oats, petrol, straw, and hay. German soldiers bivouacked all over the city, including in front of the cathedral, surrounding its bronze statue of Joan of Arc, on her horse, holding her bent sword high. Soldiers and horse-drawn carts squatted in the square, horses whinnied and clopped, farriers' hammers clanked, and everything smelled of horse manure, petrol, and grease. In this scene, the chortling German soldiers surrounded fires and gobbled sausages, black bread, and wine.

Abbé Landrieux and his fellow priests felt hurt to see their Joan of Arc standing there lonely, lost in the middle of the German bivouac, surrounded by Prussians, as if she were their prisoner. German commands spread around the city to force—under threat—the billeting of German officers in commandeered homes, where they appropriated families' food, water, and wine and displaced them from their beds.

A week later, Landrieux learned that the Germans would be putting all their wounded into the cathedral. He went to headquarters to ask for reconsideration. Weren't there other places for better quartering where the wounded German soldiers could be assisted? But on arrival he sensed quickly that there was electricity in the air. German senior officers were distracted and edgy, flustered, talking abruptly. Soldiers with fixed bayonets scurried about and fenced in automobiles that brought to the German commander the mayor, the secretary-general of the city, the deputy mayor, and the president of the chamber of commerce. The Germans were assembling one hundred French hostages. By order of the German commander in chief, the mayor posted his proclamation that the hostages would be hung and that the town would be burned, partially or totally, and its inhabitants hung on any attempt at disorder. To choose the hostages, the Germans ordered the city leaders to present themselves and name other prominent citizens.

That evening, word circulated of signs that the Germans were ordering their men to evacuate the town, with fighting in progress around Reims. Late in the day, workers, under German orders, brought fifteen thousand bundles of straw into the cathedral to cover the floors in the three naves. The clatter of workers and soldiers removing hundreds of wooden chairs, and piling them in heaps in the choir and sanctuary, resounded through the great space. But that evening, before the Saxons could put their wounded in the cathedral, all German soldiers evacuated the town. The French Army had arrived eighteen miles west of Reims while convoys of Germans filled the road southwest to Vitry-sur-Seine, drawing the French hostages with them.

A citizen the next day brought a large Red Cross flag to the cathedral's north tower and hoisted it next to the white flag the Germans had left. When the French troops entered the city, they replaced the white flag with a French Tricolor. And the Red Cross flag, although in shreds, remained and was soon replaced with a larger one that had been pieced together by locals from a clergyman's vestment and a rose cassock. But it also was quickly ruined by the wind.

Landrieux tried, starting on the fifteenth, to get the straw removed from the cathedral. The work finally began the next day, but the French military quickly issued an order to stop. French commanders had heard a report that a German senior officer had let slip a comment "expressing pity for the coming disaster." From that, the French commanders suspected the Germans of planning some new attack and determined, as a deterrent, to add more German prisoners to the wounded Germans who were already in the cathedral.

The next afternoon, French military moved a dozen wounded Germans from the hospital into the cathedral on stretchers and open carriages, followed by more of the same the next day. The military carried out those transfers very conspicuously, in Landrieux's view, to be sure the Germans' spies—who lurked in Reims—would see the movements, in the hope that they would report to German command and deter any plans to create a "disaster."

There were no doctors available in the cathedral for patients—only a chaplain, a deaconess, and a couple of nuns. More than a hundred wounded men lay on the floor of the nave with only blankets, accompanied by a German major, himself bandaged, wounded in the head. French soldiers guarded the doors.

On the eighteenth, with Mass under way, a shell crashed through a window of the archbishop's palace adjoining the cathedral, penetrating interior stone, killing three men, and wounding fifteen. Repeated explosions hit the roofs and buttresses. Landrieux saw the wounded men lying in the cathedral panicking, believing themselves lost, mad with fright, not knowing where to find cover. Those who could not move groaned, begged, and cried.

Landrieux arranged for the wounded to be bundled into the clock tower staircase, which seemed to him safest in view of the direction of the firing. Those who could move, moved together. The others drew themselves to the staircase, bucking and jerking, hauling on all fours, wound coverings as their boots. Those whose legs had been amputated, shifted ahead with their stumps. The priests helped the disabled, dragging those unable to move by themselves, and though the wounded were barely clothed, the priests sat them down on the naked stone stairs. Five German officers among the wounded called out that they were under no illusion: they were convinced that fellow German units were aiming at the cathedral. Landrieux and his helpers had to repeat the process of moving the wounded a second time that evening and again the next morning.

Most shells fell in the neighborhood of city hall and the military barracks. Others fell throughout the town. Three struck the cathedral.

Landrieux had just left the cathedral by foot to visit the stricken hospital when a shell fell behind him. He retraced his steps in the smoke and found a man bleeding, stretched out on the steps, gashed in the stomach. Soldiers carried the man into the church, where the wounded German major could assess his injuries. By evening, the wounded man was taken to the hospital, nearly dead. Some wounded had been reinjured by falling stones or by pieces of lead severed from windows. Their heads bled. Landrieux and Abbé Schemberg gave last rights to those who were Catholic. A wave of sunshine through the windows lit the carnage and suffering. The wounded lay on piles of straw, in all stages of suffering. Their bluish-gray uniforms contrasted with the black of the attending priests' robes. In the background on the steps outside, French soldiers in their red uniform trousers stood by.

The wounded German major begged Landrieux to send an emissary to the German front to tell them they were shooting at their own soldiers. But the major acknowledged that they probably already knew it and that it was the cathedral they were trying to hit, even at the cost of killing their own soldiers. How could this be a strategy? Wasn't it unthinkable for civilized commanders to order such a thing?

When explosions hit, the cathedral's pillars quavered. Landrieux and his colleagues heard the thunderbolt and thud of jolts pummeling the naves, the blows absorbed by the resilience of the arches' vaults. At one point, the noise of falling stones thundered so loudly that Landrieux and his companions thought the apse was collapsing. He ran outside to see. A flying buttress of the first retaining wall had broken and fallen through the roof of the lady chapel, its remaining lower section pointing toward the sky. Stone chunks littered next to a crack in the roof, exposing timbers, broken masonry still moving through. The remaining rubble perched nearby, threatening further collapse.

During Mass on the next morning, the nineteenth, the bombardment began again. Landrieux told the altar boy assisting him, "Leave me. Go. Get into shelter." But the boy said, "I would rather remain," and stayed until the conclusion. The bombardment lasted throughout the day. During a lull, some of the staff ran across the plaza to the archbishop's palace to get bread for the wounded, who were moved again to the tower. At two o'clock,

Landrieux and the other priests entered the chapel to pray. The a cappella lament of their chants conjured withdrawal, sadness, and serenity as backdrop to the brutal clash and concussions of the attack's striking shells.

That's when the fire started. At about three o'clock word spread that smoke was coming from the scaffolding of the north tower. They rushed outside to see. Landrieux and Abbé Thinot huddled outside the west portal, searching to spot whether an incendiary shell had hit. To Landrieux, there was no doubt: Massive scaffolding of heavy lumber—which had been in place for a year of repairs, covering the north half of the west facade—had now been hit. The shell had lashed through the wooden scaffolding half way up the north tower, erupting in a flash fire. The two men ran down the steps, flinching, and were cowering away from the portal when the cathedral's forty-foot round stained-glass rose window burst from the fire's heat, showering sparks into the cathedral's interior.

With that, the straw beds ignited. Fires flared in the wooden roof. Lead sheets that covered the roof's oak frame boiled, scattering a fine rain of molten lead inside the cathedral. On the exterior, streams of the molten lead ran under vaults and out the mouths of stone gargoyles that had overseen the church for centuries. Firefighters struggled in vain to contain the fires. The nearest fire station—now empty—had been destroyed by bombing, its firemen struggling to deal with other fires in the Wool Quarter of town. Overwhelmed rescue services anguished over their incapacity to help.

Water pipes burst. Winds drove the flames up the staircase of the north tower, whose draft fanned the inferno surrounding the scaffolding as the fire consumed the carpentry of the cathedral's superstructure and destroyed the archbishop's palace. The combustibles that had been left throughout the cathedral, including the straw in the nave and chairs in the choir, fueled the flames. All ignited, including the wood columns that framed the main door.

Landrieux and Thinot, hoping they could help, tried to climb the scaffold. Above them, four cylindrical fires swirled, blazing one above another in stages. The two abbés tried with their arms to dismember the dense girders but could not, their calls for help drowned out by the roar of shell explosions convulsing the town.

The two men retreated, in the hope that the wooden scaffolding not supporting the building would burn, fall away, and leave the building standing. They tried, with the help of prisoners, to gather and cast the straw out clear of the building into the terrace. But outside, the fire was intensifying and eventually reached the facade. As they felt the fire approach, red tints appeared in the light, as if permeated with blood, which flushed the windows at the entrance. And with a loud cracking report, the scaffolding broke and crashed to the surface of the Place du Parvis plaza in front of the west facade.

Landrieux and the other priests collected the wounded beneath the organ and also in the apse. Those who could, dragged themselves. Others, who were ill or missing limbs, were hauled on stretchers.

The flames devoured the apse, scaled up the steeple, and spread over the roofs. The flames' tentacles stroked the lead plates of the roof as if with hot tongues, melting the scales away, little by little, and revealed the raw enormous cluster of woodwork whose frame stood out, across the entwined arcades above the vaults, like a colossal bony structure of fire. Streamlets of lead ran in the grooves as through conduits and discharged through the gargoyles, dribbling down as if tears and then spreading on the floors and flying back in granular fragments as dust, with fiery particles passing through the air encircling in the airborne soot.

When the priests realized that the woodwork of the roof was aflame and would be lost, they turned to save the pieces of the Sacrament at the altar and then the gold and silver altarpieces, and other medieval relics stored in the sacristy as the cathedral's treasure. Landrieux and Thinot, joined by Abbé Andrieux and one Mr. Divoir, forced open the doors of the cupboards and ran outside to find hands to help. Several workmen responded, helping to move the treasure. The molten lead splashed and mixed with sparks flying all around, in the smoke, lit by the flames. The sparks pricked on their faces and hands as the priests and helpers traversed the courtyard carrying their pieces of treasure.

All told, the time that passed between the priests' ascent into the scaffolding and the moment when the fire died out was about an hour. The cathedral burned at both ends, though the middle was still intact. Landrieux eventually concluded that it wasn't the scaffolding that had set fire to the roofs: it was a shell falling on the apse and then two other shells hitting the roof of the central nave. Four distinct fires had consumed the cathedral.

And if the fire had not been catastrophe enough, after carrying the treasures, Abbé Landrieux saw a small group of French soldiers in their red uniform trousers lined up, kneeling, their rifles raised, facing the cathedral entrance. At first, he didn't realize what was happening. But when the door opened, he saw the wounded assembled in the lobby, not being allowed to come out, as the fire roared behind them. They stood frozen, staring into the rifles.

Landrieux confronted the sergeant, yelling, "Wretched man, what are you going to do?"

"We have our orders."

"It is impossible," Landrieux said. "There is a mistake. What has now occurred was not foreseen. They must come out. You will not fire upon unarmed wounded men, even if they are Germans! On the battlefield it is war, but here it would be a crime."

"We are obliged to do it. Those are our orders."

So Landrieux placed himself in front of the door and yelled, "Very well; you will commence with me!"

After a pause—as an opening—Landrieux assured the French soldiers that none of the German prisoners would try to escape; he and the other priests would escort the wounded to city hall and hand them over to the military. The prisoners, through an interpreter, agreed and followed in a procession, those who needed supports using brooms, sticks, and boards as crutches, others being carried on stretchers.

The wounded prisoners and priests confronted a hostile crowd of townspeople, who surged forward, bringing the procession to a standstill. Fearing the crowd and seeing a French military captain with a squad riding by, Landrieux called to the captain to intervene. The captain warned Landrieux that the crowd, growing in anger, would never let the wounded prisoners and priests reach city hall and that the abbé, therefore, should give up his futile quest. Landrieux and his flock pressed forward, hesitated, resumed, and then halted. Crucial minutes passed, the two groups at an impasse.

The captain spotted a nearby factory. He ordered his squad to use their mounts to separate the crowd and Landrieux's column, forcing all parties to freeze in place. The captain ran to the factory, appealed to its proprietor to open his manufactory doors, and, having been satisfactorily persuasive, before his horsemen had to resort to force, shuffled the German prisoners to safety. On the night of the nineteenth and twentieth, stretcher-bearers and soldiers transferred the 124 wounded to ambulances for evacuation by rail to a safe zone.

Despite the menace of that mob, most of the townspeople of Reims had made no trouble: they either had run to escape the German approach on the city or had been hiding in their homes.

That evening a French pilot, a Commandant Capitrel, flew over Reims while returning to his base and reported seeing the burning glow of the cathedral: It was a silent, glowing furnace, without flames or smoke. Its contours, outlined by the cathedral's nave and the transept, stretched over the city as though a giant blazing cross—the Cross of the Redemption. It was as if disaster had stretched out beneath the heavens and forged itself into a symbol of hope.

The giant cross formed by the cathedral fire had awakened the world to the new dangers posed by modern warfare and eventually—but only after subsequent disasters—played a part in stirring to action the government powers charged with protecting historic monuments in France.

Cathedrals are, in Malcolm Miller's words, "embassies," noting that in medieval times bishops were thought of as "celestial ambassadors." Churches are vehicles of culture and evangelization. Each such building, for its congregants, is the locus of intimate remembrances. France's great cathedrals have served as venues, pantheons for national solemnities, for coronations and royal marriages and burials, and many cathedrals—such as Notre-Dame de Reims, the Basilica of Saint-Denis, Notre-Dame de Paris, and Notre-Dame de Chartres—have been assets of economic necessity, in need of civil defense.

Before 1914, it had been unthinkable that any army would intentionally target a cathedral, let alone one of France's great cathedrals like Reims. And yet Reims Cathedral was hit by seventeen shells in the weeks following that first bombardment. For four years, with only brief respites,

Reims was besieged by German guns, which sometimes fired for a few hours, sometimes all day long, at the rate of one shell every three minutes, and again at night.

After that initial week of attacks, Abbés Landrieux and Thinot carried on ministering to the faithful of Reims. In this "total war" that the French were suddenly facing, the German shelling of Reims Cathedral would, in the end, account for some of the greatest damage the war would inflict. The Germans did not loosen their grip on Reims until October 1918, after 857 days of bombardment. During that time, life around the city was a terrifying disaster: Over three hundred people were hit directly by shells, and portions of the city were largely abandoned. But a remarkable number of townspeople remained, in hiding. More than five thousand people were killed in the bombardments and resulting fires. The German justification for shelling the cathedral was that the French were somehow using it for military purposes—as an observation tower to aim French artillery. The French denied it. There was no evidence to support the German allegation.

The day before the first shells would be fired on Reims, on September 3, 1914, the French government had evacuated tapestries and artworks from the town and other locations as part of a southward convoy. But the stained-glass windows had not been removed. The Historic Monuments Department began taking defensive measures (beyond evacuation of nonfixture artworks) at the cathedral only in 1915— many months after the outbreak of war—even as the bombardment continued. The measures included removal of statues and installation of sandbags and supports. Most stained-glass windows had by then been destroyed, but some had survived. But the authorities feared that construction of scaffolding in the cathedral might give the Germans the false impression that the cathedral was being used for military observation, furnishing the Germans with an excuse for further bombardment, and so remedial work on the windows was postponed.

At that point in the war, much of the population of Reims had remained in the city, and they stayed on for another year still, continuing their lives and work, adapting themselves courageously to the trying and dangerous circumstances. But in April 1917, the shelling resumed, eventually rising to a level previously unimagined, which included a stretch of four days punctuated with seven-hour periods in which German barrages struck at five-minute intervals. For quite some time after this, any further work on proactive preservation of historic monuments and stained glass was subordinated to more pressing matters.

What else would it take for the authorities to protect the French cathedrals and their stained-glass windows from war damage?

PART I

WORLD WAR I

Chapter One

Chartres Cathedral and Its Windows

In early 2015, I visited Chartres Cathedral on back-to-back days with my wife. We walked up the hill from the train station toward the sanctuary in the center of the old city. The curved cobblestone streets leading to the cathedral were lined with two- and three-story stucco buildings, and near the top, an ancient wall enclosed the church and its school, seminary, and archbishop's palace. The twin spires stood watch.

Construction had begun in the early twelfth century to build a cathedral over the Romanesque church on the site that dated to the fourth century. For those who built it, the work was in effect an act of penitence, for them to feel assured of the forgiveness of their sins. The privilege to participate was granted only to those who were willing to forgive enemies. Any man who carried bitterness in his heart was deprived of the right.

At the west entrance, we entered through the lower-right quadrant of an aged wooden door, as tall as a giraffe. A frieze above displayed weathered stone sculptures that recalled the death and resurrection of Jesus, and over our door a carved image of infant Jesus on Mary's lap professed the cathedral's dedication to her, like the more than 180 other images of her that dress the building inside and out.

The dim light surprised us. Scaffolding draped with curtains extended along the sides of the nave and transept and reached up high from the floor to cover most of the windows. We could hear chiseling and scraping coming from behind the curtains. A sign announced that the stained glass was being restored as part of an EU–funded project. We could see only the low windows on the sides of the ambulatory and those forming a crown high above the altar at the far east end of the building.

My disappointment that so many windows were covered soon faded as an insight came to me: the sounds of the workmen and the covered scaffolding reminded me of how the windows had been removed in both world wars. I wondered what it must have been like for teams of workmen to be dismantling the windows and packing and hauling them in wartime inside the expanse of the cathedral. Now I could hear, in the clanking of tools and the voices of workmen hidden from sight, how it might have been done.

In the vast interior space—almost eight stories tall—lancet-shaped stained-glass windows occupied most of the ascending stone walls. The paramount purpose of the walls was not to support the roof but to feature—to extol—the great windows. Most were more than three stories tall. When the windows are uncovered, one's eyes follow their two parallel rows wrapping around the building from west to east, circumventing the apse and returning to the west facade, where the great western rose window is poised over its three large lancet windows. In the center of each end of the transept, north and south, a rose window stands above its own set of five smaller lancets.

On a normal sunny day, with no scaffolding, a visitor who enters the cathedral is greeted by an ocean of light that changes during the day with the movement of the sun. Early in the morning, the visitor seems to be gaining access to the interior of a huge ship, with the high band of lancet windows glistening like a ship's sails in sunlight. The light that strikes the high windows on the east end above the altar is so bright that it becomes saturated with colors, bleaching into a white brighter than the human eye can process. Then, as the visitor's eyes pass to each successive window, the saturation subsides and the rich colors of the glass capture the light like a bright parasail aloft into the great space illuminating the sanctuary, first in a wash of transfiguring color and then moderating for the human eye to focus on the images of the windows' story panels, which portray ancient tales and depict medieval benefactors who paid for the windows and artisans who forged the windows from sand and iron.

Almost a millennium ago, the windows taught vital lessons to masses of illiterate congregants eager to learn. To be in this place on a sunny day was like standing inside a jewel as it rotates through the day, the light evolving and transforming as it transits the sky, each movement altering light patterns reflecting off of surfaces inside the sanctuary, the movement and color changes continuously reinventing the experience every few minutes, dawn to dusk.

The cathedral's wonders did not begin with the windows. Its location, on the hilltop with subterranean grottoes where Chartres now stands, was once the site of a sacred forest, a patch of holy ground where—according to mystics—powerful currents come out of the earth, and the cathedral itself has been a fountain of innovation in building, sculpture, window making, and other fields. The cathedral school at Chartres, which was founded in the twelfth century, has served as a European center of learning.

The cathedral also represents the evolution of high Gothic art, containing not only the windows but also around four thousand sculptures, whose faces show a new stage in Western culture. Rodin called it the "Acropolis of France." The cathedral is the best preserved of all Europe's Gothic cathedrals. Most of its sculptures are intact. The Royal Portal illustrates twelfth-century technical innovation of the column statue, combining support and decoration in a single stone block.

The cathedral for centuries has held precious relics that have brought a stream of pilgrims and money to Chartres.

The cathedral's groundbreaking innovations included side doors in its transept, features created to display the array of windows to project light in a new way, higher vaults to provide more room for stained glass, and among the earliest flying buttresses for the same purpose. And its two towers, of different heights and differing architectural styles, illustrate an older symbolism, the dimensions of the taller tower relating to the solar calendar and those of the shorter to the lunar cycle. Their sun-moon and masculine-feminine symbolism echoes pagan traditions.

And the windows themselves tell thousands of stories. Malcolm Miller likens this cathedral to a modern public library. He said, "Its texts are written in the stained glass and sculpture of the 12th and 13th centuries. Printing had not yet been invented; paper did not exist in Europe. Most of the population could not read or write, but people knew how to 'read' a window. The lives of the saints were well known, and the educated could understand the more complex symbolic interpretations of the biblical texts."

The windows' colors are uniquely intense, especially the blue. The light pouring through the windows casts reflections in moving patterns throughout the day over the limestone walls, the floor, and the columns inside the cathedral. The blue, made eight hundred years ago, is said to no longer be replicable today. Even the purest and brightest natural colors, such as the madder-root orange, are actually blends of many colors, such as yellow, blue, red, and white. They can be distinguished under a microscope. By contrast, chemical colors often consist of only a single color.

The glass, although it appears flat, is not. Its uneven surface and impurities mixed with its coloring elements (gold for pure red, cobalt for blue, and manganese for purple) cause the glass to shimmer. These impurities highlight that in striving for perfection, imperfection, accident, and vulnerability play a vital role. The itinerant glassmakers lived close to forests, where they obtained their supplies of wood, resulting in the bumpy glass, full of bits of leaves and dust motes.

In all, the light at Chartres has special significance. Joan Gould describes it as inner space and outer light, not light in the twentieth-century sense showing us a view, but "light for its own sake, sent through windows that filter the colorless air of day and make the rainbow inside it visible to our eyes."

I imagined a Sunday in late August 1939, when the cathedral and its priceless windows faced the peril of a threatened new German invasion. I could feel the history surrounding me. In the glow of candles and lingering scent of burnt incense, I imagined hearing shuffling feet of generations of congregants who'd passed through its portals for christenings, confirmations, marriages, funerals, and more and the thousands of craftsmen who'd devoted years to constructing this monument and the hundreds of artists who'd forged and fashioned and painted the windows. And now on this imagined August Sunday in 1939, war would threaten

Chartres again—just as war had in 1918. Even a single bomb hitting any nearby site would obliterate the stained glass.

My wife and I strolled down one of the pair of ambulatories to the other end of the structure and back through the opposite passageway. In the limited light that filtered through the remaining stained glass, we smelled the incense and heard indistinct voices of priests and visitors faintly echoing through the building, and I felt the cool air on my face and the underlying peace of the ancient space.

We descended a flight of worn stone steps but were blocked by a locked heavy iron gate through which we peered down to the crypt through a long dark passageway with its stone floor, rubbed smooth by centuries of passing feet, and the long, low, barrel-vault ceiling.

We returned to the nave and bought our tickets to climb the 195 spiral steps of the north tower. As we climbed, I imagined Colonel Griffith must have seen and felt the same as he inched his way up slowly, his weapon aimed up, step by step, fearing German soldiers were hiding up there, ready to fire. We emerged onto the tower's sunbathed balustrade, its dominant view before us. As we lingered at the top to drink in the sights, I ran my hand along the rough, cool vertical granite exterior and across the horizontal stone surface of the balcony banister, and then I reached up to touch one of the ancient stone gargoyles that overlooked the cathedral and the city and countryside below.

We took a few photos and then descended the same spiral stairwell. With each step down, I touched the surrounding stone wall, and I peered out through the series of small leaded tower windows that lined the stairwell to see the green copper roofs and plaza below. I imagined that these were the same things the colonel must have seen and touched and the sounds he listened for as he climbed down and tasted his relief from the fear he must have felt in his throat as he risked his life to save this monument.

CHAPTER TWO

Groceries: Quanah, Texas, 1914–1918

ONE SEPTEMBER MORNING IN 1914, NOT LONG AFTER LABOR DAY, Welborn Barton Griffith Jr.—Web to his fellow sixth graders—walked toward the two-story Old Reagan School near the center of Quanah, Texas. Up the street, a railroad engine waiting at the depot hissed steam, and horses clopped down the road pulling wagonloads of ranch supplies.

It had been less than a month since war had erupted in Europe. Just that morning the *Dallas Morning News* had reported that the French Army—with aid from six hundred taxi cabs helping move troops to the front—had counterattacked thirty miles northeast of Paris and forced a German retreat sixty miles to the Aisne River. But the young boy, not yet thirteen, had his mind on more local concerns.

Web's schoolmates jabbered about the previous weekend's family picnics, swimming at Lake Pauline, Lake Copper Breaks, or old Gyp Rock, and getting a chance to help their dads in the harvest and ride in the cattle drive. As they walked up the school steps, they were greeted by their teachers—Web's aunt Ella Smith among them—who hoped a cheerful welcome would distract their charges' thoughts from the war, which was already affecting Texas ranchers and its cotton and wheat farmers. The war represented change, something all too familiar to folks in Quanah.

Quanah had sprouted up as a railroad town in the north Texas prairie and marsh country below the Red River, east of what would become the Dust Bowl, where the Oklahoma panhandle joins the pan. Quanah's 1,500 inhabitants voted it the county seat in 1890, when windblown native grasses, prickly pears, and scattered mesquite trees were the area's primary vegetation. Web's parents, Welborn and Lula, were originally from outside of Temple, where Welborn had sold groceries wholesale for W. A. Harkey, and had started their life together some 130-odd miles north of their hometown, in Dallas, where Welborn then sold groceries at the store of a friend, James Wilson. After a time, Welborn acquired a farm to the east, near Cobb Switch in Kaufman County, but he sold it a year later because Lula preferred living in town.

The Welborn Griffiths moved to Quanah in 1909 with Web and his two little brothers, Philip and Lawrence. There Welborn's brother Fuller—who went by F. O.—owned a grocery he'd bought out from and operated with two brothers. Upon arriving in town, Welborn worked for F. O. for a year and then bought in as partner at F. O. Griffith & Co.

Now, in 1914, change was driving Web's world. Familiar smells of cattle, horse, and sheep manure were being overpowered by coal smoke, fueled by the arrival of hundreds of settlers annually, enticed to Quanah by cheap railroad tickets and promotions for ranchland, principally promoted by the *Quanah Tribune-Chief*—run by Harry Koch, grandfather of the entrepreneurial Koch brothers. Quanah's settlers tried to convert their farms in part by plowing ranch grass into fields for cotton or wheat, but many failed and moved on, hoping to sell later, seeking work in the interim.

That year in school, Web was readying for seventh grade's serious learning: English, ancient history, and algebra. He was the oldest child in the family, which by now had grown by two girls—"Baby" Dorothea and "Tiny" Virginia Harrison.

Each day after school, Web would walk home on dirt streets lined with sidewalks and houses to the Griffiths' home at 700 Cain Street— a two-story clapboard house his father had built for the family—with its painted trim, fruit trees, and row of whitewashed locust trees the Griffiths had planted, and two pine trees that shaded the front door. On one side of their fenced-in grassy backyard stood the Griffiths' metal-and-wood A-frame swing, which offered a place for Web to talk alone with one or both of his parents, away from siblings, its pair of wooden seats facing each other, connected by a hinged foot platform.

Dallas—two hours away by train—was the largest of Texas's few cities, but in 1914 four million Texans had spread across the state in five hundred towns like a layer of jam on toast: thin, but enough to taste. Each town occupied its own world—especially true of Quanah, home to three railroads. Quanah was becoming an urban marketing center for ranchers and farmers, with its new stone-and-brick three-story county courthouse on a tree-shaded block. Graded streets and residential neighborhoods a ten-minute walk from downtown had replaced the windswept dust and sparse vegetation.

Quanah's four thousand residents were now experiencing growth and adopting modern innovations. Web could see his parents' drudgeries easing somewhat each year, with public schools, telephones, a fire department, electric lighting indoors and out, and a waterworks under construction. Those who needed work could find it at ranches and farms, a cottonseed-oil mill, two cotton gins, packing houses, a wholesale dry-goods dealer, a flour mill, two grain elevators, and—in Acme, several miles west—twin gypsum-plaster and cement factories. Two wholesale grocery houses fed the town, together doing $2 million yearly, half of which was the business of F. O. Griffith & Co.

Web helped his father and uncles at the store after school and on Saturdays, which meant almost everybody in town who came to buy at the store knew the young boy and grew familiar with the Quanah branches of the extended Griffith family. Over a period of six years, Web clerked part-time—first with chores, cleaning, and restocking shelves, and then filling orders, riding delivery wagons, and learning how Welborn and F. O. ordered from suppliers. He worked alongside his brothers and cousins, including Orville (F. O. Griffith Jr.), who was six years Web's senior.

Web's world in Quanah was different from his schoolmates'; his experience in the store had taught him some things. The store did most of its trade with ranchers. Most goods came by train from Dallas, Houston, and Denver: produce, dry goods, coffee, and oil for lamps and heat. Working at the store meant Web encountered people from places all over, rural and urban alike; he heard talk of crop prices, costs of food and supplies, civic elections, and county fairs—with shows like Quanah Parker and his Indians returning from buffalo hunt at Goodnight Ranch. The store showed Web he could support himself and would give him opportunities to learn about the world outside of Quanah. And this—together with being the oldest of five kids at home—may have planted a seed from which his penchant for leadership grew. And it showed Web that his father had earned respect throughout town.

Around the time he started high school—taking further courses of English, along with medieval and modern history, Spanish, and higher algebra—with World War I waging on, Web's attention turned from just the store, the town, and the things his friends liked to bigger things, like war and other lessons of an international nature. At the store, on breaks, Web would likely have read newspapers and overheard, or joined in, conversations about events reported in the Quanah paper and those of nearby Dallas and Fort Worth. His world was expanding beyond his hometown.

The Griffiths subscribed to *The American Boy* and other magazines and made books plentiful in the house, because they were eager for their kids to attend college, which neither Lula nor Welborn had completed. Welborn refused to read fiction but read every day. He said time and again that he would rather go to work without his trousers than without having read his *Dallas Morning News*. Welborn appeared a thoughtful man, his clear, focused eyes recessed beneath dark eyebrows, and his broad, unwrinkled forehead capped by a head of already-graying, wavy, coiffed hair, receding hairline, and shaved face—the gravity commensurate with his status as an already-mature businessman and civic leader. But Welborn now carried more concerns, conscious of a wider world. His friends were never in doubt about his convictions on current affairs.

Welborn shared with his son stories from his daily read through the Dallas and Temple newspapers and from the biweekly *Quanah Tribune-Chief*, which was likely the first paper Web read.

How would a young Web have reacted to its October 1914 story that reported from the war near Reims in France, where German and French lines were a few hundred yards apart? Fighting had stopped about nightfall, and German soldiers were entering their field kitchen for a warm meal. A French captain waved a white flag and mounted his trench. A

German officer came to meet him. The French captain told the German his men were very hungry, having not eaten for days, and asked for food.

"How many are you?" the German answered.

"About a hundred," said the Frenchman.

"All right, call out your men."

So the French laid aside their arms, came over to their German enemy, and sat down to supper. For that night, they weren't fighting. At the table, the French captain told the German officer his men were so famished they would not have been able to continue fighting without something to eat.

Could it really have been that way? I'll have to ask Dad. Could it be that there really are just and honorable wars with commanders and soldiers who exercise restraint?

That December in another of Web's magazines, *The Youth's Companion*, he would have read about the shelling of Reims Cathedral:

Nothing . . . during the war has aroused more discussion than the partial destruction by German shells of the Cathedral of Notre Dame at Reims. . . . The beautiful woodwork of the interior is consumed by the fire, and most, although not all, of the stained glass is ruined.

. . . It is an old saying that the choir of Beauvais, the nave of Amiens, the portal of Reims, and the towers of Chartres would together make the loveliest church in the world.

And Web would have taken interest in a piece about British Boy Scouts serving in the war in France that appeared in the November issue of the same magazine:

Most of [the Boy Scouts] are only from twelve to fourteen years old; but they have . . . taken the gendarme's place as a director of traffic and dispenser of information, for the gendarmes are most of them on the firing line . . .

I witnessed an incident in Havre . . . I ran across the most desolate . . . British soldier I had seen. He was perched on the top of a tarpaulin-covered ammunition wagon, drawn by four horses, and he was lost . . . after an all-night downpour.

"I sye," he called, "you bloke on the sidewalk!" (I was the "bloke.") . . . "Where is No. 4 camp?" I did not know, and said so. . . .

At this juncture, two Boy Scouts appeared. They knew all about No. 4 camp, and they promptly took command of the ammunition wagon. One of the boys mounted the nigh wheel horse, and the other perched on the driver's seat in front. . . .

"Get under that canvas and go to sleep!" said the Scout in the wagon. "We'll take you where you belong." . . .

The lads are as resourceful as a North American Indian, and as ready to accept hardship as a veteran of four years' fighting.

The Griffith boys did summer fieldwork at ranches, like the ranch of their father's closest friend, John R. Good, along Groesbeck Creek, a half dozen miles from town. Good had built a house at the ranch and used an 1885 stagecoach building for his barn. He was a town father, game warden, gun-club founder, member of the First Masonic Lodge, and a musician in Quanah's first band. On occasional weekends at the ranch, for Web and the other boys, trees and shrubs along the creek provided relief from the weekday dust and dry winds of Quanah's streets and surrounding fields. Welborn loved to ride horses, and he named all of them John, in honor of John Good. He also hunted wolves and owned wolfhounds, which he kept at the Good ranch.

Welborn and his sons rode horses, hunted with dogs, and fished alongside John Good and Good's four children. John's second wife, Josephine, had died of illness in 1913, and her death opened Web's eyes to what it was like for Sydney—her son and Web's friend—to lose his mother and for John to lose his wife a second time.

During those summers, Web worked with his brothers, and they had their share of sibling quarrels. Once Web accused his brother Lawrence of not pulling his own weight in the fieldwork, harvesting wheat with a traveling crew and their horse-pulled thresher. Another time, brother Philip accused Web of the clumsy handling of a horse—"uncoordinated but determined," Philip said—which Web took as a challenge. These incidents fired Web's temper, which would be a notable trait throughout his life.

Congress created Junior ROTC in 1916, and Web would have read about it, but there was none in Quanah. His father was often working at the store or on civic projects, and mother Lula was tutoring neighborhood kids, substitute teaching, making bandages in her Red Cross homeland war-support group, conserving war materials, planting trees with her 1904 Club, campaigning for women's suffrage, cooking for her family, baking bread, or skillfully making clothes for Web and his siblings. As a result, much responsibility fell to their oldest son. And even when his parents were not so engaged, Web's plans might often be thwarted by an urgent customer order that had to be filled or a direction to watch over his siblings at home.

His friends, like John Good's sons, seemed to be free, and cousin Orville, F. O.'s son, was preparing for college.

Web appreciated early the need for leadership, being the oldest of five and with cousins in an extended family. His store work and ranch work meant his intelligence and leadership were spotted by superiors, which, in some way, helped him develop a talent for planning. But tension between work and play—sports, hunting, and doing the things teenagers do—probably muddled him as much as anyone his age. As his responsibilities grew, he was—like other adolescents—focused on learning who he was, sifting through identities to find one that suited him. Web's view of the world was probably changing, away from marbles, backyard ball games, and bike rides to a new sphere. In early high school, he was above average in his English and Spanish classes, his personal best being history class, his weakest early algebra. Writing did not appeal to him. He would rather talk—often fast—in his Texas drawl. Later, in his third year at Quanah High School, he excelled in advanced algebra and plane geometry and improved in English.

The outside world was encroaching, and Web was noticing it at school, home, and work.

After America declared war in the spring of 1917, cousins Fuller and Welborn J. Griffith, the former, Uncle F.O.'s son, and Web's friend Sydney Good all enlisted. Welborn J. would sail from Boston in June 1918 with the 345th Field Artillery Battalion. Web wanted in too, but the war had come too soon for him.

That July, Web took the train to Temple for a two-week visit with his parents' families, where he got to know his mother's brother, Uncle Harrison "Tex" Smith, who had trained as a civil engineer at Rensselaer Polytechnic Institute in New York and formed a Texas company to build roads.

Back in Quanah, Web sat on the backyard swing, perhaps first with his mother and then with his father, and asked for their permission to move to Dallas to finish high school. He had bigger ambitions than working at the grocery.

In December, Uncle Tex came to visit the family in Quanah soon after Welborn had taken a trip with F. I. Hendrix and Charles Welch, two other Quanah business leaders, to inspect the plains across the proposed Quanah-Roswell highway. It's probable Tex used the trip to discuss bidding for another highway-building project.

In August 1918, Web, suitcase in hand, boarded a train to Dallas, where he would live with the James Wilson family, friends of the Griffiths from their Dallas years. Web earned his keep clerking in the Wilsons' grocery—the company for which his father had sold groceries at wholesale before the family move to Quanah—and meanwhile enrolled at Bryan Street High School.

Web had learned a kind of willfulness in Quanah—the gulp-your-sobs, hold-up-your-head kind of stubborn composure—and how to care for himself and to take care of his siblings and customers. Now he was opening a new chapter of his life in Dallas, where he would soon learn to lead men.

CHAPTER THREE

Risks: Paris and Chartres, 1915–1918

ON JANUARY 15, 1915, FRANCE FOUNDED ITS MILITARY AVIATION school at Chartres to train three thousand pilots—becoming its most important such school—but the choice of Chartres would obviously increase the risk to the cathedral. The Germans had already been bombing London, and in March they bombed Paris, beginning with a raid by zeppelins that caused nearly a dozen deaths and thirty other casualties. Thereafter Paris protected itself with barrage balloons.

That spring, new voices began drawing attention to war's impact on monuments and artworks and began advocating for proactive monument protections to meet new conditions of war. In May, Camille Enlart—a fifty-six-year-old archeologist, lawyer, and photographer—organized France's first exhibit of photographs to document and publicize German military destruction of French buildings and art. Enlart would later become a mentor to the young Achille Carlier, who would play a significant role in the protection of the Chartres windows. Enlart's efforts to publicize war damage to monuments failed, however, to mobilize widespread support. His was merely another voice in a chorus of world outrage surrounding the Germans' destruction of Reims Cathedral and other great buildings that did not sufficiently move the French public, who still supported the war and could not yet see the value of devoting precious wartime resources to minimize damage to buildings. Also that May, Albert Thomas became undersecretary of state for artillery and munitions.

Around this time, Louis Billant invented a new, improved type of hand grenade, the pear-shaped "P1." Its spoonlike arming lever and percussion igniter were impact-detonated, so long as it landed with the heavy end down on sufficiently hard ground. Undersecretary Thomas solicited Billant to produce large quantities of the new grenade. And so Billant built a factory in a triangular lot beside his workshop on Rue de Tolbiac in a densely populated industrial and residential district in south Paris packed tightly with buildings ranging from three to a half dozen stories tall. The factory consisted of wooden sheds and employed a staff of reportedly more than two hundred workers, of which eighty were women and young girls, most younger than age fifteen, working night and day in two shifts.

On October 20, 1915, at a quarter past two in the afternoon, the factory exploded when operating at full capacity; a quarter of an hour later it exploded again, with equal violence. Reports of the cause conflicted. One journal said the first explosion was caused by the fall of a bundle of grenades from a truck on which a cargo had just been loaded. The explosions blew the factory into fragments and generated a cloud of toxic fog over the area. Another newspaper reported that, in the alley separating two groups of buildings, a truck loaded with different crates, passing over a gutter, violently exploded. The same factory had experienced two prior accidents, with victims.

The Prefecture of Police, anticipating the risk inherent in this type of facility, had prescribed limits on the quantity of explosives stored. It had ordered that explosives magazines be separated from the detonator shop, that separate workshops be maintained for each manufacturing operation, and that grenades be shipped out twice daily to limit the number on hand to five thousand. But the national government was asking for more grenades for the troops, and the shop responded, increasing production to thirty thousand per day.

President Poincaré arrived on the scene, going to an old movie theater that had been converted into a morgue, accompanied by the minister of the interior, Undersecretary Albert Thomas, and local officials. A newspaper reported that the president "and those who accompanied him bowed, moved to tears, in front of these mutilated bodies, almost all corpses of women," with forty-five dead and another sixty injured, many of whom were wives or daughters of soldiers mobilized at the front. A month later, Cathédrale Notre-Dame de Paris hosted a national funeral service for the victims, with officials in attendance, but though the shock waves from the Rue du Tolbiac explosions brought names and faces of victims to the public's attention, the tragedy did not result in significant reform. Billant, rather than moving the armaments factory to a rural setting, rebuilt the plant in his home city of Bourges, farther from the front.

Nearly a half a year later in the town of Saint-Denis, about six miles north of Paris, a few soldiers were moving boxes of grenades in an area dense with homes and commercial activity when they must have dropped a box. It exploded and triggered other explosions that "disemboweled" buildings and blew a nearby streetcar off its tracks, splitting it like a log and tossing twenty-pound stones into neighboring streets, killing cart drivers on their seats and leaving horses lying on the road, body parts shredded. People rushed toward the noise to deal with the dozens of wounded. Twenty-eight people died, including eighteen civilians and ten soldiers. Only the nearby police station, constructed of solid stone, remained standing; all other buildings and houses within hundreds of yards from the blast were flattened. The shock wave blew out windows at the town hall of Saint-Ouen, three miles away.

Again dignitaries traveled to the site to lend support, including the city mayor and the president. Two weeks later, on March 8, 1916, notables conducted another national funeral for the victims, in which Undersecretary Albert Thomas delivered a speech. But the state refused to recognize its responsibility for the explosion and to compensate the victims.

The Basilica of Saint-Denis lay less than four miles away. This was one of the great remaining ancient churches of France, where almost all the kings of France from the tenth to the eighteenth centuries, and many from before then, are interred. Still, no proactive steps were taken to prepare it or other historic buildings, or their windows, for the risks of factory explosion or other war damage.

A year later at Reims, ninety-four miles to the east of Saint-Denis, German bombardments resumed on April 15, 19, and 24, 1917, the worst group of bombardments causing the cathedral at Reims the most damage of the war.

Six months after those attacks, in early October 1917, Count d'Armancourt, president of the Archeological Society of Eure-et-Loir, convened a meeting of the society in Chartres. Twenty or so ASEL members gathered, including Father Yves Delaporte, a thirty-eight-year-old priest who had been ordained in 1904 and was serving as archivist for the Diocese of Chartres.

At the meeting, the paramount concern was for the safety of the cathedral's windows. An artillery-shell factory had emerged and expanded at Lucé, a suburb on Chartres' southwestern edge. Although Undersecretary Thomas, in his authorization order for the factory, had specified in detail the nature and maximum quantities of explosives permissible in the plant, the locals were worried about the likelihood of an accidental explosion or the Germans bombing it. Either event could blow out the stained-glass windows and structurally damage both Chartres Cathedral, which was less than three miles from the plant, and the Church of Saint-Pierre, a mere third of a mile south of the cathedral, even closer to the plant. The society determined at the meeting to urge the prefect, as chief executive of the department of Eure-et-Loir, and appointed by the national government in Paris, to write to the undersecretary of fine arts in charge of historic monuments to warn him again of the dangers posed by the plant and to ensure that all precautionary measures prescribed by the authorization order be applied.

Within weeks, the prefect had written the undersecretary, arguing that the factory posed an extreme danger to the cathedral and Saint-Pierre. The undersecretary responded that he did not believe the cathedral and the church were in danger, because the authorization order issued by the armaments undersecretary would have meant that those materials were being handled safely and that the factory was surely applying all appropriate safety measures. The maximum charge of the various explosives permitted at the factory, the undersecretary continued, was calculated such that the workshops of the neighboring depots would not even suffer shocks in the event of an explosion.

But for those who lived in Chartres, such assurances were no comfort. They perceived three dangers that compounded the risks of German attack: the artillery factory on the southwest of Chartres, the growing military airfield on the east, and the growing mainline railroad traffic from Paris to Bordeaux through the Chartres depot and switchyards, located less than a mile west of the cathedral.

Three months later, in January 1918 at Reims, the Historic Monuments Commission took action in Reims to salvage the remains of the stained glass of the windows of the roofless cathedral. Workers salvaged the remains of the stained glass that were still intact, including some of the nave's best. Because the authorities thought scaffolding would have furnished the Germans an expedient for more barrage, the Fine Arts Administration arranged for a small group of courageous firemen from Paris and two glassworkers to attempt a salvage operation. In foggy weather, and before daybreak, the team climbed high up to the iron framework of the windows, dismantled what remained, and lowered it to the floor of the nave.

That same month, at the Basilica of Saint-Denis, fifty-eight miles northeast of Chartres, many of the most valuable stained-glass windows were removed and stowed in the cellar of Turenne located within the crypt of the Basilica of Saint-Denis. And they hadn't acted a moment too soon: less than three months later, Gotha bombers would arrive over Paris and bombard by night, wreaking damage in unpredictable locations throughout the city.

The protection efforts in Saint-Denis served as beacons for other activists around France. And on February 22, 1918, the Historic Monuments Commission convened a meeting, attended by twenty of its members. The commission president was Charles Bernier, a man in his early sixties who served as a lawyer at the Ministry of Public Instruction and Fine Arts and as an emeritus jurist. He was known as the "father" of France's Law of 31st December 1913 on Historical Monuments, which first authorized automatic classification of private property to enable the Fine Arts Administration to impose protection on a monument's owner and even carry out work on the monument to guarantee its preservation. Also guest attendee at the meeting of the Historic Monuments Commission was Pierre Paquet, the commission's chief architect who in 1920 would go on to become its inspector general and who since 1914 had been working to restore France's war-damaged historic buildings.

The Historic Monuments Commission met in a ballroom at the Ministry of Culture's main offices in the seventeenth-century Palais-Royal on Rue de Valois in Paris, an apt setting for the task before them: The room's sixteen-foot ceilings were ringed by gold plaster moldings, and beveled glass spanned from wainscot to ceiling, along with rich tapestries, reminding all present of the grandeur of historic monuments the commission was to protect.

During the meeting, President Bernier read aloud a letter from the president of the Society of Friends of Reims Cathedral asking permission to have debris, consisting mostly of lead scrap that came from Reims Cathedral, to be sold for use in making small souvenir reproductions of the cathedral, with proceeds to be donated to the cathedral. The Historic Monuments Commission approved, also sanctioning additional appropriation for the removal, packaging, and transport of the remaining stained-glass windows from Reims Cathedral to Paris. Camille Enlart, also a member of the commission, reported that his comparative sculpture museum at the Trocadéro Palace was currently storing two hundred cases of stained-glass windows in its cellars. Enlart proposed, and the commission approved, that the museum's basement be cleared of rubble to allow for installation of the windows from Reims. The commission appointed a delegation comprised of Enlart and three other members to inspect the space at the Trocadéro museum and give the appropriate approvals, which they did on March 2.

Later in March 1918, the Germans began using their rail-mounted Big Bertha cannon to shell Paris, causing death and destruction. After the cannonades, more Gotha bombings hit Paris on April 12. The attacks of the Gothas would make a deep impression on one Parisian, fifteen-year-old Achille Carlier—then a high school student and future architectural historian and crusader for the protection of French medieval monuments, who in the next war would lead the fight to spur the Fine Arts Administration to proactively protect the Chartres windows. Twenty years after living through the bombardment, Carlier would write that he had felt indignation upon seeing how inadequate were the measures put in place to protect the gates of Notre-Dame de Paris from possible obliteration during the nightly air raids.

On March 15, not two weeks after the meeting of the commission at the Trocadéro, Father Lamey, parish priest in nearby La Courneuve, was riding the tram at 1:40 in the afternoon about a hundred yards from the church in Aubervilliers. A mile and a half north, at a grenade factory at 25 Rue Edgar Quinet in La Courneuve, three men carrying a box of hand grenades heard a click; they dropped the box and ran for their lives. The contents exploded and triggered more blasts, resulting in the detonation of twenty-eight million hand grenades, killing fifteen people and injuring another fifteen hundred. People forty miles away reported hearing the explosions. Four miles away, observers reported seeing two vast plumes of grayish-black smoke, turnip shaped and rising thousands of feet into the air, carried by winds, spreading a pall of smoke and fog over the flattened blackened rubble of the town and surrounding farmlands. The explosions destroyed the many brick buildings of the town, including a local maternity hospital—though, miraculously, no babies there were hurt. The explosion also blew out numerous windows at the Basilica of Saint-Denis and other area churches, but many of the basilica's stained-glass windows had already been removed.

The grenade factory was supposed to store no more than two hundred thousand grenades at any given time. Two weeks before the explosion, the artillery authority at Vincennes, which managed the depot of grenades at La Courneuve, had warned of danger, reporting that more than eighteen million were being stored at the site.

Six days after the explosions at La Courneuve, the Germans launched their spring offensive, which would reach to within fifty miles north of Paris, the deepest advance by either combatant force since 1914. But by late April 1918, the danger of a German breakthrough seemed to have subsided.

In April and early May, at Chartres workmen were already prepositioning iron scaffolding pipes in the attics of the ambulatories on the lower sides of the cathedral. From there, if ordered, they planned to move the pipes to required locations, row by row, to begin removing the cathedral's stained-glass windows.

The Historic Monuments Commission convened another meeting in mid-May, attended also by commission president Charles Bernier, a Mr. Berr de Turique, and Paul-Louis Boeswillwald, chief architect and inspector general of France's historic monuments. Also present was Eugene Will Lefevre-Pontalis, architectural historian and professor of medieval archeology, who had taught at the School of Chartres for two decades and had served on the commission since 1911. Nonmembers also participated, including Pierre Paquet (who would go on to become the commission's inspector general in 1920) and Gabriel Ruprich-Robert, chief architect of France's historic monuments in Eure-et-Loire and other locations and assistant to the Inspectorate General, tasked with the monuments' preservation.

The La Courneuve accident and the others before it were a slap in the face to the Historic Monuments Commission. Mr. Ruprich-Robert introduced a proposal made by Émile Brunet, chief architect of the department of Eure-et-Loir, recommending that the commission order the stained-glass windows of Chartres Cathedral to be removed and requesting funds to pay for the work. The members approved. Brunet called it a precautionary measure, motivated by the proximity to the cathedral of the Lucé artillery factory.

On May 25, the ASEL membership met again to discuss the procedures to be used in the removal, approve funds for the work, adopt a plan to photograph each window before removal, observe the work, and ensure that it would be performed only by specialists. In addition, Étienne Houvet was designated to photograph each window as a whole and each individual panel before it could be separated from its window.

Shortly after the meeting, employees of three master-glassmaker workshops began removing most of the stained-glass windows from Chartres Cathedral, storing them off-site. The work was performed by the Lorin workshop in Léves, run by Charles Lorin, founded by his father in 1869; the Parisian workshop of Albert Bonnot, who had been involved in an 1886 restoration at the cathedral; and the Parisian workshop of Jean Gaudin.

The upper windows were removed from the exterior, the lower from the interior. When the windows were removed, workers inserted canvas mounted on frames into the window openings. For the upper stained-glass windows, workmen installed scaffolding outside the cathedral and lowered it from the roof by means of construction equipment consisting of specialized hoppers. For the lower windows, they lowered scaffolding pipe down to the floor of the cathedral, or to each successive level of constructed scaffolding, by rope through openings in the vaulted ceilings of the ambulatories. They painted a number on each panel and prepared a tracing in duplicate of the panel's images and design, placing one copy of the drawing inside the box holding each panel and affixing another on the outside of the box. Among the challenges they faced were the need to remove the brittle glass from hardened cement.

As the work at Chartres progressed, danger increased of further German advances. The Germans were planning an attack against the British through Flanders. But to disguise that intention, the Germans launched a long offensive against the French across the River Marne, which had been the scene of the heavy fighting four years before, in 1914. On July 15, 1918, the Second Battle of the Marne began with an attack by fifty-two German divisions across the Marne using temporary bridges near Dormans. But soon the British Twenty-Second Corps and several new American divisions reinforced the French and followed with a large Allied counterattack, including twenty-four French and ten US divisions with a force of 350 new French tanks. The counterattack forced the Germans to retreat almost back to their July 15 starting point while suffering 168,000 casualties and 30,000 of their soldiers taken prisoner.

Less than a week after the counterattack, the membership of the Archeological Society of Eure-et-Loir again met to debate dangers to the project at Chartres, including whether to pursue the project, and confirmed that it should continue.

Ten days later, the Allies began a major counteroffensive with the Battle of Amiens, using new artillery techniques and operational methods, including surprise attacks, and using Canadian and Australian mobile assault forces. The offensive, eventually growing into what was called the Hundred Days Offensive, was seen by many as the tipping point in the war and signaled the end of trench warfare.

Later that August, on two successive nights, enemy planes dropped several bombs at Chartres, damaging roads and some buildings but not the cathedral.

On August 30, the commission convened another meeting at the Palais-Royal. President Bernier had received a letter from Henri-Louis Bouquet, bishop of Chartres, asking the commission to halt the removal of the windows and offering to bear responsibility for the abandonment of the removal and replacement of any windows already removed. His reasons likely centered on concern for breakage or loss of the windows. He may also have shared the belief, discussed below, that the cathedral and its windows would be protected by the Virgin Mary and that mortals should refrain from interfering with Divine will. Bernier had also received a letter from Émile Brunet, chief architect in Eure-et-Loir, alerting the president to the August 15 and 16 bombings by enemy aircraft. Bernier concluded, and the members agreed, that under the circumstances there could be no question about stopping the removal and that the commission should even expand the operation to also remove the windows of the Church of Saint-Pierre and take steps to protect the statue-covered porches of both structures.

For five months, through the war's end and the armistice, they continued the removal work, completing it before either of the two buildings could sustain further war damage. They rescued a total of twenty-nine thousand square feet of stained glass among the 174 windows of Chartres Cathedral and an unknown portion of the windows of the Church of Saint-Pierre. One accident occurred during the removal at Chartres. Specialists dropped a twelfth-century panel, the Virgin, from the stained-glass Tree of Jesse Window. It would be repaired or replaced by a replica. Any crates in which the window panels were stored appear to have been discarded after the windows were reinstalled.

Over the next five years, with the oversight of architect Émile Brunet, the craftsmen of the Lorin, Bonnot, and Gaudin studios restored and reinstalled the stained-glass windows in Chartres and Saint-Pierre, beginning with resealing the windows with hydraulic lime and cement to ensure a better seal and reinstalling the Chartres windows in a modified, more logical arrangement developed by Canon Delaporte according to his research, to better reflect the windows' original pattern that had not been followed in previous refurbishings.

The authorities learned lessons in their World War I removal and reinstallation of the windows. First, Canon Delaporte's scholarship of the cathedral and cataloging gave them courage and the confidence to identify and document the complex, delicate collection of windows. The process then was to remove, package, and store them and to repair many before reinstallation. The canon's scholarship into the iconography, interpretation, and cataloging of the panels was essential to retaining the stories illustrated by the windows. Second, they developed a conceptual framework to identify, label, describe, and place the windows into context. Third, those carrying out the removal, repair, and reinstallation created an early solution to the problem of replacing hard cement with soft caulking to make the task of future removal and reinstallation even conceivable. Before the 1918–1924 project, the risks of breakage of the older windows in the collection may have seemed almost insurmountable.

The last lesson was a subtler one. Over the years, many church supporters and congregants used their faith to assure themselves and convince others that through some miracle the cathedral would protect itself and that intervention by man would impair that process. But as the machines of war became more efficient, the grip of those old notions appeared to weaken, which allowed the authorities to adopt more pro-active policies in response to citizens' calls for action to protect historic monuments. Would those changes hold for the next war?

Ironically, the great work of Canon Delaport and other supporters, such as the Marianites of Holy Cross—a group of devout laywomen dedicated to the Virgin Mary who had always had a close relationship with Chartres Cathedral—may have detracted from the cathedral's protection, in that it overly reassured those who opposed so-called passive defense. They were deterred from building shelters to protect vulnerable structures and creating detachments of residents to prepare for and deal with aerial bombardments and just wanted to withdraw into prayer in the hope that the war would bypass the cathedral. In the long run, these detractors were in a sense correct, in that Chartres Cathedral escaped direct bombardments, and in large part the escape was due to factors other than the passive defense measures. Perhaps, as the Marianites claimed, it would come to pass that the Virgin Mary would look over the cathedral during all future wars that would cross France.

One aspect of the window work certainly benefited the cathedral in World War II: The removal of the windows and their replacement with flexible expandable material would have the effect of allowing shock waves to pass through the cathedral with less resistance. That likely proved important in helping the cathedral endure nearby bombing and bombardment and leaving it better able to bear damage from rain, snow, and the elements during the last fraction of World War II after the liberation of Chartres.

A handful of young men who gained important experience in the military during World War I would go on to play vital roles in saving the stained-glass windows at Chartres in World War II. They included Achille Carlier—who as a teenager was so dismayed by the vulnerability of Notre-Dame de Paris to the German bombardments of World War I—and René Planchenault, Ernest Herpe, and Lucien Prieur. Others, in civilian roles, learned from the World War I window removal and restoration in ways that would prove valuable in the next world war.

Chapter Four

Griffith Faces the World: Texas, New York, Manila, and Shanghai, 1918–1935

In late summer 1918, Web arrived in Dallas, already home to 150,000, its central area packed with brick buildings, mostly five stories tall, and church steeples. There were none of the open lots Web had been used to in Quanah. Trolley cars screeched past horse-drawn wagons, while autos and trucks clamored on paved streets lined with curbs and sidewalks. Electric signs and streetlights kept the night alive—a new world for Web.

Sometime after he arrived, Web seems to have wanted a new name, because soon he would be called Griff (likely because that's what he wanted), but Quanah folks, and relatives, would continue to call him Web.

Within days, word reached him that his friend Sydney Good from Quanah had died at El Paso's Fort Bliss, which was the Army's cavalry center and a rail hub for soldiers returning from Europe. Flu had broken out the prior spring and was now spreading to pig farms and converting into a human pandemic, with a rapid course, some victims dying within hours of contracting it.

Griff rode the train back home to Quanah for the funeral. Graveside at Memorial Park Cemetery, on its windy hill with a few scattered trees along the road, Griffiths and Goods and a large group of Quanah friends watched Sydney's casket lowered into a plot near the grave of Alline, Sydney's mother, who had died when he was four.

Back in Dallas, James Wilson oriented Griff to his job as clerk at the Wilsons' retail grocery store. Griff got settled in the Wilson home as well. The Wilsons had been long-standing friends of Griff's parents and watched over him but likely gave him more latitude than they had given their own children. He likely had his own room in their house to be alone, read, and study, and he would have been able to explore the city. He probably missed his family but would have been glad to not have to devote time to caring for his siblings, and he surely wouldn't have missed the extra harvest work required of Quanah children and mothers that fall, with manpower to harvest the cotton having been absorbed by the war.

Web's work at the store and school filled his days. Time off wasn't in the cards. He would have ridden buses and the noisy streetcars, but he probably did a lot of walking between home, the store, and school. Trucks and autos were everywhere and were breaking down in the street and clogging traffic amid the dwindling number of horse-drawn wagons and riders, signs of continuing transition, and the grime of congestion contrasted with Quanah's dust and wind and open horizons.

That fall, he started twelfth grade at Bryan Street High School, located in a four-story rectangular brick building downtown that was two to three times the size of Quanah's Hardeman County courthouse, the biggest building Griff had seen up close until then. He began with English, geometry and trigonometry, bookkeeping, military science, and physics and inorganic chemistry, both with a laboratory component.

About this time, the influenza pandemic hit Dallas. Newspapers reported cases in two counties by early September. In Dallas, there were calls to ban gatherings, but pressure mounted to save the September 28 Liberty Loan parade, in which five thousand civilians and 2,500 enlisted men paraded down South Harwood Street to launch the government's fourth campaign to sell Liberty bonds for the war effort. The gathering was good for the campaign but bad for public health. On October 3, Dallas had 119 reported influenza cases and one death. By October 9, there were one thousand. On the tenth, all Dallas theaters, playhouses, and other places of public amusement were ordered closed, and on the twelfth all public and private schools were closed, by which time the total number of cases had exceeded 2,700, the pandemic peaking in the fall, but new cases continuing to arise into winter and spring.

On October 31, the schools reopened.

Before news of the November 11 armistice reached Dallas, Griff had longed to join the military but knew that for him World War I had come too early. Still, he was determined to be ready for the next war. Finally, availing himself of the Junior ROTC cadet training at his new school, he was able to do something about it. When he put on his cadet uniform as Private Griffith of Company B, with high black collar over white shirt and solid vertical stripe down his chest, his extraordinary good looks showed as never before. He already stood at six feet, one inch tall, and he was handsome with his short, curly hair, dark eyebrows, broad forehead, and pronounced chin, with the beginning of what would become a distinctive dimple; yet his complexion still reflected a boyish softness.

Even without his family, Griff thrived in Dallas, keeping busy at the store and school—while at the store in Quanah Griff's brothers took up the slack caused by his absence. Later in his first year at Bryan Street High, and in the half year that followed, Griff's studies included Spanish, civics, and economics, and he shone in geometry, physics, military science, and bookkeeping.

During the year, he rode the train south to College Station, two-thirds of the way to Houston, to visit his cousin Orville (F. O. Jr.) at Texas A&M and to see what life might be like as an Aggie in the Corps of Cadets—the next step after Junior ROTC—if he were to matriculate there. Orville was three years older than Griff and had F. O. Sr.'s prominent forehead, closely trimmed hair, but his thicker eyebrows framed the focused, no-nonsense look he shared with this entrepreneurial father. Orville showed Griff around campus, with its line of stone buildings surrounding its Greek-style domed administration building, paneled halls, huge classrooms, dining halls, cavalry barns, and training and parade fields. It had to have made a strong impression on Griff.

Back in Dallas at Bryan Street High, Griff found time for football practice and made the Wolf Pack team, at left tackle for the 1919 season.

After fifteen months at Bryan, Griff's demeanor had developed a seriousness, a focus, and a sense of concentration that distinguished him.

On a Friday in January 1920, Griff graduated from Bryan Street High School, and on the following Monday he enrolled at A&M, intending to major in agriculture, rounding out his course schedule with classes in chemistry, rhetoric, composition, and literature. Upon matriculation, however, the majority of his time was spent as an ROTC Company D cadet, among the school's mile-wide, open-grass parade grounds and training woods. Drills included calisthenics, escort to the colors, pitching tents, bayonet practice, and mapmaking. Signal corps maneuvers included the military's new use of radio, map reading, and telegraph practice. Artillery drills including marching with rolling caissons, fording rivers with mobile cannons, and firing practice. And parade formation and cavalry drills included work with sabers, saddling instruction, and equestrian class.

Griff also continued in football, this time as one of twenty-eight reserves on A&M's team, which was Southwest Conference cochampion (with Texas) in 1920, never scored upon, aggregating a score of 275–0 in eleven games.

He studied at A&M for twenty months and in the spring of 1921 got himself nominated to the United States Military Academy at West Point by Eugene Black, US congressman for East Texas's First District and a teacher, lawyer, and wholesale grocer. Griff was soon appointed to West Point without examination by James Young, US congressman from Texas's Third District and a lawyer from Kaufman, where Griff's father had briefly farmed.

Griff entered the academy in July, and within weeks he had written to his family that he was having the time of his life and, being "initiated" as a plebe, could scarcely sit down, but he knew he would get over it, and the next year, he wrote, he would be as bad as those who were hazing him. He continued to write his family, and the next January, Griff's ten-year-old sister Tiny wrote with news: an electrical fire had broken out in the family's Quanah store and burned it to the ground. By then, his father had parted ways with F. O., and with insurance proceeds from the fire, he began his replacement venture: a novel kind of self-service retail grocery in which customers entered through a turnstile, picked out their own items, and took them to the checkout counter themselves. Welborn had opened in Quanah one of the first franchises of the new Piggly Wiggly chain.

Though Griff apparently remained close with the family through letters, he rarely saw them. Over the summers of his undergrad years, he remained on the East Coast, living in Larchmont, New York, with his uncle Tex Smith, who had moved with his wife to suburban Westchester County from Temple, Texas, to become partner in the New York engineering firm Sanderson & Porter, which handled large projects like the Pennsylvania Railroad tunnels. Each summer Griff worked in the company's New York office for Leslie Myer, the man in charge of construction of the Hoover Dam. .

In the fall of 1923, Griff began his third year at West Point, by which point he'd been promoted to lieutenant, having earned his strongest ratings in "military bearing" and leadership. Every year he was rising in class rank among his 270 fellow cadets, excelling most in athletics. In fact, over his four years as a cadet, sports would consume most of Griff's nonacademic time: He played four years of football as an all-American and was on the wrestling team for three, and he played lacrosse, ran track, and joined the rifle-sharpshooting and pistol-marksmanship teams. In wrestling, he won an individual championship in his second year, in the unlimited-weight class, in which he "threw" a fellow named Barry, of Yale, the reigning intercollegiate champion. In his senior year, with Griff as offensive tackle, the football team suffered only one defeat all season—thirteen to seven, to Knute Rockne's Four Horsemen of Notre Dame, allowing them a single touchdown—and they tied Yale and Columbia, beat Florida by a touchdown, and won four additional shutouts.

Griff's West Point yearbook extolled his athletic record, and pictured is a handsome young man with eye-catching curly hair noted for his work on "Beast Detail" hazing underclassmen and his propensity for action: "When the game ahead calls for a good scrap and furnishes a thrill, there you will find Griff."

All this exercise and outdoorsmanship had their effect, and Griff's height, build, and magazine-cover face landed him a part as an extra in a Hollywood movie, *Classmates*, filmed partly at West Point. It was screened in February 1925 at Quanah's Texan theater.

By early 1925, Welborn Sr. was feeling the effects of Quanah's increasing cost of living. For a year, he had cut business costs where he could, eliminating delivery services and cutting expenses and prices where possible. But now two locals, J. G. Wilkerson and Tom Mitchell, were opening a new store in town—part of the chain of Massie-Cope M System Food Stores—where they sold groceries and meat and offered to take their customers' orders by phone and include delivery. By September, Welborn sold the store and, five months later, the family house, and the family moved back to Temple, where he opened several M System Food Stores of his own. Here were better schools and nearby colleges for the children, and Lula was back home, but she would not be so active in club or church work now, because she helped part time in the stores' office.

After graduating in June 1925, Griff obtained leave and managed a trip home to Quanah before he was to report for duty in August. What with the Griffith family's impending move to Temple, this would mark his last extended visit in Quanah.

Griff volunteered for paratrooper training, but on arrival for duty at San Antonio's Brooks Field, he was rejected as too tall. So he opted to take infantry training at Fort Benning instead.

Once in Georgia, Griff met Alice Torrey, daughter of Major Daniel H. Torrey, a lawyer and Fort Benning adjutant general whose father and maternal grandfather had also been infantry officers and West Pointers. Alice's spirit and energy caught Griff's attention. At West Point, Griff had focused on athletics, weapons, and achievements, but now it was perhaps time to expand his circle of interests to include women. There were certainly worse picks than Alice: her father could advance Griff's career, and Griff and Alice made a startlingly good-looking couple. His former classmates had long teased him that his looks would get him lassoed by a woman before long, and why not by petite, pretty Alice, who with her movie-star appeal and dyed-blonde hair could have been mistaken for Mary Pickford? The couple married in 1929 at Fort Benning, the bride wearing a Gatsby-style gown complemented by a Juliet cap and twelve-foot-long veil that would have been Hollywood standard fare, the groom dressed in gold-trimmed ceremonial uniform, complete with saber and white gloves.

The same year, the statuesque Griff was tapped as the Army's photo model to display its newest postwar uniforms for field, dress, and work.

Soon Griff was transferred for more infantry training, first to Fort Leavenworth, near Kansas City, and then to Fort Leonard Wood, in the Ozarks, north of Springfield. Then it was on to Jefferson Barracks, near Saint Louis. Alice accompanied him on his transfers until she became pregnant, during which time she moved in with her parents, who were then living at Fort Leavenworth, where the major was serving as adjutant. Griff and Alice's daughter was born in 1931. They named her Alice.

But Griff's joy was cut short when in September of that year his mother was injured in a rollover auto accident near Temple. She died four days later, at the age of fifty-five. Her funeral took place in Temple, but it is not clear whether Griff was able to attend. By mid-1931, he had been reassigned to serve as a first lieutenant and military observer with the Thirty-First Infantry in the Philippines. The instruction he would receive there was considered the best overseas training available for any Army officer, and selection as an observer reflected recognition of Griff's talent and intellect, and he must have seen both for the opportunity they afforded.

And so in early July Griff, Alice, and the baby sailed from New York, first with a stop in San Francisco, and then on to Manila, along with fifty other officers, many with their own families. Their accommodations aboard the USS *Republic* were first rate, as the six-hundred-foot-long troopship had before been a North Atlantic passenger liner with United States Lines. In the Philippines, Griff was assigned to Manila's Fort McKinley and then to Fort Stotsenburg, fifty-plus miles north, where his primary function was to engage in military-defense planning in case of Japanese attack.

In fact, soon after the Griffiths arrived in Manila, Japanese troops invaded China, and on February 1, 1932, General MacArthur ordered Griff's regiment to deploy within four days by sea on the USAT *Chaumont* to guard the Shanghai International Settlement. Griff was appointed provost marshal, head of the military police. The Thirty-First were to serve as peacekeepers, augmenting the security force of the

Shanghai Volunteer Corps at a time when the SVC was protecting the settlement in the face of fighting between Japanese and Chinese troops, and also to provide reinforcements for the Fourth Marine Regiment and a British force.

Although adjacent parts of Shanghai were demolished by fighting between Japanese and Chinese troops, the International Settlement remained an island of security. By April, Griff and other officers had sent for their families to come from Manila by commercial liner and had billeted them at the Cathay Mansion, a hotel in the International Settlement. There the children attended the American mission school, and the women shopped together on Shanghai's renowned market streets. A Chinese caretaker named Amah Le Su cared for little Alice.

In July, when the crisis had passed, Griff and his family returned by ship to the Philippines with the full regiment. Griff and Alice again took up residence at Fort McKinley. Alice and Griff engaged a Philippine nurse for little Alice, to whom she became attached. But the household peace was not to last. Griff and Alice had begun to fight, and Alice was growing increasingly unhappy in her marriage. Alice was a sociable woman, with little interest in domestic life, whereas Griff's predominant trait was seriousness: it was becoming increasingly clear that the couple was a mismatch.

A month later, Major Torrey and his wife sailed from New York to Manila for a long stay and visited Griff and Alice. This stay likely afforded the opportunity for private talks with their daughter, because, by November, Alice had left Griff for the first time. Soon she returned, however. She told her parents that Griff had promised to be a model husband if she would only come back, but "no sooner would I come back than he would start all this again."

Alice left again, with the baby, to return stateside, where she took up residence in Reno. In the 1930s, Nevada's divorce laws were more liberal than the rest of the country's, and many women moved there, where, after establishing a six-week residency, they could apply for divorce and be almost assured of getting it. With his own thirty-second birthday approaching, Griff took stock of his life thus far. In a letter to his father, he revealed his growing disillusionment, wondering "if the Army is worth it all. It's a hell of a life in some ways but in others all I could ask."

Griff felt isolated and was greatly disappointed over Alice's threat to divorce him. Welborn Sr. grew concerned enough over his brokenhearted son that he urged Griff's youngest sister, Tiny, to travel to Manila to be with her brother. "You've got to go," Welborn Sr. said, worrying his son might be distraught enough to take his own life.

Tiny came to live with Griff in Manila soon after Alice left, to keep house for him. Tiny loved life in Manila, driving her own car through the streets of the old city, with walled gardens alive with rose-purple rhododendrons and large China roses, and down Dewey Boulevard though the American Ermita district, with the bells of Santo Domingo Church pealing and traffic at a near standstill, buses competing with taxis, trucks, cars, jeeps, and pony carts, no one in a hurry. She took her first office job there, working as a secretary for a Mr. Kemp, a politician, and after a while resigned before his scheduled time away for the hot weather months. With his recommendation, she landed a teaching job at the American Business School, attended by most of the "Army girls"—wives, daughters, and followers of stationed military men.

Tiny's sibling companionship cheered Griff, but he was still somewhat unsettled: After almost two years, he was finding defense planning boring, and so, when the opportunity arose, he took over management of the Army and Navy Club, an assignment Tiny considered a "lifesaver" for her struggling brother. The club, housed in an old Spanish-style two-story building located on Manila Bay, operated its own restaurant, several bars, a reading room, a bowling alley, a swimming pool, and tennis courts. The work did not excite Griff, but at least it kept him busy—especially in the spring of 1934, in the weeks leading up to departure of the American fleet for China, where it was to stay until the fall, and when most other Americans were leaving for the hot season. Tiny was busy, too: During that time, she had a date almost every night for four weeks straight. While in Manila she planned to find a husband among the American officers stationed there.

Griff enjoyed having Tiny stay with him. They got along surprisingly well. When Tiny started getting serious with one of her beaux, Charles DeKay—nicknamed "Count," a naval officer whom she would eventually marry—Griff got a kick out of teasing his sister about how many dates she went on with other officers while Count was off on a Navy cruise, calling them her "affairs." But his teasing aside, he was learning at lot from his kid sister, to his surprise. She was showing him, undoubtedly, that his family was his foundation of support, even though he would spend most of his adult life away from them.

Alice, meanwhile, had established residence in Reno with the baby, supported by her parents, and in November 1933 had sued for divorce. She had testified, without cross-examination, that Griff had treated her with extreme cruelty since the earliest months of their marriage. He had insisted that everything be done his way and ruled with an ungovernable temper. He was physically violent all during their four years of marriage—more than ten times—twisting her arm, knocking her down, even breaking one of her teeth.

Griff had received his copy of the divorce complaint while on assignment abroad, but he couldn't appear in court. She won the divorce and custody of the baby. He would never recognize the Reno divorce as valid.

In late 1934, Griff was transferred back to Shanghai, and late that year Tiny married Count DeKay in Manila and the following February moved back to the States, setting up home in Washington, D.C. Griff served for nine months as provost marshal in charge of the military police and lived in an Americanized part of Shanghai. But he quickly grew bored with the assignment and decided he was ready to return to the United States, where he would be faced with rebuilding his life.

But before boarding his return ship to San Francisco, he was ready for his next adventure.

CHAPTER FIVE

Warming Cauldron:
Paris and Chartres, 1919–1936

IN 1919, THE REPAIR AND REPLACEMENT OF CHARTRES CATHEDRAL'S windows began under the leadership of Émile Brunet, chief architect, with assistance from Canon Delaporte, the cathedral's historian. Brunet was a working architect schooled in medieval archeology and art history. Delaporte, a priest educated in history and art, was a dedicated archivist and scholar.

Others before them had repaired or restored the windows through the centuries, but in the course of some such repairs, restorers had placed a number of the refreshed panels of certain windows back in "inaccurate" positions, according to Canon Delaporte. That is, scenes and figures depicted in the stained glass had been misidentified, in part because earlier restorations had relied on the writings of one or more art historians unfamiliar with the precise literary sources or who could not identify all of the scenes on the panels before them, and so when the stained-glass was put back into the casings, the order was skewed, losing the original artists' iconographic intention. Brunet and Delaporte took advantage of the removal of the windows during World War I to instruct workers under Brunet's supervision to reorient or rearrange certain panels so that their scenes, in Delaporte's view, would appear in a more "logical" position.

For example, in one window, the Charlemagne Window—number 38 by Delaporte's ordering schema—located in the apse next to the steps leading to the Chapel of Saint Piatus of Tournai, we see a series of scenes depicting the Jerusalem crusade cycle, including a scene in which Charlemagne and Constantine speak with two bishops, one in which Constantine dreams of Charlemagne, and others depicting known priests conducting famous Masses. Over the years, certain scholars who had compared these scenes with literary sources had questioned the order of the panels, because the sequence of events depicted failed to match the historical sequence described in the sources; furthermore, they had noted, certain priests had been misidentified and certain bishops associated incorrectly with either Charlemagne or Constantine. This iconographic debate had raised complex theological issues that, as time would show, would not be settled by Delaporte's determinations. Nevertheless, the architects who carried out restorations under Brunet appear to have begun to effect "corrections" such as Delaporte's as a matter of practice.

During the interwar years, the French had reconstructed 1,200 churches, 1,000 factories, and 350,000 homes among the thousand villages shelled and bombed. The authorities who directed that work operated under a creed of restoration that had been evolving since the nineteenth century, during which time a school of thought led by architect Eugène Emmanuel Viollet-le-Duc had aimed to "augment" a building's appearance or character with the aim of better expressing its originally intended purpose. But in these interwar years a new line of thinking began to emerge—that architects should engage in "total preservation," restoring structures to their original appearance, often in the name of reversing "errors" made in previous restorations.

Preserving France's cultural heritage was a prominent concern after the destruction of World War I, and citizen advocates for the protection of France's historic and cultural monuments came from a variety of backgrounds, including architecture, archeology, business, and the arts. Most were men, but also a few women became prominent in the cause. Many were citizen soldiers—veterans, reservists, or both. Many had served in World War I and then joined the civilian workforce. Some would rejoin the military at the outbreak of World War II and continue performing monument preservation work in uniform. They were a disparate group, and even if they were not formally trained in architecture, they committed themselves to the fight to save their national architectural treasures. Achille Carlier was one such man. Born in 1903, he had been a high schooler in Paris in 1918 when he'd seen workmen placing protective sandbags around Notre-Dame Cathedral. German aircraft and artillery had been blitzing Paris nightly, and Carlier had grown incensed when he had seen the workmen quitting their labors promptly at 5:00 p.m. even though the work was far from complete, their sandbags never reaching the higher, most ancient and precious parts of the building.

Fifteen years later, Carlier had grown into a mustachioed man with thick eyebrows, often wearing a fedora and scarf, who, though thin of build, possessed a zealous, all-out spirit and forceful energy which cast him at the front of the crusade to safeguard the Chartres stained-glass windows. He had studied at the École Française de Rome and won a Grands Prix de Rome in architecture and French Artists Medal of Honor. Early in his career, he had spent time studying Gothic architecture in Cyprus and had published on, among other things, the subject of the French character of the Cypriot landscape, arguing for it to be treated as a province of French archeology. He later maintained an office in Paris and became an ardent supporter of the preservation of French medieval monuments.

Carlier specialized in the architecture of the French Middle Ages. In the 1930s, he led a fierce fight against "interventionist" practices of the Historic Monuments Service. His numerous articles published in the interwar period defended the vision of restoration championed by John Ruskin, English art historian and prominent social thinker and philanthropist. Ruskin advocated that the British should adopt the Venetian architectural style, celebrating its "imperfection" as an essential feature of Gothic art, in contrast to the mechanical regularity of neoclassical buildings. He extolled the value of creative freedom and artistic fulfillment enjoyed by individual workers.

As an architectural historian, Carlier became a proponent of reversing what he viewed as the distortions caused by prior so-called restorations and became a harsh opponent of the school of Viollet-le-Duc. Carlier militantly defended medieval art, drawing attention to the need for the protection and careful restoration of the Gothic monuments of France.

He advocated with such passion that he was seen by government officials as an adversary who spoke in exaggerations. One might argue that Carlier's fervor and foresight played a productive role in driving the Fine Arts Administration to move ahead at a pace faster than it would have without him—and to productively tolerate more risks, such as breakage, loss, and theft of the stained-glass windows—if for no other reason than to counter the heat of the spotlight his advocacy imposed on them.

René Planchenault was another key technocrat in monument preservation. In 1923, he was a new graduate of the School of Chartres when Marceau Prou, director of his school, introduced Planchenault to Paul Léon, director of fine arts, who selected Planchenault to take over assembly of the Supplementary Inventory of Historic Monuments, a task Planchenault performed with distinction. To reward him for that work, in 1930 Minister Prou appointed Planchenault inspector of all movable objects considered historic monuments, a role in which he would serve for fifteen years. Starting in 1932, Planchenault took on another heavy burden: preparing a national plan of "mobilization" to centralized protective measures for historic monuments to be implemented in case of conflict.

Throughout the 1930s, as the French continued to repair damage done during World War I to cultural monuments, including churches, Hitler's rise to power in Germany became a growing concern, placing increasing pressure on France's Department of Fine Arts. Its officials, anticipating another war, hurried to finalize plans to protect French historic buildings and sites. The rise of air combat in wartime and recent advances in weaponry were forcing them to focus on averting consequences of bomb explosions near buildings, such as rumbles that could bring down unsteady buildings or blow out windows.

As early as 1923, the French government had made general plans for wartime preservation, but because of faith in France's strong defense strategy, no specific measures were adopted. In March 1935, Germany reintegrated the Saarland into the Reich, reintroduced conscription, and reestablished the German Air Force. The French reacted by enacting a passive-defense organization that April, which established a High Commission on Civil

Defense in the Ministry of the Interior to coordinate between ministries. It encouraged construction of shelters, protection of vulnerable structures, and creation of detachments of local residents to prepare for, and respond to, effects of aerial bombardments. Although planning was under way, in the view of citizens who considered Chartres Cathedral and its windows to be national treasures, the government was doing far too little.

The people of Chartres became increasingly concerned. Carlier, though a Parisian, and editor of his own quarterly publication, *Les pierres de France* (The stones of France), shared their passion and focused his attention on the windows of Chartres. In alliance with the Paris newspaper *L'Écho de Paris*, Carlier launched a campaign to spur the Fine Arts Administration to take action to save the cathedral and its windows. Carlier and the newspaper pressed dual campaigns. First, they planned to take aim at the military, hoping to force it to relocate the Chartres airbase, which threatened the destruction of the cathedral. Second, they pressed the Fine Arts Administration to create plans and assemble equipment and personnel to be able, on short—very short—notice, to remove the windows and pack and store them in a safe place before any military attack in or near Chartres.

In April, Georges Huisman, who just the year prior had been appointed director general of the Fine Arts Administration, wrote Carlier soliciting his ideas for protecting Chartres' windows. Then, in May, the Archeological Society of Eure-et-Loir again became involved: ASEL president Charles Louis invited Carlier to present his proposal. Carlier contended that officials in the Fine Arts Administration were engaging in wishful thinking if they thought they still could apply World War I planning to successfully protect monuments from future war damage. He argued that destruction suffered by French monuments during World War I—as bad as it was—could no longer be the standard for expected wartime destruction. If a new German attack were to come—which was feeling more likely every day—the attack would be much swifter than those made in the World War I and would come initially from the air. The air base at Chartres, located less than a half mile from the cathedral, would be a prime target.

The solution, Carlier insisted, was to relocate the air base at least twelve miles away from the city, to one of the many possible sites available in the wheat field–covered plains surrounding Chartres. The editors of *L'Écho de Paris* joined Carlier in that argument. If the airfield were to remain where it was, he and the newspaper contended, only one solution remained: the immediate removal of the threatened windows, even in peacetime.

Chartres' rail hub presented a second grave risk. The rail depot was only six hundred yards from the cathedral. France's rail system was then under competitive pressure from the growth of roads and autos—which would soon lead to the nationalization of the railroads. Due to the competitive atmosphere, the rail depot could not be expected to be moved any time soon. At Chartres, two main rail lines from Paris branched off, toward Bordeaux and Brittany.

Carlier summarized his plan for the ASEL: Given the risk that the rail depot, together with the air base, would be targeted by an invading force, he was convinced that the danger to the cathedral would be imperiled immediately at the start of an invasion. So he devised a plan to protect the windows on the assumption that there would be no more than a two-hour alert before the attack.

Carlier's plan—he called it a "study"—anticipated a number of obstacles. First, no one could count on the air base being relocated; the government must therefore plan to remove the windows from the cathedral and place them in safe storage. That plan presented its own set of challenges, including the need for equipment and trained personnel, since most trained men experienced with such work would be subject to immediate mobilization at the outbreak of fighting. So, Carlier determined, the authorities should organize a special military unit assigned to the removal operation for at least a couple of hours after the initiation of any attack. But, he proposed, until the authorities could create such a force, they should recruit a staff of nonprofessionals and young people to be trained and supervised by professionals to carry out a rapid, large-scale, almost choreographed, removal. This approach would allow a much larger workforce to be assembled quickly. He envisioned a team of 350 people, which could execute the plan within the two hours.

After all, Carlier contended, the actual work of removing the windows required, in most cases, only a limited skill level, given training and supervision. The program would call for teams trained to work together. Training, he said, should be conducted with high schoolers a couple of hours per week in lieu of physical-education classes. And Carlier determined that a new type of scaffolding would be needed—one that could be assembled quickly, yet be sturdy enough to securely hold workers simultaneously at multiple levels. The scaffolding must be collapsible so multiple sets could be prepositioned in the attics and other rooms of the cathedral and swiftly lowered into position to be erected in front of all windows. The keyhole opening at the apex of each ceiling vault above the various windows could be used, he said, to drop the equipment down using ropes for the removal of the low-lying windows. Other equipment necessary to removing the upper windows could be stored in unused rooms in the cathedral towers. That equipment could be passed through the doorways onto the balconies. Since all scaffolds would have multiple levels, separate teams of workers could occupy all levels and work simultaneously on separate windows.

Carlier suggested that the authorities designate and train a special supervisory staff—who need not be architects or building professionals—to replace the architects and building experts likely to be called up for military service in the opening hours of an attack. He advocated procurement of a large supply of custom-fitted cases to hold the removed windows, fabricated from metal, not wood, so as to be light and fireproof, with custom inserts to safely and firmly hold the panels of each window. The crates should be as small as possible to facilitate their being lowered through the keystone holes. Cases needed for larger window panels should be fitted with hinges to be foldable, small enough to pass through keystone openings. He contended that windows, once in the cases, should not be removed from the cathedral. Transport would present too great a risk to the windows. Instead, they should be first placed in the cathedral's crypt. In the meantime, the authorities should explore the ancient excavated spaces below the crypt—sufficiently far underground to withstand bombing and fires, Carlier felt—and clear them of debris to make them available to hold the windows.

During the removal, sentries should guard all doors to keep out unnecessary personnel, even townspeople seeking refuge in the crypt in the event of a threatened attack. The guards should also enforce one-way traffic in the stairways, to maintain safety and facilitate rapid movement. Since the removal work might have to be done at night, Carlier also said blackout lights, equipped with blue bulbs to be invisible to overhead aircraft, should be positioned throughout the cathedral, powered by a petrol-fueled power generator at the cathedral, independent of the city's electrical grid.

The architects should not perform as line workers. Instead, they should limit their role to standby in reserve and should only handle emergencies and contingencies, such as designing and directing the laying of shoring were the cathedral bombed. Architects should also refrain from ordering any new activities or directing alteration of any established plan of action for which teams would already have been trained. Those teams, Carlier insisted, must remain free to carry out the preestablished plan, and not be distracted by new directions from supervisors.

Within a few weeks of Carlier's presentation to the Archeological Society of Eure-et-Loir, he sent the study to the director general at the Fine Arts Administration, thereafter placing unceasing pressure on the authorities to take action. He sent letters, made calls, and worked with local citizens to do the same.

The Fine Arts Administration did not respond swiftly.

After four months of no action, Carlier increased the intensity of his campaign. He published his study as a twenty-eight-page article in *Les pierres de France*, the entire first page of which was an aerial photo of Chartres oriented to show the cathedral virtually next to the railroad complex. He wrote,

> The Cathedral of Chartres is one of the most precious works of art to be created by Humanity . . . [and] represents the pinnacle of dedicated work of many generations and a privileged time in history, one of those pieces of cultural heritage [that] is properly inestimable and [that] nothing on earth could replace. Sadly, citizens of other countries have a greater understanding of this than many French! Hence, those who come, often from

far away, to contemplate this great work are met with the sad surprise of . . . its immediate neighbor . . . a military aviation camp . . . continually amid an uninterrupted fracas of engines, test flights, exercises. . . .

But it gets worse. These monuments . . . were not constructed, to all evidence, by generations equally as indifferent and unprepared to value them as ours. We owe it, however, to the future, and this transmission must be the first and most sacred of the duties of our civilization.

This impudent folly, this danger [that] the neighboring aviation camp brings headlong to the monument, is obvious to everyone. In the initial hours of first hostilities, it is one of the sites [that] will be struck by the enemy . . . and more precisely the area immediately around the cathedral will be one of the chief goals of a sudden attack. Moreover, we have only too cruelly learned, during the last war, how fiercely the enemy can target both the noncombatant population and the great masterpieces that contribute to our glory. Suppos[e], however, that the formidable bombs that fall on Chartres in a moment of surprise fall only on their strategic target. Even in this instance, where the cathedral will not be touched, without a doubt, *all the stained-glass windows will have been shattered.*

In November, prominent citizens of Chartres formed a new organization they called the Safeguarding French Art Society. SFA initiated a publicity campaign targeted to appeal to various French scholarly societies. Later the same month, Carlier set out to design the new kind of scaffolding that he intended to be assembled quickly and easily by minimally trained volunteers, and he presented the design to both the ASEL and the SFA. The device would consist of metal tubes connected in units that could be stacked on top of one another. Each unit could support a stack of six wood-plank work platforms, with units stackable to a height of thirty-five feet or more, which would enable a half dozen pairs of workers to operate concurrently. An attachable narrow ladder of thin metal tubing would run from bottom to top to provide access.

By early December, Carlier had fabricated a prototype of the new scaffolding and assembled it in an alleyway in town. To test for stability, he climbed it with two other men, stood atop, and posed for a photo. He made final modifications to the design and placed an order with a manufacturer to fabricate a model for testing.

He wrote to the director general of the Fine Arts Administration, requesting permission to conduct a test at the cathedral. In his letter, he explained that he'd been authorized to place the initiative under the patronage of the SFA, which would participate in financing the project. A week later, Carlier took delivery of the scaffolding prototype for final evaluation and modification and then ordered two units built. Again he wrote the director general, this time informing him that the SFA had now placed funds at his disposal to purchase the custom scaffolding and run the tests, and he promised to personally cover any overage from his own funds should the tests prove more costly than anticipated.

By the end of January, Carlier had received many inquiries about and criticisms of his published study, but none yet from the Fine Arts Administration. So on January 31 he published a twenty-five-page supplement to his study of the Chartres dilemma in *Les pierres de France*. In this "Supplement No. 1," he refuted many of the criticisms lobbed at him, further explained his position, and considered further complications that had come to light: It was urgent that all installed windows be prepared for easier removal by replacing their cement anchors with malleable material. This would reduce the risk of damage to the windows in their actual removal. He further urged the authorities to detach and prepare for movement any built-in furnishings in the cathedral that might obstruct the window-removal work.

Carlier's public-relations efforts found an audience, and both of his aims—to force peacetime relocation of the air base and rapid removal of the windows upon first word of any German invasion—gained support. In February 1936, two weeks after publication of the study supplement in *Les pierres de France*, reporter Anne Fouqueray wrote a story for the Paris newspaper *Le Journal*. In the article, she included the same aerial photo of Chartres' proximity to the airfield that Carlier had put on the cover of the supplement. Fouqueray led her story with the ironic observation that the cathedral that had withstood fires from seven lightning strikes between 1539 and 1833 now faced growing danger from proposed expansion of an airfield, which project was awaiting the approval of the prefect. "Now," Fouqueray wrote, "what these desires could not do, a modern projectile, in a minute, alas!, would accomplish . . . and the mere explosion of one of these formidable war engines, falling in its neighborhood, would annihilate in an instant the incomparable windows . . . which include no less than 5,400 panels of the thirteenth century." Plying pressure on the military to relocate—or at least not expand—the air base, she went on to describe Carlier's window-removal scheme.

On March 7, Hitler ordered German troops into the Rhineland. France at the time was suffering through a financial downturn and did not have the monetary reserves to maintain the value of the franc. Short-term loans alone prevented France from defaulting on debts and causing further decline in the value of the franc. French newspapers and public opinion, though denouncing the German aggression, with a few exceptions did not call for war. Most newspapers called for the League of Nations to use sanctions to force Germany to back down and for France to strengthen existing alliances. France's political left opposed war. The French premier announced that French forces and resources would be at the disposal of the League of Nations as long as Britain and Italy did the same. So long as the Rhineland had remained unmilitarized, France had been secure in the knowledge that it could easily reoccupy the territory and threaten Germany's industrial area. But Germany's mobilization had removed this safeguard.

In Chartres, with its right-wing mayor, Raymond Gilbert—and its largely agricultural economy—the mood was likely no less polarized than in Paris and the other metropolitan areas of France. In reality, conservatives were likely no more eager for war than their liberal counterparts; yet they undoubtedly felt they had no alternative but to support the League of Nations and the agreements of the Locarno Treaties, since the only way France itself could again demilitarize the Rhineland would be to mobilize, which would be politically unpopular and cost far more than France could spend. The left, however, was on the ascendency—as the 1936 elections would show. The citizens of Chartres, however, were of one mind: townspeople of all political persuasions felt the need to act to protect the cathedral windows.

On March 9, Carlier arrived at the cathedral by truck with the two experimental scaffolds. At Carlier's request, Jean Maunoury, architect of historic monuments in Chartres, had arranged for all the metal scaffolding to be set up in the attic above several windows that were to be removed as a test of Carlier's procedures. Further, a pulley was to be installed in the attic ceiling to permit a rope to be used to lower equipment through the keystone opening in the vaulted ceiling 120 feet above the base of the lower windows. Maunoury also arranged for Yves Mellot, a Chartres fabricator, to install a metal sheet in the keystone opening to protect the surrounding stone from rope damage. To test the scaffolding's functioning for the removal of a pair of high windows, they would install another pulley from the edge of the roof for a rope to reach along the outside wall through a small trapdoor eighty feet below that had been cut in the ambulatory roof near the base of the windows. They would hoist scaffolding up from below and would lower any removed windows in their cases down through the trapdoor.

Days later, Carlier put out the word for helpers to assist in the tests. He visited Mellot and asked for a team. Within two weeks local leaders created a special committee whose lone purpose was to rescue Chartres' stained glass, which brought together nine volunteers and sent Carlier a written commitment of further support.

By March 28, Carlier had everything in place for the test removals. At the cathedral, he met the volunteers and two employees sent over from Charles and François Lorin's master glass workshop, along with the inspector of the Fine Arts Administration and a photographer. An observer timed and documented every step of the test removals. The volunteers lowered all scaffolding parts from the attic to assemble them at the two test windows. They assembled one on the floor of the nave at the base of one of the six-by-twenty-foot lower windows to give the workers access to the entire window. They positioned the other parts beneath the trapdoor for hoisting to a sill at the base of a pair of seven-by-twenty-seven-foot upper windows, where they assembled it to face the windows, resting on the five-foot-deep stone sill along the bottom edge of the windows.

One photograph taken that day shows three of the volunteers standing on their newly assembled six-layer scaffolding, perched high on the cathedral wall. They looked out like Lilliputians, dwarfed by the windows between two of the cathedral's flying buttresses. One of the men standing on the top level grasps one of the scaffold's vertical struts with both hands and, gazing down, looks like a reluctant high-diver questioning his resolve before his first plunge. The Lorin employees, wearing their white smocks, climbed up, chipped away the cement that secured the glass panels, removed them, and placed them in metal cases that Carlier had produced for the tests, which were then lowered through the trapdoor and shuttled to the crypt.

That same day, the team ran a separate test, employing in place of the scaffolding a two-man enclosed platform atop a mobile hand-cranked telescoping crane on wheels. They invited the Lorin employees to climb inside to be hoisted up so they could remove a lower window and then repeating the process on a higher window. For each test, the workers removed the windows and packed them in the cases that were then lowered to the floor and subsequently moved to the crypt. After the tests, all of the windows were reinstalled.

The tests having been completed, Yves Mellot assured the Fine Arts Administration that the people of Chartres would provide any support necessary to save the cathedral. Carlier and Chartres' stained-glass-rescue committee deferred to the administration for evaluation of the test results. Carlier followed with a letter to the administration director, relinquishing all rights he might have to the scaffold design.

But there was tension. The tests had revealed new risks and showed that the time required to remove the windows was four times that estimated by Carlier.

Within a week, the Historic Monuments Commission decided—based on recommendations in a report by Eugéne Rattier, chief architect and inspector general for France's Fine Arts Administration—that the administration would employ Carlier's scaffolding for the upper windows and the telescoping platform for the lower windows. It would order twenty such scaffolds for the upper windows and four telescoping platforms for the lower windows. The Historic Monuments Commission appointed Rattier and Émile Brunet to study arrangements for the cases to hold the windows.

The next week, in mid-April, the committee concerning itself with Chartres' stained glass sent the director general of the Fine Arts Administration a set of resolutions the committee had passed, endorsing Carlier's resolve to ensure that the stained glass would be removed within the two hours of word of any attack and imploring the director general to plan for "the rapid and simultaneous removal of all windows" because that "enormous task ... far surpasses the capabilities offered by existing professional businesses" and that without volunteer assistance and advance preparation by the local population, the administration would be "caught completely off guard." The Chartres committee promised also to install a set of stained-glass windows at a separate designated location on which to promptly train teams of volunteers—who were not (within the initial hours of the war) subject to being mobilized—to pass a test of skill to be judged by the Fine Arts Administration.

Two weeks later, Carlier fretted that he'd not heard any decision from the Fine Arts Administration's director general, so he published in a second supplement to his Chartres study in *Les pierres de France*: "Supplement No. 2" ran some thirty-four pages and also included a full-page aerial photo showing Chartres Cathedral's proximity to the military air base. He included a copy of his letter to the director general of January 24, 1936, and another letter sent to the director general on April 17 from the Chartres' stained-glass-rescue committee, asserting that "any stained-glass still in place two hours after the opening of hostilities will inevitably and irretrievably be destroyed by the explosions produced on the nearby airfield." That letter continued,

It would be criminal to resign oneself to the loss of such an inestimable and irreplaceable treasure, the unique testimony of an incomparable spiritual exhalation, bequeathed from the past to the future and to which our age has the even-more sacred and formidable duty of conservation. . . .

In the certainty that you will appreciate and make full use of all the possibilities of collaboration that are being spontaneously and voluntarily offered, we assure you, Mr. Director General, of our very strong attachment to the Cathedral of Chartres.

Carlier also reported that forty-two newspapers had participated in his publicity campaign in France and abroad. He wrote that with this publication he hoped to inform anyone interested in Chartres Cathedral's preservation of his progress. But his ardent and sustained efforts to raise public awareness to garner support and funds for the project may have gotten under the skin of the Fine Arts Administration's staff, concluding the piece as follows:

IX. What Will Be the Signal for the Removal?

The administration could do nothing, we said, to save the windows of Chartres in less than two hours without the immediate assistance of the population. Therefore, we address . . . a question . . . to the administration: TO WHAT SIGNAL, FROM WHAT EVENT, WILL WE HAVE THE RIGHT TO PROCEED WITH THE EFFECTIVE REMOVAL OF THE STAINED GLASS? Will it only be the alert, that is, the entry into the war? Could it not be an earlier stage, the decree of mobilization, for example, supposing that it precedes heavy attack?

For it is quite evident that, from the decree of mobilization, for example, telephone and telegraph lines will be exclusively given over to the service of the military authority and that OUR UNHAPPY OFFICE OF FINE ARTS, so often considered secondary in our era among the State machine, WILL THEN BE MATERIALLY UNABLE TO MAKE KNOWN ANY ORDERS. It must therefore be established in advance that this or that next step of tension automatically leads to the implementation of a particular safeguard measure. . . .

It is now well known that on 28 March, during the tests, one of the most directly responsible officials, questioned in this vein, replied: "The question is solely a matter for the Fine Arts Administration, and the city does not need to worry about it; the

Fine Arts Administration will send specialists from Paris." To do what? To make an inventory? To discover that there will no longer be any stained glass in the windows and that everything will have shattered?

So to those who think that they have to wait for orders, one can only respond by admonishing them to wait for nothing and no one before gathering, readying, and preparing themselves.

It would not be surprising if the administrators and staff had taken umbrage at his tone.

The men and women of the Fine Arts Administration may not have communicated their decisions and actions to Carlier or to the committee dedicated to saving Chartres' stained glass, but, as we'll see, they had already been moving forward with the project—even if many of their decisions conflicted with Carlier's notions of how to proceed. But would their planning move quickly enough to save the windows before war struck?

PART II

THE INTERWAR YEARS

CHAPTER SIX

Spy Hap: Shiojiri, Japan, 1935

IN JUNE 1935, ARMY LIEUTENANT WELBORN B. GRIFFITH JR. ARRIVED in Osaka on a ferry from Shanghai, spent a night in a hotel, and walked to the train station through neighborhoods pervaded with the smells of incense, steaming rice, and fermented soybeans. He found the platform for the morning train to Shiojiri, a city in Japan's interior highlands, and boarded the first coach, which jerked with a burst of steam and heaved from the station. Griff arched over the aisle and looked for a spot in the overhead rack for his backpack, to keep an eye on it. A man in a blue suit, white shirt, and tie boarded behind him at the end of the coach and walked past. This man placed a leather satchel in the rack and took a seat ahead, looking over his shoulder, peering at Griff as if probing for something to report. Something about the man's eyes, the way he kept looking over his shoulder, puzzled Griff. The man looked down, yet peeked up again, furtively, as though he didn't want to be caught staring.

Griff was perhaps not overly surprised to be an object of curiosity in Japan. Now six feet, three inches tall, he'd likely already attracted his share of stares on this trip and was headed to see parts of real, non-Westernized Japan; in the Philippines bush he had been intrigued by its indigenous people—the first he had seen since Comanches in Texas—but in Manila and China he had been confined to areas whose cultures had been attenuated by English, Spanish, and Americans. Now he was determined to encounter people and cultures untransformed by the West. He gazed at passing country through a portside rail yard and industrial and residential zones and rundown neighborhoods—no surprise, given Japan's depressed economy.

A pall permeated the coach. A man in threadbare clothes in a seat across from Griff would look up from his newspaper with haggard eyes, glance at Griff, avoiding eye contact, and a woman glimpsed at Griff watching him and then looked away.

Soldiers sat at the rear. Passengers avoided eye contact with them, too. Nationalist groups were infiltrating the Japanese military, rejecting party politics, pressing to unite Japan under the emperor, and staging coups and assassinations, transforming the country to a police state.

The train headed northeast. After a stop in Kyoto, it headed east, out of the dense urban region and past open lots, a lake, and another city (Nagoya) and then continued northeast, past factories flanked by queues of military trucks and planes with red zeros. After several stops, the train climbed a winding valley through hills into a narrowing, steep notch. Finally, a high village emerged among slopes of *matsu*, persimmon, and cherry trees. The sign read *Shiojiri*.

Griff meandered through town, snapping pictures of forested slopes, homes, and locals. He glanced toward a man skulking a block behind who wore a gray robe, but Griff didn't give him much thought. The quiet, wagon-wide street passed between weathered clapboard sheds and narrowed to a paved lane rising along a creek bed on the facing hillside into forests that surrounded the town.

Griff was drawn by sounds of metal clanging from a small building tucked between houses and peered inside. It was a ceramics works. In a large room, several men in shirtsleeves supervised a dozen or two shop-apron-clad workers carrying trays of parts. Other laborers fastened, stacked, and inspected amid the clanking and whooshing of a furnace that piqued Griff's curiosity. He put down his backpack to snap a picture inside.

A man yelled something Griff didn't understand, something sounding like "Same nasahl!" The man—in a robe—came running, shouting, waving his arms. He drew his revolver, pointed to Griff's camera, and snarled a few orders Griff couldn't understand. Griff guessed the man was telling him to cease taking pictures, so he set the camera down.

He reached for his own service forty-five, only to remember he'd left it in his trunk at the Shanghai barracks across the East China Sea. Now, from inside the doorway, Griff faced the gunman and shrugged to show he had no clue what the gunman was ordering.

The workers fixed their eyes on the robed gunman, who edged toward Griff.

"Does anyone here speak English?" Griff called out.

An elderly man in the back raised his arm over his paper-strewn desk. "Yes, a little bit," he said. The glare of the old man's desk lamp reflected off his metal-rimmed spectacles, obscuring Griff's view of his eyes. Griff summoned him, and the old man shambled forward. "Can I help?" the old man asked. "I am Jiro Katsu."

"Thank you. Can you tell me in English what he's ordering?"

"He says you must tell him why you're looking inside our establishment. He says pictures are forbidden. All works are secret."

"Well . . . please tell him I'm just visiting. I've never seen a furnace like that. I'd like to know what you're making, how the furnace works—that's all."

The gunman yelled again.

"He says you must not ask questions," Katsu translated. "You must tell him what you are doing here. He says he is Agent Yoshida, special police. You must go out through the same door and leave."

Griff recognized Yoshida. He'd been on the train: that same man who'd boarded in Osaka, wearing a blue suit and tie and carrying a leather satchel. Yoshida again tilted his head down, yet peered up, but this time staring at Griff. Now Yoshida was wearing that robe over his suit and tie. Griff could see them beneath his robe.

"Please tell him I'll stop," Griff said to Katsu. "And ask him to put down his weapon. I'm just a vacationer."

Katsu, in Japanese, relayed Griff's consent to Yoshida, who barked further instructions.

"He says you must put your camera away. This factory is secret. You must go."

"Thank you. I'll go. I'll just pick up my backpack and leave slowly. See?" he said, reaching for his backpack. "Please tell him."

Yoshida spoke again to Katsu, signaling for Katsu to come to the door. Yoshida inserted his gun beneath his robe as he conferred with Katsu.

Katsu turned toward Griff. "He says you need to tell him where you are going now."

Griff said he would retire to his hotel, which he assumed was back in town near the train station. He had the name and address on a letter in his backpack and offered to pull it out to show the policeman.

Katsu spoke further with Yoshida and finally said, "He will go with you to your hotel. Show him the letter, and he will know where to go."

Griff pulled the letter out and introduced himself. Katsu bowed, smiling in relief. He showed conspicuous deference, even obeisance, toward Yoshida. Katsu then spoke some words of reassurance to the employees, and most shuffled back to work.

Yoshida scanned Griff's letter for an address, nodded, and returned it to Griff. He then glanced back toward town and set out in the lead, waving for Griff to follow. As Griff fell in behind him, he noticed another of Yoshida's surreptitious nonlooks, with head pointed down and eyes peering up whenever looking Griff's way. Griff hesitated, not quite sure what Yoshida was up to. Was Griff free or not?

The two walked back toward the center of town, Yoshida walking several steps ahead of Griff. The mountains loomed above the village, with ridges that faced each other and joined like the tip of a giant wishbone. After a time, Griff lost track of where he was. Things were closing in around him. This wasn't his boyhood big-sky Texas, but as he passed between buildings he could see the forested slopes of the hills surrounding the town, reminding him that he was heading back toward the train depot.

They arrived at a two-story wooden corner guesthouse, its small entryway leading to a dimly lit sitting room. Three wicker chairs faced a shoulder-high rice-paper window opposite the reception desk. With a bell on the desk, Griff summoned the owner-manager, a short, middle-aged man with eyeglasses who was wearing a *yukata*. The manager recognized the letter and asked Griff in English for his passport and to sign a room register, and then he peered at Yoshida, who was scrutinizing their every move.

After Yoshida had withdrawn, the manager whispered to Griff that he'd made Yoshida out to be a secret police agent, probably with the Tokkō or Kenpeitai, since he wasn't a local. He could see Yoshida tracking everything, and he mentioned the black notebook visible in Yoshida's pocket. Griff smiled with a wink.

"We do not receive many visitors here," said the manager. "People in this prefecture keep to themselves, mind their own business, obey orders, and expect others to. They let police do the observing." He added, "Oh, and this agent thinks you are a spy."

In his room, door closed, sweat dripped from Griff's forehead. In the bathroom, he splashed some water on his face and looked in the mirror as he hung up the towel. He saw Yoshida through the window, watching from across the street.

He thought about Alice, their journey to the Philippines with the baby, the fights, and her walking out and filing for divorce. It weighed on him. He had never faced anything like it before in his life. Perhaps he should feel humiliated, disgraced by her allegations, or maybe they were just the made-up, run-of-the-mill incidentals in Reno divorces. He was probably already determined to return stateside, clear his name, and regain custody. But first he needed to clear his head. His prime objective in Japan was just to take time off and see something new.

At dusk, he went to an eatery that smelled of grilled fish and sat at one of its few tables, Yoshida still shadowing him. Griff ordered the same grilled sardines, rice, and miso soup he saw a nearby patron eating and dug in when it arrived, maybe figuring that—Yoshida's tail notwithstanding—the factory incident was over. But he saw the cook-server behind the counter looking back and forth between Yoshida and Griff, fear showing on his face.

Griff returned to his hotel, Yoshida still tagging him. In his room, Griff could have reasoned, *The people in town resent these secret police. No wonder there was such tension. It wasn't about me. It was about their fear of that agent.* Even with Japan's economic recovery under way, pressure from Tōhōkai—Japan's fascist party—right-wing zealotry, and terrorism were creating an atmosphere of anxiety. It had begun with an assassination attempt on the emperor several years before. Griff had decided to visit

Japan anyway. He'd seen fear in the faces of the factory employees, guest-house manager, and cook. *I'm no damn spy*, he thought. *And there's nothing secret about that dang furnace. I'd just never seen one like it before.*

A night's sleep helped, the bed firm—a simple futon. He woke early, probably looking forward to his day, and at a breakfast bar suggested by the manager learned that a Japanese breakfast is a dinner meal with smaller portions, not the porridge of soybeans or rice common in China. That morning he ate rice, more soup with cabbage and onion, green tea, and juice.

He emerged to return to the guesthouse when a uniformed police-man, accompanied by Yoshida, confronted him. The policeman introduced himself in English as Officer Akio Nakamura and Yoshida as an agent of the special police, Tokkō (Peace Police), from Osaka.

"You will come with us," Nakamura instructed and directed Griff first back to his guesthouse to gather his things.

Griff might have objected but didn't—yet—and simply told the manager he'd be back. Flanked by Yoshida, Griff followed Nakamura out the door, probably wondering what they'd ask and where it was all headed. His pulse throbbed in his throat. Could this be a real police affair? Sino-Japanese relations were strained. His military passport and Shanghai duty—likely known to the Japanese—could raise suspicions.

They took him to a bare-front building shared by the town govern-ment and police that baked in the late June sun. Inside, two kimono-clad clerks nervously tried not to be noticed, perspiration on their brows, eyes confined to desks. Nakamura and Yoshida directed Griff to a dark, windowless room with a table, four chairs, and dented desk lamp, where they told Griff to sit. They walked out and closed the door behind them.

Smells of stale tea, cigarette ash, and neglected sweat pervaded, but the place wasn't as unnerving as dank police-interrogation chambers back in Shanghai, in which Griff had observed quaking Japanese suspects questioned by Chinese and Americans.

Nakamura and Yoshida returned with a third uniformed officer, whom Nakamura introduced as his superior, a Captain Yoshirou Kimura, chief of local police. The man spoke no English, so Nakamura translated. The men looked at Griff and observed him, pencils poised.

They asked him to identify himself, and then the captain rapidly fired a series of questions, translated by Nakamura: Where did you come from? What brought you to Shiojiri? What unit are you in? Why look at the factory? Don't you know factories in Japan are secret? Where is your uniform? Where are you going next?

Griff made contact with each question pitched to him, listening carefully, and answered one at a time, without dramatic points—just speaking truth. He recapped his Shanghai-to-Osaka trip, day in Osaka, train to Shiojiri, walk around town, tourist picture taking. At the factory, he had heard a noise and was curious and so looked inside. The furnace had seemed odd. He'd grown up in a small Texas town, working in groceries. He'd never seen one like it.

When all had been asked and answered, the chief spoke to the others, and they gathered their notes. Nakamura bowed in haste and excused himself and the other two men, offering Griff a drink. Griff waited in darkness.

They returned to examine Griff's possessions, from the contents of his jeans pockets to his backpack: his C rations, dictionary, clothes, and family photos and a carved driftwood piece from Quanah. They puzzled over his toiletry bag from the Philippines, which led to questions about his role as a military observer. An observer does just that, Griff explained. He observes and acts as a liaison. It was a training assignment. They asked about American intentions regarding Japan. He knew nothing.

They seemed perplexed by Griff's explanation, their brows furrowed. They remained polite but were clearly puzzled, unable to grasp that nothing he'd revealed to them could be of concern, clearly still suspecting he was on a spy mission.

He kept cool. Patience would see him through. He had seen suspects under questioning. The more he maintained that he was being honest, the deeper seemed their confusion and the more intensely they demanded further explanation, until he ran out of neutral things to say. He held his tongue. *I can explain it to you, but I can't understand it for you.* The interview dragged on for two hours, until they excused themselves once again.

Once again the three returned, Chief Kimura and Yoshida remaining standing, Nakamura sitting down across from Griff.

"That will be all, Lieutenant. You may leave now. But I will be accompanying you for the rest of your stay in Japan. We hope you will not mind; my superiors have ordered that I escort you while you remain in our country."

Griff hesitated, then asked, "Can I take my things?"

"Yes," replied Nakamura.

"I have some other places I'd like to visit. All right?"

"Yes, Lieutenant. You may go where you wish. But you may not photograph factories. Do you understand?"

Griff nodded, packed up, and returned with his gear to his guesthouse, Nakamura at his side, who asked Griff to address him as Akio from now on. Griff agreed, if Akio would call him Griff.

Akio accompanied Griff to lunch—urging him to eat one of the rice balls with pickled plum in the center that school children eat to reinforce their patriotism—and then ushered Griff on a walk to the Hiraide Iseki archeological dig on the edge of town, a collection of ancient settlement ruins, where Akio now served as Griff's interpreter and guide. But although Akio gamely answered Griff's questions and was quick to offer translations, he gave Griff no reason to trust him.

They boarded the train to Osaka, where Griff checked back into the same hotel in which he had stayed upon first arriving on the island. In the morning, Akio was waiting in the lobby when Griff finished breakfast, ready to show the American old Osaka Castle and other sights in the city.

Griff finally broke away only upon boarding the ferry back to Shanghai. From the deck, he watched the receding Osaka harbor and then the last trace of land fade into the horizon. He filed away the week's events for reflection.

The passage back to Shanghai provided him time for a breather, to turn over in his mind the predicament of his military career. But what most likely absorbed his mind was the miserable state of his marriage. What a comparison this grim, solitary voyage was compared to the cruise to Manila three and a half years before, with Alice and the baby when—trapped on the ship without official duties to occupy him—he had spent a lot of time doting over the baby and remaining attentive to his wife. Back then, his relationship with her had been smooth, except for the normal getting-used-to-each-other ruffles any newlyweds must endure. But now he would be replaying their time together, scanning his recollections for early signs of the strife to come. At the same time, he likely would have reflected on his forestalled determination to make a name for himself, and the tension between that ambition and staying close to his family, turning over in his mind the compromises that would be required to take up with a new wife, perhaps with turbulence, urgency, even desperation on his mind.

Did he have his eyes on some kind of dream? Alice, gorgeous Alice, was from a blue-blooded eastern family with military roots going back generations. Her father had served in the Philippines upon graduating from West Point and recently graduated from Fort Leavenworth's Command and General Staff School. There were sufficient grounds to think Griff's marriage might enjoy attraction and commonality enough to make a happy union. But life with Alice had not turned out as he had imagined. She was strong willed and used to getting what she wanted. Her parents gave it to her. And Griff was headstrong too. He had thought she would know what to expect as an officer's wife, but he'd been wrong. Their marriage had been a terrible mistake.

On the ferry, his eyes on the blue horizon, Griff had hours to reflect. And what of his adventure in Japan and his narrow escape? No, he wasn't a spy; he was a military observer in the US Army's 130-year-old observer program. The duties of observers had historically included intelligence gathering, but that role had shifted to attachés, who—a generation before Griff—had taken on intelligence gathering for the Military Information Division. Observers were directed to develop themselves professionally through their peacetime observation of foreign military. By selecting Griff as an observer, the Army had marked his talent, competence, and intelligence. It did not make him a spy, but no doubt his experience in Japan, Manila, and Shanghai complemented his savvy.

However useful the adventure in Japan may have been for Griff's professional whetting, his choice to expose himself to such an incident and his conduct during its course may have revealed something inside him—an unknown that would emerge again and perhaps grow and impel his conduct during the coming war. Griff's personality was enigmatic, combining brusque forthrightness and a propensity to follow rules with tenderness and an almost-clumsy indulgence. Yet his adventure in Japan illustrated an extra dimension to his character. Observed objectively, Griff's decision to go to Shiojiri in the first place, to photograph the factory, and especially to adopt a blazon posture during arrest and cavalier demeanor during his interrogation manifested a proclivity for taking unnecessary risk. Such detachment from reality in a military officer might be somewhat over-the-top and maybe even border on a wish to cause self-harm.

On the ferry, the businessmen and gaggles of revelers drank and bandied at cards and looked forward to Shanghai as their Far Eastern Babylon. The ferry approached Shanghai at dusk, with lights of oncoming ships and Chinese junks flickering on the Yangtze River. One riverbank came into view, then the other, and the ferry turned to the left and entered the Huangpu River, where Shanghai's lights beckoned. On the right bank, lamps glistened, and smoke rose from Japanese factory chimneys.

Chains clattered on the dock, winches whirled, and gabbling dock laborers surged to unload cargo, like squirrels scurrying for food. Griff passed up the rickshaws, climbed into a taxi, and in his Texas drawl attempted to direct the driver to the Shanghai Volunteer Corps barracks. The taxi drove up dirt-scattered streets lined with shops, bars and teahouses, tailors, and watchmakers. Signs in French and Russian, Chinese and English, hawked wares and services. The driver turned down the main street in the English neighborhood, Shanghai's Broadway: a curving oceanfront boulevard where traffic was light, with streetcars passing seven- to ten-story stone and brick office buildings, with guardsmen outside banks and offices that faced the river, whose shores bustled with junks and bantam market boats.

They passed onto the streets crisscrossing the Chinese sector, where evening life was just getting started, with open shops, lantern-covered walls, signs scrawled in Chinese characters, crowds sprinkled with salesmen and waiters chanting on sidewalks in front of eateries, steam rising from vents. They passed into the French Concession, with its entertainment palaces and shops of clothes and books, beauty parlors, hair salons, bakeries, cafes, dance halls, and cinemas.

Griff tipped the driver, slung his backpack over his shoulder, and entered the barracks, where he retrieved his stored gear, changed into his tropical work uniform, and repacked. Then he handed off his gear to a crewman for transfer to the ship in Chinwangtao—up the coast via Tientsin, 180 miles east of Beiping, an all-day train ride north—and, for his last day, he bid colleagues goodbye.

When Griff woke in the Shanghai barracks the next morning, he packed his jeans and other gear for the sea trip back to the States, perhaps now better grasping the narrow margin by which he had escaped danger in Japan. The blue jeans he had worn in Japan resembled the denim fatigue uniforms the Japanese marines had worn in the 1932 Shanghai skirmish between the Japanese and the Chinese in which his peace-keeping force had served. Now it may have been clearer to him that the Tokkō police in Shiojiri could well have interpreted choice of attire as a stick-in-your-eye provocation, escalating an already-tense situation with the Yank. Things could so easily have turned horribly wrong. But now, in the safety of Shanghai, he was in a better position to appreciate the risk. But why did he take it? What had driven him to it?

CHAPTER SEVEN

Zay Transcends Confrontation: Paris and Chartres, Spring 1935–1937

IN EARLY 1936, ACHILLE CARLIER COMPLAINED THAT THE FINE ARTS Administration had failed to respond to his demands or in any other way endorse his plan to preserve the Chartres stained glass from destruction. Still, records reveal that the administration had felt increasing public pressure to act as Germany rearmed and remilitarized the Rhineland. Amid this change, although they had not acceded to Carlier's plan, the Fine Arts Administration's archives show a flurry of wartime preparations behind the scenes. It had been less than a year since France had adopted the April 1935 law making civil passive defense compulsory; the act compelled local authorities to begin organizing civil-defense measures, including establishing a committee of passive defense in each adminis-trative department throughout the country. And so by the time Carlier's Chartres campaign had gained public attention, the Fine Arts Adminis-tration had already assembled an experienced team as impassioned about protecting historic monuments as were Carlier and his backers.

Georges Huisman, archivist-paleographer and associate professor of history and geography, had since 1935 been leading the Fine Arts Admin-istration as its director general. Sporting a mustache and usually a bow tie, Huisman smoked a pipe and cast an erudite aspect. In the late 1920s, he had served as chief of staff to a series of ministers and, in 1931, as secretary general of the Élysée—the most senior position in the cabinet—under President Paul Doumer. Later Huisman had been chosen to lead the

Fine Arts Administration in the government of Prime Minister Édouard Daladier. Before the outbreak of World War II, Huisman would work to establish the Cannes Film Festival—brainchild of Minister of National Education and Fine Arts Jean Zay—and at the beginning of the war Huisman would join in the attempt to form a French government in exile, starting with his departure fleeing with more than two dozen deputies and senators aboard the SS *Massilia* bound for North Africa.

Other key players assisted in the running of the Fine Arts Administration. They included Jean Verrier, who had been a prior director general of the agency as well as one-time inspector general at the General Inspectorate of Historic Monuments; Pierre Paquet, an architect who had also served as inspector general of historic monuments and had restored important buildings; Eugéne Rattier, architect and former assistant to the inspector general of historic monuments, who had restored Notre-Dame de Paris in 1923; and Émile Brunet, a chief architect who had also restored other important buildings.

Before *Le Journal* had published Anne Fouqueray's February 17 article bringing to the French public's attention the potential danger that the encroaching military airfield posed to the nearby Chartres Cathedral, Huisman's team at the Fine Arts Administration had already been planning for the protection of Chartres from wartime damage, procuring equipment and materials for removing the windows. On the day the article appeared, Huisman and members of his staff were in discussion with master glassmakers regarding methods for safely removing the windows. Days later, Huisman asked Solidevit, a Paris steel-scaffolding company, to send representatives to Chartres to study the scaffolding design proposed by Achille Carlier.

Within a week, Auguste Labouret, an internationally recognized Parisian stained-glass artist and innovator, gave Huisman a memorandum of recommendations concerning the Chartres windows. He recommended that the speed of the operation be balanced against the care the fragile windows would require. He further advised that, although entrusting several Parisian glassmaker workshops with removing the glass would offer its advantages, the sudden mobilization of the rescue operation would likely be slowed to the point of compromise by organizational complications in the assembly of a large, scattered team with varying travel times and modes of travel. In the end, Labouret also suggested specific courses of action to be taken in case of bombardment and made recommendations for the necessary manpower and scaffolding. He argued against removing any windows at night.

Meanwhile, the Parisian scaffolding firm Solidevit performed its on-site study for the Fine Arts Administration and on March 9 proposed, for a fixed price, to conduct a trial run of the assembly of its recommended type of scaffolding.

On May 1 the Fine Arts Administration completed its review of vendors' proposals solicited for production of special crates to hold the windows and ordered one thousand, to be constructed with nonflammable packing materials and so-called fireproof wood.

Several weeks later, the administration rejected the need for an on-site generator to power lights during a night removal, maintaining the machinery's upkeep would be difficult and also that the delicate procedure of the window removal should never occur at night in any case. The administration also purchased other necessary materials for the protection project, to store near or within the cathedral.

In France's national elections that May, candidates of the left and center parties—which joined as the Popular Front—won a majority of parliamentary seats, the Socialists holding the plurality and forming a coalition with Radicals to appoint Socialist Léon Blum as prime minister.

In June, Blum appointed Jean Zay new Minister of National Education and Fine Arts. Zay was a journalist and lawyer from Orléans with a wife and two young daughters who in 1932 had been elected deputy of Loiret and then reelected in May 1936. Zay gave up his law practice in 1936 to enter government service. Blum had chosen Zay largely because of his youth. Zay had been known as one of the group of young Turks who had sought to renew the Radical Party and in 1935 had pushed it to join the Popular Front. A Freemason with Jewish roots, Zay urged left-wing unity, supported Spanish republicans, and would oppose the Munich Agreement of 1938.

Zay wore distinctive heavy-rimmed, round-lensed eyeglasses, and he stood out in many additional ways, not as an anticapitalist or militant but as a man who consistently reached to operate on a high moral plane and resist what he perceived as trends toward decadence. The introduction to his file in the French National Archives describes him as having "an energetic and positive nature" and as "an endearing man, dazzling with talent, of finesse and intelligence, but attentive and sensitive, sometimes profound." Zay was a pacifist but, with Hitler in power, opposed fascist states and considered the League of Nations a failure.

Zay contributed leadership, energy, inspiration, and a radical activism to the Ministry of National Education and Fine Arts. His administration applied modern principles of planning and logistics, focusing on procuring personnel, training them across organizations, purchasing equipment and supplies from dual sources, securing financing, coordinating with the military, and engaging local volunteers for training on-site.

Zay also reanimated the government's preparations for preservation of artworks and cultural monuments and guided them in a new direction, building on the work René Planchenault had begun years before. What set Jean Zay apart was his passion—his sense of great purpose in whatever he set about doing. For him, the work of monument preservation was part of the core function of education—to help the people, from all walks of French life, to try to make sense of the world that seemed again in the 1930s to be gyrating out of control. He operated according to a moral compass, and it is entirely fitting that his ashes would eventually be installed in the Paris Panthéon, immortalizing him as one of the great players in the French Resistance. At the onset of World War II, he would quit his ministry post to join the military, suffering a tragic fate when the Vichy regime arrested him, tried him for treason along with a host of other left-leaning political players, and imprisoned him.

Zay wrote a wartime prison diary, published in 1946, in which his meditation displayed what one commentator called "an amazing degree of literary panache and verve." Zay identified with Captain Alfred Dreyfus, who had been unjustly imprisoned in 1895. Zay jotted in his diary a description of Dreyfus by another French author to the effect that "persecutors could not divest him of his priceless inner freedom." Zay exhibited that inner freedom. While in prison, not only did Zay maintain the diary, but he also wrote a detective novel that was published under the pen name Paul Duparc. In addition, he grew radishes, tomatoes, and flowers in a tiny gravel path.

Zay arrived as the new minister of National Education and Fine Arts at a time when the Fine Arts Administration was increasingly focusing on the Chartres windows among its wide range of projects. Following Achille Carlier's March trial run of the window removal at Chartres, Pierre Paquet, within the Fine Arts Administration, wrote a May 23 report to the commission detailing the Fine Arts Administration's efforts to respond expeditiously to the urgency advocated by Carlier and the Chartres stained-glass-rescue committee; that same day the Historic Monuments Commission approved purchase of the equipment proposed by Émile Brunet—excepting a generator and the telescoping cranes, which were still under consideration but were later approved as well.

In early July, on request from Zay, the defense minister agreed to make 124 soldiers available to the Fine Arts Administration for removal and crating of the Chartres windows, adding that by October the number could be increased to 250.

But the Fine Arts Administration had greater responsibilities for preservation of France's cultural patrimony beyond the provincial concerns of one cathedral in one city. Beginning in 1936, the interior, defense, and education ministries began a coordinated effort to incorporate a national "passive" civil defense, consisting of nonmilitary measures to protect French heritage from aerial attacks. The Direction des musées—or the Directorate of Museums—directed public art museums throughout France to assemble lists of art objects (paintings, sculptures, and archeological and decorative objects) that would need to be evacuated in the event of war. The Fine Arts Administration also had to decide whether it would evacuate private collections as well as those of public museums. But while it struggled to realize its mandate, political change intervened.

Overall, although the Fine Arts Administration's planning by the end of 1936 had aligned in many ways with the preservationist steps advocated by Achille Carlier, the leadership team at the Ministry of National Education and Fine Arts and at the Historic Monuments Commission determined Carlier's plan to be unrealistic; his plan was too aggressive and risk-prone to gain traction. Carlier had insisted that a team of 350 workers—many to consist of volunteers—when summoned, would be able to gather at Chartres Cathedral, clear three thousand wooden chairs from the nave, move the confessionals out of the way, lower most of the scaffolds through the ceilings and others from the storage rooms, reposition and assemble the scaffolds, and gather the one thousand crates and packing materials from storage areas in designated groupings to designated points, all in the first hour, and then mount the scaffolds and simultaneously remove the hundreds of windows, lower their thousands of glass panels, pack them in crates, and deposit them in the crypt, all in one additional hour. The Historic Monuments Commission instead chose to prioritize security along with speed. So it called on the workshops of France's master glassmakers to propose an alternative plan.

Nevertheless, the agitation of Achille Carlier and his team of volunteers and Chartres Cathedral's civic supporters appears to have performed a valuable function—and would again in the near future: They had forced the Fine Arts Administration to expedite and make critical preparations—to build trapdoors and keystone sleeves and to order manpower, equipment, and supplies. More important, Carlier and supporters had deployed the knowledge and support of Chartrains whose lives were intimately woven with the cathedral. And Carlier seems to have forced the professionals to listen to the citizens and grapple with their fears. But now it was up to the Fine Arts Administration to fit all the Chartres players—government, citizen, and military—into the larger national need to preserve monuments under mounting threat of German invasion.

In January 1937, director general of the Fine Arts Administration, Georges Huisman, determined that the government would undertake to evacuate all works of art "worthy of state protection" from all museums and many private estates in eastern and northern France and move those artworks to the south and west into protective sites, including one hundred castles, as well as prepare for the protection of culturally significant historic buildings, like Chartres Cathedral. Although preparation began right away, another year and a half would pass before a law would be adopted to provide a national legal framework for the passive-defense program, giving the state the necessary authority, including powers to requisition privately owned buildings for storage of art and to designate personnel, including volunteers, reserve soldiers, and even veterans, who could be called up for nonmilitary duties within two years of completing military service.

In addition to the Fine Arts Administration's behind-the-scenes preparations to protect France's national treasures, the Historic Monuments Commission authorized purchase of supplies for rapid removal of Chartres' stained glass and payment of fees to the architects working on the project.

Blum stepped down as prime minister in mid-1937, but Zay stayed on in the Ministry of National Education and Fine Arts, and during the next year he moved the wartime-national-preservation project forward. Two months after Blum's departure, Zay issued a set of secret, far-reaching instructions on the protection of France's monuments and works of art against war damage. He ordered his staff to classify monuments and artworks under a kind of heritage-triage system and designated eight administrative departments from which artworks were to be withdrawn and, for each, a corresponding department in the country's interior to which the artworks were to be directed. Zay premised his directive on the belief that no part of the country could be sheltered from aerial attack and that precautions must be taken against attacks near munitions factories on the basis of lessons learned from the damage to the stained-glass windows of the Basilica of Saint-Denis after the 1918 La Courneuve explosion. Zay wrote, "It is better to pursue measures that may ultimately prove useless rather than leave oneself exposed to be taken by surprise." In another report, Zay prescribed building protective walls of sandbags around fragile buildings, removing stained-glass windows, and using various means to prevent fires.

In October 1937, Zay established general principles that he later directed be disseminated in a secret directive throughout the north of France. This report was likely based on the work of René Planchenault, begun as early as 1932. Zay ordered Georges Huisman at the Fine Arts Administration to promulgate the secret order by recirculating a memo previously issued in 1935 by Inspector General Eugéne Rattier of the

Historic Monuments Administration in which Rattier had without success requested that the architects of the Historic Monuments Administration assemble an inventory of French artworks and answer detailed questions concerning buildings housing the works. Zay now instructed staff countrywide to promptly follow their head architects' orders and provide Huisman answers to Rattier's 1935 questions, all to facilitate central ordering of equipment and supplies for evacuation and passive defense of those works.

A critical matter remained to be resolved, however: The Fine Arts Administration had not yet secured sites in which the evacuated art, including the stained-glass windows, could be stored. The Ministry of Defense chose the western and central regions of France as those in which storage depots would be established.

In the second half of 1938, Fine Arts Administration and Directorate of Museums staff began to search for suitable facilities within those regions that met the militarily mandated criteria: The sites had to be away from urban centers and strategic targets, yet easily accessible by rail or road, sturdy and large enough to withstand nearby explosions, close to water for firefighting, and in climates neither too cold nor humid for paintings. But even when storage buildings satisfying all of these difficult criteria could be found, they couldn't be used until Ministry of Finance officials offered indemnity payments to property owners, who were required to permit curators and guards, with their families, to live on-site indefinitely. For stained-glass windows, that storage facilities meet all of the criteria was essential. But even as late as 1938, no destination for the Chartres windows had been secured.

The Fine Arts Administration had to engage in comprehensive multisite planning for evacuations they knew might have to be implemented at any time. The sites needing protection included Paris's Sainte-Chapelle, Chartres' cathedral and Church of Saint-Pierre, and the cathedrals at Bourges, Amiens, and Metz.

They worked on the far-reaching project throughout 1937 and the first three-quarters of 1938, engaging dozens of contractors and vendors to plan, procure, and place supplies and equipment in storage near the various cathedrals for quick access when needed. But such planning and procurement was only part of the problem posed by this vast undertaking. The need for personnel trained to carry out the necessary work was a thornier problem and perhaps a greater source of uncertainty: most Frenchmen of suitable age and physical ability to the tasks were subject to conscription and immediate call-up in a military mobilization. This posed a potential risk too great to ignore. Furthermore, the exodus of artwork to be conducted via trucks and trains across the country would require guards and teams of workmen. To manage the problem, the authorities called on military workforces to prepare the artworks for shipment and for assembly in the storage depots. They created a new military unit that would be known to France's wartime Grand Quartier Général (GQG) as the Service des Monuments au G.Q.G.—or the Historic Monuments Service—whose mandate would be to protect the convoys who would evacuate, first, France's moveable art and, second, its cathedrals' stained-glass windows.

Captain Lucien Edward Louis Prieur, a Parisian-born architect and World War I veteran, headed the new unit. Prieur worked closely with civilian officials, including Ernest Herpe, a widely experienced chief architect who would join the Historic Monuments Service in 1939 and eventually head the Fine Arts Administration.

Many planners and project managers were involved in the Chartres project. In 1938, over at the Fine Arts Administration, Director General Georges Huisman appointed Paris architect Jean Trouvelot as Chartres project leader for both the cathedral and the nearby Church of Saint-Pierre, to be assisted by Jean Maunoury, and Michael Mastorakis, another state-trained architect at Chartres, to assist Maunoury in turn. Contractors responded with bid proposals. Some were accompanied by lists of proposed workers.

They anticipated that specified essential workers would have to be issued security clearances by the military and granted waivers from mobilization and transportation permits to enable them, with their families, to travel to Chartres.

The equipment and supplies needed for the window-removal work would not fit in the cathedral's attic. So the Fine Arts Administration arranged for two storage facilities: First, it gained access to the nearby granary and cellar of Loëns, five hundred feet northwest of the cathedral, in which to store the empty wooden crates. Second, it leased from the military a portion of Building Q in the Rapp District of Chartres, a half mile southeast of the cathedral, next to the Church of Saint-Pierre.

By mid-March 1938, fears of German invasion heightened further when Germany incorporated Austria. On April 10, Édouard Daladier became France's prime minister, and he kept Zay on in the Ministry of National Education.

The international crisis over the Sudetenland in September 1938 would serve as a technical run-through for the protection of historic sites across France. On September 6, with war appearing imminent, France's Division of Public Buildings distributed fire extinguishers and materials for sandbags to cities throughout the country and recruited workers to create protective ramparts.

On September 9, Enterprise Mathieu & Marçais, a Paris construction contractor, delivered to Jean Trouvelot a complete proposal to supply managers, manpower, and equipment to oversee major portions of the Chartres project, with lists of equipment and personnel—including each man's address and biographical profile—to be processed for security clearances, mobilization waivers, and transit permits.

Between 1936 and mid-1938, crews brought material, tools, and equipment to Chartres Cathedral and the nearby cellar of the Loëns and Rapp Building for use in both the cathedral and the Church of Saint-Pierre. Contractors cut holes for as many as three dozen exit hatches in the attics and roofs of the north and south ambulatories for hoisting tools and equipment from below the floors of those ambulatory attics, and inside the cathedral in the attic of each ambulatory they installed metal sleeves in the keystone holes of such ambulatory vault, through which scaffolding would be lowered to the cathedral floor when needed.

Without elevators or power winches, workmen hauled hundreds of lengths of tubular pipe and fittings for scaffolding, in interchangeable pieces, up circular stairways to the cathedral's attic, whose ceiling extended more than forty feet above the vaults of the nave.

Atop the nave, in the main attic, workers traversed boardwalks resting on the crossbeams above the ancient vaults, where they stacked designated pipes and fittings above their respective assigned keystones, which would later be opened, through which to lower the equipment by ropes down to the floor of the nave. Other equipment and supplies they carried up circular stairways to be stacked in the towers' storage rooms, some to be hoisted up through the exit hatches cut into in the ambulatories' ceilings, the other portion to be lowered through openings in the balcony floors through keystone holes of the ambulatory vaults.

They placed supplemental materials in storage as well: ropes, hoists, buckets, dozens of exit hatches, pumps, and hundreds of fittings. And they detached the wooden confessionals from the walls of the nave and placed them on wheeled platforms to facilitate moving them to make way for scaffolding.

Trucks delivered the thousand custom-constructed wooden crates for the stained glass, containing insulating panels of Celotex insulation. Laborers brought work lights and six large tool chests for hammers, clamps, chisels, strapping machines, and steel strapping. To the cellar of Loëns they carried more than one hundred thousand sandbags, together with more than fifty thousand square feet of vitrex (particle board) for covering window jambs to close up the bays once the windows had been removed, plus nine tons of sawdust and cork fiber for use inside the crates as packing material.

The Fine Arts Administration and the architects working on the Chartres project also drew up a survey listing all bay fixtures and the more than 7,500 stained-glass and painted-glass panels to be removed from both buildings, numbering each window and its individual panels and specifying the number, size, and category of crates for use with each. And in the cathedral attic they posted a notice listing all of the stored material.

The authorities had tried to think of everything the teams would need, even while they still pondered where they would store and hide the windows.

The French National Assembly had by then passed the War Powers Act, and in July 1938 the Defense Ministry appointed a director of passive defense to coordinate the protection of civilian lives and property with the committees of passive defense that had been set up in each French administrative department.

Le Journal published another Fouqueray article, this time describing Carlier's plan in strikingly simple terms. "With a sum of 400,000 francs and a workforce of 350 men," Anne Fouqueray wrote, Carlier "ensured in one hour the rescue of 5,700 panels that dispense mysterious clarity to the nave of Chartres, provided that the acquisition of the equipment and training of the teams [are] carried out in time." She claimed that the "usefulness and the possibility of the application of this project [had] been officially verified in the spring of 1936," referring to the tests performed by Achille Carlier's team, which had, she said, "in thirty-five minutes established the metal parts constituting the special scaffolding against one of the high windows, and in forty-five minutes on one of the low windows, and that they unsealed the stained-glass windows to arrange them in metal cases built for this purpose."

One can only imagine how infuriated Jean Trouvelot and his Fine Arts Administration colleagues must have been when they read Fouqueray's oversimplification of the project. And why was there apparently no concern about revealing the plan to Germans who would read the newspaper? But the fact remained that Trouvelot and the administration had yet to make the fundamental decision about how to proceed with the removal project: Which of two solutions should they adopt for removal of the windows? Should they remove the windows quickly, without first detaching from the stone window jambs the external flashings that surrounded the windows, risking breakage, or should they defer actual window removal until first removing the flashings, one by one, and securing the glass with pins to ready them for later safe removal?

Until the third week in September 1938, the Fine Arts Administration had been able to defer that decision. But then the steam began to whistle in the teapot of Western Europe. The time for a decision had arrived.

CHAPTER EIGHT

Griff in Training . . . But for What?
Wyoming to Georgia,
August 1935–January 1940

ON JULY 8, GRIFF BOARDED THE USAT *US GRANT*, AND THREE WEEKS
later he arrived in San Francisco and boarded a train to Temple, Texas, to
visit his father and other family. By then, Welborn Sr. was living in the
family house in Temple with only Philip, Griff's twenty-eight-year-old
brother. Lawrence and his sisters had all married. At the time, Welborn
Sr. and Philip operated three different M System Food Stores, two in
Temple and one eleven miles southwest, in Belton, halfway between
Temple and Salado, the Griffiths' ancestral home.

During his stay, Griff visited Philip at one of the Temple stores.
Philip would stand at the scale in the central rectangular island of
counters in the store fronted by a glass display case that offered sausages,
cheeses, and cigars. Two other employees in white aprons worked the
floor, assembling orders for customers, pulling canned goods from shelves
on the left, dairy from the refrigerated display in the back, bulk items and
tools from the back, and produce from wire bins in the front. Philip—in
his white shirt, tie, and white apron—weighed and tallied. Since the time
Griff had been working in the family's old Quanah store, advances in
packaging and distribution had streamlined such stores, now affording
the customer a broad selection and swift special ordering of containers,

light bulbs, canning supplies, and just about any other goods one might want in a home kitchen.

Welborn Sr., now sixty-seven, his blond hair thinning and showing more of his already-high forehead, was still taller and thinner than Griff. He usually listened and offered advice to his son. The visit afforded the two opportunities for talks, perhaps sitting in the A-frame swing Welborn Sr. had brought from Quanah, with his dog, Rosa, nearby. Griff may have brought up his marital strife, his efforts to cultivate a relationship with little Alice, and his frustrations with the lack of opportunity for advancement in the Army. Welborn Sr., then seven years a widower, would have been enjoying his work with Philip and relished living so nearby his married daughter and grandchildren. He also loved dogs; in Temple, he always owned either a fox terrier or a Scottie and had named every one of them Rosa, in honor of John R. Good's wife.

Soon following the visit, Griff reported to Fort Frances E. Warren, adjoining Cheyenne, Wyoming, along Crow Creek. The post–Civil War fort had been a major Army cavalry post and, in World War I, a mobilization center for artillery and cavalry training, with twenty thousand horses in brick stables, five parade grounds, barracks, officer housing, and a hospital. By 1916, it was the Army's largest cavalry post in the United States, but after the war, all cavalry had left, and by Griff's time it had become an infantry post. Griff moved into one of the several dozen officer's houses arranged in a circle surrounded by shaded lawns, and he set to work training infantry.

The following year, in 1936, he transferred to the Pole Mountain Target and Maneuver Area, a sixty-two-thousand-acre site east of Laramie, where he acquired further training, including in artillery and chemical warfare and a field officers' course. Little did Griff know that the field-officer training in Wyoming would be so important to him. The repetition of the drills he and his fellow soldiers performed instilled muscle memory. He enjoyed his time there, much of it in forests, open plains, and mountains covered with trees and rock formations with scenic views, hunting, and riding. While stationed there, he learned fly-fishing. Several times over the Wyoming summers he went down to Laramie to buy fishing tackle, and on those trips he paid visits to the mother of his brother-in-law, Tiny's husband, Count DeKay, who had been reared in Laramie.

By 1938, Welborn Sr. had contracted Parkinson's disease. His muscles had become so stiff that in bed he could be propped into a sitting position and would stay that way with no danger of falling. Philip gradually took over the stores and within a few years would sell them.

Griff's life at Pole Mountain, although enjoyable in summer and fall, might have taken on a be-careful-what-you-wish-for element, with the north-plains winters and never-arriving spring. Eventually, he questioned whether he was chasing some unattainable dream. The Wyoming wind and snow probably drove him to wonder what to do next and question whether to go on with his military career. In the difficult interwar years in the Army, with limited budgets, officers with personal drive like Griff's— when confronted with lack of advancement, moribund assignments, and endless relocation—reached their end. He pondered resigning in order to pursue another career, his patience for action and for some bigger challenge or purpose nearly exhausted.

On leave, Griff went to Virginia to see little Alice, who was living with her mother and grandparents, Major Torrey and his wife. Griff still refused to recognize the Reno divorce as valid and was fed up with his separation from his daughter, so he sued little Alice's mother in court in Alexandria and won the right to see his daughter at reasonable times and to have her with him for three months a year, so long as he would arrange transportation and increase monthly child care payments from $25 to $35.

Filing suit against Alice Torrey, daughter of a major from a family of military officers, took guts. Griff would have had to ponder the risks to his career before confronting her, but he pressed his case and won.

In mid-1938, Count DeKay, who had been living with his wife, Tiny, in Washington, D.C., landed an assignment as military attaché in Paris and would soon be leaving with Griff's little sister for France. So Griff took the train from Cheyenne to see them off, taking the opportunity to see little Alice, then aged seven and living with the Torreys nearby. When Griff arrived, Tiny and Count were spending a long weekend at the D.C. home of Count's uncle, Emory Land, known to his family as Uncle Jerry. Land was a Navy man, a recently retired vice admiral and naval architect who had made contributions to submarine design and who in February 1938 had become chairman of the US Maritime Commission. Griff joined them for part of the weekend, including a Chevy Chase Country Club party hosted by Jerry's wife, Betty. Over that period, Griff likely talked with Uncle Jerry about career opportunities in the defense industry and government.

Griff picked little Alice up at her grandparents' home to spend the day with her while Tiny, Count, and the Lands attended a Senators–Red Sox ball game. The next day, Tiny and Count moved out of their rented house, and Griff and Count loaded the DeKays' car with their Europe-bound luggage and drove from Washington to the home of Griff and Tiny's uncle Tex and his wife, Edie, in Larchmont, New York, where Griff had lived during his West Point summers. Tiny accompanied Alice on the train to New York, reaching Larchmont by late afternoon. For Tiny, it was a sad time to be leaving her family behind in the United States. On the train, Alice read the funny papers to her aunt to keep Tiny from crying.

Count and Griff arrived in the afternoon in time to drink one of Tex's mint juleps before dinner. When Alice and Tiny arrived, Alice overflowed with excitement about their house, moving from room to room, inspecting and commenting. The adults got a kick out of it. The next day, Sunday, the weather having turned hot, Alice swam at the Westchester Club with other neighborhood children. In the evening, she stayed with the maid while the adults attended a dinner party. The next day, Edie, Griff, Alice, and Tiny swam together in the Long Island Sound at a beach club, and then Tiny and Alice took a boat ride into the city to the Battery and saw the aquarium and construction under way for the World's Fair, returning by boat late in the afternoon.

Griff likely talked with his uncle Tex about some career opportunities, or even about perhaps working again for Leslie Myer—who had been the contractor in charge of the Hoover Dam construction, for whom Griff had worked during his West Point summers.

Griff and Count drove Count's car the next day into the city to leave it to be loaded on the ship for Europe, and Tex hosted a reunion luncheon party at a downtown club with several of Count's Harvard classmates. Griff went to meet with Leslie Myer. That night, back in Larchmont at a barbecue on Tex's terrace, Griff probably consulted again with Tex about Myer and job prospects. The next day in New York, Tiny and Count boarded the SS *President Roosevelt*, seen off by everyone, including some friends they had known at Fort McKinley in Manila. Griff brought Alice to the dock an hour before sailing to see the ship, which fascinated her.

Tiny received three boxes of flowers and several corsages for the send-off, rendering her quite emotional, but she was nothing but happy with the case of Folger's coffee that their brother Philip had sent from Temple. Count locked it in the trunk of their car in the hold; they would wait to savor it in France.

Griff took Alice to see the sights in New York. They enjoyed the city together—everyone busy, determined to get some place, do something, the aural tapestry of the city, the country clubs and dinner parties, with smells of cigars and mint juleps. They returned to Washington by train. While they were together, Griff told her how discontented he was with the Army.

Within a month, Griff and the rest of the family were receiving Tiny's letters from Paris. Upon arrival they'd had to place their furniture in storage and were staying temporarily in a friend's Paris apartment, unable to get settled until they could resolve with the War Department an outstanding issue regarding Count's assignment.

Tiny and Count were aware that Europe was tense, but she had also heard from neighbors that many French believed Chamberlain's visit to Hitler would circumvent war. She had seen about her few signs of preparation for war. But she had seen swarms of reserve officers—just activated for service—surrounding the military academy near the Paris apartment where she and Count were staying. And she had learned from neighbors that government trucks were delivering piles of sand to every house in Paris to be spread four inches deep on their attic floors as a precaution against fires from bombing.

One Sunday afternoon in September 1938, Tiny and Count took a drive from Paris to Chartres to see the famous cathedral. They were eager to explore Paris and its surrounding sights, even though they could sense the fears of war in the air. They drove from Paris the sixty miles to Chartres with another American couple, Dottie and Knight Pryor. Tiny would describe their excursion in a letter to her family—one of many she sent them. In it, she asked that copies again be distributed to her siblings, including Griff.

The foursome approached Chartres at the end of their drive from Paris, and Tiny could see the cathedral towering on the top of its hill in the middle of the city.

Her first glimpse of the cathedral's west facade transformed her visit into a daydream. She entered the archway, pushed open the ancient, nut-brown wooden door, and stepped into the dark, wood-paneled entryway. She gave a tug on the inner wooden door, pulled aside the plum-purple curtain, and made contact with the cathedral's sweeping, timeworn, almond-brown stone floor and felt the vastness of the nave. The darkness enveloped her. She mused in her letter that she was transported by the windows. They exerted an unforeseen sway on her, the beginning of what for Tiny was a four-hour visit to what must have seemed a new and contrasting space in the fresh old-world environment she was already loving so much after only a short first few weeks in France.

In the cathedral, she felt the cool, damp air brush against her face, in a hush of quiet, accompanied by the sliding of shoes on the stone and the echo of people's murmurs, stirred by the rustling of wooden chairs being arranged for the upcoming late-afternoon Mass and the occasional drone of a biplane taking off from the air base a mile north.

The windows were like shoots of strangely dusky-yet-rich, gleaming, and colorful stalks of flowers rising upward. And there were no pews but instead a collection of hundreds of uniform wooden chairs. Men and boys in robes were arranging the chairs in rows facing the altar but parted them around a circular gap, leaving a space at the west end for a circular pattern of darker polished-stone channels inlaid in the lighter smoothly polished cathedral floor in what formed a labyrinth or maze forty feet in diameter.

Tiny lingered for four hours inside the cathedral with her husband and companions. She reported that she sat through the entire Sunday late-afternoon Mass, conducted in a language she could not understand.

The Mass began with the plaintive ring of a triangle, and small bells signaled the start and the transitions between portions of the service. Her eyes were drawn by the reds and clarets of the priests' robes encrusted with gold trim, and in the hall the colored rays of sun penetrating the windows illuminated the believers. She noted the reverberation of the priests' voices reading from scripture, the sway back and forth between the congregation's responsive chants, the smell of fresh incense above the altar and in the aisles as priests passed, the congregation sitting, then standing, then kneeling.

Tiny's description of her excursion to Chartres reflects her empathic, respectful enthusiasm for the French. She wrote, "Perhaps what has impressed me most about France is not the people, the ancient beautiful buildings, their artistic good taste in clothes, their fondness of children, their courteous treatment of foreigners, their universal happiness, nor their leisurely pace, but it is their gardens! . . . Ingenious use of every plot of ground to make something beautiful of it. . . . All this is what makes me love being alive and being here." Tiny's letter revealed the passion her visit to Charters Cathedral seems to have sparked.

That Sunday afternoon Mass would be the last at the cathedral for months.

Back stateside, Griff was finding that, despite his disenchantment with the US Army, his career achievements thus far had placed him in a select group of Regular Army captains, and in mid-1938 he was selected to attend the same Command and General Staff School at Fort Leavenworth, Kansas, from which his former father-in-law had graduated. In September of that year, Griff moved into the base's old "beehive" three-story red-brick barracks. Leavenworth was still a quiet, slow-paced post reflective of the "old" Army, with Griff's barracks facing the polo field near shaded Pope Avenue arched by elm trees. Griff would later see Leavenworth in much busier times.

The school maintained a traditional aura for its students—who were a select group of Regular Army majors and captains with superior records—and like most, Griff probably felt a sense of fraternity with generations of graduates who over a century had come before him. The course would be a year of instruction on combat orders, field engineering, leadership and psychology, military history, "equitation" (horseback riding), methods of training strategy, tactics, planning, and troop leading—all designed to produce commanders and staff officers for general staff duty.

Leavenworth students felt pride in their selection. Griff likely felt that thrill along with them. Most also felt trepidation that they might not measure up—a mixed feeling of satisfaction mingled with uneasiness. The school gave its students a status and a conviction that they were important and part of a great ongoing concern. Griff probably shared that sense of accomplishment and of fitting into the larger institution that the Army represented.

Griff's study and training at Leavenworth with his classmate officers consisted of classes, problem-solving maneuvers, and reading an enormity of study material, maps, and overlays. A typical day would start with rising before daylight, a shower, a shave, and a dash to breakfast, followed by a short time to glance over an unfinished assignment. Students would carry a full briefcase to their first class at 8 o'clock. The morning sessions included three classes—called conferences—many in large classrooms with a hundred or more students and three ten-minute breaks for coffee and a rest for wrists sore from note-taking. In conferences, instructors lectured and fired questions at randomly selected students. Afternoon sessions included more conferences and note-taking, followed by opportunities for physical exercise. Within a month, examinations would follow, many unannounced. Tactical problems, map maneuvers, and war games joined the mix and would constitute the final exam, beginning one day, running through the night, and finishing well into the following day.

Early in 1939, Griff received orders that once his Leavenworth coursework concluded in June, he was to attend tank school back at Fort Benning, near Columbus, Georgia, on the border with Alabama—an assignment for which he had applied that would also allow him to be closer to little Alice in Washington. He wrote to Tiny that he hoped to go to Washington, D.C., some time to pick Alice up and bring her back to New York for more sightseeing. He also wrote that he had learned that his ex-wife would be remarrying in California in May, but he did not yet know to whom. Tiny wrote back to Griff that she was curious who the "lucky man" might be. He turned out to be a divorced Navy officer, John S. Blue, who hailed from a military family with a long line of Navy officers; he would adopt little Alice and go on to have a baby daughter with Alice Torrey.

Tiny wrote back that her exploration of France had included a visit to Amiens Cathedral, where she had again been taken with the stained-glass windows.

In June, Griff and his Leavenworth graduating class of 228 paraded in their dress-white uniforms into the new War Department theater, again giving Griff grounds for satisfaction and a chance to reflect on his achievement.

Before moving to Fort Benning, he managed that trip to Washington, D.C., to pick up little Alice and take her to New York, where they saw the World's Fair. Then Griff headed to Georgia.

Tank school at Benning not only got Griff to the East Coast but also introduced him to a new branch of the Army, sparking new opportunities that would lead to important professional contacts for him.

While in tank school, he lived in a white two-story house with a wrap-around, ivy-covered screened-in porch that was shaded by trees. He had access to horses for riding and amenities appropriate for a child to visit. Starting when little Alice was about eight, Griff began making arrangements for her to make a series of extended summer visits to spend time with him. Fort Benning was their first such visit. They shared some good times together. Griff tried to interest her in activities that then might have been considered more suitable for boys, like horse riding and bike riding, fishing and hunting, but Alice had become acculturated to refined city life with her mother and her Torrey grandparents. She did like horseback riding—but in a refined equestrian spirit rather than as Griff did, out of enjoyment of the horses as pets and, with Texan practicality, as transportation.

Photos from their time together at Benning reveal Alice as an eight-year-old with a conflicted and uncertain posture, as if she were unsure of her bearings with her mainly-only-summertime father. One shows her and Griff with his big black retriever, Smudge. In another, she is standing alone in a yard wearing her jodhpurs, English riding breeches, squinting as if eager to get on with other things. In another, hugging a cat, she seems to be more at home. And in one more, holding the handlebars of a brand-new bicycle, she seems to be trying to look happy about it. In other images, whether surrounded by a litter of puppies, or side by side on a play date with another girl her age, she seems genuinely happy.

After at least one such visit, Griff sent little Alice a pair of Sonja Henie ice skates that Alice loved. Sonja, Norway's celebrated Olympic champion and Hollywood movie star, was the kind of female icon they could both appreciate, athletically inclined enough for Griff and glamorous enough for little Alice. She would remember Griff as an awkward and somewhat distant but well-intentioned father who tried during their times together to overcome his seriousness and meet her needs as well.

Griff's time at Fort Benning progressed well enough, but his time with little Alice highlighted the tension he felt between pursuing his military career and quitting it in hopes of starting a normal family life. It was a period of flux and turbulence for him, which probably weighed on him. He suffered lingering effects of the divorce and his ex-wife's accusations that he had been abusive, which could have been quite a burden to him, and from professional demands to relocate and be separated from his family.

By the time Griff finished tank school in 1940, the war in Europe had erupted, and changes were under way within the US military. It was time for Griff to move yet again. By the summer of 1940, the Army had created the new Armored Force to be relocated to Fort Knox, but for Griff there would be another destination: the college at Fort Leavenworth. The college was expanding its operations, shortening its regular course from ten months to ten weeks and quadrupling the number of students in its class to more than a thousand. Griff was recalled to serve in its academic command as one of its four faculty in the Armored Force subsection of its G-3 Section, out of a faculty of more than 150.

Griff's concerns about whether to remain in the Army or to seek a discharge would soon be resolved for him.

CHAPTER NINE

Jump-Start: Chartres,
September 1938–January 1940

SINCE GERMANY'S REMILITARIZATION OF THE RHINELAND, A SLOW pace of events had built steadily the way a brook swelling in spring might intensify into a raging flood. Journalists and government leaders who feared that Germany's remilitarization of the Rhineland would be only a beginning to Hitler's aggression saw greater dangers in Germany's annexation of Austria in 1938, and at the same time the demands for German-Czech autonomy in the Sudetenland in April turned into military threats that usurped the attention of British, French, and US diplomats. Through spring and summer 1938, French newspapers reverberated with headlines heralding the transforming international landscape.

Consequently, by mid-1938 Minister Jean Zay could wait no longer to act on the question of preserving France's most precious national treasures. He signed a four-stage advance order authorizing Georges Huisman and his team at the Fine Arts Administration to launch the removal of the Chartres windows.

The pressure inside France only increased when the German-Czech dispute reached a breaking point on September 24. In response, France partially mobilized its military, called up reservists, and invoked controls on transportation and censorship of the press. Jean Maunoury, who had been designated as assistant to Jean Trouvelet in the Chartres removal project, was one of the call-ups, but Huisman had anticipated Maunoury's mobilization and on the same day furnished Maunoury's own assistant, Michael Mastorakis, with the necessary instructions and plans to take over the lead.

On Sunday, September 25, French newspapers reported developments unfolding in Munich and Prague: Chamberlain had met Hitler, who had stiffened, now demanding that the German Army be allowed to occupy the Sudetenland and that the Czechs evacuate by September 28, which Chamberlain had put to the Czechs, who rejected Hitler's demands, backed by both the French and the British cabinets, the Czechs having already mobilized fully. In response, Chamberlain had proposed an immediate four-power conference to settle the dispute in a last-minute effort to avoid war.

At 7:00 p.m. the next evening, four men left by car for Chartres: Jean Trouvelot, Louis Linzeler, and two Parisian master glassmakers, Messieurs Delange and Bourgeot. The temperature was in the sixties; a storm was moving in with windy, cloudy skies, bringing with it showers. After an hour, the men could see the hill and atop it the cathedral's twin towers. They drove to the prefecture, where they met Jean Chadel, then serving as secretary-general to the prefect, who suggested they convene with the volunteers at 7:30 the following morning. Chadel also authorized Trouvelot and his team to request volunteers from among the military's 150 designated troops.

The next morning, amid overcast, windy skies and rain, the volunteers, contractors, and laborers, grouped in teams of five to eight, began lowering the scaffolding materials stored in the attics. They did so by means of ropes through the keystone holes of the vaults.

Within hours, the first twenty-five reserve enlisted men had arrived, with more arriving throughout the morning. Volunteers helped first in clearing the cathedral's nave of its hundreds of wooden chairs, transporting them to the crypt at the Church of Sainte-Foy, several blocks from the cathedral, and onto the esplanade of the garden of the bishopric across the cathedral's plaza.

To make room for scaffolds, teams moved away the wooden confessionals—already detached from the walls—into areas without windows. Workers also cleared candlesticks, ornaments, fixtures, interim decorations, and statues from the side altars, together with the high chandeliers and other large electric lighting equipment.

Soldiers and volunteers cleared furniture, and military trucks brought the specially fashioned wooden crates, which had been stored in the cellar of Loëns. They installed the crates in the attic through four small doors in the clerestory, located more than fifty feet above the nave's floor. In a long and difficult task, they hoisted each crate by ropes to the clerestory, each load requiring six men. They eventually used a van to assist in pulling the ropes, and they stored the raised crates in the attic of the ambulatory at the foot of each window, maneuvering through the tight passage under the attic.

The teams initially struggled with the scaffolding, but by 9:30 a.m. they were growing more skillful, assembling scaffolding with increasing speed, assembling and installing the first of the scaffolds, each thirty-two or forty feet in height, in the narrow passage at the foot of the tall windows, completing fifteen to eighteen of the many scaffolds the massive task would require, by 5:00 p.m. While installing the upper portions, they made ready the telescopic platforms for use for the lower portions of the windows—units that consisted of crude, early versions of today's cherry pickers.

In the choir chapels, which were difficult to access with telescopic platforms, workers installed six scaffolds. By the end of the second day, they had installed the last of the tall scaffolds.

As soon as access to the windows was available, the master glassmakers and glass painters, Charles Lorin and eight of his men, went to work with chisels, beginning to unseal flashings and detach the hard putty that held the windows fast to their iron framework.

While the artisans detached windows wherever scaffolding or telescopic platforms gave them access, workers continued clearing out the attic, removing wood debris, wood paneling, and other flammable materials.

Meanwhile, Jean Trouvelot and his on-site architects, Michael Mastorakis and Louis Linzeler, were ready for the next steps, but they were hesitant to begin the window removal. On the one hand, they sought to permit the artisans to remove as much hardened cement as possible, in order to minimize the damage that would be inflicted on the windows if rush removal were to be commanded. They feared that they had to be ready as soon as possible to remove the windows in the event of any attack—when trucks would have to be requisitioned away and specialists whose skills were needed for such work would likely be mobilized for other military duty and unavailable for the delicate Chartres work.

Relief from the dilemma soon came. The French government had already announced that it would not intervene in a war over Czechoslovakia. Only a few days later, on September 30, Chamberlain, Daladier, Hitler, and Mussolini signed the Munich Agreement with Czechoslovakia. In that agreement, Czechoslovakia ceded the Sudetenland to Germany in exchange for a German, Italian, British, and French guarantee of the territorial integrity of the rest of Czechoslovakia—a grasp for peace to appease Hitler.

At least for the moment, the Fine Arts Administration could postpone removal of the windows, forestall mass requisitioning of military and civilian volunteers and trucks, and allow additional time for the craftsmen to systematically "release" most of the windows from their bay jambs: it was slow, careful work replacing the flashings and sealants that had been made thirteen years before—which had employed hydraulic lime and cement for its perfect seal, now to be replaced by limed flashings and plaster made for quick and easy removal to avoid breakage—and reinserting them using that new malleable plastic material as caulking rather than cement so that later the windows could be removed by less skilled workers. The abatement in geopolitical tensions would relieve pressure from the risk that the skilled craftsmen would later be drafted for combat. While the "preremoval" readying work was being conducted, the Fine Arts Administration continued to line up and train a large workforce to be held on standby for the next phase of the Chartres operation.

As an added precaution, Trouvelot, Mastorakis, and Linzeler took the step of selecting a number of windows throughout the cathedral that could be removed immediately to establish "air holes," to relieve air pressure from nearby explosions—in the hopes of minimizing damage to the glass that remained.

These developments allowed the Fine Arts Administration the time to select the second of the two window-removal alternatives: mount all available scaffolds and hoists, complemented by other makeshift devices; make ready all packing material; remove window flashings in situ; secure the stained-glass windows with pins (the *barotères* and *feuillards*) to be restored and kept in place; and make them ready in situ to prepare for the rapid and easy removal of the greatest number of windows if as a result of war tensions or outright invasion the need to remove, transport, and hide the windows became unavoidable.

As events transpired, the time available for preparation would prove longer than Jean Trouvelot and his colleague would have dared to hope. Within a week of the Munich Agreement's signing, the number of work-men at Chartres was cut to a minimum, leaving only a few craftsmen, using the scaffolding remaining in the side aisles, to continue to release and reputty the thousands of window panels and flashings and to seal the outer edges of each window to its masonry window jamb. The scramble of workmen—with the clatter of metal tools and shouts that had rever-berated in the cathedral in the first days of the operation—now subsided into an orderly pattern that permitted church services to return and allayed fears of a wholesale panic and breakage. Part of the ambulatory stained-glass windows and sections of the high choir and transept were restored and reinstalled with soft putty and soft flashings.

The scaffolding installed in September 1938 remained in place for that year, except for a few scaffolds that were moved to repair windows.

And as it turned out, Jean Trouvelot also determined that it would be necessary to modify the strips (*feuillards*) of the windows of the ambu-latory. Meanwhile, the Fine Arts Administration took advantage of the time between late 1938 and August 1939 to complete preparatory work on the windows and other parts of the cathedral.

During that time, specialist volunteers rendered what Trouvelot characterized as extraordinary service, but their private businesses suf-fered from their having to invest time and resources into instructing the project's workers and providing for insurance.

In November 1938, Achille Carlier resurfaced in the debate to close and relocate the airfield near the cathedral, launching what he called a "national petition for the suppression of the Chartres aviation camp that threatens death to the cathedral." He appeared in a radio interview to press his petition and campaign. The senate debated the matter, but the motion to adopt was defeated.

In late January 1939, a new player had entered the picture—Jean Moulin, another World War I veteran, who had been appointed prefect of Eure-et-Loire, based at Chartres, early in 1939. He was a staunchly republican lawyer from Béziers near the southern French coast southwest of Montpellier, and he would become a renowned member of the French Resistance, unifying its many factions at de Gaulle's direction during World War II. Before coming to Chartres, Moulin had served in a series of positions in the prefectures of a number of the French administrative departments and in France's Air Ministry during the early 1930s, where he had been active in efforts to send planes and pilots to assist the Spanish republicans during the Spanish Civil War.

Five months later, the annual religious pilgrimage to Chartres honoring the Virgin Mary had to hold Mass outdoors, next to the cathedral, for the first time in centuries.

In late August, after three years of planning, the Directorate of Museums launched the national operation to evacuate artworks from museums.

But still they refrained from ordering removal of the stained-glass windows from Chartres.

CHAPTER TEN

Removal: Chartres, August 1939–January 1940

FOLLOWING FRANCE'S 1938 MOBILIZATION, THE GOVERNMENT RATCH-
eted war production into high gear, and within six months the Munich
Agreement's promise of peace dissolved into war, as many had expected.
When the Germans and the Soviets joined in a nonaggression pact in
August 1939, the French again had reason to fear that another war would
be fought in their homeland.

By then, France's military had been moving most French war
industry to the interior, which caused dislocation of workers and their
families—who were expected to follow the industry—and pressured
communities to provide schools and housing. At the same time, over
one hundred thousand refugees from Austria, Poland, and other Eastern European countries began arriving in France. And eight hundred
thousand French from Alsace-Lorraine moved to the interior, displac-
ing inhabitants and inundating local social-service resources. Com-
pounding those dislocations and efforts to move the new entrants to
the southwest, four hundred thousand exiles of the Spanish Civil War
were entering France.

By now, Minister Jean Zay had overseen three years of planning for
two large evacuations in anticipation of war: museums would have to
ship their artworks to depots in the interior, and teams would be poised
to remove stained-glass windows from cathedrals and other churches and
transport them to safe facilities.

France's defense ministry would work closely with the Fine Arts Administration to provide security and manpower. Captain Lucien Edward Prieur, an architect and World War I veteran who had headed the civilian Division of Historic Landmarks, would serve as the director and liaison between military and civilians. He had taken charge of positioning supplies and equipment at other cathedrals and churches that would be needed for removal and transportation of their windows—including interchangeable parts for scaffolding—as he had already accomplished at Chartres. He faced a challenge securing personnel, particularly because so many skilled workers had been drafted to fight, so Prieur's division was forced to develop the capability to train almost a quarter of the workers on-site.

When the German-Czech and German-Polish confrontations reached a breaking point in late August 1939, Zay launched both evacuations. The work on the windows began at Paris's Sainte-Chapelle and at Bourges' and Amiens' cathedrals. There, during the previous twelve months, teams had also reputtied the stained-glass windows. Now workers went into action and, within four days of his order, dismantled and packed the windows at those locations. Attention then turned to the cathedrals at Chartres and Metz.

On August 24, the day after Germany and the Soviets had announced their pact, the French called up their reserves. Late the next morning, a foggy, rainy Friday with temperatures in the seventies, Georges Huisman, at his Paris offices in the Fine Arts Administration, received the call from Zay. The time had come. Then Zay telephoned Jean Trouvelot with the go-ahead to put his teams at Chartres to work.

So on the afternoon of the twenty-fifth, the prefect of Eure-et-Loire ordered the cathedral closed and summoned two hundred troops to start the work. They arrived at the cathedral by midafternoon and commenced work directly, first carrying out the three thousand wooden chairs that occupied the floor of the nave and choir and storing them in the bishop's palace across the square. When room became available, some troops assisted Mr. Faucheux, the designer of the telescopic platforms, to wheel his half dozen inventions back inside the cathedral into position in front of those windows that had already been reputtied and could be removed by workmen.

Artisans from the master glass workshops soon arrived. They included men from the nearby Lorin workshop and from the Paris studios of Gaudin, Tournet, Bourgeot, and Delange. First they worked on the windows that had not yet been reputtied in the work that had begun in September 1938. Those windows that were still attached to their jambs with rigid flashings consisting of especially hard cement would have to be loosened and reputtied. Then they removed the stained-glass panels that had already been reputtied since the start of work in 1938. Those panels, largely ancient ones, would be removed only by the artisans and trained employees of the glass workshops. Their task first consisted of positioning the scaffolding to gain access to each targeted window.

As work got under way, Roger Grand, president of the local Association of Passive Defense, assembled his teams of volunteers from around the city. He also summoned a hundred building workers—who had signed commitments with the prefecture and the Fine Arts Administration. Those volunteers and the committed laborers and tradesmen climbed the hill toward the cathedral.

Meanwhile, troops already on-site began bringing to the cathedral the wooden crates for the windows, together with shredded straw and powdered cork as packing material, all of which had been stored in the cellar of Loëns. They had to start by identifying those of the crates designated to hold the first of the windows to be taken down, identified by window number according to the numbering system adopted by Canon Delaporte in 1918 for all of the cathedral's 175 windows.

The first teams to work on the windows started with the thirty-seven lower ones in the aisles of the nave, ambulatory, and side chapels. They employed scaffolding assembled inside the cathedral in those aisles. The scaffolding was forty-two feet tall, with five platforms spaced at six-foot intervals; starting at the sixteen-foot level, the scaffolding's base would be anchored to the lower part of the wall and the upper part anchored to the top of the iron framework of the window bay with ropes as soon as the first panels of glass were removed, in order to minimize shifting of the scaffolding during ongoing work, a step repeated at intervals as the workmen moved lower down the framework.

One of those thirty-seven lower windows was the Assumption Window, number 7 of Delaporte's 175, which dates to the thirteenth century, located in the south aisle of the nave near the Labyrinth. That window's twenty-seven picture panels—shaped as circles, semicircles, and quatrefoils—were sandwiched among the window's forty other background panels.

The workers began on the lower windows by hauling up the wooden crate designated to hold the Assumption Window. Each crate, when empty, weighed on average between fifty and eighty pounds. A team of men hoisted the designated crate up to the top scaffold platform using a set of ropes pulled by workmen and positioned it on the platform. Pairs of men made duplicate copies of a cartoon drawing (likely a rubbing or tracing) of the entire window and each of its many constituent panels and labeled the cartoon with the number 7, matching the window and also numbering each of its many panels, according to Delaporte's numbering. A pair of workmen on the top platform went on to remove the window's uppermost panels.

The removal of a stained-glass window requires that it be dismantled into its separate panels, each of which constitutes a separate picture or scene, composed of multiple pieces of colored and/or painted glass. In some cases, a panel consists of a single piece of glass, but in most cases it is a set of as many as several dozen pieces. Usually a window is removed starting with its uppermost panels and moving down toward its lowest panels, first labeling the panels with white paint.

They likely removed those panels by prying them from the soft flashing that sealed them to the masonry window jamb and sliding them from the iron framework that formed the circular and quatrefoil shapes of the window's panels, placing four to five panels in a simple glazer's rack. They affixed a pulley at the top of the scaffolding, threaded a rope into it, and lowered the rack while maintaining it in a vertical position. They numbered the crate with a view to storage before packing. They took each panel out of the rack, wrapped it, and placed it in its crate with packing material and then continued, panel after panel, until the crate was full.

They then placed one copy of the cartoon inside the crate, covered it with the pine lid, and sealed it with a metal strap, which they drew tight with a hand-operated clamping tool. The fully loaded crates weighed on average between 330 and 400 pounds. The men also labeled the outside of this crate with the catalog number of the window while others sealed it.

A separate team hauled the crate to the head of the stairway inside the cathedral along the south wall inside the west portal, which led to the crypt—the twelve-foot-wide and 230-foot-long gallery chapel of Notre-Dame-Sous-Terre beneath the cathedral. They gently eased each crate down the stone steps into the crypt and placed it on the floor on its edge, with its flat side leaning against other crates similarly placed, all ready to be secured, and never placing anything on top of the crates.

As they removed the panels from the aisle windows, the light poured in through the open armatures, and the cathedral was brighter than it had been since the windows had been removed that last time, during World War I. With each stage of removal, the swell in brightness further diminished the shadowy, otherworldly iridescence of the cathedral's expanse beneath the vaults of the nave.

The next teams assembled other scaffolding on the exterior of the cathedral to reach the twenty-seven upper windows of the nave, transept, and choir, installing that scaffolding onto the narrow ledge at the base of each of those windows, which they reached through trapdoors in the ceilings of the attics beneath the roofs of the clerestory. Among those was the Life of the Virgin Mary Window, numbered by Delaporte as 16, located in the south ambulatory, halfway between the transept and the altar.

For the next project, other teams assembled tall scaffolding on the exterior of the cathedral to reach the seven upper windows of the apse. Among those was the Charlemagne Window, number 38 in Delaporte's list, which had been the subject of the controversy following the 1918 removal. It was located in the ambulatory on the northeast between two apsidal chapels.

Another team of workers reinstalled tall scaffolding on the interior, against the inside of the west facade of the nave and the north and south facades of the transept, to reach the three lancets topped by the large west rose window, and both sets of five lancets each, topped by the large roses on each of the north and south transept facades. Among those was the North Rose, number 145 on Delaporte's list. It consisted of fifty-seven intricate windows, each embedded into its own individual window jamb. Those windows were arranged in five concentric circles, each consisting of a dozen matching windows, and each circle composed of windows of a distinct shape, with each divided into as many as thirty-six panels. Its images reflected Old Testament figures, in contrast to the South Rose's themes from the New Testament and the West Rose's themes of the Last Judgment. Because the rose windows consisted of a large number of panels embedded individually into their own separate window jambs, they required removing more flashings than was done for the lancet windows. And because they had not been taken away during the 1918 removals—having not been repaired since the nineteenth century—they were also in poor condition, requiring extra effort.

The remaining teams took their direction from the glass painters and their workers in the cathedral, organized into teams to assist the artisans and their employees who would remove the remaining flashings and detach and reputty those of the stained-glass windows yet to undergo such treatment. The glass painters moved on to begin removing the oldest stained-glass windows in those locations that had been prepared in advance. Any idle workers were directed to carry sandbags to the cathedral from their storage in the cellar of Loëns, to be ready to be stacked in the lower bays and around the portals at the end of the window-removal project, to protect them from bomb blasts. By the end of the first day, more than 5,300 square feet of the stained glass had been packed in crates.

The next day, the number of soldiers on-site swelled to two hundred, plus seventy workers consisting of teams of glassworkers from the Lorin, Tournel, and Gaudin workshops. The crews continued to remove stained glass, starting with the work on the thirty-seven lower windows of the aisles, the ambulatory, and side chapels, using the scaffolding inside the building. The base of those windows was sixteen feet above the floor.

On the evening of the twenty-sixth, Mr. Bourgeot, another glass painter from Paris, arrived to prepare for his portion of the work. But a snag developed the same day: army mobilization papers arrived, calling up some of the laborers for deployment.

On the twenty-seventh, Minister Zay gave the order to commence the second major evacuation: exodus of artworks that had been packaged for shipment from museums all over northern and eastern France.

Back at Chartres the work continued. The number of workers available to proceed with the removal work in support of the skilled craftsmen had shrunk to about fifty, due to recall of most of the reservists. Jean Trouvelot asked Jean Chadel to requisition additional workers, a request filled several days later.

In the afternoon, Pierre Paquet arrived to assess progress. Paquet worked for France's General Inspectorate of Historic Monuments as an inspector general since 1920 and had overseen the restorations of some of France's great landmarks. With his handlebar mustache, bushy dark beard, and invariably stiff-backed posture, he would have noted how the brightness of the daylight in the aisles of the cathedral from which the stained glass had already been removed, washing out the colors—even in the still-overcast weather—contrasted with the dark richness of the areas in the cathedral whose windows were still intact.

By six o'clock that evening, seventy troops had arrived and had finished carrying the last of the empty crates and straw into the cathedral; later that evening, when the worksite closed, the crews had packed and deposited in the crypt 5,200 additional square feet of the windows.

The next day, about fifty workers were present, continuing removal of windows. In the afternoon, the first contingent of about twenty special construction workers arrived, including masons, carpenters, roofers, and house painters, together with another skilled glass painter, Mr. Delange of Paris. By that evening, another 7,500 square feet of windows had been deposited.

By Tuesday morning, the full contingent of 180 required construction workers had arrived, including a lead fitter from the firm Entrepose to direct the assembly of the large new interior scaffolding to reach the rose windows. The workers filled the cathedral with sounds of hammers striking, crates being dragged along the floor, joined scaffolding pipes clanging, and supervisors directing workers in and out. At midday, the smells of wine and sausage, bread and cheese, and brewed coffee were accompanied by the voices of women bringing and serving food from the bishop's palace across the square and the seminary. Workers sat and ate wherever they could find space. By day's end, the workers had packed away another 5,300-plus square feet of windows.

On Wednesday the thirty-first, two additional lead fitters arrived to build scaffolding for the rose windows. The same number of workers as on the previous day continued that day and the next day to assemble the rose-window scaffolding and prepare crates to receive those windows. Minister Zay also traveled to inspect the window removal and other passive-defense work under way at the Parisian churches, Sainte-Chapelle, Saint-Séverin, and Saint-Sulpice. He remarked that those places of prayer and silence were now by necessity filled with the noise of hammers pounding on crates and of the trucks transporting crates to the crypt of the Paris Panthéon, and he spoke with approval of the "passion and action" exhibited by the crews.

Then he visited Chartres Cathedral and jotted in his notebook, "I pushed on to Chartres; a harsh light streamed through the large bay windows, no longer filtered through stained glass, bright light in even the most secret corners." And, reflecting on the storage of the Paris stained-glass windows and artworks being moved to the crypt of the Panthéon, he called those subterranean reaches "an excellent hiding place . . . where the carefully swaddled works of art slept" but remarked that, in "this underground cemetery, one of the saddest in the world, it seemed to me that one clandestinely celebrated the funeral of a civilization." He would later write in his memoir,

> I continued as far as Chartres: through the wide windows, a brutal light, no longer filtered by the stained-glass windows, entered the cathedral, blazed in the innermost corners of the apse, beamed down upon the defenceless altars. It seemed that the sanctuary had been violated, left to the forces of nature. But, a few hundred yards away, military improvidence had built an airfield, and the stained-glass windows of Chartres had been saved from certain destruction by our care.

In the tumult of a developing war, which did not yet consist of heroism but nevertheless already required a great deal of levelheadedness and method, the officials of Public Education and those of Fine Arts rendered to France many unknown services that would be wrong to consider negligible. Across the country, in advance of the war, they showed competence and dedication.

When all who were commanded to mobilize were put in place, each could take up his post, conscience in order: one in his school or museum, the other in the Army. The situation had found them ready for all that depended on them.

The day of Minister Zay's visit and the two that followed, the workers at Chartres finished building the new scaffolding and removed the rose windows while continuing to remove and crate the other windows. Many of the mobilized workers were then paid and departed, but because the Fine Arts Administration had not yet received all funding needed to pay all of the workers, it proved necessary for Roger Grand and his Association of Passive Defense to loan the funds necessary to pay the workers.

The fifty remaining workers continued with more packing and movement of the loaded crates down to the crypt, and they commenced dismantling the scaffolding. The same day, Sunday, September 3, both the British and the French ultimatums to the Germans expired. By midday, both countries declared that they were at war with Germany.

At the cathedral, the teams continued through September 5 with crating of windows and installing temporary inserts of vitrex and Plexiglas into the empty iron framework of the windows, and then they began to remove the scaffolding. In the crypt, they nailed down and strapped the crates. They also installed protections in the lower bays consisting of a combination of wooden and sheet-metal cladding and sacks of earth for protection.

On the last day of the project, September 6, the teams of workers undertook a new project: they installed exterior protections for the cathedral's main west portal and for its north and south portals, to protect their centuries-old collections of sculptures. For that work, they used the same steel tubing that had comprised the scaffolding. With it they built three large protective structures, also using flooring and battens and cable and sandbags in the construction. Workers then put the cathedral back in order for religious use, permitting services to resume during the week ending September 8.

The entire operation had been completed in eight days. By the time war had been declared, thirty-two thousand square feet of stained glass had been removed without notable accident or injury to personnel or the glass—despite the large number of workers and the immense scope of the construction site, with men working high on lightweight scaffolding. The only mishap was that some of the modern, clear glass of the borders of some windows had been damaged, having been previously sealed with cement rather than soft putty.

And this project was only a portion of the larger effort that had also encompassed the stained-glass windows at Sainte-Chapelle and the cathedrals of Bourges, Amiens, and Metz. At all sites combined, workers had removed and placed in safe storage—within two weeks—over 193,000 square feet of stained glass and had replaced many of the windows with temporary enclosures (mostly vitrex and Plexiglas), which they hoped would enable churches to continue to accommodate worshippers during the war.

Immediately afterward, on September 13, Jean Zay resigned from his post as minister and volunteered to reenter the French Army—perhaps drawn by the same "passion and action" he'd seen in the workmen rushing to save the windows and artworks of the Paris churches and Chartres Cathedral. Although Zay had likely been mobilized as a second lieutenant prior to September 13, the following year, in June 1940 he would embark from Marseille on the SS *Massilia* to Africa with other members of parliament and soldiers seeking to continue the government in exile. But upon arrival in Casablanca, he would be treated as a suspect and in August arrested by French gendarmes. In October, he would be sentenced by a military court for desertion and then deported to successive military prisons, where he would write letters and a memoir. In June 1944, right-wing militiamen would pick him up from prison and murder him in a forest. In 1945, a court of appeals would quash his conviction and rehabilitate Zay posthumously. Ultimately, in May 2015, Jean Zay's ashes would be permanently installed in the same underground cemetery of the Paris Panthéon of which he had written following his 1939 visits.

But for the time being, Chartres' windows rested in the crypt of the cathedral. Within months, three glassmaking workshops were installed in the cathedral's crypt. Glassmakers went to work to repair a portion of the stained glass—to restore the borders of windows that had been damaged during removal—an operation that would be halted by events in May 1940. Otherwise, most of the windows—excluding the three roses—were in good condition, many having been restored during their earlier removal in 1918.

In the context of the centuries-long life of the cathedral, as of the end of 1939, it appeared that the removal of the windows would perhaps be among the most important events of preservation in the cathedral's nine-hundred-year history. But would the windows be safe in the crypt? One direct hit from a bomb could collapse the cathedral and destroy the windows, and any number of triggers short of that could ignite a fire, destroying the entire collection of windows—as had occurred during the last war, both at Reims, by artillery and fire, and at Amiens, where boxes of stained-glass windows had been incinerated when the warehouse there had caught fire.

Jean Trouvelot and his team had been unable to find a suitable hiding place for the Chartres windows, so they would remain in their crates in the crypt as the risks of war continued to mount. The windows of the other cathedrals had been hidden in safe places. What other solution could be found to safeguard the windows of Chartres?

Part III
World War II

CHAPTER ELEVEN

Fort Hood and Leavenworth Faculty, with Nell: Texas, Kansas, and California, Fall 1940–1942

BY MID-1940, SOLDIERS IN ARMORED UNITS LIKE GRIFF'S WERE FOL-
lowing reports that German armor had ripped through Czechoslovakia and Poland seven months earlier and were now doing the same in
France. With signs of possible American intervention in Europe loom-
ing, opportunities for Griff to see action were improving, and this time
he stood a chance of getting into the fight. After years of frustration
and soul-searching, he was recommitting to his military career. Yet, like
hundreds of thousands of other Americans at the time, he may not have
favored American involvement in the European war.

President Roosevelt was struggling to obtain congressional approval
to assist the English, but the US isolationists were still firmly in control
of Congress, opposing intervention, and they had passed the Neutrality
Acts in 1936 and 1937, under which Americans were prohibited from
sailing on ships flying the flag of, or trading arms with, belligerent
nations. Roosevelt, however, had been fighting back in two phases: In the
first, he successfully pressed for the 1939 passage of the Fourth Neutrality
Act, which permitted the United States to trade arms with belligerent
nations as long as these nations came to the United States to retrieve the
arms and pay for them in cash. In the second, he pressed for the Lend-
Lease Act, which was passed in early 1941, permitting the president to

lend, lease, sell, or barter arms, ammunition, food, or any "defense article" or any "defense information" to "the government of any country whose defense the President deems vital to the defense of the United States."

Many Americans felt at the time that US technology was superior to European, but the Germans took them by surprise with significant advances in their military technology and, more significantly, with superior tactics, combining arms and close air support. German weapons proved in many respects to be superior, the German infantry proving able to inflict casualties at a 50 percent greater rate than Allied infantry—whether attacking or defending, and usually when outnumbered—and the United States would prove to have far fewer high-quality, trained career leaders than would be needed in the military, which had been rapidly expanded from 190,000 to more than eight million.

Griff's sister Tiny and her husband, Count, were still in Paris in June 1940. She left Paris on the last train before the Nazis took control of that open city. Count stayed on for another two months attached to the US State Department. So Griff had plenty of reason to feel a connection to the conflict. Tiny and Count soon landed back in Washington, D.C., together, before Count took on a new Pacific Navy assignment in Honolulu.

That month, at Fort Benning, the Army disbanded the Thirty-Fourth Infantry Division and from its Second Battalion formed a new unit, called the Ninety-Third Antitank Battalion. The Ninety-Third was assigned to develop tactics and techniques for a new class of weapons called tank destroyers, to prepare to counter German mobile armored units of the type that had already proved difficult to combat with existing weapons in Dutch, Belgian, and French hands. General Lesley J. McNair led the tank-destroyer-development effort, and the prototype tank destroyers featured a three-inch turret-mounted antitank gun on an armored halftrack or special tank and a distinctive shape resembling a duckbill that resulted from their carrying two large counterweights on the rear of the turret. They carried fifty-four of the three-inch rounds and a .50-caliber rear machine gun. The Ninety-Third, which was redesignated the 893rd Tank Destroyer Battalion, eventually became a recognized part of the US Army. It was the first unit to arrive at the new Camp Hood, near Killeen, Texas, which would become the Tank Destroyer Tactical and Firing Center.

In mid-1940, Griff took a reassignment to Camp Hood, halfway between Austin and Waco, about twenty-five miles northwest of Salado, familiar territory for Griff. Salado had been the town in which his grandfather Alonzo Griffith had lived and the place where a ten-year-old Griff had met so many of his relatives back in 1911, including his Griffith grandparents on both sides, in his first big Griffith family reunion.

Tank-destroyer testing and training called for wide-open space, in good supply at Camp Hood—which would be renamed Fort Hood in April 1950. Griff employed his substantial prior tank and field officer's training as part of the team that defined doctrine, tactics, and techniques for deployment of the new tank destroyers. Soon General George C. Marshall would activate the tank-destroyer force, to be headed by General A. D. Bruce at Camp Hood. Tank destroyers would eventually perform an important function in World War II in Normandy and throughout France and Germany.

In January 1941, Griff was promoted to major and soon thereafter to a faculty post at Fort Leavenworth school, in the rapid wartime scale-up of training in the US Army's effort to catch up after decades of Congress's minimal military funding. The faculty post would position Griff's skills as teacher and operations commander to be recognized by top brass in the run-up to the war in France.

By about this time, Griff had met Nell Haller Humphrey, a twenty-seven-year-old woman living in Brooklyn, originally from Greensboro, North Carolina. They probably met at Fort Benning or Camp Hood when Nell had paid a visit to her sister, Virginia Lane Humphrey Griffin, who was married to Thomas Griffin, an Army officer. Nell was different from Griff's ex-wife, Alice—in a homespun way—and she was bright. She had been first in her graduating class at Salem Academy in Winston-Salem, North Carolina. Mr. and Mrs. Clen Simmons Humphrey were Nell and Virginia's parents. Mr. Simmons's company had invented Hope Denture Powder. He had sold the company to a large consumer-products company—perhaps the Colgate-Palmolive Company—and moved his family to a home in Brooklyn to run the company from an office in Manhattan. Nell was also an attractive brunette and in New York worked as a model for the Conover Agency, known to have coined the term *cover girl*.

A slogan repeated by Harry Conover, the agency's founder, was that Conover Girls are "the kind of natural, well-scrubbed girl you used to take to the junior prom."

When Griff reached Leavenworth, he became part of the school's influential G-3 Section, focused on military operations and training. He wrote to Tiny that he was proud of his new job as professor, that he expected it to be a first-class stepping-stone in his Army career, and that he viewed the G-3 Section as the "cream" assignment, in which he would learn much and make valuable contacts. It seemed, therefore, to put Griff back in a mindset for pursuing professional advancement in the Army.

Starting in September 1940, the majority of Americans shifted their attitude about the conflict in Europe as a result of the German blitz bombing of London, which would continue until May 10 of the following year, and by the time of the attack on Pearl Harbor, more than two-thirds of Americans had come to think that America's most important task was to defeat the Nazis and that doing so was more important than staying out of a European war.

The importance of the Leavenworth school to the Army is difficult to overstate. It was, and today remains, a graduate school for officers of the Army and other military services, interagency representatives, and international military invitees. Historically, its mission had been to train general staff officers and their commanders. Staff officers assist the commander of a division or larger unit by formulating and disseminating the commander's policies, transmitting the commander's orders, and overseeing their execution.

However, in the lead-up to World War II, it had become clear that the US Army had suffered from an acute shortage of general staff officers. By December 1940, the Army reorganized the Leavenworth school to reduce that shortage. It changed the school's mission to concentrate on training general staff officers and to forego training commanders. It did so by changing its basic course from a length of nine months down to ten weeks. The shorter course permitted the school to bring in many more waves of student officers. The school also reorganized the faculty to fit within the four traditional sections of a military general staff: G-1, personnel; G-2, intelligence; G-3, operations and training;

and G-4, supply and evacuation. Below those, the school created twelve subsections, including infantry, cavalry, field artillery, armored force, coast artillery, air corps, and others. Griff taught in the Armored Force Subsection of the G-3 Section.

One man under whom Griff served was General Edmund L. "Snitz" Gruber, a man of relentless drive who exhibited the same impatience with inefficiency that would later characterize Griff. The general had taken over as commandant by November 1940 and had overseen the conversion of the school to its wartime mission, but he died in June 1941. Griff would have attended the funeral in which Gruber was interred at Leavenworth National Cemetery.

Griff had already been teaching at Leavenworth when his uncle Tex Harrison, still a principal in the Sanderson & Porter engineering firm, also became involved in the war effort. Tex assumed the role of resident partner in charge of the Elwood Ordnance Plant in Joliet, Illinois, a major manufacturer of TNT, whose campus covered an area of twenty-four square miles. The plant commenced production in July 1941, following an opening celebration in the form of a Texas-style barbecue that Tex had inspired. We don't know what impact Tex's position may have had on Griff's thinking, but it possibly opened his eyes to how his military experience could be of value in a career in civilian-defense procurement. Or it might have been a boost to his military ambitions to see that even Tex was getting involved in defense-related business.

By mid-1941, Griff had decided to try marriage again, and in August, he and Nell were married at the home of her parents. Also attending were Tiny and Count DeKay. Nell was twelve years younger than Griff. The Humphreys' three-story Brooklyn home stood along a tree-lined street with a shaded yard ringed by a white picket fence between stone columns. The house featured a double front door below a central balcony with white wood trim, and on the third floor was an ornately trimmed oval dormer window with leaded glass below a brick chimney. For the wedding, Nell wore a long-sleeved white-on-white dress with puffed sleeves and long train, along with a pearl necklace and a vintage-lace crown bridal veil. Her father, wearing a tuxedo with tails, white vest, and white tie, exhibited pride next to his new son-in-law.

Griff wore his formal white dress uniform, and Count DeKay wore his dark Navy dress uniform.

If Griff had been planning to re-up with his military career, why did he remarry? If it was family life that interested him, what drove him to continue, and even pick up the pace of, his military career?

He enjoyed family life and probably wanted to find a normal pattern to life after years of a certain amount of hardship and uncertainty, but he wanted more than just domestic tranquility: he wanted a chance to do something impactful and, perhaps, a chance to show his ex-wife's blue-blooded family that he had what it takes. He perhaps had came to an understanding that it wasn't his going it alone that had killed his first marriage, or perhaps he had just decided to try again because he really liked being a father, even if his relationship with little Alice had been at times somewhat awkward. But most significantly, it looked as though war was coming, and he would get his crack if he kept up his top-tier military work.

After the wedding, Nell joined Griff at Leavenworth, where they lived in a house with a white column–framed wooden porch on a lawn-covered lot shaded by flowering trees, probably with plenty of room for Miss Peggy, Nell's small, white, long-haired dog. There, at Leavenworth, Griff could finally again enjoy family life close to his work, this time with a wife who would perhaps understand and accept her role as a military spouse.

On December 7, 1941, Tiny and Count were at Pearl Harbor, where Count had been stationed. They were at breakfast when the attack struck. Count rushed to his ship, and Tiny hurried to the Red Cross. Fortunately, they were safe, and they informed their families of this fact via shortwave radio, followed by a letter from Tiny describing what had happened, in which she struggled to comply with military secrecy. Soon Count would be stationed on a cruiser in San Francisco for repairs before becoming involved in the first surface battle of the Pacific theater; for her part, Tiny would return to Washington to work with the Red Cross.

Uncle Tex, meanwhile, was continuing his own work with the war effort at the Elwood Plant in Illinois. But in early June 1942, part of the plant suffered a large explosion on the assembly line where antitank mines were being loaded into railroad boxcars for shipment, resulting in forty-eight dead and another forty-six injured, leaving a twelve-foot-deep crater at the explosion site. The exact cause was never determined. It was the greatest loss of civilian life at a munitions plant during the war. The explosion was felt sixty miles away.

That same month, Griff was promoted to the rank of lieutenant colonel, and by Labor Day that year, he'd left Leavenworth for a new mission while Nell headed back East to live with her parents in Brooklyn for the duration of the deployment. Griff's reputation and years of training—and his blend of experience—had led top brass to select him from among hundreds for the position of corps headquarters' deputy chief of staff and G-3 operations officer, charged with planning and training in the Fourth Armored Corps that was to be activated in September. Training would take place at Camp Young in the California desert. The new corps' headquarters—in which Griff would be a key player—would oversee and direct armored divisions under a single command. General Walton H. Walker, another Texan from the Temple area and also a West Point and Leavenworth graduate, was appointed by General George S. Patton to command the corps. It would later be renamed the Twentieth Corps within Patton's Third Army. General Walker would ultimately write to Nell that he had hand-picked Griff to be his number three man because of Griff's' superior record and ideals.

Shortly after Labor Day, Griff stepped off the train at Indio in an expanse of sand and rock in wind under beaming sun. He boarded a six-by-six truck for the thirty-mile trip to the camp, passing from the Coachella Valley, with its lengthy, linear stands of date palm trees, into desert dotted with low shrubs and sporadic Joshua trees, rising to low mountain ridges. The camp's rows of five-man wood-floored tents stood between wooden sidewalks joined to form streets. Each tent contained cots surrounding a stove whose smokestack poked through a hole at the top. The camp's administration buildings and mess hall, located partly up the slope from the highway toward the mountains, consisted of wood frames covered with tar paper. All ground surrounding the living areas and buildings was saturated with oil to control scorpions, tarantulas, and snakes. The desert, with its natural predators, sandstorms, cacti, and summer heat up to 125 degrees, was to condition (and put to the test) not only the men but also the machines and other matériel.

Later in September, Griff's father died at age seventy-five in Temple, after a ten-year battle with Parkinson's. Griff was likely unable to attend the funeral. His brother-in-law, Walter R. Humphrey, editor of the *Temple Daily Telegram*, wrote a tribute article about Welborn Sr. in his regular column, the "Home Towner." In it, Walter praised Welborn Sr. for his lifetime of honorable dealings in business and all of his relationships.

Two months after Griff's arrival at Camp Young, he learned something that may have had a lasting effect: word reached him that Commander John S. Blue, the husband of his ex-wife, Alice, who had become stepfather to Griff's eleven-year-old daughter, little Alice, had been killed in action in the Pacific. His ship, the USS *Juneau*, had sunk during the naval Battle of Guadalcanal. Blue had learned just prior to his death that Alice had borne him a daughter. So now Griff might have been feeling not only the conflict of separation from his own wife but also a new sense of conflict from this fresh reminder of the risk that his profession imposed on his family. Blue had spent the greater part of the short time between his marriage to Alice and his death deployed on ships in the Pacific. Griff could not then know when he would see Nell or little Alice again, if at all, before his own deployment to Europe, which could come at any time.

Griff saw his first extended California maneuvers with the Fourth Armored Corps from October 1942 to March 1943, conducted under the simulated theater of operations for a period of thirteen weeks.

The normal pattern would consist of first a week of individual, crew, and squad training, and then two weeks of company and battery training, followed by a week of battalion training, a week of regimental training, three weeks of divisional field exercises, and, finally, six weeks of corps maneuvers.

While Griff was at Camp Young, a Hollywood production unit filmed battle and desert scenes of a movie, *Sahara*, starring Humphrey Bogart, at the camp, with cooperation of the US Army, employing many of the corps' tanks (including "Lulabelle," the featured tank in the film). Many soldiers, including Griff, performed as extras.

By late March 1943, the desert war in North Africa had begun turning in favor of the Allies, and attention had turned to Hitler in Europe. Griff's corps would be relocating to Fort Campbell, Kentucky, for maneuvers of a different kind: although tanks would be needed, that fight would require infantry for combat in mixed terrain of plains, mountains, cities, and forests.

This time, Griff's arrival on the scene was in plenty of time for him to perform his part. If he played his cards right, now—in a football frame of mind—with Griff as the G-3, his new unit could be both the offensive line and the running back. From the beachhead in France, the corps could bust loose and outrun the enemy through its own territory.

CHAPTER TWELVE

Stunned into Action: Chartres and Paris, September 1939–June 1940

THE CURATE—A TALL, MIDDLE-AGED PRIEST WITH STRANDS OF SALT-and-pepper hair showing from the sides of his round black silk zucchetto skullcap—walked east into morning sunlight across the hilltop courtyard to Chartres Cathedral, and the rooftops of the town at the base of the hill shimmered as light reached them. Leaves of the courtyard's trees rustled a hint of early fall color in the crisp air. The sun, with its mid-September slant, accentuated in silhouette a new structure now guarding the south portal on the right side of the cathedral ahead. Similar new structures secured the two other portals. In front of him on the cathedral's west facade, a boxcarlike enclosure—fifty feet wide and thirty feet tall—shrouded the Royal Portal. A skin of fiberboard plates covered the enclosure's framework, a giant sleeve of a boxlike winter coat built to guard the cathedral from the winter tide of war. The curate entered through its doorway into a dark interior vault that was lined floor-to-ceiling with sandbags like a regiment of stubby mythical warriors standing watch around its base on the front and sides of the passageway into the cathedral's only remaining available west entrance: the portal door under the right-hand arch. The wall of sandbags inside the structure, packed tightly and bulging from behind its steel and wood framework, now protected the portal's cherished and delicate ancient array of Old Testament and Last Judgment sculptured figures.

As the priest walked through, he may have thought it a travesty that those sculptures had to be hidden now—especially under such a crude leviathan. But better they be secluded for a time under this behemoth than annihilated under German bombing and lost for eternity. Yet why was all of this happening?

The curate opened the frayed door-sized hatch through the aged portal door of the cathedral into the wood-paneled entryway. He tugged on the small inner door, pulled aside the heavy plum-purple velvet light-blocking curtain, and made contact with the sweeping almond-brown, smooth stone floor of the nave, which he recognized had been cleared of all crates, tarps, and equipment. The clamor of workers and steel pipes and machines that had intruded into the sanctuary in August and September 1939 had now mostly been silenced.

Now one could hear isolated sounds of caster wheels squeaking and foremen directing workmen to roll the wooden confessionals to positions away from aisle walls, which were now lined with sandbags from the floor to the sills of the window openings. Other workmen were bringing in some of the thousands of wooden chairs from storage across the courtyards.

The curate would have been pleased that all the windows had been successfully removed and were in their crates and safely in the crypt, and he would have been gratified to see the cathedral being restored so quickly to religious use. But he may have felt a strange disappointment that the crude, massive new structures obscured the entrance and may well have felt an even greater blow from the abrupt change to the lighting and atmosphere inside the cathedral that removal of the stained-glass windows had caused. In the greater part of the nave, choir, and apse, the cathedral was now dark, as if a huge shroud had been placed over the building. Opaque vitrex panels inserted end-to-end into the jambs of the high lancet and rose windows now blocked most light, except for thin bands of faint white daylight. The rich-colored tones that had bathed those spaces for centuries were gone. But worse, in the aisles on the sides of the nave under the clerestory balconies, the vitrex panels now covered only the upper half of the window jambs. The lower third was now screened instead by plain canvas mounted on wooden frames to provide for temporary closure of the window openings into which a few rows of translucent plastic panels could be installed. As a result of this temporary measure, much more light was now penetrating the building through its side aisles. One of those absent lower windows had been the deeply colored Noah Window, in the north aisle, famous for its rich marine hues.

Historically, one of the most striking impressions of the interior of the cathedral had been the concentrated, colorful, saturated light. It was as though the cathedral, with its stained-glass windows, was "full of picture books, with pages of colored glass," as described by Philip Ball, in his book *Universe of Stone.* "In the Middle Ages," Ball writes, "the ordinary man and woman, illiterate and never likely to set eyes on the parchment pages of a book, would have gazed in wonder at these stories of Christ and the Virgin, the saints and the Old Testament, glowing in miraculous visions in the dark stone. . . . One simply didn't see colors like this in everyday life. Ruby reds, sapphire blues, emerald greens. . . . They evoke the Scriptures in a way that even the most eloquent priest could not rival."

Stained glass, and light that has passed through it, has been regarded as a metaphor for the divine. Nowhere was that more evident than in the cathedral, because of the way the stained-glass windows changed the light as its rays penetrated them. The curate and his priest colleagues were so familiar with the movement of the light passing through the stained glass—and the way the shafts of light touched the surfaces of wood and stone and the people within the building. The effect would trigger something exquisite in them and in almost everybody.

Ball describes the reactions of those who would later visit the interior of the windowless Chartres Cathedral during World War II. They said it was bathed with a harsh, uncolored "natural light" and, as a result, was "a harsher space, its elegant lines no longer softened by the reddish violet effulgence of Gothic illumination." In fact, they felt there was "something improper" about this untransformed light, "as though it [were] the Virgin herself who ha[d] been disrobed and exposed under the harsh glare of the noon sun. The space look[ed] crude and cold, the stones pale and exhausted."

In the following weeks in the autumn of 1939 after the curate's tour, glass-workshop artists painted color-infused scenes onto the protective translucent plastic panels inserted into the lowest few rows of the window jambs, which had the effect of softening and coloring the light passing through them to shine on the congregants as they would sit in the nave.

In the first few weeks following the September Anglo-French declaration of war, the people of Chartres did not feel much impact from the warfare under way to the east. But by the end of that year, they felt an abrupt influx of refugees from areas near the German border, which began to change life in Chartres. Prefect Jean Moulin noticed that tolerance for refugees was already declining. He made a series of visits to the railway station to secure food and shelter for refugees and made a point there of displaying an accepting posture, to pressure unwelcoming railway managers. Although Jean Chadel and his staff had been of help to the Fine Arts Administration, by arranging resources and clearances for removal of the Chartres windows, Moulin himself had not been much involved with the windows until the spring of 1940. He had been compelled to deal with wider issues stemming from the displacement of French workers and evacuees and from the influx of foreign castaways. All of that would change, however, when the war arrived in Chartres and the search for a more secure hiding place for the windows would, for Moulin—like so many other causes—become a passion and a matter of urgency.

In late February 1940, Georges Huisman, director general of the Fine Arts Administration, convened a special meeting of the Historic Monuments Commission to enable Huisman's staff to report on the overall evacuation of artworks and stained-glass windows from a multitude of churches and museums across France and from private collections at their owners' request and report on protection of historic monuments in conflict zones. The meeting did not occur at the administration's Palais-Royal offices on the Rue de Valois but instead in a ceremonial location: a large chamber in the recently constructed Palais de Chaillot, in Paris's sixteenth arrondissement. It was a grandiose building designed for the World's Fair of 1937 in a "classicizing 'moderne'" style, located on the site of the former Trocadéro Palace—an iconic promontory rising above the Square of Freedom and Human

Rights, overlooking the valley of the Seine, with a view down past the Place du Trocadéro, to the Eiffel Tower and beyond.

Twenty-seven members of the Historic Monuments Commission attended the meeting called by Huisman, along with Jean Trouvelot and Fine Arts Administration staffers, who were there to answer questions about the just-completed operations at Chartres and across France and to be honored by the members of the commission for the operation's success.

One of the newest commission members present at the meeting was Jacques Jaujard, director of National Museums and the School of the Louvre. Jaujard would go on to try (unsuccessfully) to convince the Germans to maintain an inventory of artworks and the destinations to which they chose to relocate them. Instead, fortunately, the important task of recording the works taken by the Germans—and the locations to which they were taken—would be secretly carried out by a member of Jaujard's staff, who would eventually be recognized for her valuable work. She was Rose Valland, a longtime unpaid volunteer and assistant in charge of the Jeu de Paume museum; she has been described by author Robert Edsel as a woman with a forgettable, bland style and manner who ingratiated herself with the Nazis and spied on their activities for the four years of the occupation. After the liberation of Paris, the extent and importance of her secret information, which she fiercely guarded, had a pivotal impact on the discovery of looted works of art from France. She would be recognized as a hero. Following the war, Jaujard would be honored and decorated for his own protecting and safeguarding of works of art stolen by the Germans and would be appointed to succeed Georges Huisman as director general of the Fine Arts Administration.

But on this February day in 1940, Huisman opened the meeting and recognized Lucien Prieur, Ernest Herpe, and René Planchenault for their work to protect monuments in the militarized zones—which included the work at Chartres—as well as Jeanne Laurent, the young state secretary at the Fine Arts Administration, one of the small number of women in the government, who had taken charge of passive defense from the time of the declaration of war and, like Moulin and Zay, would later be active in the Resistance.

As a result of this meeting, the Historic Monuments Commission authorized another five hundred thousand francs for Chartres Cathedral to install protections against threat of bomb damage to its choir fence and another twenty million francs to repair and relead the stained-glass windows over three years, to be completed before they could be reinstalled.

The attendees at the meeting also did not foresee that France would suffer a swift, humiliating military defeat and surrender, much less that France would be divided into an occupied zone and the collaborationist Vichy zone. In addition, the Germans were already establishing a separate Gestapo organization that would be dedicated not to protecting the treasures of artwork embodying the French cultural heritage but to the systematic looting of artworks, which they intended to display in a grand "Führermuseum" that Hitler envisioned would be built in Linz, near his birthplace, Braunau.

Various members of the Historic Monuments Commission recommended publicizing the Fine Arts Administration's mass evacuation of artworks from museums, churches, and private collections. One senator urged that a report be published in the *Bulletin des Monuments historiques* and other journals. Another urged that a "luxurious" book be published that could be sold by subscription, and another spoke in support of work already under way to film removal of the windows of various of the most famous buildings, including Chartres. Had the members known that the Third Reich would sponsor its widespread theft of art from France and other countries of Western Europe, they would have sworn all to secrecy and insisted on burying all records. As it turned out, many of those records should probably have been burned in the last-minute escape from Paris before the arrival of the Germans.

Still, the Chartres windows continued to lie in the crypt of the cathedral—exposed to bombardment of the airfield and rail yard. Even into April 1940, no action had been taken to move them to a different, less exposed location.

It isn't clear why that task was taking so long. Georges Huisman and his team at the Fine Arts Administration, including Jeanne Laurent, may have thought the war was going to be a short one. They had not yet identified a single hiding place that would be large enough for all of the Chartres crates and would meet all of the fire, security, and logistical standards required by the Historical Monuments Service. They likely worried about the shortages of trucks, petrol, and drivers and feared those resources would become even scarcer by the time the site could be identified and secured. And all over France, refugees were crowding onto trains.

Why move the windows? Why not follow Achille Carlier's recommendation that the windows stay in the crypt for the duration of the war? The answer may have been that the Fine Arts Administration staffers were discovering in real time that this was going to be a new kind of war, mechanized and aerial. Bombs being readied for use in the next war, Carlier contended, already had ten times the force of those used in World War I. Separate from the risk of fire in the cathedral, there was the danger that the cathedral might entirely collapse if bombed. A Gothic cathedral of the Chartres type is a stack of precision-cut-and-polished stones, held in place by balance between the internal pressures of the arches and external pressure of the flying buttresses. The stones are masterfully carved and fitted together. They are not bolted or stapled together. If a bomb with sufficient force were to hit, the cathedral might crash down to the floor and break through into the crypt, destroying the entire collection of the stored windows inside their wooden crates.

Why not put them in the location used when the windows were removed during World War I? For one thing, it is not clear where the Chartres Cathedral windows were stored when removed in 1918. Considerable repair to the windows was required following the 1918 removal, so shipment to a distant location would not have been likely. The prospect of shipping such a large collection of stained glass to another location in 1918—especially a distant location across the country—seems more remote even than it would have been in 1940. In those early decades of the twentieth century, trucks were advancing, but roads were not yet widely developed—especially in isolated areas. The railroads were functioning, but the network of spurs to rural castles would have been less developed even than in 1940. It stands to reason that, in 1918, the windows were kept in the crypt of the cathedral.

In any event, it seems that the Fine Arts Administration in 1940 had at its disposal all necessary information regarding disposition of the removed windows in 1918 and the years that followed. Several members of the Historic Monuments Commission present at its meetings in 1937 and 1940 were also involved in the commission's meetings during World War I. They would have known or been able to determine where the removed windows had been stored between 1918 and the time they were reinstalled at Chartres.

The record is not clear on why the Fine Arts Administration had failed to identify a storage location for the Chartres windows even as late as April 1940—or, if they had identified one, why they waited even beyond that date to give the order to move the windows.

There were likely many reasons. It was such a large collection, including the largest concentration of twelfth- and thirteenth-century stained glass in a single location anywhere in the world. As such, breaking it up into segments to be stored in multiple locations may have seemed unthinkable. Jeanne Laurent reported at the February 23 meeting that there were over a hundred additional sites already serving as storage depots but most may have been already filled, which would have required that the Chartres collection be divided into pieces. Trucks and fuel were in short supply, but surely if there were a will to move the Chartres windows, wouldn't there be a way? Ironically, the events of June 1940 themselves decided for everyone whether the Chartres collection would be separated into pieces or remain whole.

In addition, the French wondered what parts of the country would become embroiled in conflict, so the Fine Arts Administration was searching for places far in the southwest, yet still away from the Atlantic coast. And there was growing unrest throughout France from relocation of defense workers and, to a much greater extent, displacement of refugees.

That all being said, it would prove to be only the shock of German onslaught and the clear prospect of French defeat at the front—and the realization that war would be different this time, without a "front"—that would convince the Fine Arts Administration to take the huge risk of moving the Chartres windows.

By the late spring of 1940, the nation's entire infrastructure was becoming overwhelmed and frayed by, among other things, the arrival of masses of refugees and spreading fear.

But Chartres was fortunate. Jean Moulin was unique in his dedication as prefect of Eure-et-Loire, and, despite his young age, he had a multitude of personal acquaintances among the prefecture staffs of various western departments. It was a stroke of luck that he hailed originally from the southwest of France and had worked a short stint as a prefect in one of its departments—as an attaché to the cabinet at the departmental prefecture for Hérault, centered in Montpellier. It was even more fortunate that he had known Marcel Jacquier, who was now serving as the prefect of the Dordogne. Jacquier, a World War I veteran, had served in the interwar years in the Ministry of Foreign Affairs in various foreign assignments and in the prefectures of various departments, starting with the department of Hérault, located in Montpellier, where Jean Moulin had attended law school at Montpellier University.

On March 22, 1940, Paul Reynaud replaced Daladier as prime minister of France. A week later, France and Britain agreed that neither would enter into a separate peace without the other. Less than three weeks later, on April 9, Germany invaded Denmark and Norway, and then the British and French forces who were sent to confront those incursions failed to stop the German forces. Shortly thereafter, Churchill replaced Chamberlain as British prime minister.

The citizens of Chartres felt the war was moving closer. Reports of the German bombing in Poland, Denmark, and Norway fueled those fears, and the Fine Arts Administration likely felt mounting pressure to find a safe place to hide the windows.

In Paris, the first air-raid sirens sounded on May 10, but planes did not appear. Even so, the Minister of Information announced to the Parisians on the radio that "the real war had begun." Parisian suburbanites reported hearing cannon fire and bombs exploding. The Wehrmacht invaded Holland, Belgium, and Luxemburg, the Luftwaffe entered French airspace, and three days later the Germans entered France.

Fear of the invasion spread rapidly though the northern French departments. The government offered only limited assistance to residents in those departments, and it forbade civilians from participating in what had been an "official evacuation" of Alsace-Lorraine. Within a week following the German attack, Belgian refugees swarmed into France.

Although the newspapers were not reporting the military movement, those refugees were spreading the word. Then, as bombs fell on urban centers, millions of civilian refugees fled from northern France, heading west and south. And soon thereafter, the French State, and any organized evacuation structure, headed toward collapse.

The staff at the Fine Arts Administration finally caught a break. Jean Trouvelot had made a request specifically directed to Yves-Marie Froidevaux, of Périgord, chief architect for historic monuments of the department of the Dordogne. Périgord architect Paul Cocula had had the original idea to hide the Chartres windows in an underground quarry. He knew that the excellent stone from quarries at Ribéracois had been used in restoration of monuments. Froidevaux had been appointed chief architect in the Dordogne only the year before but was familiar with the château in his department. By then, the Departments of Museums and Fine Arts had already hidden many deposits of artworks and museum pieces in the basements of several other castles in Périgord.

Together they identified a possible site, Château de Fongrenon, a castle in the village of Cercles, close to the town of La Tour-Blanche. The castle was listed in the General Inventory of Cultural Heritage that René Planchenault had refined. Château de Fongrenon was listed as a "classic-era" castle built in the seventeenth century, perched on a small rocky promontory and surrounded by a moat. Over three centuries, masons had drilled underground high-ceilinged quarries into the promontory, which were sealed by large lockable doors. And, critically, besides being equipped with its underground quarries, Fongrenon had a nearby railroad spur, served by a road that also led to other roads up to the quarries' entrance.

The Fine Arts Administration—working with Jacquier in the Dordogne prefecture—obtained the right to use an inactive portion of the quarry at Fongrenon for two hundred francs per month. Once they had done so, Captain Lucien Prieur and Ernest Herpe of the Monuments Service of the GQG went to work with Michael Mastorakis and the local Chartres staff to plan the evacuation of the crates. They still had to find a way to transport them. Long-distance trucks would be nearly impossible to obtain for the nearly three-hundred-mile voyage south to La Tour-Blanche. For such a long trip, Prieur's obvious choice would be conveyance by rail, but to get the crates onto a train, together with the contingent of guards and workmen to accompany them, he would have to find trucks to transport the crates to a railhead. By late May 1940, crowds of refugees at the railway station at Chartres would make it necessary to find another railhead. A convoy of trucks could not possibly find space to deliver the crates to, or near, the station. Besides, Prieur must have anticipated that the freight yard at Chartres would be an early target for German planes. No, they would need to search for another site near Chartres to which freight cars could be shuttled and parked long enough to be loaded and then hauled by a locomotive across the country toward the rail hub nearest Fongrenon.

Prieur set out to locate trucks that could navigate the narrow streets of Chartres up the hill to the cathedral, get as close as possible to the cathedral for the crates to be loaded, and then carry the crates to the railhead—once one could be located. He would need fifteen trucks, each with a capacity of five to eight tons, that would be expected to carry the crates in two trips.

By the end of May, Parisians were losing their determination to remain in the city. Refugees in increasing numbers were passing through Paris. Then news of crisis sounded with reports of the British evacuation of Dunkirk. By the start of June, war was closing in, and fear caught hold in Paris.

On June 3, a formation of German bombers attacked the Chartres airfield. There were fifteen twin-engine Dornier bombers in the German group, with only three French planes able to get off the ground, two piloted by Czechs, who suffered as many as thirty hits from heavy defensive fire generated by the German planes. Somehow, the cathedral and its windows escaped serious damage.

At about the same time, Lucien Prieur's team received word from the railway that it could deliver four railcars to a siding in the small wheat-farming village of Berchéres-les-Pierres, six miles southeast of Chartres. Prieur and Mastorakis knew what they had to do. Could they round up the trucks and manpower and get all of the crates to that village in time? Could they make the journey and get the crates loaded onto the train before detection by German planes or ground forces? And, once loaded, could a railroad engine get to that site to haul the cars far enough west to avoid being sighted and hit by attacking German forces?

Sunlight view of north and west facades of Chartres Cathedral, from the northwest. COURTESY OF MICHAEL CLEMENT.

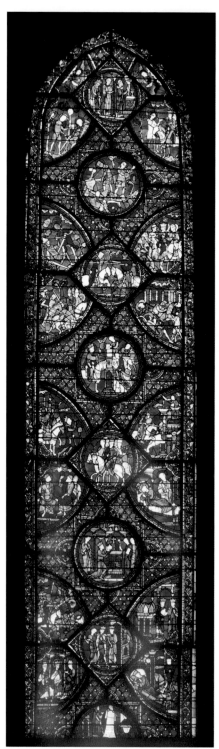

Charlemagne Window, Chartres Cathedral.
COURTESY OF SONIA HALLIDAY.

Tree of Jesse Window, Chartres Cathedral.
COURTESY OF SONIA HALLIDAY.

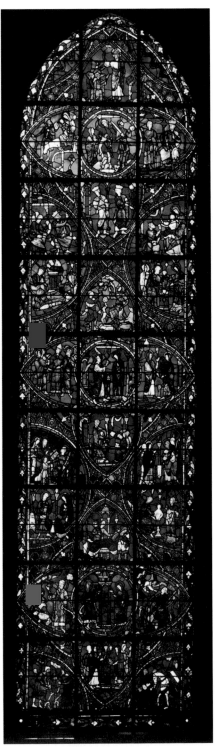

Life of the Virgin Mary Window, Chartres Cathedral. COURTESY OF SONIA HALLIDAY.

Assumption Window, Chartres Cathedral. COURTESY OF SONIA HALLIDAY.

Incarnation Window, Chartres Cathedral. COURTESY OF SONIA HALLIDAY.

West facade and towers, Chartres Cathedral in sunlight, view from the west. COURTESY OF MICHAEL CLEMENT.

Apse of Chartres Cathedral with late-afternoon sunlight, view from the choir. COURTESY OF MICHAEL CLEMENT.

Blue Virgin Window (Notre-Dame de la Belle Verrière), detail, Chartres Cathedral.

South transept rose window and lancets, Chartres Cathedral. COURTESY OF PATRICK COINTEPOIX.

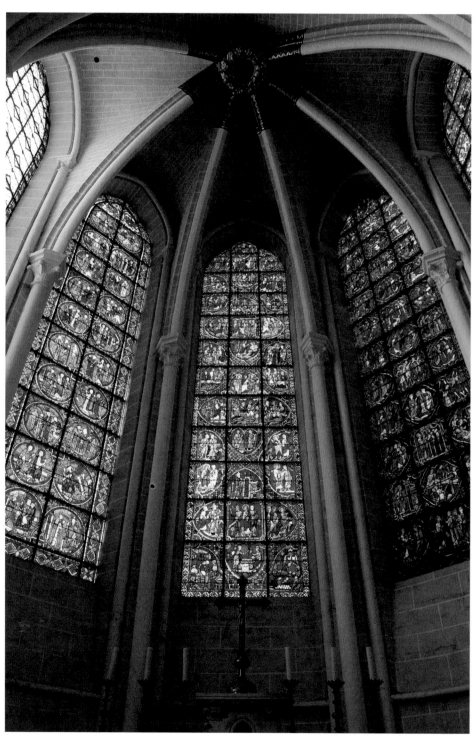

Altar and windows of a radiating chapel, Chartres Cathedral. COURTESY OF PATRICK COINTEPOIX.

CHAPTER THIRTEEN

Transport: Chartres and Berchères-les-Pierres, June 1940

IN THE JUNE 3 BOMBING RAIDS, FIVE WAVES OF GERMAN PLANES OF twenty-five or more each attacked Paris around 1:00 p.m. and again just before 2:00 p.m., part of Operation Paula, Germany's plan to destroy the French Air Force, the first against any belligerent capital and the first to hit Chartres since World War I. Antiaircraft fire blotched the sky with gusts of white smoke, which, together with attacking French fighters, forced the German bomber crews to remain above thirty thousand feet, preventing them from accurately hitting military targets. Over one thousand bombs fell in the area, eighty-three in western Paris and the balance in a circle around the city, including the Citroën automobile factory. Planes attacked the airfield of Issy-les-Moulineaux, between Paris and Versailles. Other bombs fell at Le Bourget Field, east of Saint-Denis, on the city's northern edge, and other airfields as far southwest as Chartres, where at least twenty bombs fell on that city's west edge. From the highest point in Paris, atop Montmartre on the north riverbank of the Seine, observers could see flames and smoke from bombs bursting at points over a five-mile area with columns of smoke from five fires. The all clear was given at 2:18 p.m.

Two days later, on June 5, a second bombing raid on the Chartres airfield killed eight and injured many more. In his role of prefect of Eure-et-Loire, Jean Moulin visited the wounded in the hospital. The raids were worse twenty-one miles north in Dreux, with over one hundred dead and much of the town center destroyed, including most hospitals. In the days following, journalists reported that 254 persons had been killed in that day's bombardments. Nearly two hundred were civilians. In the operation, German formations had attacked twenty-eight railways and marshaling yards, but all of that damage inflicted was light. None were out of action for more than twenty-four hours.

Even while the June 5 raid was under way, Jean Moulin, Jean Chadel, and their prefectural staff were probably working with Roger Grand to arrange for Chartres volunteers to come back to help remove the windows from the crypt for transport to a safe haven. Moulin had much to do, first consoling wounded in the hospital and then mobilizing teams of volunteers and soldiers, tools, and equipment. Some who had helped with the window removal during the eight days in August and September 1939 probably would come back to help, but the situation in Chartres had deteriorated since then. The climate of fear caused by the bombings of June 3 and 5 and the stresses of a threatened invasion—including displacement of large numbers of people from the east and from Paris through Chartres and surrounding areas—made it difficult for civic leaders to find Chartres residents willing to volunteer for the tasks that would require them to be away from their families for a full day and possibly into the night. It would be a rush of collective multicultural sweat, blisters, aching arms and feet, and diesel exhaust—at the cathedral, at the railhead at Berchères-les-Pierres, and along the train route south.

Captain Lucien Prieur's military group would have been inundated, and Ernest Herpe's Fine Arts Administration could do only so much, working through private contractors, given the wholesale disruption of Paris life.

On the morning of June 8, a Saturday, Jean Moulin would have been disheartened that the weather was fair. He would have been hoping for rain and fog—or, at the least, overcast skies—to degrade visibility from the air, to shroud the cathedral and the streets and roads south of town from the eyes of German pilots who were continuing to terrorize Paris and towns south and west to force the French to surrender.

To accomplish the day's enormous workload, Moulin and his team must have known they would need 115–140 men. So, probably on Moulin's instruction, Jean Chadel's prefectural staff would have solicited in the train station and refugee shelters for men seeking work to come to the cathedral on Saturday, and maybe Sunday, likely for two shifts of ten to twelve hours of work, one shift to start early in the morning, the other in midafternoon. Ironically, they could be turning to foreigners and displaced persons for a significant part of the manpower needed to save the windows, a French historic and artistic treasure.

Moulin would have been lucky to have managed even a few hours of sleep in the predawn hours of that day, having had to work well beyond dark—even on those long days of June, night after night, especially since the bombing—his head probably swimming as he arrived at the cathedral. The tidal wave of emergencies swirling around him would have been enough to turn anyone's mind to a blur: he would have shuffled through crowded prefecture hallways to Chadel's and other staffers' desks, reaching truckers and drivers by telegram and phone. He would have taken calls and meetings in his office with people begging for help, exchanged messages with Lucien Prieur to press railroad managers to summon to the cathedral the few soldiers who'd remained in town, to haul crates and serve as guards on the train carrying the windows to Fongrenon. He would have ordered soldiers to guard the trains along the journey and the trucks at either end and implored Roger Grand to line up more volunteers of his citizen contingent to come back to the cathedral to haul the crates onto trucks and to provide food and drink for the workers.

But Jean Moulin had stuck with it. He was no ordinary man. He was determined to get the windows out before the invasion could overrun Chartres.

Moulin walked up the hill from his rooms at the prefect's residence. The smell of cordite lingered in the air from Wednesday's bombs, a smell Moulin knew from his nearly two years of work for Air Minister Pierre Cot. Moulin's official residence lay in the shadow of the cathedral, a residence he called "comfortable enough" but "ostentatious and in bad taste." His own Citroën would have just been an impediment at the cathedral, with the fleet of more than fifteen lorries soon to arrive. Even a small grouping of trucks in those small spaces would cause a tangle, but the much larger conglomeration of trucks summoned to the cathedral for the busy day ahead would create a dangerous confluence, requiring planning and control amid the mass of men and machines on the site that day and into the night.

The earliest sunlight reflected off the sun-bleached masonry and white stucco of the buildings and limestone of the cathedral's towers and sculptures and illuminated the weathered pale-green patina of the great roofs of the cathedral and the rust-red roofs of the surrounding buildings. Early rising Chartres residents emerged from their homes to begin the day, but the sounds of hammers and vehicle engines were already fracturing the tranquil morning of the town. Dogs barked, buckets clattered, milk bottles rattled, and brooms swept as the townspeople began their chores amid the sounds of work at the cathedral.

Moulin came within a couple of blocks of the cathedral, and he could hear sounds of activity: carpenters called out measurements, saws sliced lumber, hammers struck nails, and boards slapped and clanked as workers hauled lumber off trucks. Michael Mastorakis had assigned the earliest task to the carpenters. They were to build a set of three wooden ramps to enable men to push handcarts bearing the window crates out through the cathedral's west door and down its steps onto the courtyard for loading onto waiting trucks. Joiners had been hard at work since before dawn among piles of tools and supplies—wheelbarrows, sawhorses, tool belts and -boxes, water cans, nail buckets, and piles of boards scattered around the front of the cathedral and on the broad floor of the nave inside the west entrance.

The day's work would be to haul the nearly one thousand wooden crates out of the cathedral's basement crypt into the courtyard to be loaded onto trucks. From the crypt, a vaulted hallway led through an arched passageway and up a five-foot-wide set of more than a dozen stone steps, leading through an iron gate to another set of eight stone steps up to the main floor of the cathedral, one hundred feet from its west entrance. At the top of those steps, teams would place each crate onto a handcart to be rolled to the entrance. There, they would have to push it over the three new ramps. The first ramp ran over the entrance door's threshold into the portal's shroud. The second ramp ran down the cathedral's half dozen front steps beneath the temporary shroud or rampart toward the outside entrance. The third ramp ran over the threshold of the shroud's outer door to the courtyard. From there, each cart would be rolled to a waiting truck.

The second task facing Moulin and the military and civilian teams would have been to organize those of the workmen they'd instructed to arrive early. They divided them into teams and instructed them on what to do and how to do it—all in time for the arrival of the first couple of trucks whose drivers they'd told to arrive before 8:30 a.m. The remaining drivers would have been told to schedule their arrivals later—in intervals throughout the day.

Moulin and Mastorakis, along with Captain Prieur, likely had estimated that the work would take all day and continue into the night. They planned for the fifteen trucks to make two trips from the cathedral to the rail spur. Risks of additional German attacks were growing. They had to pack the crates in and move as quickly as possible to come back to the second load. Traveling during daylight, they would have to somehow minimize chances of being spotted from the air. Later, the waxing crescent moon on June 8 would provide only 7 percent of full moonlight and furnish a cover of darkness, but only if lights were avoided or modified under blackout protocol.

The loading and transporting would have to be done quickly. Moulin likely knew that the situation in France—from the view of leaders in Paris—was deteriorating fast. News was already spreading that French prime minister Paul Reynaud had dismissed his supreme military commander, Maurice Gamelin, and replaced him with Maxime Weygand, and Reynaud had named Philippe Pétain, hero of World War I, as deputy prime minister. As would become apparent, neither Weygand nor Pétain felt the Germans could be defeated. They began looking for a way out of the war.

By the time Moulin and the others had gathered at the cathedral on June 8, the security situation had become perilous. Trains filled with refugees were departing Paris's Gare d'Austerlitz train station with no announced destination. When the prefectural assistants arrived at the cathedral from Jean Chadel's office by midmorning to meet Moulin, they would have told Moulin that calls were coming in from Paris: German shelling could be heard in the Paris suburbs.

That morning, Moulin, Mastorakis, and Prieur would have been faced with a crowd of men lined up outside the cathedral—likely an amalgamation of Czechs, Poles, Belgians, and French from Alsace-Lorraine—eager to start work, yearning for pay of any kind. Many would have spoken no French, so the matter of issuing orders would have been somewhat complicated, with those who could speak some French and another language doubling as translators. Michael Mastorakis, Louis Linzeler, and Roger Grand probably got the crews working right away. There was plenty to be done.

Mastorakis led the first five-man crew of workers down into the crypt. There, the windows rested in more than one thousand fully loaded crates, stacked on end like huge slices of bread in loaves. The smell of freshly cut pine saturated the damp, dark air of the crypt. Each pine crate rested on its narrow edge, the glass carefully packed tight inside. The two rows consisting of crates resting flat side to flat side, along the long walls under the sixteen-foot barrel vaults, looked like two lengthy rows of giant volumes resting in two gigantic bookcases facing each other; these newly assembled volumes, however, now contained not pages with words but precious panes of nine-hundred-year-old glass, displaying variegated, tinted graphic stories, each sealed in a wooden receptacle for safekeeping to ward off war damage. For every few crates, workmen had hammered slats of wood in place to secure against falling if crates were to be removed or jarred.

The gallery's walls beneath its barrel vaults, some sixteen feet tall, were mostly covered with frescos starting at shoulder height. Each team of five men, cautioned to avoid scraping the walls, began by hauling a crate by hand from its position in the row of crates across the smooth-worn old herringbone-brick floor. Four of the men in each team, working in pairs, two men on each side of the crate, flung ropes over their shoulders, the partner of each man on the other side of the crate doing the same, draping the rope over his shoulder and around his back and then wrapping it around his wrist to increase traction for lifting and control. The men then lifted the crate and hauled it along the gallery toward the hall doorway. The fifth man in the team stood by for relief, in case anyone faltered or to guard against obstacles. The team edged down the hallway, step by careful step, and then up the first flight of smooth stone stairs, their surface polished by centuries of shoes of priests and pilgrims, and subsequently through the crypt's iron gate and up the second flight of steps to the cathedral's first floor, sounds reverberating throughout the open expanse far above them up to the nave's vaulted ceiling.

Workmen called out questions, and supervisors answered with orders and encouragement and prodded them to keep moving, with wheels of carts creaking, coils of ropes being cut to carrying length, the smooth surface of the amber-colored stone floor reflecting dust kicked up and fibers from ropes floating in the air, with wisps of cigarette smoke illuminated by thin shafts of natural light peering through cracks between the temporary vitrex window coverings, and everything infused with smells of incense, sweat, drying pine boards, cork powder, and grease under the high vaulted ceilings of the nave.

At the top of the stairs, the team placed the crate onto a waiting handcart, which they rolled toward the front door and then guided up and over each of the three newly constructed ramps, down to the level of the courtyard, finally rolling the cart across the rough cobblestones of the courtyard to a waiting truck.

At least half of the thousand crates would have to be loaded and hauled out in a first convoy of trucks by midafternoon in order to arrive six miles south at a railhead at Berchères-les-Pierres, and from there the crates would have to be unloaded and transferred to the first train cars. After that, the trucks would have to return to the cathedral for the second load of crates and return to the railhead and unload for the trains to depart during the night.

The first couple of trucks arrived at the cathedral early and took their positions side by side in front of the west entrance shroud. Each driver then climbed into the back of his truck to meet a pair of additional workers and prepare their ropes to receive the first crate. As the first cart with its crate arrived, two men waited in the cargo hold of the truck with the driver. The men used ropes to pull the crates on to the trucks.

At any given time, several handcarts were making their way from the doorway of the shroud out to the waiting trucks. In all, the project would have required as many as 115–140 men.

By midmorning, Michael Mastorakis had probably made enough progress with Louis Linzeler—assembling teams of workmen and arranging for their supervision—to attend to other issues. The effects of the June 3 and June 5 bombings on the cathedral were a concern. Mastorakis and Linzeler, with binoculars in hand, at some time would have walked slowly along the interior and perimeter of the cathedral, peering up at its walls, inspecting for any damage that may have been sustained from impact of the exploding bombs affecting the temporary vitrex window coverings, or in the structure of the cathedral. Because the cathedral was sealed with temporary window coverings, the air pressure and vacuum force resulting from bomb explosions were a concern. Mastorakis and Linzeler may again have considered prophylactically removing some of the window coverings to permit free passage of shock waves to avoid damage to preserve the remaining temporary coverings and the supporting armatures.

Soon it was noon, and Mastorakis called for a break for the teams of porters. Jean Moulin, his staff, and the curate worked with Roger Grand's volunteers and with nuns and priests from the seminary to arrange for townsfolk to supply food and drink and servers to distribute to the workers. Wash buckets filled with water provided cooling wet relief, cotton rags providing a sense of order. Double French doorways of the bishop's palace across the courtyard were flung open to reveal long tables staffed by smiling matrons and daughters, perhaps even a few girls flirting with the workers. Water and wine poured from jugs into cups, soup filled bowls, and stacks of baguettes and cheese and sandwiches of coarse bread and sausage and mustard quickly dwindled and were replaced with new stacks. Reused cans as serving vessels were heaped with pickles and slaw, celery and carrots, the cans rattling as they emptied into cups carried away by the hungry workers. Bowls of red and yellow fruit, sweet green peppers and peas in pods, resembled dessert. Simmering coffee, with its mist rising, was poured into cups, its aroma spreading across the workers, who were eating, drinking, and probably resting on chairs in the shade of the courtyard between shifts, some perhaps lying in the shade along the walls of the courtyard to catch a quick nap before resuming work.

The men deserved this break. This great effort of men working as a team in unison—like the rituals that had been repeated for centuries at the cathedral, through wars and disputes and campaigns of terror and fires and storms—was what it took to watch over the great cathedral and its art. The dedication and sweat of men—generations of men—through the centuries. And these men were doing their part. Some had grown up in Chartres, attending the cathedral's weekly events for years. Some were occasional visitors. Some were simply accidental visitors, looking for a few francs to feed their families while looking for other work, having left their homes in the east as the German invaders moved in, thankful to have their wives and children alive and nearby, at least safe for the day, with the prospect of a roof over their heads and something to eat until tomorrow's search for more.

By early afternoon, the time was approaching for the first convoy of trucks to be heading down the hill and out of the city, south to Berchères-les-Pierres. That tiny village wasn't much more than an intersection of two dirt roads a few hundred yards off a paved one. A few dozen scattered buildings surrounded the intersection, including barns for storage of wheat, a gateless-train crossing, and a small pale-brown-stuccoed train station of two stories plus attic, with a three-door waiting room on the first floor facing the track, with several brick-lined windows on the second floor, each framed by a pair of green wooden shutters. The station's attic could quarter a seasonal extra stationmaster. A single rail track ran past the station, toward Chartres on the north and Courville-Sur-Eure on the west. Twenty yards south of the station, the dirt road, without crossing gate, passed over the track next to a one-room railroad switch hut. Nearby, along the track, a spur a few hundred yards long joined the track where boxcars could be parked to be filled with seasonal wheat to be hauled to markets. A sea of fields of freshly planted green wheat stalks surrounded the village on all sides. Distant explosions could be heard to the east.

By midafternoon, a small black steam-switching locomotive came to a halt at Berchères-les-Pierres, pulling two boxcars with wood siding painted a fading brown. The switchman jumped off and stood next to the

SNCF letters painted in red on the side panel of locomotive's tank. The engineer looked out from under the visor of his flat-topped engineer's uniform cap, as the engine's steam slowly hissed, a dog barking nearby. He called out to the switchman, asking whether there was anyone in the station. The switchman shrugged and walked over to the station, knocked on the locked doors, and called for anyone inside. There was no answer— no one inside the station or anywhere nearby.

The waiting engineer looked through the window of his locomotive cab behind its black steam-simmering engine and saw thin streaks of smoke rising in the sky far to the north and east. Deep-toned, faint thumps of artillery and muted bomb explosions recoiled far off in the distance. The switchman, finding no one, looked around, puzzled.

The engineer asked where everybody was and whether this was the right place. He'd been told to drop the boxcars and return the engine right away to the yards where it was needed for repair work and repositioning cars and other equipment.

He called out to the returning switchman, "15:00 latest, they said. If no one comes in twenty minutes, we'll spur the cars and leave them unlocked."

The switchman shrugged in agreement.

Within minutes, the sound of an approaching car caught their attention. A black Renault sedan pulled off the main road in the distance and headed toward them, trailed by its approaching dust cloud along the dirt road. A young man jumped out, introducing himself as an assistant to Jean Chadel, confirming that, yes, this was the right place and that the first trucks would be arriving within the hour and that preparations for their arrival would be needed. The engineer answered that the switchman could stay for a short while if someone could drive him back to the marshaling yard at Chartres before the afternoon was out, but the engineer had to get the locomotive back right away; the engine was needed there. He or another engineer would return to Berchères-les-Pierres later with two more empty freight cars.

Jean Chadel's assistant directed him first to position the cars as close to the road as possible, to minimize the distance crates would have to be hauled, but the engineer said he couldn't do that. He couldn't leave them on the through-track. He'd have to park them on the spur. A rough dirt road came close to the spur. They'd have to haul the crates by hand from there to the boxcars. So the assistant jumped back into the sedan to return to the cathedral for additional men.

The engineer and switchman moved the boxcars onto the spur, disconnected and unlocked them, and then left. Good luck, they said. They'd be back. The switch engine chugged off to head back to Chartres.

Back at the cathedral, the assistant told Jean Moulin that the boxcars had arrived but more men would be needed to carry the crates from the dirt road to the railcars on the spur. Vehicles would be needed to shuttle at least two dozen, and maybe three dozen, workmen to the train siding.

A half dozen of the trucks had been loaded with crates. As the loading of the others continued, Michael Mastorakis directed two supervisors to round up a dozen men each and to locate vehicles right away to shuttle those men to Berchères-les-Pierres. Only one van could be located initially; Mastorakis directed its driver to take him with a dozen men while two of Moulin's assistants left with the other dozen to gather up any cars they could find to transport them. Meanwhile, one of Lucien Prieur's team sent men back to the Rupp District to commandeer an additional military vehicle or two. The first six trucks, loaded with crates, pulled out from the cathedral as a convoy, accompanied by two military personnel carriers (one in front, one in back), journeying down the hill and south to Berchères-les-Pierres. Several porters hopped into each truck with handcarts and dozens of ropes for hauling crates.

When the trucks arrived, the supervisor directed the first to back onto the road next to the spur as close as possible to the boxcars. The first team of five moved in with its ropes. Two helped on the truck, the others lowering the first crate to the ground, and two hopping down to help haul the crate to the rail car, the fifth in reserve in case of a trip or fall. The five-man team carried off the crate, and a team approached the truck to repeat the process for another crate; then others continued until each truck was empty. By the time the first group of trucks had been emptied and was ready to depart to return to the cathedral for more crates, another half dozen full trucks had arrived. The first trucks returned as a group, leaving the men and military vehicles at the railhead to unload the next.

Teams of three climbed into the boxcars such that when others arrived with each crate, two climbed up into the boxcar to help haul and stack the crate on its edge in a riding position inside, the third man to tie ropes to secure the loaded crates while more were loaded. The crew returned to the truck for another crate and repeated the process. Each of the two railcars would have to carry almost 270 crates, plus two armed guards and at least one agent of the Historic Monuments Service to oversee arrangement of the crates and watch over them and to be available at the destination to ensure that the crates were properly handled and stored. Prieur's men also loaded fire extinguishers, along with a handful of days' provisions to sustain the guards and crew.

The second group of trucks arrived at Berchères-les-Pierres from the cathedral, and Moulin and Mastorakis arrived by car. They would have been worried that the whole project was taking longer than planned and that dangers of additional German attacks in the area were growing. By dusk, an engineer with his brakeman returned from the marshaling yards in a larger locomotive pulling a tender loaded with coal and two more empty boxcars, which it backed onto the spur and dropped off. The larger steam locomotive—an SNCF 141 R class 2-8-2, painted dark grey with red trim—could travel long distances better than the small switch engine.

The engineer told Moulin and Mastorakis that reports were coming into the rail marshaling yards: air strikes were hitting rail lines in the east and at some surrounding Paris. Moulin gave the order that the first two rail cars should be fully loaded with as many crates as possible, no matter how the crates had to be stacked, and the locomotive should depart without delay for Courville-sur-Eure, the first leg of its journey to La Tour-Blanche. Perhaps he thought it could wait at Courville-sur-Eure, or at some location farther west, for the second pair of rail cars to be brought from Berchères-les-Pierres to meet it. From there, the route would take the train to Le Mans and points south. At dusk, the locomotive pulled out from the spur and headed south, hauling the first two boxcars loaded with 539 of the crates, leaving the remaining two railcars to be loaded. Aboard were the engineer, a brakeman, two military guards, and the representative of the Fine Arts Department.

On Moulin's order, the local stationmaster called the Chartres marshaling yard from the tiny station at Berchères-les-Pierres requesting that a second locomotive be dispatched to pick up the two remaining boxcars when loaded and haul them to La Tour-Blanche, hoping that the second train could meet up with the first train somewhere along the route to Courville-sur-Eure or a point west or south. The second convoy of trucks with the remaining 395 crates arrived at Berchères-les-Pierres. The crews worked into the evening hours, continuing to pull down the crates and haul them to the railcars to be stacked, finally finishing when the fifteenth truck of crates had been unloaded. The second train, when fully loaded, departed, but very close to the railhead it slowed to a halt. By then, continuing German disruption of the rail system by damaging tracks and equipment had blocked the routes west and south. Late in the evening, Moulin was forced to conclude that there would be no way for a locomotive to get through to Berchères-les-Pierres, pick up the remaining boxcars, and proceed to meet the other train.

But he was determined to press for a solution. He ordered the train to pull back to the railhead and the men to remove the crates from the boxcars and transfer them all back onto the trucks, which were to make the run directly all the way to La Tour-Blanche rather than back to the cathedral. But the truckers whose trucks had been hauling the crates that day were unable, for various reasons, to make such a long-distance run. So Moulin's staff made calls for trucks to other firms in Chartres and surrounding towns as far as forty miles away—including Dreux, Nogent-le-Rotrou, Charray, and Gallardon—without success. But Moulin kept calling. As the hours passed and the men loaded the trucks with the crates, the roads became increasingly unsafe for convoys. As the German invasion pressed westward, the roads became more clogged with refugees fleeing Paris and points east.

Finally, Moulin again conceded. He abandoned his plan to ship the remaining crates to La Tour-Blanche and instead ordered the trucks to head back to the cathedral. German attacks intensified during the night. Only hours after the trucks departed from the railhead at Berchères-les-Pierres with all of the remaining crates, an attack hit the station at Berchères-les-Pierres. A train carrying munitions situated near the rail cars that had contained the crates burst into flames from an explosion and destroyed all nearby railcars, including the two that had contained the crates.

For the time being, all of the windows had escaped damage, but all of the participants would have been terrified to learn that the half of the priceless collection of stained glass that had been left behind at Berchères-les-Pierres—and possibly all, if the first train had not departed when it did—could have been pulverized or burned into tens of millions of particles of blackened sand, no different from the medieval sand from which the ancient glass had been forged almost eight hundred years before.

Welborn B. Griffith Jr., circa 1919–1920, in cadet's uniform, at Bryan Street High School or Texas A&M. COURTESY OF ALICE IRVING.

Welborn B. Griffth Jr., 1925, West Point yearbook, *The Howitzer*. COURTESY OF KEVIN COFFEY.

Welborn B. Griffith Jr., modeling infantry
combat uniform, circa 1928–1929.
COURTESY OF ALICE IRVING.

Griffith family, circa 1931 (Welborn Jr., lower row, left; first wife, Alice, upper row, left). COUR-
TESY OF GARY HENDRIX.

Welborn B. Griffith Sr. (L) and his wife's brother, Harrison (Tex) Smith. COURTESY OF GARY HENDRIX.

Welborn B. Griffith Sr. COURTESY OF GARY HENDRIX.

Custom scaffolding designed by Achille Carlier, used for the front second window of the choir, during removal tests conducted March 28, 1936, at Chartres Cathedral, as shown in Carlier's "Supplement No. 2," page 68 of the reprint. Achille Carlier (1903–1966), architect. J. Sorbets (20th century), photographer. Preventive measures that would make it possible to rescue the stained-glass windows of Chartres Cathedral in the event of a sudden attack. "Supplement No. 2" (1935). © MINISTÈRE DE LA CULTURE / MÉDIATHÈQUE DE L'ARCHITECTURE ET DU PATRIMOINE, DIST. RMN-GRAND PALAIS / ART RESOURCE, NY.

Custom scaffolding designed by Achille Carlier, used for low windows in the east aisle of the north ambulatory during removal tests conducted March 28, 1936, at Chartres Cathedral, as shown in Carlier, "Supplement No. 2" (1935). © MINISTÈRE DE LA CULTURE / MÉDIATHÈQUE DE L'ARCHITECTURE ET DU PATRIMOINE, DIST. RMN-GRAND PALAIS / ART RESOURCE, NY.

Faucheux telescoping cranes in 1936, in the nave of Chartres Cathedral, used to reach clerestory windows and lower windows during removal tests, March 1936. COURTESY OF LES ARCHIVES DÉPARTEMENTALES D'EURE-ET-LOIR.

Jean Zay at first meeting of the council of Prime Minister Chautemps, at the Hôtel de Matignon, Paris, official residence of the prime minister, 1937. PHOTO: AGENCE MEURISSE.

Jean Moulin, 1937.
PHOTO: STUDIO HARCOURT 1937.

Interior entrance to crypt of Chartres Cathedral in its present-day condition. COURTESY OF
PATRICK COINTEPOIX.

Large crypt of Chartres Cathedral in its present-day condition, filled with chairs arranged for services. COURTESY OF CORINNE HALL.

View from north tower of Chartres Cathedral, showing rail yard, 2015. VICTOR A. POLLAK.

View of Fongrenon Manor (Dordogne) and the cliff line sheltering its quarry.
COURTESY OF THIERRY BARITAUD.

West entrance to quarry at Fongrenon Manor (Dordogne). COURTESY OF
THIERRY BARITAUD.

Large entrance room of quarry at Fongrenon Manor (Dordogne) served by
its west entrance. COURTESY OF THIERRY BARITAUD.

Boxes containing the stained-glass windows of Chartres Cathedral, deposited in 1939, stored in the quarries of Château de Fongrenon in the municipality of Cercles (Périgord), 1940. Positive monochrome on paper. Inv. no. 16L12226. From photographic report of J. Tourvelot of window removal and concealment in quarry. © MINISTÈRE DE LA CULTURE / MÉDIATHÈQUE DE L'ARCHITECTURE ET DU PATRIMOINE, DIST. RMN-GRAND PALAIS / ART RESOURCE, NY.

Welborn B. Griffith Jr., circa 1943, in street uniform and major's overseas cap. COURTESY OF GARY HENDRIX.

View of Chartres Cathedral from the southeast, vegetation in the foreground. COURTESY OF ROBERT LAILLET AND LES ARCHIVES DÉPARTEMENTALES D'EURE-ET-LOIR (ARCHIVE OF EURE-ET-LOIR).

Welborn B. Griffith Jr. in G-3 tent, with deputy and clerk preparing orders, circa 1942–1943. COURTESY OF THOMAS N. GRIFFIN.

Eugene G. Schulz as a young GI, wearing sergeant stripes during World War II.
COURTESY OF EUGENE G. SCHULZ.

Temporary burial of Colonel Welborn B. Griffith Jr. at Saint-Corneille, France, August 17, 1944. COURTESY OF EUGENE G. SCHULZ.

Colonel Welborn B. Griffith Jr.'s body, covered by US flag and flowers, next to the street in Lèves, France, on which he was killed, with chairs on which villagers sat vigil all night, waiting for Americans to retrieve the body. COURTESY OF THOMAS N. GRIFFIN.

Ceremony posthumously awarding the Distinguished Service Cross to Colonel Welborn B. Griffith Jr. by pinning medal onto the coat of his widow, Nell Griffith, at Fort Hamilton, Brooklyn, New York, November 1944. COURTESY OF ALICE IRVING.

Blown-out temporary replacement windows in Chartres Cathedral, 1944. Achille Carlier (1903–1966), architect. Photography from figure 21 in "Le drame des vitraux des Chartres pendant la guerre," *Les pierres de France* 13 (April–June 1950). Window bays of the nave of Chartres Cathedral, after the complete removal of stained-glass windows in 1939. Inv. no. page 30 07R03701. © MINISTÈRE DE LA CULTURE / MÉDIATHÈQUE DE L'ARCHITECTURE ET DU PATRIMOINE, DIST. RMN-GRAND PALAIS / ART RESOURCE, NY.

Wooden crates holding window panels in storage in 1946, one revealing water damage. Achille Carlier (1903–1966), architect. A copy of this image appeared as figure 23 in "Le drame des vitraux des Chartres pendant la guerre," *Les pierres de France* 13 (April–June 1950), 31–35. Boxes containing the stained-glass windows of Chartres Cathedral, deposited in 1939, stored in the quarries of Château de Fongrenon in the municipality of Cercles (Périgord), 1940. Positive monochrome on paper. © MINISTÈRE DE LA CULTURE / MÉDIATHÈQUE DE L'ARCHITECTURE ET DU PATRIMOINE, DIST. RMN-GRAND PALAIS / ART RESOURCE, NY.

Choir and altar of Chartres Cathedral in winter 1944–1945 and 1945–1946.
COURTESY OF LES ARCHIVES DÉPARTEMENTALES D'EURE-ET-LOIR.

Plaque honoring Colonel Griffith, mounted in Lèves, France, on the building in front of which he died. Translated into English, it reads, "Here was killed on August 16, 1944, the American colonel Welborn B. Griffith." COURTESY OF EUGENE G. SCHULZ.

Distinguished Service Cross. PHOTO: SHISCHKABOB.

Chapter Fourteen

To Quarry or Back to Crypt, for a Long Wait: Fongrenon and Chartres, June 1940

NEARING DUSK ON JUNE 8 AT THE RAILHEAD, AFTER CREWS ON THE ground had heaved and shoved their crates and the teams inside the second car of the first pair of boxcars had drawn and hoisted the ropes, the last of the crates slid into place. The pleasure of accomplishment fell on the men like a warm cloak on a cold evening. Most had been hauling the crates since early that morning, but they knew the job was only half completed and that after a short break they'd need to shed that cloak, fight off the fatigue, and join the other two crews already at work loading other crates onto the remaining pair of boxcars. Anyone not hauling a crate kept his eyes aimed on the northern and eastern skies, searching for planes. Any noise in the sky brought fear that a German fighter would be diving to unleash a bomb load or let loose with an effusion of strafing on any rail activity below.

Inside the tiny two-story Berchères-les-Pierres train station, the engineer, accompanied by his stoker, chattered by phone with dispatchers in Chartres to confirm the route and status of tracks and traffic in the coming hours on the route to Courville-sur-Eure, the first leg of their run, and to work through the uncertainties of the more than 360-mile route to La Tour-Blanche—where a small station and yard with cranes operated for the port of quarry stones—the closest railhead near Fongrenon where the rail cars could safely stop and be unloaded into trucks. The engineer and stoker wanted to get under way quickly, but the late-afternoon sun brought added danger. Luftwaffe pilots could take advantage of the low-lying sun and its longer shadows for their gunners and bombardiers to spot targets of opportunity—the silhouette of locomotive smoke or steam, the reflection off moving rail cars, the shine of the tracks. The engineer had to be cautious before nightfall. During daylight, the military guards would ride on the roofs of the boxcars to watch for danger, and on each train two representatives from the Fine Arts Administration per train would oversee the crates. Under darkness, the crew would need to eliminate all lights except those on their instrument panels. Sparks from the coal fire would be dangerous enough.

The engineer walked back toward the locomotive from the station, lifting his cap to cool himself with some fresh air, revealing his silver hair as he wiped his brow with a sleeve.

"Clear and locked yet?" he called.

"Not yet. Almost," the brakemen answered. He stood opposite the rearmost boxcar, squinting into the sunlight, and could see the engineer walking back from the station to the locomotive. The brakeman pulled off his faded red bandana that had been tied as a sunshield around his neck and wiped the sweat from his forehead and neck.

In the locomotive, the engineer broke away from his conversation with the stoker, who had returned to climb back into the tender to take up his shoveling position in front of the furnace. The engineer held onto the safety handle mounted next to the cab's open window and leaned out to look back alongside the train toward the attached boxcars, squinting to spot the brakeman. He told the stoker it was a good idea for the dispatchers to use a code name in their calls and telegrams from now on, in place of the names of Angoulême and La Tour-Blanche and Cercles, and not mention the name Fongrenon to anyone. The stoker nodded and pulled off his gloves in his coal-dust-blackened work clothes. In case anything happened to the engineer on this run, the stoker would be the one to have to step in to take over the controls.

That phone call to the dispatchers back in Chartres would be only the latest of many such calls to be anticipated along the route that night. The uncertainties of the route far outweighed the knowns.

The crates finally rested in the first two boxcars, loaded and secured with ropes, the cars locked except for a rear door on the last car for the train crew and guards and the overseers from the Fine Arts Administration to gain entrance. The two guards climbed onto the roofs of the boxcars, and the brakeman called the all clear, as the locomotive steam simmered. The engineer was about to release brakes, engage driveshaft, and press throttle when he remembered that Jean Moulin's assistant had told him to make one last phone call to Jean Chadel's office before leaving—to receive any last-minute instructions or changes in plans. So he told everyone to wait and hopped down to run to the station to make the call.

Ten minutes later, he returned with the all clear and climbed into the cab of the locomotive and, with a release of steam, set the train in motion. The group of workmen and truckers looked up from their crates and ropes to wish him good luck, and as the train pulled out, each guard, sitting atop his boxcar, scanned the sky for planes. The sun began its descent in the western sky, a ball of diminishing orange lowering over the tops of the few clumps of trees scattered over the expanse of green wheat fields, with shadows of the few trees beginning to stretch toward the east and shadows of the countless neatly planted wheat stalks drawing intensifying lines, as if to suggest an incongruous sense of order in contrast to the frenzy of the workmen trying to load the remaining crates onto the two cars left behind.

Minutes after the first train slipped away with half the crates, German planes struck rail targets around Paris and Chartres, which—rail managers within hours concluded—resulted in freezing all rail equipment for miles, the freeze trapping the second train a short distance under way from Berchères-les-Pierres and compelling it to return.

The crew leaders reached out to Moulin for further orders. They had to react quickly, reasoning that because the number of remaining crates was down to a little over five hundred, it should be possible to load them all back into those of the remaining trucks still at the railhead, and, if not, then to chase down and stop any of the other empty trucks on their way back to the home base that had already left and order the drivers to return to the railhead. If Moulin and his team could find adequate petrol, and if the roads to the Dordogne were not yet bombed or clogged with refugees, it could be possible for the trucks to drive the balance of the crates most of the way to Fongrenon, to be met there by the crates that were already on the train. So they sent word back to the workmen at Berchères-les-Pierres to retransfer all remaining crates back onto the trucks, to be driven cross-country to the Dordogne.

Meanwhile, Jean Moulin's team set out to track down any trucks that had already left Berchères-les-Pierres and send them back to take their portions of the second half of the crates. They also made calls to line up a supply of petrol at refueling stops along the route, and they telephoned or cabled prefects, police, and military units to inquire whether roads were still passable, but the bleak news did not take long to arrive: by the time the crates could be reloaded, all roads surrounding Chartres—not to mention all from Paris—heading south and west, had become hopelessly choked with fleeing refugees in cars and on foot, many with pushcarts, pets, and livestock. So Moulin ordered loaded trucks to not make the long drive to the Dordogne but instead to somehow navigate their way through the blockages back to the cathedral, where teams must in some way hide the crates before daybreak. *Now secrecy must eclipse speed. They must hide the crates so all citizens—and the Germans—will believe the windows have left Chartres.*

Back at Berchères-les-Pierres, the team of laborers worked into darkness to finish hauling each of the remaining crates back out of the second two boxcars and into the trucks. And Moulin's team worked through the supervisors to contact departed empty trucks to return to the railhead to gather the remaining crates and establish a plan to get them back into the crypt; only this time, the work had to be done in the dark, quietly and secretly, and they needed to return all of the remaining crates to the crypt well before any congregants arrived for the first morning Mass.

With the change of plans to rush the crates back, Moulin and his team—in almost an instant—probably had undergone a transformation, focusing now on an entirely new and more direct threat. Windows must be protected by secrecy against German threats—of theft or destruction. Everyone outside the teams now loading, driving, and emptying the trucks must be led to believe that all the windows had been shipped out by train. Word of the aborted second train must remain a secret from all except the priests and the cathedral's curate, whose job it would be to maintain secrecy. Quickly after abandoning shipment of the remaining crates, the team would operate within the existing small cell of men already at work.

They contacted the curate and Michael Mastorakis. How could the 518 crates soon to arrive back at the cathedral in the convoy of trucks be hidden again in the cathedral—but this time secretly? The priest knew the crypt held the secret.

The crypt consisted of two long galleries running in parallel from east to west—one on the north side beneath the nave, the other running parallel on the south. Between the two, beneath the choir of the cathedral, the walls of the galleries wrapped toward each other to join in forming a semicircular wall. Within it lay the oldest portion of the cathedral, the subterranean chamber known as the Crypt of Saint Lubin. It dated to the ninth century, the deepest crypt and one of the oldest visible vestiges of the cathedral, part of the original pagan shrine that was on the site from earliest times, which later became the crypt of the Carolingian church that predated the cathedral.

That nave had been destroyed by fire in 1194. Two priests are said to have rushed into the burning building and taken hold of its most sacred relic: the tunic, or Sancta Camisa (a cloth over sixteen feet long), posited to have been worn by Mary at the birth of Jesus (or, some say, at the Annunciation) and given to Charlemagne, the first Holy Roman Emperor, by Byzantine emperor Nikephoros I when Charlemagne had passed through Constantinople, returning from Jerusalem. The two priests had retreated with the relic into the crypt, where they would remain trapped while the fire burned above. There—in the Crypt of Saint Lubin—they were sheltered from danger, including burning and falling timbers, molten lead, and burning coals. Three days later, they emerged from the crypt holding the Camisa.

When the trucks with crates arrived back from the railhead, the priests with the keys guided workers back into the cathedral during the night to stack crates in the inner crypt through two small doorways, sealable by iron gates. There they stored the remaining windows of the cathedral and of two other Chartres churches not on their way to Fongrenon. In the workers' rush to get them back into the inner crypt, they could not place them in any particular order, but still they managed to get them in, and the priests locked the gates and disguised and fenced off the inner crypt to minimize chances of its secret being revealed. They and Mastorakis put out the word to all concerned that the whereabouts of the windows must remain a secret.

After the train carrying two cars full of crates had left the station at Berchères-les-Pierres, it had headed south and west to its first destination, Courville-Sur-Eure, where the engineer might have planned to wait for darkness and then try to make most of the run at night. Perhaps the engineer was a pressure-tested veteran trainman. Along his route, stations were jammed with refugees, and Luftwaffe spotter planes and fighters were attacking more rail installations, with French warplanes fighting back. Chaos reigned throughout the rail system in the eastern and northern regions of France and expanded southward and westward from Paris.

The route to La Tour-Blanche likely would have taken the train through river valleys. They would probably have traveled from Berchères-les-Pierres to Courville-Sur-Eure and then on to Le Mans, and after that along the Loire River to Tours. Then they would have headed over the hills south of the river to Poitiers and into the Charente River valley to Angoulême, and then through La Rochebeaucourt-et-Argentina, farther south in the direction of Bordeaux to the small town of Cherval, and then twenty miles farther to La Tour-Blanche, the crates there to be unloaded onto trucks for the haul to Fongrenon. Somewhere along the way, they would need to stop to take on more water for the engine, and maybe more coal, in case there was none at La Tour-Blanche, for their return run. Best they do so far from any lights and away from any crowds of passengers.

With Germans threatening from the air, shouldn't we take routes with the most tunnels, to be able to run from tunnel to tunnel?

In case of attack, one could aim for the next tunnel—or even back to the last—to be able to stop and wait inside until risk subsided. But congestion and delays or accidents or clogging rail traffic—with thousands of refugees everywhere, overrunning stations—could strand this engine and its boxcars with no escape. They probably had to choose between smaller routes, on the one hand—many with a single track but with less traffic, although more vulnerable to interruptions—or, on the other hand, routes with two or more sets of tracks. But the latter option would have been carrying more traffic with greater risk of stranding the train. A key choice would have been to take routes having at least some tunnels.

The engineer searched the late afternoon and evening skies for danger from the air, mindful of how far away the next tunnel would be in which to be able to take cover. The initial arrival time was Sunday morning—as early as possible, to give the work crews scheduled to meet the train time to evaluate how to manage the unloading process in a place out of sight. The crew expected that the unloading at La Tour-Blanche would take longer than had the onloading at Berchères-les-Pierres. But lengthy unloading time would not be the only problem. Air-raid alerts along the way compelled the train to make incessant stops on the tracks to stay out of sight of planes, so three days would elapse before the train could arrive at La Tour-Blanche.

It fell upon Jean Maunoury and Paul Cocula, ordinary architects of historic monuments for Eure-et-Loir and Périgord, respectively, to orchestrate the hiring and supervision of laborers to transport the crates from the small station at La Tour-Blanche up to the quarry. In the Dordogne, the tiny town of Cercles adjoined the village of La Tour-Blanche and Fongrenon on the east. Cercles' mayor of five years had been Francis Mazières. Who were the men recruited to unload the crates at La Tour-Blanche and transport them by truck to Fongrenon? Based on Jean Moulin's political orientation and that of his counterpart, the precept of the Dordogne, they would have been leftists and farmers. The area of the Dordogne that surrounded the site featured truck farming and dairy and livestock production, with a large forested area to the northeast and vineyards to the south.

The train arrived at the railhead with the crates of windows intact, and somehow, the boxcars, parked in the small rail yard amid cranes and piles of newly quarried stone, lay sufficiently out of the way of rail traffic and out of view to passers-by to avoid scrutiny of German warplanes. From the train, the men loaded the crates onto wagons drawn by oxen and cows in a multiday process to the base of the embankment that led up to the quarry.

Château de Fongrenon was located within the village limits of Cercles. The road to the castle ran through La Tour-Blanche to Fongrenon, which was just over the boundary line with Cercles. Stone walls and a moat enclosed Fongrenon's several-acre compound. Half was tree-shaded, on which stood the castle's half dozen three- and four-story white-brick buildings, framed with ornate stonework, red terra-cotta tile roofs overseen by several classic tile-roofed Aquitaine-style "pigeonnier" or dovecote-topped towers extending another a story or two above the buildings, the tallest of which resembled a medieval defense tower. In 1940, it was likely unoccupied, so the crews on-site to unload and guard the windows would have had to fend for themselves for food, water, rest, and sanitation and would likely have spent their time at the site without telephone or radio communication.

The compound sat atop a 470-foot white limestone promontory overlooking otherwise flat or rolling landscape. Large cultivated fields and livestock pastures, interspersed with small woodlots, surrounded it on all sides. Beneath the compound, carved into the limestone, lay the castle's underground quarry, consisting of a network of a dozen rooms cut into limestone with fifteen-foot ceilings, rough flat rock floors, and vertical walls with straight cut marks revealing where four-foot-square limestone blocks had been cut and removed. The quarry's two entrances penetrated the cliff of the promontory on the west and south beneath a tree-covered ridge, which hid both entrances. The men brought the crates in through the west entrance, which was cut forty or fifty feet into the ivy-covered limestone cliff.

Under the direction of local manager Alexis Moreau, the men unlocked the quarry's large ivy-clad steel doors three hundred yards up an embankment off a gravel lane at the base of the cliff and transported the crates on handcarts with ropes. Through the doors, they entered the space carved into the limestone. It had an L-shaped floor plan consisting of two long, high-ceilinged corridors. The west door led into one hallway running north-south (perpendicular to the west entrance) one hundred feet to the right and two hundred to three hundred feet to the left. The longer hallway, on the left, met another perpendicular corridor joining on the right, which led to a large double doorway fifty feet past the junction.

Through the doorway, the corridor continued for another three hundred to four hundred feet deep into the rock wall. Along both hallways, masons had carved a dozen square-cornered rooms of various sizes deep into the rock, half on each side. The long hallway to the right led to eight such rooms, four on the left and four on the right. The temperature in the quarry was a constant fifty-five degrees Fahrenheit. The men wheeled the crates all the way back to be stacked into three of the farthest-back such rooms, consisting of the penultimate room on the left (numbered as room one), the last room on the left (numbered three), and the last room on the right (numbered two).

From the west entrance, a ramp led down to the floor of the large front quarry room, whose level was five or six feet below the base of the door. The floor surface was relatively flat but bumpy, also resulting from the cutting and removal of blocks of limestone, but free enough of obstacles to permit use of a handcart for teams of men to haul each crate from the entrance back to the storage rooms—but not without difficulty.

The men hauled the carts as far as possible up the embankment and rigged ropes and pulleys with which they hauled handcarts to the top of the embankment by tying the rope to another vehicle that edged its way down the hill, pulling the rope to lift the cart and its crate. At the top, they transferred the crate to another handcart, eased it down the ramp, and pushed it through the hallways of the quarry into its designated back room. In the three innermost rooms, they stored the crates on edge in rows in a single layer, stacked side by side against each other—not atop each other—on what appeared to be the dry limestone floor, as they'd been stacked in the crypt of the cathedral, and secured them with wood framing. In room one, they stored 100 crates; in room two, 120 crates; and in room three, the remaining 309. The windows in their crates finally rested at Fongrenon under twenty-four-hour guard.

Ironically, the idea of rushing the windows westward to be stored to protect them from war damage was perhaps not as sound as believed at the time. Within weeks of the time the windows arrived at Fongrenon, the German-occupied zone that would be established under the armistice would not only cover the north and east of France but also extend through Normandy and down along the Atlantic coast southwest all the way to Spain. The demarcation line between the occupied zone and the Vichy zone ran north-south, through the Dordogne a little more than ten miles west of Fongrenon. All effort to escape from the rush of the westbound Germans closing in from the east and north ended up drawing the windows closer to the eastbound German units coming from the Atlantic coast for the occupation. So the staff guarding that half of the windows hidden at Fongrenon had to be no less preoccupied with secrecy and security than the staff guarding the other half of the windows concealed in the crypt at the cathedral.

In Paris, on June 9, the beginning of the end commenced. Senior government ministers debated the need for civilian evacuation but subordinated that need to that of evacuation of government officials and offices. Georges Mandel, minister of the interior, objected to plans to evacuate Paris's civilian population. In fact, he ordered punishment of prefects, mayors, and police commissioners who ordered evacuations or assisted fleeing civilians. Prime Minister Reynaud, on the one hand, wanted the military to defend the city and fight the Germans to the end, but, on the other hand, he wanted to spare Paris from destruction and its citizens from bloodshed.

On June 10, Weygand and Reynaud declared Paris an open city, and the French government fled Paris. Parisians followed in the thousands, jamming roads out of the city, in cars, buses, wagons, and carts and on bicycles and foot. The slow-moving columns of refugees took ten hours to cover less than twenty miles. That day, just north of Chartres, air raids hit again, causing the worst damage yet. In the afternoon, Jean Moulin drove with his friend Antoinette Sachs to his apartment in Paris to recover papers belonging to himself and his former Air Force boss, Minister Pierre Cot. Antoinette would later travel with those papers on the liner SS *Massilia* to seek exile in Algiers.

In Dreux, twenty miles north of Chartres, raids caused one hundred fatalities between June 9 and 11, and much of the center of the town was destroyed, including most hospitals. Moulin drove frequently to Dreux during those days but found much to do in Chartres. A group of high-ranking military officers and civil servants in retreat from Paris passed through Chartres on June 10, causing a serious blow to the morale of Moulin's staff.

On June 12, the French military issued a general order for withdrawal. Sirens stopped warning of air raids when the Air Force deserted the Chartres airbase that day, but aerial bombing continued. Moulin devoted the day to arranging hospital care for patients arriving from Berlin, and the next day Moulin received a letter from Colonel du Tille, the local commander, ordering evacuation of the department's civilian population. The colonel called Moulin the following morning to confirm the order and tell Moulin that since the time he'd left his post on the Belgian frontier, Moulin was the first prefect du Tille had found at his post.

By June 14, the population was quickly emptying from Chartres. Bombing destroyed much of its center, with the most intense bombing in the afternoon hitting bridges and houses, killing another thirty-three. Moulin closed the railway station and promised to provide meals to refugees at the prefecture that evening. When he returned to Chartres on the evening of June 14, a cloud of smoke rose above the city. Moulin's whole staff assembled at the prefecture, preparing to leave. Moulin grew angry when he learned that Bishop Harscouët was also leaving his cathedral, along with the right-wing mayor, Raymond Gilbert, whose sister and daughter-in-law had been killed in the air raids. Moulin had to accept the order for military retreat beyond the Loire River.

After some time, next to the cathedral two specialist glass artisans of the Lorin workshop established a small work space in the basement of the bishop's palace, to which they quietly—likely in the dark, late at night—removed one crate at a time from the inner crypt and transported it to the work space, where they made repairs and took photographs; when they'd completed the repair work on all panels stored in such a removed crate, they returned it to the inner crypt and removed another of those that were accessible. Over the four years of the occupation, the glassmakers would repair the window panels concealed in those crates of the inner crypt that they could reach furtively, but the storage portion of the crypt had been disguised and fenced off in order to avoid "indiscretions," as Jean Trouvelot would call them, and the glassmakers could not have replaced any of the remaining crates without attracting attention, so repair of panels in these remaining crates was deferred.

On Saturday, June 25, Jean Moulin estimated that only seven- to eight hundred of Chartres' population of twenty-three thousand remained. Refugees and sick people too ill to travel were pouring into the cathedral's crypt, seeking shelter. Moulin managed to keep the municipal hospital operating with the help of nuns and a military dentist, mainly serving people too ill to travel and refugees, including many who had congregated in the crypt of the cathedral. He arranged to move them out. He also arranged for eight hundred loaves of bread to be brought in from another town and was seen walking through the streets carrying the loaves to distribute to people passing through from the region around Paris. The next day was filled with deserting soldiers—or those who seemed disinterested—escaping civilians and incidents of looting, and Moulin's car was stolen from the prefecture by French soldiers.

On the seventeenth, Moulin was waiting in his office at 3:00 a.m. when he heard tanks. He had been expecting Germans but saw French units retreating. Three hours later, a regiment of Senegalese soldiers passed through, appearing to Moulin to be trying to fight rather than be taken prisoner. The next hour, German soldiers arrived in a motorcade. One of the German officers assured Moulin that the Germans would treat civilians with respect. The next morning, Moulin heard that Senegalese members of the French Army had made efforts to prevent the Germans from entering Chartres, but soon Moulin saw Germans driving through on motorcycles. In the early evening, as Moulin was sitting down to eat, German soldiers came in, arrested him, and demanded that he sign a "protocol" stating that black French troops had raped and murdered a group of French women and children. The Germans took him to a remote location to see mutilated bodies of the women and children, ostensibly as evidence of the alleged massacre, but Moulin concluded that the women and children had been victims of a bombing. The Germans, meanwhile, had shot and killed most of the Senegalese.

The Germans were infuriated with Moulin and locked him in a cellar with some of the corpses, but he still refused to sign. He tried to run off, and they shot him for attempted escape; then they took him back to Chartres and beat him again, finally leaving him in a makeshift cell, an isolated one-room house on the hospital grounds, with a surviving Senegalese soldier. The soldier gave Moulin the only mattress, and Moulin fell asleep.

When Moulin woke, he tried to kill himself by cutting his own throat with broken window glass. The Germans found him and took him to the hospital. After treatment, they drove him away and eventually dropped him at the prefecture. Within a week, Moulin had sufficiently recovered to resume his duties. Soon Frenchmen nationwide would hear about his beating and attempted suicide, one of many incidents that would lead to his recognition for civic courage alongside de Gaulle among the foremost resisters. The cut on his neck resulted in a scar. Photographs of Moulin taken thereafter show him wearing a scarf around his neck, which became his trademark image.

In November, Moulin was removed from office by the Vichy government for failure to comply with its order for all prefects to dismiss left-wing elected mayors of towns and villages. Jean Moulin was a man of determination, and he proved it during the war, as none other. In the next several years, he would travel secretly to London and meet with de Gaulle.

In December, the German occupation forces demanded that the manuscripts and books from the Chartres library that had been moved to the Château de Villebon the year before be returned to Chartres as a propaganda move to reassure the population that they need not fear Nazi occupation. Those in charge of the library could not refuse the order.

CHAPTER FIFTEEN

Maneuvers: Kentucky to New York, April 1943–February 1944

BY THE END OF FEBRUARY 1943, THE BATTLE OF GUADALCANAL HAD finally ended. It was the first major offensive by Allied forces against Japan. Griff's brother Philip would soon be in the Pacific theater as a US Navy petty officer, and Griff's brother-in-law, Count DeKay, would serve there as an admiral.

On the other side of the world, the North African campaign had already been under way four months and was finally progressing—and the Army was nearly finalizing its Italy invasion plan—the first invasion of Axis-controlled Europe. In two weeks, the Allies would launch their scheme to deceive the Germans into thinking the Allied attack would start on Sardinia and Corsica, the Italian and French islands west of mainland Italy. In their scheme, they would plant the body of a man who appeared to be a British Royal Marine pilot in the waters off a Spanish beach, with an attaché case cuffed to his wrist containing top-secret documents, but it would actually be the body of a homeless man from Wales who'd committed suicide. The documents—an elaborate British diversion called Operation Mincemeat—succeeded in fooling the Germans into redirecting their forces to defend Sardinia and Corsica, but by the time they did so, the Allies' invading force had set sail to come ashore at Italy's largest island, Sicily.

For Griff, his Fourth Armored Division had amassed good records as aggressive, disciplined fighting units with high morale, so General

Walton H. Walker—the Texan from nearby Temple—relinquished command of the Desert Training Center and ordered the corps to move to Camp Campbell to undergo continued physical training and schooling in equipment, weapons, and tactics. He and his headquarters staff—including Griff, with his G-3 operations team—welcomed the change as a step nearer to shipment overseas. Griff used his desert training as a spark to transition into high gear to generate plans for field training to ready the corps for combat.

Troops with gear-filled trucks pulled out at 5:00 the next morning to drive to Indio, California, where they boarded a troop train. Griff's assistant, Eugene Schulz, relished the train's Pullman sleeper cars, an upgrade from the tent cots and heat of Camp Young. The train passed through Yuma, Phoenix, El Paso, and Little Rock to cross the Mississippi at Memphis, on to Clarksville, Tennessee, where the men boarded trucks and buses with their gear for the ten-mile drive northwest to Camp Campbell, an area of more than one hundred thousand acres spreading across adjoining parts of Tennessee and Kentucky.

The new camp had been built during the previous year, with capacity for 45,000 enlisted men and 2,400 officers. Griff, Schulz, and the others took up their spots in the barracks, two-story white frame buildings joined by paved streets. Each man would have a bunk bed, footlocker, and coatrack, improvements over the tent accommodations of Camp Young. The GIs and officers relished the prospect of mess halls, hot showers—finally with ample water, which desert camp had lacked—and dayrooms stocked with reading material, chairs, writing tables, and couches. Post exchanges offered a lineup of food, chips, chocolate, beer, and Coke. Posters announced movies coming to multiple theaters.

The Fourth Armored Corps under General Walker's command included five infantry and two armored divisions besides the corps headquarters general staff, which constituted an independent unit. Colonel Griffith, as the senior G-3 headquarters operations officer, was in charge of corps plans, operations, air support, and the situation map—issuing orders to subordinate commanders and seeing that they were carried out. The G-3 covered infantry, armor, artillery, cavalry, antiaircraft units, and the G-3 Air Corps (air reconnaissance and tactical fighter-bomber air support). In short, the G-3's primary responsibility was to administer the tactical plan by converting all steps of the plan into objectives and steps in detailed written orders to field commanders who would be charged with implementing the directives in specified sequence through available men and resources.

Serving with Griff was young Major Melville I. Stark, who had been Griff's deputy since his early days at Camp Young. Griff, Stark, and Lieutenant Lee directed setup of the G-3 office (called the "three-shop") and map room, by its three clerk-typists: Sergeant Joe Messner—chief clerk—Gene Schulz, and Don LeMoine, together with John Massa, cartographer.

At Camp Campbell, training began with drilling, calisthenics, and an obstacle course and was followed by classes: first aid, fieldstripping and reassembling submachine guns and machine guns, driving jeeps and half-tracks, learning tank operation, employing maps, reading aerial photos, and identifying enemy aircraft. Each man dug a three-foot-wide foxhole chest deep in tank-wide rows and climbed in to experience a tank rolling overhead. Hikes with packs of gear and bricks figured prominently, of usually five to ten miles, some with time limits; each man had to complete twenty-one such hikes overall from April through mid-July. One afternoon, all headquarters personnel, including Griff, were ordered to undertake one such hike with pack and rifle, initially ordered to be nine miles, but after a short break, the order extended the trip to twenty-five miles, to be completed within eight hours of the earlier start. Any man not meeting that limit eventually had to make repeated attempts until successful—one requirement to qualify any soldier for deployment overseas.

Corpsmen got accustomed to long overland trips, often in rain and mud, night marches under blackout, digging slit trenches in woods laced with thorny tree roots, and enduring rationing of water and food. Commanders usually intensified exercises by ordering the unexpected.

By late August, after six months, the corps had completed its initial physical training and battle indoctrination, and so General Walker ordered eight weeks of simulated battle training, from September to

October 1943, to be called the Tennessee Maneuvers, in which the corps headquarters staff and units from the Second Army would face each other in simulated combat.

The maneuvers would take place in the bluegrass region near Lebanon, Tennessee, forty miles east of Nashville and ninety miles southeast of Camp Campbell, in terrain heavily wooded with red cedar trees blanketing hills and deep gorges with large rivers and streams, which would figure in most of the maneuvers.

During the eight weeks of training, the two forces faced off in simulated combat, in a new operation each week: movement to contact, engagement of forces, attack and defense of a river line, coordinated attack of a prepared position, delaying actions, and breakthrough then withdrawal over a considerable distance.

In mid-October, all units of the Fourth Armored Corps were renamed and modified to be known as Twentieth Corps for action in Europe.

In mid-January, orders arrived for the corps to ship overseas, and early on February 1, Griff and the remaining corps headquarters staff—with the enlisted men and other officers in their Class A olive dress uniforms and jam-packed duffle bags in tow—boarded a fleet of six-by-six trucks for the drive to the Hopkinsville train station. There they boarded special trains. Exactly where they were going, and when, none of the enlisted men knew. Sleep came quickly on the train.

Days later, in darkness, a jolt rattled the shade-covered rail-coach window Griff was leaning against, and he couldn't sleep anymore. He raised the shade to look out. In the foggy darkness blanketing the train, the beam of a swaying flashlight shined on the ground. A switchman was walking toward him through the darkness, the light diffusing across the ground like waves of seeds spread on a lawn and illuminating his work boots, the crunch of his steps over oily, snowy gravel loudening.

A sliding side door jounced open near the front of the coach. A conductor leaned in, announcing with muffled voice into the darkness that the train would be stopped for thirty minutes, for engine switching and taking on water, and cautioning the passengers against jolts from coupling of railcars, in case they cared to step out for a smoke. The train would be under way soon; meanwhile, lights would remain off.

Few of the thirty or so officers in the coach were awake, many packed two to a bench. For Griff, at least one perk of being the G-3 was getting a seat to himself, although he still had to contend with the man stretched out in the seat facing him. He had to sleep upright but managed to get his legs under the facing seat diagonally to keep out of the aisle to avoid being awakened during the night by men tripping over his feet on their way to the can.

He checked his watch. It was almost 03:00. Through the cold fog, lit by a solitary bare light bulb on a pole along the rails, he could see a half dozen switch posts and other rail lines parallel to his coach's track. It seemed they were in the beginning of some sort of switchyard. All was quiet. He guessed the train had reached the middle of Pennsylvania by now, which would have put them about eight hours from the coast, where they'd be unloading to ferry boats to take them to Fort Slocum on David's Island in Long Island Sound.

Of the thousands of soldiers on this and the other trains that had left Fort Campbell early that damp, cold February morning the day before yesterday, only a few senior officers (including Griff)—not even all on his car—had been told where the train would be heading. All they suspected was that they would eventually end up somewhere in Europe, probably starting in the British Isles.

No, this was an "eyes only" operation. Except for those few senior officers, including Griff, not even Griff's own clerk-typist knew where the train was headed or what their orders would be when they unloaded.

What excitement would lie ahead, Griff wondered. Finally, the real fight, a shot at recognition. Three years into the war, and all those years of training might actually pay off. He had wanted to tell Nell what the plans were. Why the hell not? *She has no contacts in Brooklyn with any military.* But if the troops themselves weren't allowed to know, then he couldn't rightly tell his wife and daughter. So he hadn't. He'd written Nell a letter a week ago saying that he expected to be on the East Coast soon, but that was all. Even though he was bursting to share with her his excitement and fears.

He imagined the two of them at dinner somewhere in Brooklyn having a quiet conversation—just the two of them. He wished he could spend a night at home with Nell, alone. He missed her touch and her voice and the fragrance of her hair and neck. They could sit together on the porch in the evening, in the lull of the Eighty-Sixth Street Brooklyn traffic and trolley shuffling past in its normal orderly slowing from the daytime bustle. He longed for his dog too, the way its red hair shimmered in the afternoon sun as it lay next to him on the porch, its snout on his leg, after chasing the ball around his in-laws' small backyard.

He leaned back against the window for more shut-eye, having settled finally into a relatively comfortable position. Silence returned to the car, but it was soon interrupted by a revving of the engine at the front, another thump from railcars connecting, more screeches, and finally resting silence.

His daughter, Alice, came to mind. He wondered how much she'd grown since he'd seen her last. His thoughts turned to selecting a few limited facts to share with her about his deployment. Maybe he could tell her he'd be leaving soon by ship, heading to England. But that notion didn't sit well. What good would it do for her to know, anyway? And how could he expect a thirteen-year-old to keep that kind of secret, especially on Governor's Island, where she was surrounded by children of other officers? Surely she'd get the impression that it'd be okay to share the information with her friends. *And then for sure her grandfather, Lieutenant Colonel Torrey, would find out—either from Alice or from others—that I'd shared the information with her.* Then it could get back to Twentieth Corps. And Griff'd be in the soup.

Nope. Operational security won't permit it.

But . . . really?

Random flickering lights filtered through the car, illuminating the sleeping officers. Griff thought about the sleeping men spread throughout the coach. This was the brain trust of Twentieth Corps, he thought. Fine officers, most of them. And they were also just a group of fathers and husbands, brothers and sons, each probably missing his family too.

While darkness abided, Griff absorbed a few more hours of sleep. The sound of muffled conversation eventually woke him, some of the men pulling out their mess kits and working their way back to the kitchen car to bring coffee and breakfast back to their seats.

He wasn't quite ready. He kept his eyes closed and thought through a plan to call Nell from Fort Slocum. He would propose to take both her and Alice together out for an evening of dinner and dancing at a New York hotel, something first class, like the St. Regis or the Plaza. First he'd call Nell and sound her out on the idea. If she were keen, he'd call Alice to arrange it. But little Alice would have school tomorrow. So he'd have to plan for Saturday, the day after, since the pullout to the ship would have to be completed by the following Friday, the tenth.

If things weren't too crazy at the fort, maybe he could take Nell home to Brooklyn, to spend the night with her before returning to Slocum. If not, he'd just have to take her home, say goodbye, and return to Slocum. He thought about it and decided it sounded good.

So he took his mess kit back to the kitchen car for a cup of coffee and a plate of powdered eggs and bacon and toast and then worked his way back with it to eat in his seat.

After another few hours of the coach's rattling and jostling, he ate a box lunch in his seat, and then, finally, at 14:00 hours, the train pulled into the station in New Rochelle.

For now, there was work to be done.

Chapter Sixteen

Goodbye to Both: New York City, Early February 1944

LATER, ON FEBRUARY 3, GRIFF FOUND AN EMPTY OFFICE WITH A PHONE, and he put in a call to Nell, who was at home, and told her he was at Slocum and perhaps could come into the city on Saturday and spend some time with her and Alice in Manhattan. Nell thought that was a good idea.

Late the next afternoon, he reached Alice at the Torreys', where she lived with his ex-wife and her grandparents, Lieutenant Colonel and Mrs. Torrey, on Governor's Island, where Lieutenant Colonel Torrey served as adjutant. Alice was happy to hear from her dad and thrilled about the plan for dinner and dancing. "At the Plaza? Really?" He asked her to be ready by 4:30 Saturday afternoon. He'd come to the island to pick her up.

He called Nell again to confirm the plan with her and asked her to get herself to the hotel where he and Alice would meet her for the early sitting. She seemed a little off during the call—almost as though she was taken aback by the prospect that Griff seemed unsure when, or maybe even whether, he could spend time at home with her. She didn't know where he was being sent, but his coming to the East Coast made her think he might be heading somewhere in Europe, maybe sometime soon. Griff didn't think much about her reaction. His focus was on getting through the next few days. There'd be time eventually, he was sure, to get things squared away with Nell.

After a full couple of days of meetings, Griff got back to his quarters at 14:00 on Saturday in time to shave, put on his dress uniform, and have a driver take him to catch the 14:45 ferry to New Rochelle, where the other passengers were waiting in the cold for the train to Grand Central. As he waited on the platform, he felt the energy of being back in New York—people shuffling about to their offices or to theaters and other entertainment, with determination and deadlines—where during his West Point summers with Uncle Tex he had been exposed to a life sharply contrasting with the slower pace of Dallas, not to mention Quanah.

When the train arrived at Grand Central, he found his way onto a subway to get to the Battery dock to catch the ferry to Governor's Island. Sailors and soldiers were passing through, probably heading to bars and dance halls. Groups of girls looking for fun were flirting and hand-holding with sailors and soldiers, eager for Saturday night. At the Battery dock, upon boarding the ferry for the twenty-minute run to the island, Griff a took a seat indoors after confirming the boat would be running back and forth until late, and he thought about where he'd want to sit with Alice after picking her up. From the landing dock, he spotted the driver waiting for him in Lieutenant Colonel Torrey's green military sedan for the short drive to the Commander's House.

The car pulled up to the red-brick three-story residence, surrounded by tree-shaded lawns and fronted by a long service walk leading to its white-trimmed front porch, guarded by six two-story white columns, with its chandelier suspended from an iron chain over the front door. Griff stepped up onto the flagstone porch, and his ex-mother-in-law—also named Alice Torrey, like her daughter and granddaughter—emerged from the door in her prim skirt and jacket over a white blouse, as though she'd just returned from her bridge club, with her welcoming smile, reaching for a hug. Griff kissed her on both cheeks as she led him into the foyer.

"It's so great to see you, Griff. Little Alice will be down in a minute. She's finishing her hair."

There was no sign of Griff's ex-wife.

When his daughter, little Alice, bounded down the stairs in her sequined formal dancing dress, she rushed to her father and gave him a warm hug.

"I'm so excited to see you, Dad. I've been dreaming about this evening since you called. You look so tall and important in your dress uniform."

Griff straightened his shoulders. "You look wonderful, too. Wow, what a dress!" After glancing at Mrs. Torrey, he told Alice they could catch up on the way to the hotel, and he assured Mrs. Torrey that Nell was looking forward to seeing them both—that Nell would be coming from her parents' Brooklyn home herself and meeting him and little Alice at the hotel. As he helped Alice with her coat, he apologized to her grandmother for moving on so quickly: "The car is waiting, and the ferry won't."

Mrs. Torrey said not to worry; she wanted him and his daughter to have as much time together as possible. She showed them to the door and walked them to the waiting car.

At the dock, Griff led Alice to an indoor bench, out of the wind, on the starboard side, next to the windows. The boat got under way from Governor's Island toward the city, and the bow aimed toward lower Manhattan, whose building shadows stretched toward them like long fingers, reaching through the water, pulling the bow toward the Battery dock. Lights glimmered in downtown building windows, now in the dusk beginning to increase in intensity through the buildings' shadowed east faces.

He turned to look at Alice sitting next to him, her patent leather shoes reaching to touch the floor. He remembered the day she was born. She returned his look with a smile as he examined her eyes. He wondered what she was thinking. How had she been, with her mother, who'd been grieving the loss of Commander Blue, her second husband, in the Pacific? Little Alice couldn't really have known him that well, because her mother had only been married to this man for three years.

Wow. Alice had grown so much since the last time he'd seen her.

He took off his glove and reached to hold her hand as they each looked at the water. Her sequined evening dress and pearl necklace, visible through the opening of her wool coat, made her look almost like a prom girl. Her necklace reminded him of her mother, who'd worn pearls at Griffith Texas holiday gatherings. Alice's hat, carefully positioned for warmth without mussing her coiffed blonde hair, made Griff wonder: Was it her mother or grandmother who'd helped her dress for the evening?

Alice returned his smile with her own and a sigh. She was happy to be with him and excited to be out for their Saturday evening in New York.

When they arrived at the Plaza, Griff and Alice found Nell in the lobby, lounging in an overstuffed chair near the bar with her radiant brunette hair, her slender body shown to advantage in a stylish, reserved evening dress of a shapely cut and glowing beige sheen.

Nell spotted Griff in his uniform—tall and handsome as ever, and all energy—with his dimple and cocked hat she'd missed so much. She raised her arms, her eyes tearing up as her smile greeted him, alive and warm, in anticipation of his kiss. Her smile at first sight gave him a wave of welcome. She rose, greeted and hugged Alice, and then let Griff hug her tight and close with a long kiss, holding and holding and holding her.

They strode toward the elevator, which opened under a shiny brass sign that read "The Persian Room."

The elevator operator, in his royal-blue uniform with epaulets and matching cap with patent leather visor, reached over to close the shiny brass-cage safety door, acknowledging Alice's presence with a nod and welcoming smile. She admired his formal attire and then looked around to notice that, except for his and her father's army uniform, there were no others in military dress or regalia, which made her feel even more privileged to be here with her father in his. The operator didn't need to ask which floor the group was going to. He swiftly closed the outer door and navigated up to the Persian Room's level.

Alice took in the sights and sounds. Later in life, she recalled that it felt like entering a golden gate into a Persian palace. She was beguiled by the high-ceilinged art-deco Persian style in deep iridescent tones of blues, greens, and purples and was transfixed by the ladies, in their gowns and mink furs, men in their fine suits and tuxedos, seated at tables or in elegant booths, each candlelit with white table cloth and sparkling glassware. The tables and booths surrounded a circular dance floor, already alive with music of the jazz and swing-time orchestra. It was a magical scene. A cigar and cigarette girl, with a tray strapped to her front, was selling smokes. A man with a flash camera was going from table to table, offering souvenir photos.

Alice sat at the table and smiled at Griff and Nell, seeming to enjoy herself, with the people surrounding her having a grand time. Nell kept her eyes locked on Griff, and he noticed her glances at him. There was something she seemed eager to know. Was it how long he was going to be in town, what he was up to, whether there was any word that he'd be going to war? He could see concern in the way she tilted her head, looking at him. He didn't know how to respond, bound by his constraints.

There were almost no young people of middle school age or younger, so Alice felt very grown-up to be there and told Griff she was proud to be sitting with him, his brass buttons prominent against his olive-green jacket and his khaki tie. Nell joined in that she was happy also to be there with Alice and Griff after so long a separation.

Griff noticed he was the only military man present—at least the only one in military dress; a little awkward shift of his shoulders revealed how he felt out of place. With a highball in his hand, standing on the plush carpet, he pictured the other Twentieth Corps officers, still hard at work, back in the dark fort office at Slocum, low lights hanging over the map table in the dimly lit room with cold concrete floors, as they went over plans and preparations for the transfer of men and machines across the ocean, their families far off and distant from their thoughts.

The trio ordered dinner, starting with a shrimp cocktail for Alice. When the orchestra began to play its slow, quiet rendition of "Green Eyes," Griff smiled and asked his daughter to dance, reaching for her hand. She nodded with raised eyebrows and a smile, arm extended. They joined the dozen couples on the dance floor. Once in rhythm, she leaned close and asked again what his destination would be. He said he wasn't permitted to say. Besides, a New York restaurant—especially the dance floor—was not a place for discussing any such thing. "Spies are everywhere," he whispered to Alice. "Plan security is critical. Big plans are being made. I've got to be part of them."

Alice swung her head back to meet his look, in silence, and continued to dance, sighing, stretching her arms high to hold him close.

He looked out with a blank stare over her head, wondering when he'd be able to see and talk with her again after this night.

He guided Alice back to their table. Nell was waiting, hoping for a dance with her husband. He looked at her and at Alice.

He shook his head. "Alice is asking where I am going." Leaning toward both as he sat down, he whispered, "I can't tell either of you. We must not talk about where I'm going." Looking at Nell, with a tilt of his head toward Alice, he added, "Lieutenant Colonel Torrey will surely know if we have. If he suspects, word will get back to the corps. I can't jeopardize the mission or my opportunity."

Nell nodded in understanding and attempted a smile. Alice looked around the room as if in a dream, with cocktails, dinner, desserts, the surroundings, the ladies' dresses, the feel of the purple and red velour upholstery of her bench under her hand.

The orchestra resumed with muted trumpets playing "Star Dust," and Griff went to Nell and with a hand and a nod requested a dance. She tilted her head with an I-thought-you'd-never-ask look and led him to the dance floor, starting with a tight, slow hug and a sigh. It was their first time even a little bit alone together in sixteen months. She was savoring the dance and looking forward to a long evening with Griff—and trying to freeze the memory of the feel of him holding her, wondering how long it would be until they could do this again. She dreamed of the two of them being home together at least in Brooklyn or near another base somewhere, hoping it would be soon.

Their return to the table coincided with the arrival of their first course of dinner and the wine. While they ate, Nell engaged Alice in conversation about her mother's family and Alice's interests outside of school. Griff, largely silent, enjoying Nell's genuine interest in Alice and her life, feeling a streak of endearment and tenderness that he hadn't often experienced since their wedding.

They worked their way through their elegant meal, and Griff and Nell got up to dance, while Alice admired the partygoers, the ladies' dresses, and the surroundings as she savored the last of her dessert.

When they returned, Alice and Griff left for one last dance, without talking.

Griff glanced at his watch: it was nearing 21:00. Looking up at both women, he said, "Well . . . I'll get the coats," and rose to head toward the cloakroom, saying he'd meet them at the elevator, as the orchestra played "Frenesi" to encourage the patrons shuffling in and out to keep things moving. The hallway outside the Persian Room was clogged again with departing guests and a queue of others waiting to enter, eager to be in place for the next sitting. The elevator operator greeted the departing guests with his own song, triggering a lot of smiles for the ride down.

Griff led Alice and Nell to one of the waiting taxis to return to the dock for the 22:00 ferry back to Governor's Island, Nell to join them for the return trip to help see Alice home.

On the ferry, Alice sat between Griff and Nell, resting her head on her father's shoulder as the boat rocked, the reflected lights of the city receding as the ferry crossed toward the island. They were each deep in thought, but none had much to say.

At the Commander's House, Alice's grandmother answered the door with a smile for each of them. She gave Nell a hug. Lieutenant Colonel Torrey was waiting with her.

Little Alice, with a coquettish grin, said, "We had a marvelous time, except that Dad wouldn't tell me where he's going," following with an innocent glance at the lieutenant colonel and then a light-hearted sneer at Griff, who frowned in reply.

Griff looked at the lieutenant colonel, whose approving nod signaled that he endorsed Griff's discretion.

Alice hugged Griff and Nell goodbye. "Thank you for a dreamy evening," she gushed. "I'll remember it always. And please write, Dad. Please be safe and take care of yourself."

"Sure will. And you too. When I return, we'll have another grand time. Please tell your mother to take good care too."

Alice went upstairs. Nell shared a goodbye hug and kisses on the cheeks with Mrs. Torrey, and Griff a handshake with the lieutenant colonel. They hurried to the waiting car and then were off to the ferry.

Onboard, Griff held Nell, her head resting on his shoulder. He savored her warmth, tightly gripping her gloved hand, feeling the boat rock with the harbor waves.

Earlier that afternoon, he'd thought that he would have time to ride with Nell in the cab back to Brooklyn, spend the night with her there, and then in the morning catch a cab or the subway to Grand Central and the train back to the fort—and that he had some saying goodbye to do. And his dog was with her in Brooklyn, so he'd wanted to say goodbye to the dog too.

But now, his mind had turned to all the things he needed to do, starting early the next morning, when he'd have quiet office time before the others awoke. He had to return to his unit.

So he came up with a modified plan: If the ferry got them back to Battery Park in time, he would have time to ride with Nell in the cab back to Brooklyn, say goodbye there, and then catch a cab to Grand Central and the train back to the fort in time to catch the last ferry at 0:30. He'd tell Nell that he hoped to get back during the week, but tonight just wouldn't work for him to stay in Brooklyn.

But it was already 22:10. He even balked at the notion of riding in the cab back to Brooklyn. So instead he turned to Nell to tell her his further modified plan for the night. He told her he needed to get back to the fort. He would put her in a cab back to Brooklyn, and he'd take a separate cab to Grand Central and catch the train from there to New Rochelle, then the ferry to the fort.

"I'm gonna miss you, Nell."

She'd expected this. She didn't want it, but she'd expected that he'd head back to the fort and call her in a day or two to arrange another chance for them to get together. In her lips and inward cheeks, he could see her fear-against-hope expression that she'd been looking for him to come home for the night. But they both knew that just sitting there together would have to do, just holding each other, absorbing the moment. She repeated that she'd been missing him—and would miss him even more still. But she understood. Just sitting with him, enjoying the remaining moments, would do for her what she needed most. She didn't understand, but she knew that now wasn't the time for questions and discussion.

At the taxi stand, she asked when she'd see him again.

"I don't know, but I'll be in touch as soon as I can. I was hoping to get back again in the next few days, but it's not likely."

She closed her lips. Her worry engulfed him, and he felt a spike of his own tears and a flush warmth welling up in his face. But he could answer her worry only with another hug. This sight and touch of her could be his last.

"Remember, I'll be in HQ, not at the front." Tears in her eyes drove him to reach in and roll down her taxi window before he closed her door.

"Chin up. Stay beautiful. Love my dog until I get back. I love you."

"Love you too. Be safe."

Her taxi pulled away. He checked his watch and signaled for another cab to get him to Grand Central.

Sunday at 06:30, Griff awoke in his single bunk, the dank, cold February ocean air lying between his face and the thin faded-green wallboard that crawled up the wall of his thin, dark room, illuminated by the first wave of dawn light finding its way in through the two-foot-square dirty window that faced the narrow walkway between huts. He heard the first sounds of the ferry crew preparing the dock for the arrival of the earliest boat. Facing the wall with his head still on his pillow, in his mind he could still see Nell's attempted smile as they'd said goodbye at the taxi stand, more left unsaid between them than said. He went over their conversation on the boat. He didn't feel good about not committing to see her alone for a night before shipping out, but as he reconsidered it, he was already having trouble imagining how he could get away to Brooklyn for a full night in the next four days and still finish all that needed doing between now and time for the troops to load onto launches to be taken to the big ship.

Still, the longing in Nell's face, the effort she was making to bear up to being without him, and what must have been her fear of the unknown were difficult for him to compartmentalize from the rest of his whirling thoughts. He thought again about what facts he could share with Nell to at least give her some peace of mind about some of the things that were undoubtedly worrying her. How about at least telling her they were heading out to Europe on the tenth? Nothing about how or where they *would* be going, or when they'd arrive. *Maybe*, he thought. *Maybe. Let's see how it goes today and tomorrow*, he decided. And he tried to fold up those thoughts, put them in his pocket, and get on with his work. He rolled out of bed, his head swimming with confusion.

Monday night, he found his way back to the dark office. He sat in the dimness trying first to fortify himself for what he expected would be an awkward conversation with Nell, only to stall, lighting a cigarette, trying to sort out emotions, but he couldn't quite do it. There was something that had been bothering Nell on Saturday night. He wasn't sure what it was, but there was something—it had something to do with her thinking that he'd changed, he knew, something about his focus on the war and not on her or them or coming home. He'd never had this feeling before about Nell. It was different from before, with his first wife, Alice, who'd always found things to be unhappy about. But with Nell, it had been different. She'd been content with whatever time they had together, whatever opportunities there were. When they'd first met, Griff wasn't as wrapped up in his military career, and there certainly wasn't a war going on. But now there was, and he was finally part of it and determined to get into the fight. She'd seemed to understand before, but now there was a new tension between them that he hadn't sensed before.

He placed the call to Nell, determined to tell her he wouldn't get out to Brooklyn to see her this time, and that was it. His outfit would be moving out soon, with his chance to get into the war and make happen what he'd been training and planning for all these years. And he was damn excited about it and hoped she would be too.

He said, "It's me."

"I was hoping you'd call tonight," she said. "When can you come home?"

"Well, that's why I'm calling. It's not gonna work. I'm not gonna be able to get there this time."

"Oh? Well, then, how about this weekend, or next week some time?"

"You see, Nell. Um, that's just it. We'll be moving out soon."

"Really, so soon? Who's going?" she asked. "How long will you be gone? Where are you going? When will you be back?"

"Nell, it's just that—"

"I got the impression from you on Saturday night that it was a matter of getting settled. But now it sounds like you're just passing through. Is that it? Can we get together when you get settled, wherever you're going?"

"No, that's not going to work. We're leaving this week, the whole corps. And we're going to Europe. I can't tell you more than that, Nell."

"Geez." She paused.

Griff heard only silence on the line for what seemed a full minute, followed by a sniffle.

"Nell, are you there? Are you okay?"

"Yes, I'm just feeling a bit of a shock, is all. I didn't realize you were just passing through on your way overseas. I'm sorry, Griff. I don't want to be a burden. I just . . ."

So Griff went on to tell her that he was being presented with the most important opportunity he'd ever had and that he was darned excited about the whole thing, and that corps security prevented him from saying any more to her, and that he'd probably already told her more than he should have. This was going to be his chance to get into the fight for real. He'd been learning and training and preparing all these years for real combat, and this was going to be it.

Nell tried to be excited for him, but mostly she just didn't understand. Why couldn't he plan for at least a little time at home? Didn't he want to? She thought his role would be well back from the front lines in headquarters, not in the fight. But was he going to be in danger? Why would he want to do that? Wasn't that for younger, single men?

She'd been looking forward to the day they'd finally be together. Now that they'd found each other and gotten married, she'd thought they *both* wanted to settle down—both of them wanting it just as much. But now he seemed strangely reluctant to commit.

Gripping the receiver, Griff felt a bit guilty about everything—as though he'd been trying to conceal something from her, something beyond the required corps secrecy. He felt strangely uncomfortable and sort of contrite. This was unexpected. He'd been so excited and had wanted her to share his excitement. But then he realized that she had no reason to be excited for him. She was just worried about him.

Now she'd have to get used to the idea that he'd be gone for a long time and that he'd be exposed to a lot of danger.

During another pause in the conversation in his mind, he caught a quick vision of her coming home from her office job to her parents' house in Brooklyn, eager to sift through the mail for a new letter from him. She'd be hoping to learn that he'd been stationed far back from the fighting—doing something important and satisfying, yes, but not something that would get him injured or killed.

So he gave a little thought to what he could say to her that would give her a little assurance, a little something good to be hoping for. But his mind went blank.

And Nell, too, was trying to think of something to say that would keep him from worrying about her—especially since he had so much important work to do, and so many men (and their families) depending on him. But she, too, had trouble thinking of anything else to say, except that she realized that for the first time in his life, he would now be getting the chance to use all that he'd learned and been training for, and training others for. And she realized that this was an important war and that each of them had to do everything they could to support the war effort and to support our men fighting in it, especially her Griff. And she really, really didn't want him to have to worry about her. She'd be fine, really. After all, they were two ordinary people: two of the many, many people who'd been going through the same thing and would have to keep going through it until this big awful mess of a war got won and over with.

"After all," she finally said, "I guess all of my thinking and hoping was based on the premise that our lives are somehow special and more important than anyone else's. But we're not. We found each other a little later than others, and we're just who we are."

"You're right," Griff told her. "We just have to do our part. Hopefully, it'll all work out and we'll be together, soon as I get back."

He paused and she paused.

"You do understand why I can't tell you more now, don't you?"

"Yes," she said, "I'm grateful that we had our night on the town, with Alice, and we'll just have to leave it at that, won't we?"

And with that, he felt that he'd said about enough and had nothing more to say. And neither did she. And they said goodbye. And that was it.

Two days later, Thursday, February 10, 1944, all troops at Fort Slocum were assembled and given orders to pack up immediately, to ship out at 20:00 hours.

That night, Griff and all the other officers and enlisted men of the corps climbed aboard a convoy of launches that shuttled them down the Long Island Sound, into the East River and past the Brooklyn Navy Yard. They were off to war.

CHAPTER SEVENTEEN

War Hits Again: The Dordogne and Chartres, June 1940–May 1944

TO MANAGE THE OPERATION AT CHÂTEAU DE FONGRENON, THE FINE Arts Administration assigned Jules Pillot to be supervisor. He had been chief keeper of Château de Pierrefonds, a castle in the northern French department of Oise. The Fine Arts Administration also rented a house in La Tour-Blanche in which Pillot would live. The state arranged for the house to be officially rented in the name of Mrs. Eva Faure, in an apparent attempt to maintain secrecy. In confidence with Alexis Moreau, manager of the Fongrenon quarry, Pillot recruited people to serve as the guards at Fongrenon between June 1940 and July 1941. The quarry at Fongrenon would continue to operate for extraction of stone, but operations only continued in an entrance area of the quarry, which apparently eliminated the need for additional watchmen during the day, so long as the men who quarried the stone inside could be trusted, which itself presented a persistent risk. Pillot arranged for a succession of night watchmen to arrive at the end of each workday to watch over the crates during the workweek and on weekends. The seven watchmen consisted of Pillot, Moreau, and five others. To provide shelter for the guards, the workmen constructed a small shed in a recess in the quarry, equipped with a woodstove for heat and, likely, cooking.

After a year, Pillot asked to be reinstated back to Pierrefonds, apparently to be with his family, and the Fine Arts Administration appointed a Mr. Eschlinger, followed by a Mr. Vonau. Before those assignments, both

Eschlinger and Vonau—from Alsace and Lorraine, respectively—had been posted at the Hautefort depot, in Château de Hautefort, a castle forty-five miles east of Fongrenon, near which members of the Alsace and Lorraine fine arts administrations had taken refuge at the beginning of this latest war.

In 1943, the guards in the quarry observed that some of the crates had deteriorated from moisture seeping into the quarry. The cliff into which the quarry had been dug overlooked a reservoir that collected water from an underground river passing under the surrounding valley. On request of the administration, architect Foidevaux came to inspect the quarry and determined that seventy of the crates needed repair, so he arranged for a local carpenter to mend them with poplar planks. He also recommended that the quarry be ventilated, and so the men dug a ventilation chimney, which extended from the last of the watched rooms upward to the top surface of the cliff.

Throughout the occupation, the Germans compelled French authorities to hand over to the German ministry in charge of collections of museums and monuments detailed inventories of the French collections that had been placed in the numerous depots. Thierry Baritaud, whose scholarship in 2007 had rediscovered the use of the Fongrenon quarry as a depot, argues that the Germans knew of the existence of all the deposits of works of art, including Fongrenon. Yet he has concluded that the Germans never came to Fongrenon to inspect the crates. Although the turnover of information had been required by the Germans ostensibly for safekeeping and security, certain elements of the German regime went on to use the information to organize thefts of art during the war. It may have been only a matter of time before word of the Chartres treasures at Fongrenon would have worked its way through the German hierarchy within the occupation zone and into the Vichy government.

It was likely fortunate that Fongrenon was ten miles inside the Vichy zone. However, as noted by historian Elizabeth Karlsgodt, although most Vichy members believed the state should protect the nation's cultural heritage, historians and other analysts since the war have classified certain Vichy figures as collaborators and others as resisters, but there were gray areas of activity between the two categories in the context of occupation, even without German pressure. The Vichy players who were more likely to have been engaged in assisting German confiscation of artworks would have been those who were anti-Semitic, and confiscations applied mostly to Jewish-owned art, not state property or cathedrals.

One night, probably after 1942, Alexis Moreau, manager at the Fongrenon quarry, slipped away from his security-guard post when his grandson, Jacques Moreau, came to relieve him. Alexis was on his way to join the Maquis, the guerilla band of French Resistance fighters, a group to which Alexis's son also belonged. The young Jacques, armed with a shotgun, stayed awake all night inside the little shed, but it seems that for the remainder of the occupation no one denounced Alexis Moreau or his son for their participation in the Resistance. Had the Germans inspected the quarry, trouble could have arisen, because by September 1944 one or more workers or guards had drawn several satirical drawings on the walls of the quarry that denounced the Nazi regime. The drawings were discovered by Baritaud in 2001. One consisted of a cartoon image representing Hitler, with an adjacent inscription that read, "By his fault, here 130 cases."

The crates would rest in the quarry without further incident as the war dragged on, but the other half of the windows back at Chartres faced peril. On May 26, 1944, during the aerial combat that preceded the Normandy landings, the American Ninth Air Force attacked the airfield at Chartres. The bombs hit Place des Halles and Rue au Lin, not half a mile from the cathedral, causing enormous damage, including forty-nine deaths, and a fire that destroyed most of the library of Chartres and the library annex in Chartres' city hall. Other planes also dropped their bombs too early and hit Porte Guillaume (in the lower town) and the rue du Bourgneuf.

The fire consumed the library collection, including half of the two thousand medieval books and parchments that had been relocated in 1939 to the Château de Villebon but had been returned to the library in 1940 on orders of the occupation authorities; ironically, as recently as February and March 1942, the library had celebrated this return with an exhibition of the books and manuscripts, proceeds of which had benefited prisoners of war. By the time the fire was under control, nearly half the manuscripts had been destroyed. The rest were left in varying states of distress—some barely singed, others charred into agglutinated blocks and badly damaged by the water civilians had used to fight the fire. Volunteers moved in to save what they could from the smoldering ruins. Although thousands of texts were recovered, the inferno carbonized most and rendered them unreadable.

Initially the library fire was thought to have been caused by either a British plane that had dropped its bombs after being hit by German fire or a German plane that had released its bombs accidentally, but it appears to have been the work of the American planes. Photographs of the city hall reveal that only the library's front and back facades remained standing, with supports for the burned-away roof pointing to the sky like the rib cage of a dead whale on the sea floor.

Later Allied bombing of Chartres and its airfield in the lead-up to D-Day would blow out the cathedral's west-window coverings and damage the iron armatures of the window jambs, but the stained-glass windows that were concealed in the crypt of Saint Lubin had escaped damage—for now.

Within two weeks following the fire at the library, the remains of the damaged books and manuscripts were sent for restoration to the Bibliothèque nationale de France in Paris. Technicians separated leaves of parchment fused together by the heat, but hundreds of fragments had suffered successively from heat and water and been converted into a glasslike substance—translucent and no longer naturally elastic—so that the fragments crumbled on impact.

The citizens of Chartres were left in fear over how much worse it could get.

Despite their great concern, many French were stepping into the fight to resist. But that resistance was dangerously fragmented. Since 1943, Charles de Gaulle had referred to the four hundred thousand French Resistance fighters opposing German occupation as les Forces françaises de l'intérieur—the French Forces of the Interior, or FFI. But Jean Moulin would be the man credited with uniting all French partisan activities under de Gaulle. Prior to 1943, Moulin had played the leading role in trying to coordinate all the scattered Resistance forces in France under the Mouvements unis de la Résistance—or the MUR.

A period of days after Moulin's June 1940 arrest and torture in Chartres by the Germans and his subsequent attempted suicide, Moulin had resumed his prefect's work, only to be removed from his post in mid-November of that year for refusing to carry out the Vichy order to dismiss all left-wing elected mayors of the towns and villages within his prefecture. He followed by joining the Resistance. By September 1941—operating under the name Joseph Jean Mercier—Moulin had been smuggled into England to meet General de Gaulle. The general, impressed with Moulin, assigned to him the responsibility of unifying the various Resistance groups. Moulin received from de Gaulle a simple order that he would carry back to France on microfilm in the false bottom of a box of matches: "Mr. Moulin's task is to bring about, within the zone of metropolitan France not directly occupied, unity of action by all elements resisting the enemy and his collaborators."

In January 1943, the British Special Operations Executive had parachuted Moulin back into France, where by May 27—working under the code names Rex and Max—Moulin had persuaded the eight major Resistance groups to unite and form the Conseil national de la Résistance (the National Resistance Council), which first convened in a historic clandestine meeting, at a Paris apartment, among sixteen representatives of more than a dozen Resistance groups—large and small—from both the south and the north of France, including communists, socialists, radicals, trade-union confederations, and three parties of the political right. In days, Moulin sent a detailed report on the meeting to de Gaulle. Six months after his return to France, while Moulin had been in another meeting with Resistance leaders in the home of a doctor near Lyon, the Gestapo arrested him, along with the others in attendance, and imprisoned him in Lyon, where Klaus Barbie, the head of the Gestapo there, interrogated and tortured him. But Moulin revealed nothing of value. On July 8, on a train transporting him to Germany, Moulin died, either from injuries sustained during the torture or by suicide.

Moulin achieved legendary status as the leader of Resistance, its most famous fighter, and its symbol, revered as a patriot with great courage and fortitude. Schools, colleges, streets, and squares in France are named after Moulin, and he is considered one of the foremost citizens of Chartres. In a speech delivered in Paris in 1964, on the occasion of transfer of Moulin's ashes to the Panthéon, André Malraux spoke of the final day of Moulin's torture by the Germans, when Moulin's lips "never let fall a word of betrayal: on that day, his was the face of France."

Moulin is known in France as a model of moral rectitude, civic virtue, and patriotism. Even at the beginning of the war, in his role as the youngest prefect, he demonstrated the skills of organization and leadership that would prove so effective later in the struggle: he could convince others of the vital need to have an overall plan and to execute it as a united group in a common struggle.

CHAPTER EIGHTEEN

Collared at HQ: Marlborough, UK, and Normandy, Spring 1944–July 1944

BEFORE MIDNIGHT ON FEBRUARY 10, 1944, FROM THEIR LAUNCHES IN the Long Island Sound, Griff and his men crowded onto a Navy ferry that steamed down the East River for four hours into the night, past the tip of Manhattan at Battery Park, and into the Hudson to Pier 88 at Forty-Ninth Street. The men could make out the ship on which they would find passage to England, the 80,800-ton luxury liner the RMS *Queen Mary*, in gray paint, converted into a troop ship, stripped of deluxe furnishings, with each stateroom fitted on three walls with floor-to-ceiling hammocks, five-high, to accommodate its share of the sixteen thousand men coming aboard. During the night, a blizzard moved in and caused a twenty-four-hour delay, but eventually the ship got under way down the Hudson, passing Governor's Island where little Alice lived with her mother and grandparents. She did not know her father was on the ship sailing past the island and past the Statue of Liberty and Ambrose Light on the way to the war.

For a full week, the ship sailed in a zigzag course at more than thirty knots, with its sixteen thousand passengers receiving two meals per day, wearing life jackets at all times, carrying their own mess kits to and from meals, and conducting daily drills.

On February 18, the ship reached Gourock, Scotland, in the River Clyde, where Royal Air Force aircraft met the ship to escort it. Colonel William A. Collier—the corps' chief of staff, Griff's immediate boss—

came aboard to greet the men, who were then cheered by large groups of British civilians lining the streets. Women with the Red Cross handed out coffee and doughnuts and led the way to a line of trucks, accompanied by the wail of bagpipes. The men climbed twelve at a time into the trucks that took them to troop trains for an overnight trip to the new Twentieth Corps headquarters at Marlborough Downs, on the north edge of the Salisbury Plain, twenty miles north of Stonehenge and fifty miles west of London.

At Marlborough, Walker continued to demand soldiers and staff carry on with hard, physical training. Without notice, he ordered the corps headquarters to leave its garrison at least once a week and establish a command post in the field, under battle conditions, under camouflage, and practicing dispersion. These maneuvers included simulated infantry and tank attacks against concrete and other dug-in machine-gun pillboxes, along with artillery fusillades. Top brass, including General Patton, observed the exercises. He had arrived in England following his African and Sicilian campaigns. The corps' Fourth Armored Division set up firing ranges along the coast and shot at targets floating in the water while the corps fine-tuned for its mission for battle in cramped English countryside settings.

Coming to and from HQ, Griff would have seen in Savernake Forest, three miles from Marlborough, hidden under the crown of the wood's one-hundred-year-old oaks and beeches, the second largest ammunition dump in the United Kingdom. Enormous stacks of shells and bombs arranged by dimension grew in scope almost daily to be ready to supply the invasion force.

On April 8, Griff composed by hand, in neat block letters, a V-mail note to Nell:

Sweetheart:

Big business—four letters and the shirt package came today. Now I'm all set. Thanks.

Now I'm O.K. but sucrets should be a good guarantee for the future. Also the vitamines [*sic*] sound interesting. Please send some of both.

I've seen several other interesting places in England. Guess all discussion of them is banned. When events pass a historical place I try to see it. In fact carry a guidebook given me by an elderly Englishman.

Love you, Pinka,
Grif

Early on a spring afternoon at Marlborough, Griffith walked up to the green Nissen hut that served as HQ, stretching before him like a long tubular car wash. He gave a nod to the sentry at the brick center entry portal. A sign over the door read, "XX CORPS HQ—G-2 & G-3, Authorized Personnel Only."

Griffith heard a truck horn sound and looked over his shoulder. Army trucks and jeeps approached from left and right, converging at the intersection of dirt driveways. Behind him, beyond the intersection in the camp, dozens of Nissen huts descended toward rows of tents and parked trucks. Soldiers scurried across muddy gravel driveways with boxes and gear. Three low-flying C-47 cargo planes growled overhead, circling to head north the fifteen miles to Swindon airfield and drowning out sounds of passing vehicles. Each plane towed its own cargo-loaded glider to prepare for release and practice landing.

The sentry at the front door wore a dark "MP" armband, which his helmet displayed in white. He saluted and greeted Griffith and opened the door for him. Griffith answered with a salute and stepped into the hut, whose six-foot-wide corridor spanned its length. Blackout curtains covered the twelve shoulder-width windows along the corridor.

Another member of the military police sat on a folding chair behind the small desk to the left of the door, below one of the covered front-wall windows. Griffith noticed that the sitting MP was slumped in his chair pulled back from the desk. The MP's eyes were closed, and he appeared to be asleep. His carbine lay across his lap, with upturned palms wrapped around the weapon.

Griffith was appalled but silent. He tiptoed past the sentry, down the corridor, to the door bearing a sign reading, "TOP SECRET—Authorized

Personnel Only," which led into the large map room that comprised most of the hut. With his key, Griffith unlocked the door and closed it behind him. His eyes met those of the only person inside the room, Private Eugene Schulz, who was continuing to work as one of Griffith's two clerk-typists. Ceiling lights in a row shined down on a rectangular conference table, which occupied two-thirds of the room, surrounded by desks with typewriters and small tables along the wall, each with a small desk lamp, telephone, and file trays. A bank of metal file cabinets along the sloping corrugated back wall framed a second central locked door. Six shoulder-width square-gabled windows lined the wall, each covered with a blackout shade inside.

The map room's central table held a twelve-by-six-foot military map of southern England, northern France, and the English Channel. Griffith had instructed Schulz to keep the map covered when not in use. It pinpointed every important English military installation, camp, and depot; every Channel port, dock, and marshaling area; and, in the portion covering the Normandy coast, every coastal and inland gun emplacement, bunker, and other defensive position.

Griffith looked around and asked Schulz whether any officers were nearby. His assistant answered no, with a quizzical look. Griffith summoned him with his hand to come along and, with his index finger to his lips, to be quiet. Leading the way, Griffith drew his service .45, stepped out the map room door, and closed it quietly; then he signaled Schulz with a touch on his shoulder to wait. He stepped around Schulz, and on the right both could see the MP guard in his chair pulled back from the desk, beneath the window in the entryway, still slumped with eyes closed, asleep, his carbine lying across his lap with his upturned palms still wrapped around it. Schulz watched as Griff edged toward the MP, reached out slowly, grabbed the carbine, and jerked it out of the guard's hands. The guard startled awake, groping for his weapon to no avail, and looked up with a horrified gaze. Griffith held his own weapon with both hands, ready, as if poised to attack. The guard looked toward Schulz, who stood frozen in the corridor between Griffith and the map room door, gazing back at the guard.

Griffith glared into the eyes of the guard. "What's your name, soldier?"

The soldier, shaking, mumbled his name and looked again at Schulz.

Griffith pointed to the door with the guard's carbine and asked the guard whether he could see the sign on the map room door. The guard acknowledged yes—it read, "TOP SECRET." Griffith reminded the soldier that it was his duty to guard the building and keep unauthorized personnel out; then he stiffened his neck and hunched his shoulders back. Hesitating briefly, but without waiting for the soldier to answer, Griffith turned to look at Schulz and told him to head back into the map room and call the MP office.

Schulz pulled a key ring out of his pocket, unlocked the door to the map room, and hurried inside; in a minute he'd returned to the corridor.

Two minutes later, Griff heard a vehicle skid to a stop, its occupants emerging with the slam of a door. Three MP-helmeted and arm-banded soldiers swung open the front door and burst into the corridor, weapons drawn, followed by the outside sentry with his weapon and an astonished look on his face. The MPs looked at the colonel, still standing in front of the sentry holding the man's carbine.

The lead MP, with a sergeant-striped shoulder patch on his shoulder, approached Griff.

"Sergeant, I am Colonel Griffith, G-3."

"Yes, Sir. I know, Sir."

"This is Private Schulz. What's your name, Sergeant?"

The sergeant answered with his name and MP unit number.

"Sergeant, this private is one of your sentries, and he has a big problem. Schulz and I just found him asleep at his post." Handing the weapon to the sergeant, Griffith said, "Here, take his weapon. Confiscate it, and take him into custody for violation of his first general order—being asleep at his post while on duty, posted as a sentry."

"Yes, Sir. We will, Sir."

"Sergeant, I guess I don't need to explain to you what building we are in and that it makes this sentry's problem a pretty serious one—serious as the business end of a .45."

"Yes, Sir. I do, Sir."

The sergeant stepped forward, reaching to pull the guard up from his chair.

"C'mon, Private."

Helping the guard up from his chair, the sergeant signaled one of the other MPs to take the sentry's weapon from Griffith. The third MP opened the door. The sergeant called to the outside sentry, pointing for him to move to the inside sentry position, and ordered one of the newly arrived MPs to remain as the new outside sentry. As they headed outside, the sergeant told the arrested MP to get into the jeep with the remaining MP, and Griff heard them drive off.

As the new sentry entered the building, Griffith glanced toward both Schulz and the new sentry to confirm whether they were listening.

"Schulz, be careful now. You'll have to remember what you just saw." With that, Griffith touched Schulz on the shoulder to guide him to return with him back into the map room, leaving the new sentry standing in the corner next to the desk while both the hut front door and the map room door closed.

"Let's get back to work. I'll have to write this up for Colonel Collier and General Walker."

Inside the room, Griffith turned to Schulz. "Gene, there'll be a court-martial. You and I are probably gonna have to testify."

"Sir, do you think so?"

"Yep. We're at war. What we're doing here is too damn important to let something like this go. Too many soldiers are risking their lives here to let our guard down. You know what we've been planning in this room."

"Yes, Sir. I do, Sir."

"With the sentry asleep, any damn person might've gotten in here. Our secrecy could've gone up in smoke. Think of the thousands—hundreds of thousands—who'd be in danger if our plans leak."

"Yes, Sir. I understand. But, Colonel, I feel bad for the guy and what he's up against. Any of us can fall asleep. He couldn't have been out for more than a few minutes. And the door into this map room was locked. I feel sorry for the guy."

"I know, Gene. But we all have responsibilities."

"Yes, Sir. I understand. But the guy's just as young as me. What do you think'll happen to him?"

"I expect he'll need to serve some time in the brig and probably will miss the fight, and he could be dishonorably discharged."

Gene Schulz returned to his desk and started in on his work. He looked back at Griffith, who sat slumped in the chair and stared out the partially covered window next to Schulz's desk, pausing for a moment. Griff arched his back, pulled his head back to shorten his neck, and closed his lips into a sternness. He reached for a pad and pen and wrote quickly while Schulz waited to begin trying to decipher the scrawl and type it out.

A month later, weeks before D-Day, at a separate camp, in a hut the same as the war room, a court-martial of judge advocate officers convened to try the sentry, who stood accused of violating the 86th Article of War—being asleep while posed on guard as a sentry. Both Griffith and Schulz were subpoenaed to testify at trial.

Sixty-eight years later, in his memoir about the war, Eugene Schulz would recall how nervous he'd felt on the witness stand as he testified that he had seen the soldier sleeping on guard duty outside the war room.

"I felt awful and sad and wondered what would happen to this young man who was probably my age." Schulz never heard what kind of sentence the guard received, but he is sure the guard was sentenced to some confinement in the brig.

"This event," Eugene Schulz wrote, "was never talked about openly at corps headquarters, but it was a sobering experience for me."

Around the same time that the MP faced court-martial, on a sunny day in early May 1944 General Patton arrived at Griff's corps command post. He couldn't be mistaken for anyone else. He was six-foot-two in his short jacket, three stars on his cap, wearing cavalry boots and a belt holstering a pearl-handled pistol. He had recently been appointed commander of the US Third Army. Before that, he had commanded the fictitious "paper" First US Army Group, or FUSAG, in an operation code named Fortitude South. It had been dreamed up by Lieutenant General Frederick Morgan, the British general in charge of planning the Allied invasion. Under the plan, the fictitious army had been positioned around a phony dock built near Dover with major contributions by set designers from British movie studios. The array included dummy trucks, tanks, cannons, and other equipment made of inflatable rubber, canvas, and wood, which in part floated on oil drums, with large dummy oil tanks nearby to appear to be available to supply fuel for Patton's tanks. As part of this scheme, Patton gave a number of speeches. The Germans were deceived into believing the assault would occur at the beaches of Pas de Calais rather than on the Normandy beaches.

Patton was now at corps headquarters to invite General Walker and Twentieth Corps to be part of the Third Army. For the meeting, Patton had called together the three corps commanders he had chosen in addition to Walker: Major General Wade H. Haislip of Fifteenth Corps, Major General Gilbert Cook of Twelfth Corps, and Major General Troy Middleton of Eighth Corps. Also joining was Brigadier General Otto Weyland, who headed the Nineteenth Tactical Air Command, which Patton attached to the Third Army to coordinate fighter planes to work closely with the ground troops, in a new unit that was placed within Griffith's G-3 Section for combat operations in France. Gene Schulz was surprised by Patton's high-pitched voice, which he guessed must have bothered the brusque general—so aggressive in wartime that he'd been nicknamed "Old Blood and Guts." But as Patton addressed Walker and the other corps staff officers, Schulz probably heard plenty of profanity.

It was only a month before D-Day that Griff had finally learned what the corps' role would be: Patton wanted Walker and Twentieth Corps to spearhead the Third Army's drive across France after the bridgehead was secured. Griff's corps would come ashore a couple of weeks after the beach assault to be in the front forces to push across France in pursuit of the Germans, who were expected to be in retreat.

After this visit by Patton, preparations intensified. General Eisenhower had come to England to take firsthand command of the Overlord operations, including final planning for landings on the French coast. Inspections stepped up, assessing efficiency in tactical-training maneuvers, billeting, living conditions, morale, and health of the troops. By the end of May, most of the planning for D-Day had been accomplished. From their bases scattered about England, the various Twentieth Corps units funneled into a marshaling area and ports from which they would move onto ships. Corps officers traveled to meetings in London. General Walker flew to the Normandy beachhead to observe the fighting. The corps war room buzzed with activity, the maps plotting positions of enemy and Allied units to be followed through the action.

On May 29, Eisenhower issued follow-up instruction to the Allied Expeditionary Force regarding preservation of historic monuments, making reference to the Allies' recent experience at Monte Cassino—as he had in a prior order on the subject. In the May order, he wrote:

1. Shortly we will be fighting our way across the Continent of Europe in battles designed to preserve our civilization. Inevitably, in the path of our advance will be found historical monuments and cultural centers, which symbolize to the world all that we are fighting to preserve.
2. It is the responsibility of every commander to protect and respect the symbols whenever possible.
3. In some circumstances the success of the military operation may be prejudiced in our reluctance to destroy these revered objects. Then, as at Cassino, where the enemy relied on our emotional attachments to shield his defense, the lives of our men are paramount. So, where military necessity dictates, commanders may order the required action even though it involves destruction of some honored site.
4. But there are circumstances in which damage and destruction are not necessary and cannot be justified. In such cases, through the exercise of restraint and discipline, commanders will preserve centers and objects of historical and cultural significance.

Six months before, in the Italian campaign, during the pause before the Fifth Army's assault on Monte Cassino, General Eisenhower had issued his first order, in the form of a letter to all commanders, regarding protection of cultural property. In it, he had reminded the commanders that the fight was being waged in a country that had contributed a great deal to the world's cultural inheritance and was a country rich in monuments, "which by their creation helped, and now in their old age illustrate, the growth of the civilization ... which is ours." He reminded the commanders that they were bound to respect those monuments "so far as war allows" and that should they have to choose between destroying a famous building and sacrificing their own men, "then our men's lives count infinitely more and the buildings must go." But he pointed out that the choice wouldn't always be so clear-cut. "In many cases," he continued,

> the monuments can be spared without any detriment to operational needs. Nothing can stand against the argument of military necessity. That is an accepted principle. But the phrase "military necessity" is sometimes used where it would be more truthful to speak of military convenience or even of personal convenience. I do not want to cloak slackness or indifference.
>
> It is a responsibility of higher commanders to determine through AMG Officers the locations of historical monuments whether they be immediately ahead of our front lines or in areas occupied by us.

On June 11, Griffith sent a handwritten V-mail note to Nell:

Sweetheart,

Staying busy. Managed to get hold of a Scotch cap and muffler, one for you and one for Alice. Will mail them first chance. I think you will like them. Would have liked to have gotten cloth to match but that is rationed. Perhaps can get hold of some before school back.

Love you and miss you.

Grif

Midday on July 15, 1944, Griffith and the others of the corps headquarters staff, with their field gear, drove into Southampton in a column of jeeps, staff cars, trucks, and half-tracks. Along narrow streets, British men, women, and children waved farewell. When the column slowed to a halt from time to time along the way, the people gave the soldiers tea and biscuits. By late afternoon, the column (including Griffith's staff car) drove into the marshaling area outside Portsmouth, fifteen miles south-east of Southampton. They spent the night in a large open field jammed with vehicles, equipment, and troops. They next day they checked their weapons and waited through another night.

On the seventeenth, they moved to the Southampton docks, but because their ship was not ready, they spent the night on the adjoining pier, watching cranes hoist vehicles onto ships and down into the holds. At daybreak, Griffith's and the other headquarters' vehicles were loaded onto a liberty ship, the SS *John A. Campbell*, which spent the night with a group of vessels in the shelter of the Isle of Wight.

Through the night, corps personnel anticipated the fight on a scale far surpassing what even Griff could have felt two decades before at West Point on game days before he had led the cadets' offensive line onto their big stage.

Chapter Nineteen

Race Across France, Resistance Meetup: Normandy, July–Early August 1944

At 8:00 a.m. on the morning of July 19, 1944, the SS *John A. Campbell* weighed anchor, circled west of the Isle of Wight, joined a convoy of liberty ships with a destroyer escort, and sailed the eighty miles across the English Channel. Six hours later, the convoy reached the eastern side of the Cotentin Peninsula of France and dropped anchor off Utah Beach, surrounded by hundreds of other watercraft of men and equipment.

On the boat that day, Griffith, in his barely legible handwriting, squeezed a dozen short sentences onto a one-page V-mail letter addressed to Nell in Brooklyn, his script ever difficult to decipher:

Sweetheart:

My new fountain pen has disappeared. Can you through the Base Post PX or Fort Hamilton get me another like my old one which is okay, so *don't* send yours. Be sure of this. I have one but want the second as insurance.

For our savings for taxes I'd like the *tax exemption* bonds left. They draw 2% and cost face value. I'm afraid we all tend to forget that many Bonds are earmarked for taxes. I'd bet we have to pay the taxes. Anyway we can sell tax exemption bonds if we endorsed them.

Love my Pinka. I certainly have a . . . lot to come home to. Lots of memories. I'm lonely. Love you

Grif

Please send a package of cigars . . . worked for a gift.

This was forty-three days after D-Day. There was no harbor at Utah Beach, so the US Navy had built a breakwater composed of sunken ships to protect unloading freighters. The time for unloading Griffith's ship had not yet come, so he and the others spent the night onboard, waiting. The next morning, the weather turned bad, so they had to wait another forty hours for the storm and the rough seas to subside.

Finally, on July 22, the morning dawned with clear weather. A convoy of small landing craft approached the port side of the *John A. Campbell*. Griff and his men descended into a landing craft via a stairway lowered from the top deck of the ship and from there took the short trip through mine-cleared channels to the steel piers that jutted out from the beach.

Past the beach, each man threw his duffle bag into one of a long line of cargo trucks and climbed aboard, twenty to a vehicle. They left the beach area on a narrow two-lane road beyond the dunes and traveled inland for about an hour to the west side of the Cotentin Peninsula, where the corps set up its first command post. The CP consisted of tents under camouflage netting interspersed among trees of an apple orchard in Saint-Jacques-de-Néhou. They were sixty miles northwest of Saint-Lô, in the hedgerow country of Normandy, where close-grown bushes or shrubs, tree roots, vines, and earth enchained into barriers chest high or higher. Along the hedgerows, an array of burned-out tanks interspersed with piles of discarded helmets, broken weapons, and crushed, empty ration boxes spoke to the now-repositioned American paratroopers who had landed in this drop zone during the invasion.

For twelve days, the corps had to wait while Allied forces attacked stiff German resistance at Saint-Lô. During that time, Griff and the other corps staff officers visited the various division camps around the peninsula and engaged in face-to-face planning and operations meetings with commanders of all armored, infantry, cavalry, and artillery units attached to the corps. They reviewed strategy and coordinated tactics for pursuing the Germans in a synchronized push.

On August 2, the corps broke out of its bridgehead and started its rapid sweep across France. Griff, as deputy chief of staff, oversaw the movement of the field headquarters command post to successive new sites to keep it close to the fighting front. One afternoon near the end of that period at Command Post 1—or CP 1—General Patton strode into the headquarters war tent to confer with General Walker and the assembled corps department heads, including Griff. Walker—only five-foot-two and portly—looked to strangers a bit diminutive, standing next to the taller Patton or the even taller Griffith, but, nevertheless, Walker was venerated by his subordinates from top to bottom.

That day, from the CP, Griff managed to bang out a letter to Nell, typed in all capital letters on a V-mail page:

SWEETHEART:

THESE ARE BUSY DAYS NOT AS EXCITING AS IDE [*sic*] LIKE BUT I HOPE LEADS TO MORE ACTION IN TIME. IM [*sic*] LEARNING QUITE A BIT AND GETTING EXPERIENCE WHICH WILL BE USEFUL.

THE PEOPLE I FEEL SORRY FOR IN THIS MESS ARE THE KIDS BUT THEY SEEM FAR FROM FEELING SORRY FOR THEM SELVES [*sic*]. EVEN THE SOBER ONES SEEM TO CARRY ON WITH OUT [*sic*] COMPLAINING. WOULD DO OUR SPOILED BRATS IN TEXAS GOOD TO SEE WHAT OTHERS HAVE TO GO THROUGH. I WONDER IF THESE EXPERIENCES WILL LEAVE A BAD IMPRESSION ON THE KIDS IN LATER LIFE. THEY ARE DARN FINE NOW.

IF NOTHING ELSE WAR TEACHES A GREAT RESPECT FOR THE OTHER FELLOW AND DRIVES HOME THE REALIZATION THAT THERE ARE SOME PRETTY GOOD PEOPLE IN THIS WORLD. NOT THE LEAST AMONG THEM BEING BRIG GEN CANHAM.

RECEIVED THE CHOCOLATE AND TWO MORE LETTERS. YOU WORK OVER TIME [*sic*]. HOPE THE BEACH IS FUN AND A RELAXATION BUT NOT A STOP FROM THE GOOD THINGS OF THE SCHOOL. STILL THINK THE FIRST COAT A GOOD THING.

Some new people I've known before almost every day see borders frequently. Peoples, Harvey some times. Many others, just happened to talk of them wouldnt [sic] miss this for the world but miss you. Please send [indecipherable, but may be "packages"].

Lots Love you.
Grif [handwritten]

In this letter, his praise of legendary General Canham is revealing for what it says about his view of leadership.

On August 3, the corps moved and set up its second command post, CP 2 in a pasture near the commune of Fleury, also on the west side of the peninsula. On August 5, it moved again and erected its CP 3 thirty-six miles south in a woodland-encircled meadow near Saint-Martin-de-Landelles. There the Germans battered the corps over three nights of bombings, during which German planes flew more than 290 sorties against US positions. During those nights, flares dropped by German bombers transformed the night sky into flashes of daylight, as bright inflamed streaks from tracer bullets hurtled skyward from the ninety-millimeter antiaircraft batteries that were always positioned within a few miles of the corps' headquarters CP.

Eugene Schulz, newly promoted to sergeant (technician fourth grade), tried to rest in preparation for the morning's staff meeting. He would be expected in the early hours in the sixteen-by-twenty-four-foot war tent in front of huge maps displayed on a large board covered with transparent acetate sheets, on which the latest troop positions would be plotted. On opposite ends of the war tent were openings with a flap, to which two smaller office tents were attached—one for the G-2 Intelligence Department, the other for the G-3 Operations Department.

Following the meeting, back in the G-3 tent, Schulz, at his fold-up table, would type up Colonel Griffith's orders on one of the staff's Remington portable typewriters lodged in the base of its open hard-shell case, the tent jammed with other GI clerks busy at adjoining workstations. Schulz would bustle to disseminate those orders to waiting helmet-clad

Twentieth Corps field commanders or their couriers poised in idling jeeps and motorcycles, ready to deliver the orders to forward positions.

On August 6, Twentieth Corps was ordered to head south across the Sélune River, but before nightfall its engineers had to quickly build a double Bailey bridge to replace the span that had been destroyed by German bombers. Once the corps broke across, its infantry and armored divisions progressed so fast that Chief of Staff Collier ordered half of the corps headquarters staff to come with him to set up a new CP 4, in a wheat field thirty-one miles south, near Vitré, twenty-five miles east of Rennes.

At about this time, Griff's other sister, Dorothea, was expecting a baby. Griff somehow found time in France to purchase and have mailed to her a small silver chest as a gift for the baby. Dorothea adored her brother Griff. She was impressed that even during the fighting he had such close feeling and affection for her and her baby to make the effort to send that gift.

Three days after Collier's order to set up CP 4, the other half of the corps headquarters staff followed from CP 3 to CP 4. While driving south, this half of the corps encountered little German resistance. Griff rode in his jeep, and French civilians congregated on the roadside, greeting American troops with shouts of joy and tears, handing the soldiers flowers, wine, and eggs. Streams of American armored vehicles, artillery trucks, tank transports, jeeps, and six-by-six troop trucks navigated around burned-out abandoned German tanks and trucks.

While the corps headquarters directed operations from CP 4, the corps engaged in a fierce fight for the city of Angers, which it captured on August 9, taking 1,800 prisoners. Angers was the first large, strategic center captured by the corps. It had been a communication, supply, and transport center for the German Seventh Army, with a naval radio command center that controlled the German Atlantic fleet, a submarine training regiment, a large Gestapo headquarters, and an air command.

On August 10, corps headquarters moved again, twenty-four miles east to its new CP 5 in a cow pasture a few miles east of Laval. Shortly thereafter, enemy lines broke down, and German divisions retreated to the vicinity of Chartres, and two days later, corps headquarters relocated seventy miles east to the area of the town of La Ferté-Bernard, where on August 13 its CP 6 emerged.

Since coming ashore in Normandy in July, Twentieth Corps—as part of a three-corps force—had swept eastward almost 220 miles with unexpected speed to the city of Le Mans. The corps' goal had been to secure plateaus in the areas generally on a hundred-mile north-south line roughly fifty miles west of Paris, extending from Dreux on the north to Châteaudun on the south. This area provided airfield sites from which to maintain air support for operations east of the Seine River. Following the Normandy invasion, German forces had entered the so-called Argentan-Falaise Pocket surrounding the town of Falaise. In early August, in the Battle of the Falaise Pocket, the Allies had encircled and destroyed two German armies, killing an estimated ten thousand German troops and taking fifty thousand prisoners. Allied forces were now trying to cut off at the Seine those German forces that were seeking to escape from that pocket. Twentieth Corps had been initially ordered to secure Dreux as the initial step toward blocking the German escape by securing the bridgehead at Le Mans and liberation of Angers and had taken up the role of protecting the south flank of the US Third Army.

On August 13—prompted by the discovery of a considerable number of Germans between the Argentan-Falaise Pocket and the lower Seine—General Patton changed the corps' mission to instead seize Chartres and secure a bridgehead there across the Eure River. Patton believed that by attacking the Germans quickly the Allies would have the opportunity to complete the destruction of the forces that had escaped the Falaise Pocket and estimated that seventy-five thousand enemy troops and 250 tanks could still be encircled west of the Seine.

About six miles ahead of the corps lay twenty miles of the deep Perche forest, and around the middle of it stood the town of Nogent-le-Rotrou, then a German Panzer division headquarters, which was only about five miles from Plainville, site of underground caves being used by local Resistance fighters as a hideout. After the forest, the corps' road would continue in open fields for about ten miles to Courville-sur-Eure, the site of the next command post, where French Resistance fighters had been busy attacking the Germans and planning more attacks.

One such attack had just occurred in Nonville, about 120 miles south, where a Resistance sniper had shot a German soldier who had been passing in a truck. The Germans had pounded on, and nearly knocked down, the front door of a farmer's house, demanding that he give first aid to the soldier. And around Courville-Sur-Eure, German tanks and armored vehicles had been reported concealed under trees. A little over two miles beyond Courville-sur-Eure, near Loulappe, a Resistance fighter had ignited a German ammunition convoy, which had burst into flames and destroyed a barn full of wheat.

The corps headquarters staff established its CP 6 two miles outside the town of La Ferté-Bernard, in the rose garden of an old closed château. The five-story white-stone château, with steeply pitched two-story slate roofs, featured a tall, narrow picture window in a gable in the grandest of its three roofs that commanded a view from its high-ceilinged great room from which sixteenth-century nobles likely had looked out over their feudal lands. The château and garden, in which the men of the corps had pitched their tents, exposed them to the history of the countryside through which they were fighting.

Late on the night of the fourteenth, a small group of FFI fighters came into the HQ tent while Gene Schulz worked the night shift in the attached "three-shop" (or G-3) tent. A young, attractive blonde French woman led the fighters. She was slender, in her twenties, dressed in a well-worn, tightly buttoned uniform jacket, while a tuft of her hair showed from beneath the peasant's head scarf that she had tied in a knot under her chin, its ends waving over her shoulders. She wore an armband—with its blue, white, and red Tricolor, that displayed the initials FFI and the Cross of Lorraine, with its distinctive twin horizontal bars—and in her right hand she held an automatic pistol ready to fire.

The woman introduced herself as Madame Clavel, deputy commander of the FFI battalion. She and her companions said they were eager to provide the corps with information about the enemy. The corpsmen had heard about this knockout woman, and they would come to refer to her as the Veronica Lake of the Corps, after the American pinup movie star. Madame Clavel was strong-minded and dominant, and in time the Americans—weak in the knees at the sight of her—would come to regard her as the actual boss of the FFI battalion. Her true name was Silvia Monfort, and after the war she married FFI battalion commander Maurice Clavel. She also operated under the pseudonym Sinclair, and she would later earn decorations as a Resistance figure and go on to a postwar career as a stage and screen actress, director, and grande dame of French theater.

The FFI fighters moved behind the German lines to harass German forces and carry out acts of sabotage. One FFI observer worked alongside Captain de la Vasselais, a French liaison officer to the corps while it occupied its CP at La Ferté-Bernard. The FFI observer and the captain were patrolling in the vicinity of Le Chartres-sur-le-Loir, one hundred miles south, in a jeep driven by the corps' Sergeant Sidney Bornstein, when a German machine-gunner ambushed them, killing the observer and wounding both Vasselais and the driver, who still managed to return in the jeep to the American lines through enemy fire, taking eighty-six bullet holes along the way.

Madame Clavel asked to see the commanding general or chief of staff. She sought a load of bazooka ammunition and several thousand rounds for their tommy guns to carry out a night attack against a German-held town. The Maquis of Plainville, with 150 men, led by Maurice Clavel and a local leader codenamed Duroc, had just launched an attack at Nogent-le-Rotrou, three days before the corps' arrival. Whether the corps supplied the ammunition she requested that night is not clear. The British SOE and American OSS were supporting the FFI at the time with air-dropped weapons and supplies, but the FFI used mostly its own weapons. Along the corps' route toward Chartres, around the time it had positioned its CP 6 at La Ferté-Bernard, Resistance groups conducted at least three additional operations. The raid for which Madame Clavel sought the ammunition may have been one of them.

In the Loire Valley and in Paris, the FFI and other Resistance forces aided the Allies in their pursuit to the Seine and helped protect the Third Army's southern flank. They did so by disrupting enemy railroad and highway movements and enemy telecommunications and by developing open resistance on a wide scale by providing tactical intelligence, preserving installations the Allies valued, and mopping up enemy positions the Allies had bypassed.

By 7:30 on the evening of August 14, Twentieth Corps Artillery had arrived and had set up its own command post in thick woods near the château whose garden hosted the corps' CP 6.

The next morning, when Griffith conducted rounds, three German Messerschmitt Bf 109 fighter aircraft came overhead, strafing at treetop height. Men scrambled for cover beneath the trucks. The ground had been hard when the men had arrived, so their foxholes were of negligible size. The enemy planes circled and returned with guns ablaze. Bullets zinged all around as men hugged the trucks. The artillery units escaped any injury, suffering nothing but some upset breakfast in the melee, but the troops of the Sixty-Ninth Signal Battalion on the road nearby suffered a handful of casualties.

Also on the evening of the fourteenth, on orders from the Third Army, the Seventh Armored Division was redirected east to Chartres. The German defenders were startled by the speed of the corps' armor. Usually the long barrels of the tank guns and the clanking treads were the enemy's first warning of the approaching Americans. An armored division of this type would have had in its ranks almost eleven thousand men and 160 M4 assault tanks, sixty-six M5 light tanks, thirty-six M8 armored cars, eight self-propelled seventy-five-millimeter howitzers, and fifty-four self-propelled 175-millimeter howitzers. These troops would have divided into three tank battalions, three artillery battalions, a reconnaissance squadron, and three infantry battalions, together with all services necessary for their operation.

The Seventh Armored Division reached the objective on the night of August 15, as the corps headquarters closed in the wood west of Courville-sur-Eure.

By August 15, the corps would be on its way to Chartres. The larger mission of Patton's Third Army—of which Twentieth Corps then represented a third—had been to reach the Seine to establish what the Allies called the D-Day lodgment area, the part of France northwest of the

Seine that would serve as their base for new operations in their fall and winter push toward Germany. Alongside Twentieth Corps' movement toward Chartres, Fifteenth Corps headed toward Dreux, and Twelfth Corps pressed toward Orléans. The Allies' D-Day plans had been to reach the D-Day lodgment area within ninety days, but they had done so in only seventy-four days, and for the Third Army, that speed was now creating logistics challenges that would slow its further advances.

Although the other two corps of the Third Army had not encountered significant German resistance, the Twentieth Corps was about to—at Chartres.

At daybreak on the morning of August 15, at Chartres Cathedral, priests and staff were preparing for Masses in spite of the war. August 15 is the Solemnity of the Assumption, a major feast day in the Catholic Church, celebrated as a public holiday in France.

Mass that day began at 9:00 a.m., with Bishop Harscouët serving as priest celebrant, before scores of congregants. The day of the Assumption had special meaning for the Catholics of Chartres, because their cathedral had always been dedicated to the Virgin Mary. They prayed for her to look over them, over their families, and over their beloved ancient church. The present parishioners felt somber fear, as they had in the dark days of early June 1940 when the German invasion had swept over Chartres. Now, in days just past in 1944, they had heard explosions and seen German demolition crews planting charges under bridges and at monuments, and witnesses who had come into town from outlying farms had seen debris littering the edges of roads from scuffles between Resistance fighters and German soldiers in the gaps between towns.

Back at CP 6 in La Ferté-Bernard, Griff and the other section heads conducted their predawn briefing with General Walker to discuss changes to orders. Heavy plywood easels held topographic maps propped against the long war tent wall. The maps detailed roads, fences, creeks, villages, and farm buildings. In grease pencil, clerks diagramed with specified symbols the location of each division and battalion under the corps' command and all other Allied and enemy troop positions. Field telephones rang in the G-2 department, its staff collecting reports of interrogations of captured enemy and coded messages via phone, radio, and courier from forward positions, observation planes, and informants, including German-speaking Americans who had infiltrated German-occupied territory. With constant movement of the units, the G-3 staff assistant on duty, principally Sergeant Joe Messner, was always busy wetting his rag from a can of alcohol to relocate the various units' unique x, oval, or circle symbols to an updated position.

Griffith, as senior operations officer, was in charge of corps plans, operations, and air support and the situation map—issuing orders to lower commanders and seeing to it that those commands were carried out. The G-3's primary responsibility was to construe the tactical plan into step-by-step objectives for individual units of men and matériel to carry through in a unified effort.

Walker outlined the situation in the meeting: At Chartres, the corps expected German resistance, with approximately eight hundred enemy troops in the city and French Resistance fighters and FFI active in the area. The American attack would be carried out by two groups: Combat Command A (CCA), a cavalry unit—poised two miles outside the city in Le Coudray—would skirt the city and circle counterclockwise from the south across the Eure River and attack from the east. Combat Command B (CCB) would attack into the city from the southwest and head northwest from positions in the wheat fields around Luisant, two miles outside the city, to be divided into two task forces: Force 1 (commanded by Lieutenant Colonel Leslie Allison) of the Twenty-Third Armored Infantry Battalion, to be assigned to the northern part of the city, and Force 2 (commanded by Lieutenant Colonel Robert Erlenbusch) of the Thirty-First Tank Battalion, to be assigned to the southwest around the railroad station. The order to attack would come at 3:30 p.m. on August 15.

The battle would prove fluid and complex and extend over four days, and for the first part of the battle, Griffith began by attaching himself as corps HQ observer/representative to Allison's Twenty-Third Armored Infantry Battalion.

Following the staff meeting, the workforce again broke down the CP camp, including tents, food, and other supplies and command and communications equipment, to transport them to the site of new CP 7 in a patch of woods thirty miles east outside the town of Courville-sur-Eure, thirteen miles west of Chartres. Griff knew that the task would require more than a half a day.

By midmorning, he climbed into the worn jeep passenger seat and told his driver, William L. Dugan, to drive to the site of new CP 7. Griffith's and Dugan's gear bags rested in the back of the jeep. Dugan fired up the jeep's engine and turned onto the mud-tracked highway D323. With thunderstorms threatening, the two men headed northeast along shell-scarred pavement toward Remalard through green but pockmarked and foxhole-studded countryside. From there, they would turn east toward Courville-sur-Eure on the road toward Chartres.

Griff had something to do.

He and Dugan would be in Courville-sur-Eure before noon. Griff had decided they would drop their gear at the site of CP 7 and then head forward to the armored bivouac area at Luisant two miles southwest of Chartres, where Griff needed to check with Brigadier General Thompson to be sure Thompson was clear with his orders. The corps' attack on Chartres was to start at 9:30 the evening of the fifteenth.

One of General Walker's standing orders within Twentieth Corps was that senior officers were to frequently go forward to check on the progress of operations or administrative matters at the front. All members of the Twentieth Corps staff followed this practice, from the commanding general and his chief of staff on down. The practice stood in contrast with those that had been employed by many French and British commanders in World War I, when commanders had often relied on reports from returning soldiers and junior officers (a large portion of whom were the first to be killed), which often had resulted in the commanders ignoring true conditions. Some staff officers would come to regret such practice. For example, July 1917 saw the beginning of the Third Battle of Ypres (Passchendaele), during which rains had turned the ground into seas of mud, with tanks sinking in the mire, resulting in British troops gaining a mere five miles of ground at a cost of 325,000 casualties. When senior officers had finally visited the front, they had been horrified that they had sent men into such conditions.

Griffith and Dugan drove through rolling plateaus and valleys of oak and beech forests dotted with ponds. From the open-topped jeep, Griffith could see a series of high plateaus cut by valleys and marsh floodplains interspersed with cider-apple orchards, followed by the first of what would become seemingly endless wheat fields farther to the east.

They arrived at Courville-sur-Eure, a small village on the Eure River west of Chartres, before noon, where preparations were under way for setting up the CP 7 tents beneath camouflage netting in a woodland one mile west of town.

When Griffith and Dugan arrived, the site for the CP had been secured but was abuzz with talk of an encounter with the enemy the previous evening. The two men learned that around 8:30 p.m. the night before, an American reconnaissance platoon had arrived in the village and skirmished with retreating German troops who lay in wait just beyond the river with a view of their approach. The Germans had fired machine guns, mortars, and cannons, immediately killing an American first lieutenant, James O. Gomer of Arkansas. The Americans had returned the fire. The Germans had then retreated behind an embankment, where they were silenced by fire from a field artillery battalion. Following the engagement, the Germans had retreated further toward Chartres. The American forces had bivouacked in Courville-sur-Eure for the night.

To slow the advance of Allied troops, the Germans had detonated a series of three explosions that destroyed bridges over canals and at the zoo in Courville-sur-Eure and had downed trees that had lined the road along the cemetery in Lancey, the town to the east.

Griffith and Dugan left their gear at the CP site in Courville-sur-Eure. There Griffith also met with Lieutenant Colonel Melville I. Stark—Griff's former deputy who'd since been promoted from major and was now preparing the new CP. Lieutenant Colonel Stark, then twenty-nine, the deputy G-3 officer under Griff, was short and thin and had a bushy black mustache and matching eyebrows. He was a respected and capable strategist, so Griffith instructed Stark to hop in the jeep for the twelve-mile drive toward Chartres.

CHAPTER TWENTY

Battle Prelude, First Probe of the Cathedral: La Ferté-Bernard and Chartres, August 1944

COLONEL GRIFFITH, HIS DRIVER, WILLIAM L. DUGAN, AND LIEU-tenant Colonel Melville I. Stark together left the Courville-sur-Eure CP to meet up with the Seventh Armored Division and confirm that orders had been communicated and would be carried out by General Thompson's armored battalion.

The three men drove toward Chartres from the southwest, and Griffith could see over his left shoulder the Perche forest receding behind them. While Dugan guided the jeep, Griffith could see over the windshield to the right the beginning of the low Beauce region spreading south and east from Chartres. The Beauce is a 1.5-million-acre area that changes from rolling hills into flat, rich farmland, comprising the granary of France, reminiscent of the wheat fields that had been rapidly created from cattle ranches in predustbowl North Texas when Griff was a boy.

As they approached, the two towers of the cathedral dominated the wheat fields from a surprising distance. From Griffith's vantage point, getting larger and larger upon their approach, the towers of Chartres Cathedral were the most imposing structure in the area, just as they must have seemed to approaching pilgrims in the Middle Ages.

On most days, the cathedral towers are visible from more than fifteen miles away, and from their perch they provide a clear view of positions of troops and equipment in the wheat fields. In addition, the Chartres airfield was run by the Luftwaffe during the occupation, supporting night-bombardment units that engaged in operations over England, a commando unit capable of dropping parachutists, a day-interceptor unit operating against US Eighth Army Air Force daylight bombing raids, and a night interceptor unit operating against Royal Air Force night-bombing attacks. Also important in Chartres were an antiaircraft flak-training school and an operational flak unit. The city was also economically important as a market town, with industrial flour milling, brewing, distilling, and ironworking; leather, perfume, and dye manufacturing; and studios producing world-famous stained glass.

By coincidence, on the afternoon of August 15, the German army sector headquarters conducted a planning meeting in Chartres with the commander, General Kurt von der Chevallerie, who had just arrived. At issue was how newly arriving units might reinforce the defenses west of the Seine in general and the defenses of Chartres in particular.

Hitler had ordered that his 48th Division from northern France and the 338th Division from southern France arrive in Chartres to defend against the Allied advance. This meeting occurred at the time the Seventh US Armored Division was approaching. The Seventh encountered three thousand German troops, including the flak battalion and scattered antitank strong points with an estimated fifty antitank guns and heavy antitank-mortar, machine-gun, and scattered-artillery pieces, along with rifle and bazooka strong points and sporadic minefields.

Chartres was a German "report station" or absorption point for disorganized and beaten units and stragglers withdrawing east from other surrounded and battered units. As a result, an estimated two hundred to three hundred men per twenty-four-hour period would reinforce the garrison. The German commander at Chartres was taking control of the defeated elements and, using the airfield and rail hub, resupplying and reorganizing those units for counterattack. Several German infantry and armored battalions were preparing to defend Chartres, along with personnel from the Luftwaffe flak-training center located at Chartres and two already-trained flak battalions operating on the south edge of

Chartres that had been defending the airfield. In the last few days, the flak school had been transformed into a mixed flak regiment.

As Griffith, Stark, and Dugan drew closer, the city entered into view, clustering around the cathedral-topped rocky hill. The late afternoon sun breaking through the approaching storm clouds would have illuminated the cathedral's western facade.

The Seventh Armored Division maintained a position in the wheat fields west of Chartres.

Neither the Germans nor the Americans were expecting any early major encounter as of the time the American Seventh Armored Division lead elements began probing at Chartres' outskirts. When the Seventh had arrived, it overran the defenses along the Eure River to the south of Chartres, but soon it became evident that Chartres was well defended. The corps had seriously underestimated the size of the defense force. The expected eight hundred troops had turned out to be 3,500 and growing.

At around 2 p.m., Griffith and the other men arrived in their jeep at the bivouac area on the plateau of Seresville, two miles south of the city, where an armored battalion and accompanying mobile artillery units were gathering. Reports had surfaced that the Germans in the city were starting to evacuate and were leaving many of their wounded behind. In the American armored column's approach to Chartres so far, it had encountered relatively light resistance, but now—despite the reported German evacuation—it faced determined opposition. The commander of the column had halted its forward progress to permit consolidation. Griffith told Dugan to wait with the jeep while he and Stark went to talk with General Thompson, in charge of the bivouacking units. With artillery shells landing in the vicinity, soldiers questioned whether the Germans were using either of the cathedral towers as an observation post from which to guide artillery fire toward Allied forces.

Griffith probably had several things in his mind at the time. He hoped for action, and he had been impressed with the young people and in particular the Resistance fighters he had encountered so far in France. The FFI were active all along the Americans' line of advance, often taking towns ahead of the armor and contributing valuable information on the strength and distribution of German forces. And last, Griffith was determined to do what he could to minimize the risk of the cathedral being fired upon by Allied forces.

What went through Griff's mind after meeting with Thompson at the bivouac area as he prepared to head back to the CP? Was he thinking about the briefing reminders to avoid shooting near the cathedral and his own fears of hitting it? Had he grown irritated with trigger-happy commanders who might lose sight of General Eisenhower's order to protect monuments, fearing that they might just shoot at it and be done with it? He'd no doubt heard the motto "It's easier to apologize than to get permission." Did he learn that more Germans had been sighted withdrawing from the city, giving him the notion that he and Stark might somehow surreptitiously work their way close enough to the building to listen and observe whether there was any enemy activity up in the towers?

We don't know, but he likely told Dugan to wait while he and Stark climbed into another vehicle driven by a Seventh Armored Division driver. They probably pulled out of the bivouac area and headed east for the counterclockwise swing around the city to reenter from the east while the fighting was to get under way from the east.

Griff, Stark, and their driver reached the southwest suburb of Lucé. From there, they slowly and quietly worked their way toward the center of the city along Rue du Maréchal Leclerc, heading toward the main square, the Place des Épars. The streets were empty, townspeople hidden in their homes, listening for the next of the small explosions that had popped up from time to time.

Griff would likely have ordered the driver to maneuver them quietly toward the cathedral so he and Stark could get close enough to observe whether there was activity up there. And likely they advanced close enough to scope it out but saw nothing. The driver jockeyed them into side streets to avoid German roadblocks that they expected to be positioned both at that square and at the railway station a few blocks before the beginning of the hill leading to the cathedral. They proceeded slowly, looking for German positions and snipers, but encountered none. The German defenses were concentrating near the series of bridges across the river, which ran north along the east side of the hill, and the area around the cathedral seemed very quiet, even as tanks, armored trucks, and infantry battled their way into the outskirts of the ancient town.

Then they may have told the driver to hide the jeep in an alley and stay with it while Griff and Stark took off on foot to get closer, ducking inside shaded doorways in the flat light under threatening storm clouds to stay out of sight. Stark and Griff probably decided it would be best to slowly approach and try to sneak inside the cathedral to confirm whether any Germans were in the building. The two men edged out in careful steps, guns drawn, looking around for German positions and snipers.

They inched their way toward the cathedral, looking through binoculars for any sign of German spotters in any of the windows of the twin towers of the cathedral. The two approached and searched for any snipers in the windows of the cathedral's roofs or towers or on any of their balconies or parapets. They saw no snipers and no other soldiers, nor did they see any sign of German observation equipment in or on the cathedral.

They advanced doorway by doorway. Covering each other, they prowled along the buildings of Chartres toward the cathedral, darting from cranny to cavity for shelter, finally arriving at one of the doors of the cathedral itself.

The late-morning Mass had ended hours before, and twilight vespers would not begin until 6:00, and no one was going in or out of the cathedral. It was now midafternoon, so the parishioners who had participated in morning Masses and other activities had dispersed; yet the cathedral was open, and they entered through the heavy wooden doors into the darkness, hearing only the dim echoes of distant artillery shells exploding to the south of the city.

Griff would have seen the ramparts that had been constructed over each of the cathedral's portals. He may have thought, *Something isn't right about this place*, because nothing but peace and quiet pervaded the building—even in the middle of the city still occupied by the Germans, with more coming in by the hour, into what he knew would erupt before midnight into a firefight and terror not only on the occupiers but also on the town, its people, his own men, and possibly the cathedral.

They conducted a rapid search and found no sign of Germans; they couldn't enter either tower because the stairway doors were locked and no priests or caretaker were evident. They had to get back to the CP, so, finding the church clear of apparent use by German forces, the two men returned on foot to their jeep and drove quickly away to head back to the bivouac area. Griff looked back. The cathedral quickly shrunk in size, but its towers continued to stand out against the darkening sky behind them, like a giant owl with wings high, watching over the area.

As Griffith, Stark, and Dugan drove back toward Luisant, groups of young French Resistance fighters were busy at work against the Germans. They drew fire to ferret out and eliminate German snipers from buildings, fired small arms and tommy guns at retreating Germans, threw grenades to disrupt German trucks and troop movements, and reported enemy positions to the Americans, all in spite of the threat of brutal retaliation.

For the American Seventh Armored Division, H hour, the hour to launch the operation, would be at 21:30 hours that night, August 15, 1944. A severe rainstorm was approaching.

With tanks and self-propelled guns, the combat commands breached the German defensive lines and drove through into the heart of the city. The mayor and citizens welcomed them as liberators, but after a brief interval of fighting, the German garrison counterattacked and drove the tanks back. The Germans beat up the mayor, which would cause the townspeople to hesitate to cooperate with the Eleventh Infantry when it arrived two days later.

Force 2 launched the attack as planned, from the assembly area to the southeast of Chartres. Company C of the Thirty-First was to leave Force 2 as they passed through Luisant and drove on into Chartres to help Force 1 mop up the city. Force 1 penetrated enemy defenses with infantry and established a command post in the city's northeast quarter.

Force 2 encountered heavy antitank fire in the southwest suburbs of Lucé and Luisant. It drove to the edge of the old town in Chartres but failed to maintain continuity of attack and suffered heavy losses in the very narrow streets that impaired the tanks' ability to maneuver. Force 1 remained and maintained continuous pressure on the enemy through the night, but Force 2 withdrew and resumed the attack at daybreak.

During the battle, many officers showed valor. When the vanguard tank of Major Leslie A. Lohse, acting battalion commander, was set ablaze and disabled by an eighty-eight-millimeter shell and antitank rockets, while under heavy fire Lohse helped put out the fire and took cover only after members of the crew had done so, concealing himself in an enemy headquarters. The lead tank, which carried the company commander, was destroyed after enemy forces fired Panzerfausts and antitank mines from concealed positions, killing the company commander and knocking out the second tank. That meant First Lieutenant George C. J. Racine, in his column's third tank, took over command of the column and led it through heavy fire to the center of town. Enemy volleys then wrecked a half-track in the column and cut off two platoons. Racine heard of the wreck by radio, stopped his tank, entered the fire-swept street, and signaled his location by flashlight. He made his way back to the enemy-occupied square, ignoring machine-gun cross fire from street-facing windows; he cleared out the shattered half-track, reformed the disorganized column, and led the company out of town. In all, four US tanks were destroyed. The corps retreated to regroup and rallied for a dawn attack.

The forces ran into murderous antitank fire, flares, and mines in the outskirts of Luisant, and the two rear tank companies were forced to withdraw to their alternate rallying positions. Company C of the Thirty-First went on into Chartres as planned but was unable to gain contact with Force 1 and suffered loss of both vehicles and men and became disorganized after the company commander was killed and the battalion commander's tank was blown up. The remaining elements reorganized and pulled out of the city to the south into an assembly area, and on the morning of August 16 they rejoined the combat command.

The initial fighting for the city took two days, with the Seventh Armored Division constrained from using heavy-artillery support because of concerns about damaging the cathedral.

Near the cathedral, two priests endured the night of fighting. Father Paul Douin was on temporary assignment from his permanent home, a monastery in Le Theiulin, almost twenty miles west of Chartres, and Marcel Cassegrain was a professor at the Major Seminary and master of pontifical ceremonies. Douin woke from his brief spell of sleep and wrote in his diary that "daybreak had finally arrived after a long night." It had been the first night of the four-day battle for Chartres. The two priests had huddled outside the cathedral school, avoiding bullets, and then had run through neighborhoods, looking for wounded. They saw burned-out tanks and bodies everywhere. Casualties overwhelmed the hospital.

Before dawn on the morning of Wednesday the sixteenth, Joe Messner worked the night shift as clerk to the G-3 at CP 7. Following his all-night shift on the previous night, he had been unable to get any sleep because he and the other headquarters enlisted men had been required to spend the day moving the CP, including tents, food, and other supplies and command and communications equipment from CP 6 in La Ferté-Bernard to CP 7 in Courville-sur-Eure.

During Joe's shift, in the dim light of kerosene camp lamps, he read dispatches that reported the heavy fighting through the night and into the dawn hours. He plotted the latest information in grease pencil on the situation map, sipping coffee and chewing gum to stay awake. He had become adept at translating the flow of information into moving rectangles, each containing a unique symbol identifying each fighting unit, and its class as infantry, armor, artillery, cavalry, or other.

Before dawn, General Walker gathered his section heads, including colonels Collier and Griffith, Colonel Zeller, who was the G-2 officer, and other group heads and staff around the situation map. Messner stayed for the briefing, and Gene Schulz joined upon commencement of his shift. While artillery bursts and airplane engines droned from the front lines, Walker with his staff reviewed the current situation in Chartres: Force 1 had captured its sector in the north part of the city by 1:30 a.m. after ferocious fighting in the storm followed by sporadic unorganized resistance. Although the Germans had started withdrawing in the afternoon of the fifteenth, some had succeeded in infiltrating back into the city during the night and were expected to continue. Sniper fire was to be expected throughout the day and into the night of the sixteenth, at least at routes of entry to the city and likely inside as well. Walker and the staff reviewed battle strategy, tactics, and timing.

The corps' standing order remained in place—that all units, including artillery, armor, and infantry, were to avoid shelling near the cathedral and were to employ spotters to ensure accuracy and avoid accidental hits on or near it. German machine-gun and mortar emplacements still occupied strategic spots in Chartres. During the briefing, according to one source, Griff was reported as having learned that corps artillery had received an order to destroy the cathedral, the order coming from someone who believed the Germans were occupying the twin towers as observation posts, but no record of any such order has been found. Griffith and Stark thought there was no reason to fire on the cathedral, as the two of them had been in it the day before and had found it clean.

During the briefing, Walker also reacted to Force 2's having failed to hold its position during the attack and its forced retreat, so Walker ordered the force to launch a dawn attack, and he reportedly appointed Griffith to be first-line director of military operations in the sector that included the cathedral and units of the Seventh Armored Division that were to pass through Chartres and proceed north through Lèves and toward the Seine.

Griff emerged from the briefing and as usual drafted orders reflecting decisions reached, for Gene Schulz to promptly type onto mimeograph stencils from the handwritten instructions. Liaison officers, second or first lieutenants, or even senior officers such as Mel Stark, stood by waiting for Schulz to finish and Griff to approve and shoved the orders into their courier cases to head by jeep for the front lines to deliver the orders to division and battalion commanders.

But Griffith couldn't let things just stand as they were. Something about the situation troubled him, so he took it upon himself to investigate. As he left the G-3 office, he told Schulz and Messner he would be going into Chartres on a personal mission without giving any details.

"Goodbye, be careful, and God be with you," Schulz said to Griffith.

Griffith, with his pistol and M1 semiautomatic carbine, hopped into his jeep along with Mel Stark and Colonel Robert E. Cullen, who also carried weapons, and, with William Dugan back at the wheel, drove out of the CP toward Chartres.

Cullen was the corps' adjutant general—the principal administrative staff officer, responsible for procedures affecting awards and decorations, casualty operations, and administration and preservation of records of all personnel, normally subordinated to the chief of staff and known as the G-1. The adjutant often works directly for the deputy chief of staff, the position in which Griffith also served in addition to preforming his duties as G-3.

Griffith left to determine whether German forces had now occupied the cathedral, despite the fact that his job and training were all to plan, oversee, receive information collected by G-2 through proper channels, and draft and disseminate orders to others at the front to carry out. Why did Griffith take it upon himself to investigate what Eugene Schulz, in his 2012 memoir, would call a "personal mission"? It is likely that requests had been received during the night from field commanders whose troops were being hit by what appeared to them to be coordinated fire. Those commanders could have been likely to order artillery and mortar fire to protect their troops. Sources are in conflict as to whether anyone had sought to change the standing order.

What is clear is that corps artillery was under the overall command of corps headquarters, and specifically its G-3 Section. Griffith's job was foremost to administer tactical plans and develop orders for battle in conjunction with the location and strength of the enemy as assessed by the G-2 Section and then write battle orders and assign units to execute them. G-3's function was not to engage in surveillance, much less to do it personally. It appears, then, that Griffith's personal investigation was more than a standard inquiry he could have undertaken simply by asking the G-2 to look into it.

Within a couple of hours after General Walker's briefing, two local priests began daily Mass before a small group of congregants in the cathedral's Chapel of the Sacred Heart, which was tucked along the south hallway on one shoulder of the main altar. Those attending the morning services entered the cathedral through the rampart-shrouded west portal and one of its great west doors, which opened into a Gothic 125-foot vaulting-capped nave, supported by huge marble-faced pillars running the distance of one and a half football fields along the marble floor through the nave and then the choir, leading to the altar poised at the east end.

One of the two priests who conducted Mass was Father Cassegrain, and the other was Douin, who also served in temporary assignments as vicar for the cathedral's adjoining seminary and of the hospital in Chartres. Douin had walked all the way to Chartres the prior Sunday, August 12, carrying his bag and seeing along the way charred vehicles on the roadside. He had spoken with locals concerning the movement of the Germans in retreat from the Allied forces and of the acts of sabotage and skirmishes between Resistance fighters and the Germans. He also passed through German checkpoints and learned of their actions to seal up the city—permitting people to enter but none to leave.

The morning of the sixteenth, Father Douin felt the air still moist from the night's rain. He heard another priest's voice reverberate through the vast, open cathedral, as well as bursts of rifle fire and occasional explosions in the distance. These sounds also echoed through the narrow streets, reminding the parishioners who attended the Mass that the cathedral provided both physical and spiritual sanctuary.

CHAPTER TWENTY-ONE

Clearing the Church: Chartres, August 16, 1944

IN LATE MORNING, GRIFFITH, STARK, CULLEN, AND DUGAN HAD NAVI-gated in an open jeep through the city, hearing explosions crackling in the streets and on rooftops, and finally crossed the railroad tracks a block before the Place des Épars and approached the base of the five-hundred-foot rocky hill that rose from the river at the center of Chartres. Dugan was driving, with Griff riding shotgun and Stark and Cullen in the back, each with rifle ready. In front of them, the cathedral's twin towers reached forty-five stories above the hill. Guns exchanged volleys. Artillery and mortar explosions erupted with surprising accuracy. A shell hit high above, grazing the cathedral's north tower, about halfway up. Was it American or German? A cloud of stone chips and dust floated down the cathedral's west and north facades.

It felt to Griff as though shots from small weapons were closing in. The jeep jolted and jostled around obstacles, maneuvering from position to position, through intermittent street fighting on winding, wet streets, around blind corners, probing forward and back, side to side, dodging fire. Carcasses of cars and fallen bricks lay in the rain-soaked, mud-filled streets. Smoke rose from buildings. Shots rebounded off walls, resounding through deserted passageways, with shops and houses locked, windows shuttered, and no civilians in sight.

Griff suspected at once that German spotters were directing artillery and mortar fire from the cathedral. That was the vantage point, after all.

You could see everything from that hilltop. If he was right, well, corps units presented a clear target for the Germans. All they could do was keep moving. That wasn't easy. Progress was slow through the city, due to the expected snipers. If there were German spotters in the towers, the Americans and supporting Resistance fighters might also be forced back in retreat—or, worse yet, more likely to be shot and killed.

The jeep wove through cobblestone alleyways to reach the hilltop, arriving at a gravel concourse a block west of the cathedral, the site for generations of pilgrim gatherings and carnivals. Antique walls surrounded the cathedral, encompassing a Vatican-like close (or walled-in place) above the town of centuries-old two- and three-story stone and stucco houses and other structures.

They dismounted in the concourse and entered the court on foot, shots still discharging all around. Griff motioned for Dugan to bring with him the American flag that Griff had thrown into the back of the jeep and told Dugan to keep it folded up and carry it with him.

Griff saw that GIs and FFI scattered all around the court were shooting upward. He couldn't tell whether the Frenchmen were the trained, sharp Resistance fighters whom he'd met two days before at La Ferté-Bernard, led by Madame Clavel. Or were they just disconnected, trigger-happy partisans out for revenge? And who was in charge of those GIs?

He felt his pulse throbbing, body vibrating, and vision narrowing. He played over the scene in his mind, debating whether they should follow through with his urge to get inside the cathedral and settle once and for all whether any Germans were hiding inside or in the towers and posing such a threat or if they should instead just move on—to explore what was holding up the armored column. Maybe the field officers who had called in to corps CP had been right: if there were spotters up high, directing fire, massacring corps troops, the towers damn well should be flattened!

The GIs around him were stymied. This wasn't how they'd been trained.

Griff didn't like what he saw: American soldiers exercising caution during an attack. In front of buildings on the courtyard, GIs were foiled, just taking sporadic potshots, striking the cathedral's walls up high. Stone fragments, sparks, and powder clouds were drifting down past sculptures and boarded-up Gothic windows onto the courtyard's surface.

Griff anchored himself momentarily and watched. But he saw no snipers, no enemy fire.

So he called to the gunners to stop their shooting: "Hell, there are no snipers here."

They shouted back that there were—up in the spire of the cathedral.

He looked up again and waited for shots from above.

There were none. Maybe the men had just seen falling fragments of damage from shelling that they'd mistaken for a sniper, or maybe they'd just seen companions' shots ricocheting off the walls that they'd then thought was sniper fire. He told the gunners to wait and ordered Dugan to hand him the folded-up flag, which Griff then stuffed into the back of his shirt. He would inspect the cathedral to see whether there were Germans inside. He would settle the matter.

He checked that he'd released the safety switch on his M1 for firing and set out to investigate. He prowled into the now-silent street and across the open courtyard, exposed to enemy guns, and then ran to the base of the cathedral's stone wall. He eyed the perimeter in front and behind him at ground level and looked up, all around. He started at the northwest corner of the church courtyard. Almost frozen with fear, crouching, he scuttled from one point to the next.

He sidled up to the open doorway of the rampart that covered the west portal of the cathedral, looked inside, searching right and left for any sign of life, but he saw only the sandbags stacked in between wooden framing protecting the sculptures surrounding the portals. He advanced south and then turned left at the corner to the south wall, hugging close to its base. He could sense that he was in and out of potential sight of snipers high up. He trembled and worked hard to keep his eyes and ears clear, listening for any signs or sounds of Germans. He headed slowly counterclockwise around the structure. Approaching the rampart that protected the south portico, he again stepped inside, searching slowly for any sign of sentries, but sensed none.

Inside, along the south wall inside the rampart, among the hundreds of its portico's sculptures—saints, kings, apostles, and other biblical characters—he could make out the revealing detail of one of them that caught his attention. In the central tympanum, above the middle door, in a depiction of the Last Judgment, Christ sat with arms raised, angels above him, Saint Michael at his feet, holding scales, the damned on the right and the saved on the left. Griff recognized this Jesus as the same one to whom he'd first been introduced as a kid, in Quanah's simple brick Baptist church, with its warm-hearted minister who waited at the door, welcoming congregants and later bidding them goodbye. Griff wasn't a Catholic, only an incidental Baptist, but he recognized this Jesus as the one he'd known, by whom he'd felt embraced.

He wasn't an art buff, but his love of beauty was no less than the next guy's, and he hated useless destruction and was intent on doing his part to prevent it today.

He continued around the curved wall of the chapel at the east end and then ahead around the corner of the north wall, where he gazed up at to the north tower. He saw damage halfway up. Chips of stone and dust blown by wind gusts still brushed down from the tower walls. Another chill came over him, his confidence wavering intermittently with alarm and dread.

Toward the top of the north tower, through his field glasses, he spotted one of the many carved-stone gargoyles jutting down from the roof's edge, guarding the high balustrade. The group had watched over the whole complex, including the hilltop buildings of the close, the seminary and school, the city, and the surrounding countryside, for centuries. The gargoyle's neck bent down, its eyes searching, as if to snarl, "Friend or foe?"

Griff passed through the north portico and found himself back at the west end. By God, he'd done it! He'd covered the whole visible exterior of the cathedral and lived.

But that wasn't enough. The towers, the roofs, and the inside still had to be cleared before he could call off corps artillery.

He signaled to Stark and Cullen to follow closely behind him.

"I'm going up into the top of that spire," he said to Stark and then signaled for him and Dugan to stay put outside and for Cullen to accompany him inside. He yelled to Stark, "I'll ring the bell and put out a flag. If I don't ring the bell after a while, you attack." He headed inside the cathedral and ordered Cullen to stay at the door behind him.

Rifle in hand, finger quivering on the trigger, he inched inside the north portal's rampart and up the marble steps of its porch and at first gently pushed his shoulder against the heavy door. He worried whether the creak of its rusty hinge would alert any enemy sentry inside, but he opened the door a crack, listening. Prayerlike mumbling seeped from inside. Old, damp, cool air brushed his face. He smelled incense that triggered a memory of a Wyoming wedding in which he'd stood as best man for a Leavenworth classmate and had felt awe in the strength of that classmate's Catholic spirituality.

He entered the dark transept and was absorbed by the wall of quiet. It was unlike anything he could remember, a different world—strangely intense, yet serene. He inched forward from the relative safety of the north portal door, listening and peering into the dim light, and he sensed no activity inside, except the continuing sounds of prayerlike murmuring and reverberations from shots fired outside. The terror he'd just felt, with heart rate skyrocketing and vision closing in and hands white and body humming, was now slightly subsiding. He'd been unable to think, but now thoughts seemed to be coming to him in a semblance of order. He had been an animal, doing what he'd been trained to do, but now he was returning to normal terror and being a human, starting to think again.

He slinked through the transept into the cavernous nave and through an aisle formed by chairs positioned for Masses; then he turned toward the west end. He crossed over the floor's mysterious inlaid circular labyrinth—fourteen yards in diameter—that pilgrims had explored for scores of generations. The smooth inlaid stone brought to his mind an image of parishioners and pilgrims passing through centuries into the cathedral. Through the stillness, at the back of the nave, he saw rows of red votive candle flames. They were like a chorus of glowing, floating, giant almonds, spirits gently dancing in rhythm, suspended in serene quiet, each flame in the process of consuming itself as a symbol of self-sacrifice.

To the left, at the southwest corner, he spotted a short set of stone stairs that headed down. Before descending, he scanned as much of the first floor as he could in the dimness but saw nothing moving. So he began his descent down the steps, aiming to search the basement to be sure no enemy lurked down there before facing the dangers of the rest of the building and its towers. He felt the steps, worn smooth by centuries of shoes of worshipers and priests. At the foot of the stairs, a locked iron gate blocked him at the entrance to a barrel-vaulted passage that led into the crypt. He listened for any noise or rays of light in the passageway. Hearing none, and seeing no footprints in the dust in front of the gate, he reversed course to search the rest of the nave, rather than waiting to track down keys to open the door.

He climbed the stairs and worked through the right-side ambulatory, curving around the south side of the alter in a ring around the east crown of the sanctuary, past the three apsidal chapels carved into the east walls, and past the locked door to the attached Chapel of Saint Piatus of Tournai. He continued around the altar and back into the transept at its north end and wondered whether any enemy stragglers retreating from the American attack had come inside the church in search of a fight or for rest or refuge. His spine chilled from the thought that every corner, every dark niche, might be hiding an enemy with gun ready, but he found none and felt relief.

He looked around for the stairs to the south tower and again heard mumbling near the sacristy just east of the north entrance by which he had entered. He made out two figures in shadows standing next to the wall of the sacristy leading into the choir toward the altar. They were two older men in clerical collars and ruffled dark robes—one about seventy, the other middle aged. Each held rosary beads and was waving a white handkerchief, whispering French. Griff neared them to make eye contact. Their patent terror—as if afraid he'd shoot—unnerved him, but he knew they could see his American uniform. He approached them, pointing his gun to the floor, and asked them in English whether Germans were inside. They shrugged. He couldn't tell whether they'd understood his words.

The sound of footsteps drew their eyes toward the west portal. An elderly man approached who wore an Adrian helmet and a World War I horizon-blue military uniform. Griff could tell from the uniform's fresh creases that the old man was a civilian veteran, today dressed for liberation. He'd come to tell the priests of the Americans' second sweep into the city; nothing to fear, he gestured, addressing them by name and then greeting Griff in English. Griff asked him, "Germans?" pointing up and then down. The old man shook his head, pointing down, muttering, "Locked rooms, only crates." He pointed his index finger toward the ceiling and whispered, "Occupying authorities took all keys; ordered all to keep out of both towers," but he turned his head and nodded toward the tower stairs entryway. He motioned up the stairs with a nod of his head, inviting Griff to look also.

The two priests and the old man watched Griff walk to the closed stairway door of the south tower. Griff raised his rifle in case a sentry was poised inside, able to fire through the door. Griff heard nothing and reached for the handle on the old wooden door and found it also locked. The old man saw too that it was locked and urged the priests to help by summoning the custodian to retrieve extra keys for the tower stairs. One of the men left to do so. Soon they heard someone approaching, and the old man quickly pointed over Griff's shoulder toward a fourth man, in work clothes, approaching and carrying bucket and keys. The man's jaw and clenched teeth betrayed his panic.

The old man explained in English that the custodian was terrified of the German occupiers' reprisals for violation of their order to stay out of the towers, but the priests prevailed on him to unlock the door of each of the two towers. Griff whispered that he would first search this tower and then the north tower.

After the custodian unlocked the doors, all waited quietly for any response to the sound of the locks clanking. There was none, and Griff felt another mix of partial relief and increased pressure in his throat from the prospect of the danger that might be lurking above in the spiral stairway. He turned the handle and pressed slowly on the unlocked door and peered inside and up into the dark, narrow, circular stairway, each step only wide enough to accommodate a single person. He headed up the worn, narrow stone steps. The tension felt like hot wind on his face.

For Griffith's six-foot-three-inch frame, with tall shoulders and steel helmet, this was a tight fit, especially with rifle pointed ahead. He aimed his gun upward, ready for any descending foe.

As he entered, a pair of rifle shots ripped from a distant street, the noise entering through a window. This sound flashed his thoughts back up into the bell tower, his rifle and pistol still pointed upward toward whatever imagined German gun pointing downward might be quietly descending to defend. Griff hoped any enemy soldier holding such a gun would be equally fearful of Griff heading upward, preceded by his M1, braced to shoot.

Griff figured that the stairwell would require him to make several dozen spiral rotations from bottom to top. When he reached a point about one-third of the way up, he peered out every dozen or so steps through the tower's series of small arched windows, each a foot thick, which brought in moist air from the intermittent rain. In sequence, they provided an unobstructed view along the west and north sides of the cathedral. From there, he could spot any Germans positioned at windows or on the roofs, along the flying buttresses, and along the attic, including anyone looking out its many small gabled windows.

Halfway up the stairs, he looked out across the copper roof, more than an acre on a metal frame in the shape of an inverted ship's hull. He searched for enemy soldiers who might be hiding in the attic and who could fire through arch-gabled windows that pierced the roof at fifty-foot intervals. His breathing and heart rate increased from the strain of the climb and the tension of his search. He peered through the humidity, sweat dripping from his forehead with even more concentration. With each step, he felt the growing danger of confronting any descending German, so with each step he tuned his ears and senses ahead and riveted his eyes upward, side to side along the stairway walls, searching for the slightest sound or visual cue, as would cowboy gunmen facing off against each other, ready to draw in their shoot-out in the dusty street of a Western American cattle town.

At the top step, Griff slowly creaked open an unlocked, weathered wooden door and stepped out onto the narrow outside gallery, edging forward in successive steps just a few inches each time to maximize his view and hearing. He worked his way around the gallery, corner by corner. He came across discarded wrappers from German food rations, a German chocolate wrapper that read "Shoka-cola," cigarette butts, and expended rifle casings, but no German equipment. He also found American chewing-gum wrappers and a GI-issue can opener.

So it appeared that snipers from both sides could have been up in this south tower from time to time. A swell of partial relief came over him that so far he had escaped harm. He studied those portions of the uppermost part of the tower visible to him, and still he saw no sign of anyone higher up in the tower and no sign of any stairway heading farther up to the spire, so he felt no need to explore the tower further. He looked over to the north tower and carefully scanned every window and every visible niche that might hold an enemy soldier or sign of any nearby.

He stood on the balustrade of the south tower and felt a streak of sunshine breaking through thinning clouds, a sign of the fog lifting. To his left, looking to the west, he again saw the leopard-sized stone gargoyle he'd spotted from below during his circuit, now in sunlight, its mouth still open, eyes peering down, still looking out, attentive, guarding, vigilant, as it always had been since the Middle Ages.

But he couldn't let himself feel total relief unless he could clear the north tower. So he descended the stairs, two at a time.

He met the custodian and old man at the bottom and in a whisper asked where he could enter the steps of the north tower. The custodian showed the way and quietly unlocked the north tower stairway door and opened it, and Griff scanned inside up into the dark, narrow, circular stairway, which was about the same width and had been built with roughly the same pitch as that of the south tower. Halfway up this second stairwell, he again looked out the small windows across the copper roof. Again he searched for enemy soldiers who might be hiding in the attic or its windows. Another quarter of the way up, at the fourth level of the tower, he reached the bell ringer's room, with its vault capped by a nine-foot-wide keystone. Two of the cathedral's seven huge bells in the first belfry were visible from the stairway. Still he discovered no sight or sound of Germans inside or above or across on the roof.

Finally he reached the top step. He paused to listen and nudged his way through the partially open door out to the narrow gallery, and he again looked around while navigating through the gallery, section by section. Discarded food cans, empty German Panzerschokolade candy and Stuka-Tabletten stimulants wrappers, crumpled Dresden-made Sulima

Turkish cigarette wrappers littered the floor along with ashes, butts, and spent rifle casings.

Griff shivered and patted his chest and legs with his palms to confirm that he was still in one piece. He raised his binoculars and scoured along the west facade, searching to be sure no Germans had reappeared in any window or roof or platform, or had infiltrated back into the south tower from any side rooms he might have missed when climbing up and down. He scanned the skyline and across the city along his south and west flanks for any sign of enemy action that might be retarding the American advance, but he saw none.

He felt a surge of elation on first experiencing the dominating overview the towers afforded. They revealed most streets, buildings, and vehicle movements through the city. He was struck with how effective the tower would have been for spotting artillery. His view of American units was unobstructed, and he could make out even individual soldiers working their way through the city. It had been logical for American field commanders to believe the towers were being used by the Germans to aim artillery, but so far he'd proven that the Germans were not—at least not now, since it appeared that the backbone of German resistance was being broken.

Griff inhaled a lung-full of air and felt sunlight breaking through the clouds, and he pulled the American flag out from the back of his shirt and waved it over the balcony to confirm to everyone below that he'd reached the top unharmed. He'd been correct all right. No Germans had been in either spire. He called down the stairwell inside to Cullen or the old man to get one of the priests to ring the bell multiple times to confirm it.

He felt a wave of exhilaration. He'd been right. His risk had paid off. Somehow it all felt transfiguring, as though his world were reshaping.

He could see German soldiers below, scurrying on the east side of the river, in their block-by-block retreat. He concluded that they'd blown up some but not all bridges crossing the river, mainly the historic ones.

He paused before descending. Maybe he'd learned something about himself. He'd enjoyed this. When he and the other division heads back at the CP briefing had been arguing about spotters in the towers, he might have spoken up. He pondered, why not?

In a sense, he'd gone on to defy his own orders. Maybe this was what it felt like to pursue some sort of personal glory at the expense of loyalty to corps procedure.

The church bell clanged in the belfry below. The peal reverberated through Griff's aching legs. The American and French fighters below saw the flag and heard the bell and rejoiced in relief. The flag billowed in front of Griffith's face. His realization that the cathedral was in fact still clear of Germans swelled his confidence. He basked for a moment, looking out from the narrow tower balcony, feeling the moist wind in his face, but at the same time hearing fitful rifle and machine-gun shots in distant streets below from confrontations surrounding the cathedral. They were probably just Resistance fighters outstripping their orders, or possibly trigger-happy American patrols trading shots with German snipers and stragglers. He heard the strike of artillery shells to the south and saw a few isolated American light tanks come into view as they squeezed through narrow curving streets and scraped around corners, but he couldn't see any armored column on the main streets.

He squinted through his binoculars to find the bridgehead area east of the city—somewhere east of Luisant across the Eure River in the area between Le Coudray on the west and Bonville on the east—where he had ordered the Seventh Armored Division and its Thirty-Eighth Armored Infantry Battalion to secure the bridgehead toward the east and then to patrol vigorously to the east, north, and west while awaiting further orders. He saw the main concentration of the Seventh Armored Division portion of his 12,500-man corps force. He spotted an armored column patrolling to the west and another to the east but none pushing north. He did, however, see a separate column, pointing north but standing still.

Damn. They hadn't even begun their probe northward. They're just standing there. What are they doing, just sitting there, dithering?

But now there wasn't time to ponder that. His thoughts returned to the urgent need to report to HQ at CP 7 that the cathedral was not occupied by any Germans and was not now being used to spot German artillery. He knew corps HQ had to transmit orders to the corps' own artillery to reiterate the standing command to refrain from firing at the cathedral and rescind any contrary order to attack it, and he knew that the corps had to get word up to Third Army HQ that Chartres had been taken. Once that was done, he also needed to find out what bottleneck was stalling the Seventh from pushing north as he'd ordered.

A rush of exhilaration propelled him through the door into the stairwell, and he cascaded down the spiral steps, taking them two or three at a time, his hand circling down the interior, smooth-worn stone handrail, speeding toward the base like a North Texas oil-well drill bit on the verge of a big, black, wet strike. He felt himself smiling in jubilation. He pressed through the door at the bottom step, past the priests and through the nave, across the Labyrinth, back to the transept, and through the north door, with another rush of success, and waved for Cullen to follow, emerging into the sunlight. He called for Dugan to come forward and regrouped with him, Stark, and Cullen to confirm to them that no Germans were in the cathedral and signaled to all to continue holding fire and yelling to the troops to cease fire and call off any guns aimed at the cathedral.

He told Stark to get on the radio ASAP to order corps artillery to hold off any attack at or near the cathedral while he scratched out a field message to HQ. And he ordered Cullen to get word to the tanks and field artillery to call off any attacks on the cathedral and rescind all prior orders to the contrary. He stopped to prepare a handwritten field message on a six-inch-by-nine-inch form, his twenty-third of the campaign, marked URGENT, addressed to G-3 Third Army, which read, "Chartres captured by . . . Workshop [codename for the Seventh Armored Division] 0130. Still some fighting. Dynamite closed south Chartres. Corps Trps concentrating via Coursville. G.P. 2 mi N Coursville." He signed it "Griffith, C G XX Corp" and marked it "12:45, 16 Aug.," then gave it to Stark to get it to Third Army HQ, ASAP.

This would be the last thing that Griffith would ever write.

Chapter Twenty-Two

In Command at Lèves:
Chartres and Lèves, August 16, 1944

With the cathedral cleared, Griff ordered the Twenty-Third Armored Infantry Battalion troops to continue securing the area and to push on with their mission inside the city of Chartres. To the north, time was fast approaching for the intersection a mile beyond the outlying town of Lèves, three miles north of Chartres, to have been secured. If Third Army units could hold that intersection and could reach the Seine ahead of the retreating Germans, the Allies could likely bottle up and destroy or capture all fleeing units of the German Army south of that river. Griff now had to get to the Seventh Armored Division G-3 to see whether—as he had expected—elements of that division had as of yet failed to carry out their orders.

Stark likely arranged for one of the battalion's couriers to carry Griffith's message to Third Army HQ, because Griff ordered him, Cullen, and Dugan to get back into the jeep and for Dugan to drive them to the bridgehead east of Luisant across the Eure River to find the place between Le Coudray and Bonville where that north-pointing column was sitting. Griffith told Dugan to navigate through the city on a route that would take them within sight of all crossroads to confirm that blockades had been cleared along the major routes that armored columns would encounter on their way back north through Chartres.

In the front passenger seat, Griff refocused on his mission: to check on the true locations and dispositions of units in order to more effectively direct and supervise execution of General Walker's orders. First he had to find out what the logjam was holding up that column. It should have recrossed the Eure River much earlier and passed through Lèves already.

Griffith and his companions knew they would be exposed to enemy fire as they worked their way south through the tight streets of the old part of the city. On Rue Saint-Michel, almost a half mile south of the cathedral, they passed the place where Father Drouin reported having spotted one of the last German lookouts early that morning.

The jeep turned northwest onto the Rue des Bouchers and then south two blocks toward the Place de La République, next to the prefecture, a third of a mile southwest of the cathedral.

They came across a crowd of armed civilians in the courtyard of the prefecture and stopped to determine what was happening. Every few minutes in the courtyard, small groups of partisans brought in men and women accused of being collaborators. Street-fighting sounds echoed on all sides, stimulating a scene of hysteria. Shots reverberated as a German sniper was fatally dislodged from his perch. A group of armed civilians led a screaming woman who struggled to break away. She sought to explain to anyone who would listen that she had not worked with the Germans.

Mr. Chapelier, the prefect newly appointed by the Free French, stood at the center of the courtyard and intervened on the woman's behalf, ordering the partisans to stop their manhandling and permit her to speak. She faced one of her captors and accused him of being a German collaborator. He shouted back, waving his pistol at her. Gendarmes rushed him. They restrained his pistol arm, and others took her away.

In a corner of the courtyard, a gruesome scene unfolded. Men with FFI armbands brought in three young Frenchmen accused of working for the Germans, as members of Joseph Darnand's Milice française—the most hated French militia—who had served as informers to the Gestapo, denouncing other French men and women. The three men admitted that they'd received 3,250 francs every month from the Gestapo in return for supplying the names of townsfolk working against the Germans. Resistance fighters took them into a narrow alley off the courtyard and shot the accused men in their heads. Their bodies lay piled atop each other. The spectators, young and old, looked on without a word as the corpses were loaded into an ambulance, each face covered with a copy of the most recent proclamation from Vichy. The ambulance drove them off to their graves.

Several citizens stepped forward and asked whether the three executed men had been given a trial. One local woman replied with a grim smile and a pert voice, "Yes," they had had a trial—a short trial. She said they had been court-martialed and added, "It was not necessary to hold a long trial. The lives of these men had been known for the past four years."

At an end of the courtyard, twelve women and four men had been lined up against a wall. A barber had roughly shorn off the hair of most of the women as close to the scalp as possible, carrying out a decree that they be publicly shamed for their acts. One woman stood on an overturned beer box while the barber did his work. Strewn around the box on the ground were a half dozen shades of hair—some straight, some curly, some natural, some dyed, some still with bobby pins and combs. The women—collaborators—stood helplessly against a wall. Terror showed in their faces. One woman concealed her face with a handkerchief. Another sobbed. A stout young woman in a white peasant smock held hands with her thinner mother, who wore a dark peasant dress and silver spectacles.

Overall, the scene brought together a mix of civilians dressed in coats—some wearing their Sunday best, including earrings, for the occasion—plus FFI and other Resistance fighters and police and veterans, many wearing uniforms taken out of mothballs for the first time since the German invasion in 1940. These uniformed included characters with swords and stern faces and many French youths with Tricolor armbands and pistols.

This taste of the locals' passions gave Griffith, Stark, Dugan, and Cullen a sense of the stakes confronting the people of Chartres.

The jeep continued another four blocks south to the Place des Épars, at the intersection of five streets—only blocks from the cathedral. They saw more groups gathered in the football-field-sized oval, paved plaza surrounding a statue of General Marceau of the French Revolution. Some shouted in celebration. Others called for vindication and revenge.

Griff's group spotted two abandoned American tanks that had broken down and been looted. The area surrounding the tanks revealed that a battle had been fought during the night a few blocks from the hospital. The tanks had bypassed the hospital, but the building had been hit from all sides. It overflowed with wounded lying on the sidewalks. Dugan swung the jeep west and north a block to the Rue du Grand Faubourg, where another abandoned American tank had run up against a wall during the night battle. Those of its crew who had survived had taken defensive positions around the tank to wait for the main part of the force to arrive.

Griffith again looked around for Germans and saw none, nor did he spot any German roadblocks, so they continued east on Boulevard Adelphe Chasles and Boulevard de la Courtille, detoured around the blown-out Courtille bridge, and crossed over the Eure River on a lesser bridge a few blocks south. He then sped south down tree-lined, narrow streets, past closed shops, small houses, and two-story apartments on both sides, with doors shut and window blinds closed.

In the two remaining miles between Le Coudray and Bonville, buildings stood progressively farther apart, and in the next half mile south, the houses gave way to wheat fields, and the jeep approached combat elements of the Seventh Armored Division. Those elements had formed a defensive circle like an American frontier wagon train while waiting for their order to head north and enter the city. Around the outside, like the rim of a wheel, infantry regiments were deployed, with their supporting tank and tank-destroyer units, so as to draw a ring of protective infantry around the entire division. Within this ring, transport and supply elements and command posts were dispersed. At the hub, artillery batteries would be able to fire in a 360-degree circle, and antiaircraft batteries sat deployed, ready to protect against air attacks.

By the time Griffith and his companions had arrived at the assembly area to see the forces still waiting, his jubilation from inspecting the cathedral and clearing it had turned to frustration and anger. He saw no progress, so he jumped out of his jeep to determine why.

Griffith and Stark together located the Seventh Armored Division's three-shop tent and soon determined that the division's Thirty-Eighth Armored Infantry Battalion had been assigned to reach Lèves. The two tracked down Lieutenant Colonel Samuel L. Irwin, the battalion's commander, but by the time they found him, Griff was likely fuming mad, trying to determine for himself why Irwin hadn't implemented the corps' order hours sooner. Griff and Stark knew that the whole division—which was commanded by Major General Lindsay Silvester—was a "green" one, in its first fight at Chartres, and the division's sector included the whole city of Chartres, so they had a lot of action on their hands. That said, though, as soon as Griff realized that Silvester and Irwin had permitted Irwin's battalion to just sit there, frozen in place, he lost his temper.

Griff demanded that Irwin explain the delay. Irwin no doubt tried to explain, but Griff, in his anger, wouldn't hear it. Irwin had been waiting for something but failed to convince Griffith why it justified delaying the battalion's departure. So Griffith took charge himself and probably on the spot as much as relieved Irwin of command, leaving it to the battalion's chief of staff to get it moving. And Griff may well have told Stark to remain on-site to oversee the dispatch of a column northward around the east side of Chartres to Lèves while Griff himself would set out ahead. The column would need enough men and equipment to first secure the crossroads north of Lèves and then send forward two separate units— one to head north the twenty miles toward Dreux and beyond that to the Seine, and the second to head from Chartres eastward fifty miles to the Seine crossing near Melun.

Leaving Stark behind with the battalion, Griff and Cullen climbed in the jeep, Griff carrying his carbine and pistol. He ordered Dugan to drive fast, back the way they'd come, through the east edge of Chartres and around the hill and then across the Eure and up its western bank, toward Lèves, the column to follow, and as they traveled north, to check to be sure all intersections were clear. The column had to get through to Lèves and then would send its two columns north to Dreux and east to Melun.

They likely checked both routes around the hill, east and west, and on the north side reached the Place Drouaise and then headed north toward Lèves along the two-lane N10, the main road north out of Chartres to Paris, lined by trees on one side or the other and then passing through patches of woods on both sides and relatively few buildings. The road curved gently to the right and approached Lèves's town hall from the south, near the village's center.

They suddenly came upon a remnant of fifteen soldiers from a German army corps milling in the street. Dugan hit the brakes. Griffith jumped out of his front passenger seat with his rifle and fired a series of shots to hold the Germans at bay to give Dugan a chance to turn the jeep around with Cullen in the back seat. Griff fired first, continuing until he'd emptied his rifle clip, before the Germans could respond. The enemy soldiers scattered for cover in bushes and behind trees before returning fire. Griff grabbed Dugan's carbine and fired it until empty as well and then leaped back into the jeep, which sped back south out of Lèves and around the curve along the route from which they'd come. They headed back in the direction of Chartres, searching for American troops or an outpost.

Within minutes, they spotted an oncoming American M5 light tank sitting beside the road with its turret open. It was from the Seventh Armored Division's Eighty-Seventh Reconnaissance Battalion, heading north out of Chartres. A helmeted soldier stood in the open hatch. He had removed his goggles and pulled them up and onto his helmet and was examining a map. He looked up at the approaching jeep. Griffith told Dugan to stop the jeep, called out to the tank commander—a sergeant— and asked what he and his tank crew were doing there. The sergeant said he was trying to reach the crossroads beyond Lèves—the intersection of N10 and N1154, the road north to Dreux—and that he'd been ordered to get there that morning, so he was at least a couple of hours late. Griffith told the sergeant to continue on with his crew and be fast about it.

"Get going," he said. "You'll find a bunch of Germans in Lèves. You go through firing," he yelled, "and when you turn that corner, go like hell."

He motioned for the tank to move out and looked back at the jeep, but after a few breaths of hesitation he looked back at the tank and added, "I'm going with you."

And with that, he climbed up the rear of the tank and called to the sergeant to move out, leaving Dugan and Cullen behind with the jeep. Griff may possibly have stood on a tow hitch attached to the back of the tank, but more likely he just climbed on top, while the sergeant climbed back inside and closed the hatch.

Griff was too large to squeeze inside the tank. The M5—about the size of what we would today know as a minivan—held a four-man crew but, with ammunition onboard, no space inside for an extra man, and on the outside it had neither endboard nor sideboard for standing. In fact, it probably also carried an armored case on top of its rear armor panels that hung over the back, so that, although Griff could have gripped onto hand-holds to climb up and may have found some way to stand and hold onto the back, most likely he merely knelt on the top of the tank and huddled behind the turret, where he exposed himself to attack on both sides and the rear, and likely also from the front, because the turret extended barely chest high above the tank's top surface and wasn't much to hide behind.

Griff held his M1 semiautomatic carbine in one hand and pistol in the other and looked up the road, searching for the curve leading to the spot where his jeep had encountered the German soldiers and survived the shoot-out. The tank roared toward Lèves. Griff gazed around contin-uously for signs of any of the Germans who had scattered in all directions from the would-be roadblock during the shoot-out, and he likely figured there would be other enemy positions along the way. The tank charged ahead, likely at its maximum speed of thirty-six miles per hour, with Griff on top. Had he planned to do this? Had he thought about riding on the tank, or inside it, before he and Dugan and Cullen had spotted the tank on the side of the road pointed toward them? Or was this a spur-of-the-moment decision that had somehow been stimulated by the combination of his triumph at the cathedral a couple of hours earlier, followed by his confrontation with Irwin at the Thirty-Eighth's assembly area?

He must have felt terror from being a sitting duck on the tank—or nearly a clay pigeon—exposed at the rear and on the sides and only barely able to fit a portion of his body behind the turret of the tank to hide from shots coming from the front. But he also likely felt some intense excitement. After all, he was in command, even if exposed, and some-how probably felt some protection from the roar of the seventeen-ton machine beneath him and the solid steel turret in front of him. The tank could fire one hundred or more rounds from its thirty-seven-millimeter main gun and 7,500 rounds from the 0.30-caliber Browning machine gun mounted on the side of the turret. Knowing that, Griff may have felt some sense of protection, but what about simple small-arms fire coming potentially from all around?

They passed the shoot-out site, but no Germans remained. Griff must have felt a measure of relief, and then the sun came out, but he continued to look high and low and around every building, tree, and bush as they passed through the center of town. Doors and windows were shuttered, with no residents in sight.

At the center of the village, they turned left onto Avenue de la Paix to head westward, and the sun shone in his eyes. They continued up the route that led out of town northward to the crossroads. The two-lane street narrowed, with trees on both sides, but the sun was shining through into his eyes between spaced-out single-story and two-story houses and other buildings, including, on the right side of the road, a single-story windmill structure with a pitched roof that slanted toward the street. Just beyond it was the edge of a wooded area, heavy with underbrush. A dirt pathway, hidden from view of the approaching tank, ran from the street to the right and up the hill. A small stucco, one-story warehouse stood opposite on the left side of the street. Trees and shrubs obscured the tank crew's and Griffith's view of the path as they headed west from the center of the village.

Griff knew they'd made it through the center of town with no sign of Germans, so he was probably feeling some confidence that they could get to the crossroads and find it clear, or else guarded with a small-enough enemy force to be manageable. In fact, he may have even felt a little rush—maybe even a vague kick of freedom—as he held onto the top of that tank. The tank barreled up the street and passed by the windmill, and Griff and the others could see that the street was about to curve to the left and up a gradual hundred-foot hill with a clear path ahead. Griff perhaps thought they were in the clear. He might even have found a moment to think of Nell back home, glad she was in the safety of her parents' Brooklyn house, and how nice it was going to be when the two of them could be together again. Or he may have thought of his daughter, Alice, confident that she was ensconced with her grandparents in the shady, peaceful, lawn-covered seclusion of the Commander's House back on Governor's Island; Griff was likely unaware that she was away those weeks at her favorite summer camp in upstate New York.

But out of nowhere, Griff felt the hot spike of a machine-gun round tear into his back. He probably had no idea what hit him. A young German soldier with a machine gun had been hiding in the brush along the path on the right. As Griff passed by on the tank, with no idea of the soldier's position, the soldier let loose with a burst of fire, with bullets striking Griff before he could react. Shots from other enemy rifles and a rocket launcher flew by also. Griff spun around and fired as many shots as he could from his M1 semiautomatic carbine and from his pistol, but he fell off the tank and died then and there. Bullets may have ricocheted off the tank or its turret, but the noise of the tank engine must have muffled them, because the crew inside the tank did not realize what had happened until long after. Once the shooting erupted, they must have just fought through and continued, going "like hell," as Griff had ordered, without knowing that Griffith had been hit, leaving his body behind, lifeless, on the pavement.

Locals had seen the German soldier shooting at Griff and the tank and then running away up the path. They included a Mr. Pavy and a fourteen-year-old boy named Bertrand Papillon who lived in Lèves. Pavy and another local teen, Blondel, from a distance, witnessed Griffith dying.

Some kind of passion or other internal stimulus seems to have peeled away Griff's mantle of orderly and disciplined command, his deliberate and self-possessed manner, and driven him into a sort of frenzy during the last couple of hours of his life—even perhaps through some personal transformation. Perhaps his short-tempered encounter with Irwin's battalion at the Thirty-Eighth's assembly area had triggered it, or perhaps General Walker's having assigned Griff to watch over the frontline operations firsthand had triggered it; after all, he was suddenly thrust up close inside the corps' by far most brutal fight yet, called upon to oversee the forward units to ensure that Walker's orders covering Griff's sector were being carried out, in the face of such stiff and recurring German defense. Or perhaps it was all of that combined with some feeling of triumph at having cleared the cathedral and—while at the top of the north tower—having seen the bottleneck holding up advance of the Seventh Armored Division.

Whatever it was that had driven him to such a height of vehement or almost manic frenzy, was it not a combination of circumstances, fatigue, sleep deprivation, and terror experienced by countless thousands of good men in combat, fighting for their lives and those of their men or doing their best to lead? We don't know what it was, but for Griff it all came to a crashing halt when the thunder of machine-gun, rocket, and rifle fire blew him off the tank, despite his intrepid attempt to somehow fire back until all ammunition was spent.

That afternoon, a major battle between Germans and Allied forces followed in Lèves and resulted in the destruction of the church, the boys' school, and a large part of the town. The Seventh Armored Division's Thirty-Eighth Armored Infantry Battalion carried its attack around Chartres and took the high ground to the northeast of the town and through it captured over a hundred German prisoners.

Blondel later reported that he and his brother had run out during a lull in the fighting that afternoon and approached Griffith's body lying in the left lane of the street, his chest riddled with bullets, the rest of his body untouched except for an injured finger. Griff's left hand still held his carbine, and his right hand held his pistol, which he had fired until empty into the Germans whose fire he had drawn while on the tank. They picked him up and moved him onto the sidewalk in front of the stucco building opposite the windmill.

Infantry captain Carl K. Mattocks—who led the attack on Lèves— would later report that his unit had escorted Lieutenant Colonel Irwin to General Thompson's command post, which had eventually been established a block west of the cathedral. When Mattocks left that post, darkness had set in. Mattocks traveled east and then north over the Lèves road via vehicle using only small "cat's-eye" lights. He drove through the part of Lèves where Griff had been killed but did not see Griff's body. The lights, he reported, would have prevented him and his team from seeing a human form on the road, so after Griff had been shot off the tank, Mattocks believed, his body would have remained lying on the side of the street the night of the sixteenth.

He did not know that Griff's body had been moved to the sidewalk and that by evening local residents had draped it with a blanket and later had completely covered it with flowers and placed in the middle of the blossoms a small American flag that a French family had hidden in their home. They brought chairs onto the sidewalk and held a vigil over the colonel to wait for US Army personnel to come claim his body.

Some days later, Mr. Pavy would tell villagers, including Mr. Papillon, that shortly after the shooting of Griffith, Pavy had heard a rumor that a young German soldier, whose hand had been bandaged—and who had moved on to Saint-Prest, five miles northeast of Lèves up the Eure River—had boasted, some hours after the incident in Lèves, of having shot an American colonel. Later still, eyewitnesses would come forward, including a woman who said she had seen a German soldier step out of the pathway at the side of the road after the tank passed and shoot Griffith in the back.

Griff's reasons for leading the push north by climbing onto the tank and riding exposed will never be known. But in those moments, with the apparent fluid movement of Allied and enemy units, and Germans—even in retreat—who were in the immediate area delaying the forward advance of the corps—by tactical plan, ambush, snare, or vandalism—Griff and the other American commanders had an overwhelming need to discover immediately the Germans' latest positions, movements, and strengths. What, in addition to those needs, would compel Griffith to so disregard his personal safety has been studied and investigated, but the answer seems to have been lost to history.

Chapter Twenty-Three

Aftermath—Snipers and a Scrappy Lieutenant: Chartres, August 16–19, 1944

Earlier in the day, before Griffith had left Chartres Cathedral to drive to the Thirty-Eighth's assembly area, he had reported the cathedral clear of Germans. One reason we know it was clear when he did so is that Father Paul Douin, in his diary for the day, described his before-noon encounter with the tall, rifle-carrying American officer who had come into the cathedral through its north door looking for Germans and had sought the priests' help to locate the tower stairs, had climbed the towers, and had confirmed that at the moment he had found no Germans—neither artillery spotters nor snipers—anywhere in the towers or elsewhere in the building. Douin did not learn the American officer's name but was struck by his imposing presence and had initially feared that he might have shot Douin and his fellow priest in the chaos of the moment before learning that they were clerics.

That afternoon, after he had known the American officer had left, Douin heard shots and saw street fighters shooting up at the towers and yelling about snipers hiding there, a sign that Germans must have reentered the cathedral from time to time and somehow gained access to the towers.

Through the sixteenth, the Americans had sent only the Twenty-Third Armored Infantry Battalion into the zone, not yet sufficient infantry-troop strength to conduct house-to-house searches. During and after Griffith's drive to the Thirty-Eighth's assembly area, scores of previously defeated German soldiers, who had escaped from other battles, continued to gather and reassemble at Chartres and were being resupplied and redirected by local German commanders to reenter the city—or may never have left and still hid in cellars and on rooftops sniping to sow chaos and inflict injury and death on American soldiers, French Resistance fighters, monuments, and bridges.

Thus, toward the mid- and late afternoon of the sixteenth, well after Griffith's inspection and departure, a Father Launay, along with Father Douin—and a handful of American news correspondents—had witnessed German riflemen shooting intermittently from the cathedral's towers. And at least once during that period, a half dozen Germans—who had somehow entered the towers and were shooting as a group—and French resisters were shooting back. American infantrymen and armed French civilians had crouched at corners and had peered from behind walls as they fired hour after hour at what they believed were German snipers perched up there. From the street below the towers, numerous nicks were visible in the scrollwork of stone where bullets had hit, but no serious structural damage had been inflicted. Douin reported that he'd heard that German soldiers had been ordered, in the course of their retreat from the city, to snipe from the north tower and to blow up the historic Porte Guillaume gate to the city and some bridges.

The northern tower's many openings made it attractive to the German snipers. The sniping and the counterfire peaked that afternoon as the bells rang out at 3:00 p.m. in their normal fashion, as they'd done for ages. Only this time they did so as Germans were despoiling the city.

Inside, at about the same time, Douin and Father Cassegrain felt things had calmed down a bit. They wanted to leave by the south door but thought it wasn't prudent to do so, because when Douin had looked out that door, he saw an American soldier, with a carbine, at the corner of the small street running up to the south door of the cathedral, shooting in the direction of the bell towers. The priest thought the soldier didn't know that there were Americans in the gallery and that he risked shooting at the first head that he saw up there. Having seen the priests signaling to him, he ran over to the entrance of the south door and finally understood that there may not just be suspected Germans up in the towers but also at least one American soldier in pursuit of Germans. Earlier he had heard the snipers in the tower sniping busily and armed civilians in the streets and alleys returning the fire ten for one. By 5:00 p.m., the sniping from the tower had died down, the city at last appearing to be under American control.

According to the notes of Father Douin, he and his companion priest spent the remainder of the afternoon with scraps of boards, hammer, and pincers, repairing the doors to the cathedral's kitchen storeroom and its Chapel of the Sacred Heart, which had been battered by explosions during the night.

At about 6:30 p.m., Douin was about to set out to pay a long-delayed visit to the Carmelite convent, two miles north of the cathedral, to deliver a bundle of old newspapers and clean white leaflets salvaged from the office material in his seminary quarters. But as he was leaving the cathedral via the west doors, rain started to fall again. He went back in through the same doors but learned that the north doors had been locked. He was standing by the south door thinking about what to do when he saw three people walking around the choir toward him in front of the Chapel of the Sacred Heart.

One was Father Guédou, who was accompanied by an American officer in uniform and a young girl. She was a "Nogentise," a former prisoner of the Germans at Nogent, who explained that she was acting as the interpreter for the American and that he had come to investigate reports that that morning Germans had been in the bell towers. As he left, the officer asked everyone to repeat the names and duties of the two priests, Fathers Finet and Guédou, who were interrogated, so he could make a written record. When he was done, he walked out the south door into the square where his jeep was waiting. The officer jumped into the jeep, and the driver pirouetted the jeep south, away from the cathedral, to pursue the investigation.

Father Douin talked then with Monsieur Manuel, who recounted German atrocities that had occurred that morning against Resistance members near the Place des Épars and the Avenue Maunoury, three blocks south of the prefecture. Monsieur Manuel said, "Mr. Tuvache managed to survive by pretending he was dead, but his son didn't make it, the Germans firing their machine guns without pity on the pile of cadavers in front of them. So this is war, and this time, here."

Thus, through the evening of the sixteenth—the Germans continuing to reenter the city of Chartres, counterattack, and redeploy to oust advancing American units and defend against their penetration—the battle for Chartres continued around the city, despite intervals of relative peace and quiet, which had drawn Chartres' citizens out into the streets for intermittent celebrations and displays of reprisal against collaborators.

The next morning, the seventeenth, at 06:00, a Captain Johnston of the Seventh Armored Division Eighty-Seventh Cavalry Mechanized Reconnaissance Squad, while scouting through Lèves, discovered Griffith's body and notified corps headquarters.

At CP 7 in Courville-sur-Eure, Griffith's corps headquarters colleagues and superiors took his death hard. The corps had suffered significant losses. That morning's casualty list handed to General Walker reported eleven killed; twenty wounded, sick and injured; and forty-nine missing. The corps had captured three hundred additional prisoners besides the three hundred they had already evacuated. More than one hundred other prisoners still huddled under corps detention during the night in an area threatened by enemy troops, requiring reassignment of an antiaircraft battalion for protection during the night.

Even in the feverishly busy headquarters, so close to the corps' next objective, all took time out to honor Griffith. Staff officers located the best casket available in Chartres, and an Army mortician prepared him for a temporary formal military burial, which was conducted by the corps on the afternoon of the seventeenth in a temporary cemetery in a plowed-up field surrounded by trees at Saint-Cornielle, seventy miles southwest of Chartres, nine miles northeast of Le Mans. A bugler sounded taps, and more than two dozen corps headquarters officers and staff stood at attention, facing Griffith's flag-draped and flower-covered casket, which would be marked by a simple white wooden cross until later reburial.

Back at Chartres, more Germans were showing up as each hour passed. According to eyewitness newspaper reporters at the scene, late that afternoon street fighting was still going on, and snipers were again firing persistently from the north tower of the cathedral. Rather than destroy the tower with heavy fire to dislodge the German gunners, Americans and Frenchmen used only small arms. Hence the lengthy resistance. It is not clear why the cathedral had not been secured by the Americans.

Late that afternoon, snipers were still firing from one of the bell towers as the American forces consolidated their position in the area and pressed on and after the Germans, who were fleeing in several directions. Another reporter wrote that into the afternoon a half dozen snipers were still holding out in the tower and drawing counterfire from local patriots which put fresh nicks in the tower's tracery. The houses along the streets showed marks of a tank battle and one disabled American tank was pulled up on the sidewalk.

But even on the afternoon of August 17, German attacks continued in the city. At 2:00 p.m., two American newspaper reporters were in the cathedral being shown around by the curate and cathedral historian.

They had begun in the parapet below the Roman tower, from which they'd heard Americans firing on German snipers. They climbed further into the tower hoping to get a view through binoculars all he way to Versailles, but as they reached the midway point, above the belfry on a narrow, winding stone stairway, a shell hit the other tower, sending masonry and clouds of stone dust billowing over the towers and rooftops. In less than a minute, two other shells came over, one of which hit the other tower. The reporters' driver was waiting in the street. They tried to take a shorter route down, but the curate struggled to unlock an ancient door, and they had to retrace their steps and went instead onto a catwalk around an outside railing never meant for support and within view of anyone, including any snipers, below. After climbing, crawling, and stooping, they arrived behind the main altar and made their way to the street and safety.

At 3:00 p.m. on August 17, the Seventh Armored Division was ordered by General Walker's Twentieth Corps to clean out Chartres completely, commencing its attack at 4:00 p.m. with additional artillery support.

Still, the Germans weren't giving up. Walker realized that the corps faced losing the newly liberated city, so he rushed in a combat team of the Fifth Infantry Division. Large and still organized groups of German troops occupied portions of the city and the woods to the south with many forty-millimeter and eighty-eight-millimeter antiaircraft weapons, but corps troops eliminated those pockets of resistance with hard, close fighting, supported by concentrations from corps artillery. One group of over eight hundred Germans, commanded by a colonel, surrendered as a group.

On the eighteenth, General Walker ordered his Seventh Armored Division to pull its tanks away from the city into an improvised tank park. He gave his Fifth Infantry Division the mission of taking the town with a third attack, following the Seventh Armored Division, as the Fifth Infantry Division had done with prior towns in the race across France.

This task fell to the Fifth's Eleventh Combat Team, including the Eleventh Infantry Regiment and others, to provide more riflemen, and it secured the town by a final assault on the morning of August 19, taking more than 1,500 German prisoners, with an estimated 1,800 German dead, and capturing many vehicles and stores and two airfields in the vicinity together with thirty to forty destroyed planes. A separate task force of the Thirty-Eighth Armored Infantry Battalion took control of the area around the airport. The American forces suffered approximately one hundred casualties during the battle for Chartres.

On the seventeenth alone, more than a dozen FFI members had been killed in Chartres' city center, and many more were injured, including both FFI and among the civilian population, due to artillery fire from unknown sources.

Many FFI complained that they could have avoided many losses of men had they received from the Americans the use of one or two armored vehicles, but the US Army was not inclined to receive directives from such unofficial soldiers with little experience. Firemen of Chartres intervened to fight blazes ranging from Lèves on the north to Luisant on the south along Maunoury Avenue, but lack of water made the fight impossible.

Kenneth Foree, a prominent editor with the *Dallas Morning News*, would investigate Griffith's death during the year following, and he interviewed General Walker and various corps headquarters officers and other witnesses. Foree would write in mid-1945 that "Young as colonels go, being only forty-three," Griffith was a big, bulldog, driving fighter who had everything, said his associates, that could be expected of a West Pointer, [and who'd] proved a marked addition to the desert staff, became a training expert and had so much punch that at times he had to be held back. To him there was only one kind of soldier—one who gave everything he had.

At Chartres Griffith gave everything he had.

But two decades later, *Reader's Digest* published in its August 1965 issue a story written by a renowned war correspondent, Gordon Gaskill, for its series of First-Person Articles (inviting "hitherto unpublished narrative" stories of "an unusual personal experience," for which the magazine had awarded Gaskill one of its First Person Awards). In his story, "The Day We Saved Chartres Cathedral," Gaskill claimed that he and his fellow correspondents in Chartres on August 16, 1944, had saved the cathedral by staring down a young trigger-happy artillery lieutenant.

Some could interpret it as a second history of what happened at the cathedral that day, but others, including Griffith's family—and some of Griffith's war colleagues, including William Dugan, Robert Cullen, Melville Stark, and even Colonel William Collier—would take umbrage. Some accused the author of deceit.

A more charitable view of Gaskill's story could be that—assuming his could also be true—both events may have occurred hours apart, with Griff's inspection (as told by Father Douin and reported by Dugan, Stark, and Cullen and confirmed by American and French military authorities soon after in official citations) having occurred before or around noon, whereas Gaskill's tale occurred considerably later into the afternoon. Gaskill's evoked a somewhat different scene at the cathedral that day, here paraphrased:

Gaskill and two companion war correspondents, Clark Lee and Bob Reuben, had trailed behind the Third US Army. The day before, fifty miles to the west at Third Army headquarters, an American colonel at a command tent had briefed the three about the cathedral, reminding them of the supreme commander's standing order that American artillerymen were to avoid hitting historic monuments, including the cathedral, and were to aim at only observed point targets.

If the Germans don't hurt the building, the colonel explained, "of course we won't, either, unless absolutely necessary. In such matters, we're following Eisenhower's directive to the letter."

The correspondents had arrived in Chartres on the sixteenth, following behind the lead American forces, and had just sat down to a surprising special lunch of eggs, sausage, and salad at a Chartres hotel when they were interrupted by a frantic Frenchman who ran into the dining room, crying out, "The Americans are going to shell the cathedral!"

They jumped out to the reporters' jeep and sped up the hill to the large square a few hundred yards from the cathedral. The square was filled with Frenchmen who were scared almost silent by what they saw: three American tanklike vehicles, with snub-nosed guns for close-range shelling, had come to a halt facing the cathedral and were aiming their barrels upward at the cathedral's towers.

The reporters pushed their way through the crowd to position themselves nose-to-nose with a young Seventh Armored Division lieutenant in charge of the guns who was facing down the shouts of an enraged Frenchman in a major's uniform and failing to understand what the major was saying, so one correspondent asked what was up. The lieutenant pointed up to the cathedral and said, "The Jerries must have left some artillery spotters behind, up there. We're going to knock them out."

But just how, asked the reporter, did the lieutenant know that German spotters were up there?

"Bound to be," the lieutenant said. "Can't you hear those shells falling? That means they've got a spotter somewhere around, and those towers are the obvious place."

The French major frantically spelled out to the reporter—who spoke some broken French—that of course the locals had been suspicious about the cathedral and had organized a guard that for the last several days had kept close watch on it. The major concluded, "I can assure you that there is not one single German in the cathedral, and thus there is no need to fire on it."

The reporter translated these words to the lieutenant, who scoffed, "Ahhh, I don't trust him."

The French major pleaded, "Surely you can see this is not observed artillery fire!"

The lieutenant ignored both the major and the correspondents and ordered his men to load and aim. The crowd let out a murmur of fright, and with more pleading with the reporters, the major convinced them to employ their reporters' savvy to convince the lieutenant to allow a group of civilians twenty minutes to search the cathedral inside.

The lieutenant narrowed his eyes and barked back, "What the hell are you guys butting in for? You're civilians. It's none of your damn business what I do!"

Yet the reporters were making it their business right then. One of them recounted to the lieutenant Eisenhower's standing directive that in cases like this the lieutenant was not to fire on the cathedral unless he was sure the enemy was using it militarily—and to the harm of the Allies—and said, "Even if you don't trust this Frenchman's story, you ought to know that this is not observed fire. It's falling at random. It has not hit a single American soldier or vehicle." In fact, he noted, it was hitting and killing French, and yet it was the French who were insisting that there were no Germans up in the towers guiding the fire, and he implored the lieutenant again to let the Frenchmen take twenty minutes to check the church.

The lieutenant just ignored the reporters until one of them blurted out, "I'll take your name personally to Eisenhower, and I can promise you that you'll be the sorriest lieutenant in the American Army."

The reporters had all just interviewed Eisenhower over several days. They thought they could—and would—get through to the general if they were forced by the lieutenant to do so, but the lieutenant—red in the face—answered through tight lips, "Okay. Twenty minutes, but that's all. I'll be watching and waiting, right here."

The correspondents translated the lieutenant's answer and heard the crowd's sigh of relief. The French major and the reporter hopped into the jeep and rushed to the cathedral. The locals knew the layout of the cathedral and split into two groups, one for each tower. The Americans followed the major's group all the way up the long climb through the spiral stairs and were panting for air by the time they reached the top. They found that the French major had been right: no one—German or other—was in either tower. One correspon-

dent rang the heaviest of the imposing bells of the tower, with three shorts and a long—a Morse code V for victory—and the crowd below hooted its rapture. But by then, the lieutenant and his mobile guns had disappeared.

In 1965, Griffith's brother Philip and other members of Griffith's family would become disturbed on discovering the existence of Gaskill's *Reader's Digest* story. Griffith's family wrote to the magazine's editors and asked for a retraction and also contacted Army headquarters in Washington requesting an investigation. The magazine's editors stood by their story but pointed out that their Paris-based fact-checker had told them that she'd heard a half dozen stories from Americans and Frenchmen alike to the effect that they had saved the cathedral, and she thought they could all be true, but the important thing was that the cathedral had been saved.

Army headquarters, which shortly after the battle for Chartres had posthumously awarded Griffith the Distinguished Service Cross, replied by letter to the family that the Army's award to Griffith was based on certified statements by four witnesses, which by 1965 were no longer available. Headquarters wrote that there was a possibility that both the story of Griffith's inspection and the story of Gaskill's adventure might be correct and that both "accounts described could have occurred during the heat and confusion of battle that day."

Philip Griffith would also write to Kenneth Foree in October 1965—two decades after publication of Foree's article based on his own investigation—and ask Foree what the editor thought of Gaskill's account and of Gaskill's claim that he and his companions saved the cathedral. Foree would write back:

Maybe Gordon Gaskill is right. Maybe it was saved twice. Maybe also the dust of twenty years accumulation lowers the visibility of a person and covers or softens the facts, or enlarges them, or distorts them.

But this I know damn well. That Walton Walker, a tough general if I ever met one, told me the story and if the tanks and infantry had already gone through I don't know what the hell an artilleryman was preparing to shell the cathedral for. He was in no danger and it was always a favorite sport or tactics of the Krauts to shell the crossroads behind.

I'll stick with General Walker who long since joined Colonel Griffith, and who told me that story only a year or so after the shooting was over.

It is understandable that recognition came to Griff. After all, he'd done a great deal more in addition to saving the cathedral and—to boot—had died doing it. Besides, why hadn't other Chartres locals from that crowd in the square stepped forward to honor Gaskill? Also, a search of the US Army's institutional records revealed nothing to confirm that any demands to shoot at the cathedral ever rose to the level of an order. On the contrary, many after-action reports of the various units refer to one or more orders to limit all artillery fire to "observed" shelling—shelling controlled with on-the-ground direct spotting— which was to be directed upon only fixed targets away from the cathedral. Gaskill's story seems simply outweighed by the documentary evidence and the fact that he didn't come forward until twenty years after the events he purported to report.

Yet it also seems clear from the later reports that fighting continued in the center of Chartres and around the cathedral throughout August 16, and on the seventeenth and eighteenth, despite the fact that the Twenty-Third Infantry had moved in and taken positions and set up a headquarters in the northeast part of the city. This condition certainly affords a predicate for an event such as that which Gaskill reports to have indeed actually occurred as he described it in his *Reader's Digest* piece.

At the cathedral, Griff's actions may not have been the only ones that saved the cathedral—and likely were not—but that made them no less actions of valor and importance in the long life of the sacred building. And later, at the battalion assembly area, and later still in Lèves—though he made his decisions quickly—he did not make them in haste. They stemmed from the mind and force of character that made him a fine soldier and from his training and experience that had brought the opportunity to serve his country, his mission, and the people of France.

Allied demolitions experts who arrived at Chartres also found the cathedral at risk of being damaged and possibly destroyed by twenty-two sets of explosives placed on nearby bridges and other structures. Stewart Leonard, one of their team, helped defuse the bombs. Robert M. Edsel, in his book *The Monuments Men*, recounts a later conversation over drinks in a Berlin apartment between Leonard and Bernie Taper, who served as one of the Monuments Men. Taper would ask Leonard whether he thought risking his life to defuse bombs in order to save the cathedral was worth it. That is, "Was art worth a life, Taper wanted to know . . . it was a question that haunted him." Leonard answered,

> "I had that choice . . . I chose to remove the bombs. It was worth the reward."
> "What reward?"
> "When I finished, I got to sit in Chartres Cathedral, the cathedral I had helped save, for almost an hour. Alone."

Overall, it seems that circumstances requiring two life-defining decisions confronted Griffith in the last hours of his life, and both circumstances Griffith attacked with fast—almost spur-of-the-moment—decision making. One of those decisions—to risk his life by searching in the purported fire zone all around the outside of the cathedral and then inside the building when enemy soldiers had been seen inside and were suspected of still being hidden there, and to employ his position of authority to call off any artillery attack on the cathedral—would place Griff's name permanently into the backstory of a great monument, on the long list of people whose valor, dedication, and willingness to take deadly risks created, maintained, or saved the cathedral. Griff's subsequent decision, at the assembly area, to take over command of the armored infantry column and to go ahead of it in his jeep—and, critically, to jump onto that tank and to lead from its top—would cost him his life and would place his name in the long list of soldiers who died with valor while carrying out their mission. And because of Griff's outsized energy and drive, his still-young age and tremendous promise, his principled life and the respect and admiration he'd earned from his superiors, peers, and subordinates, he would be remembered as a great soldier.

General Walker handwrote a letter to Griffith's widow on August 18, expressing his condolences. He revealed to her that when Griffith died he was on a tank leading an infantry unit against a detachment of the enemy, which was holding up the American advance. He also told her that "Griff was my choice as Deputy Chief of Staff and Operations Officer. I leaned heavily upon his judgment. He was a wonderful soldier. His ideals were of the noblest. His record was always superior, and his loss is a severe blow to the XX Corps . . . he died as he would have wished—a soldier performing his duty in a heroic manner." In November 1944, Griffith's widow received the award to him posthumously of the Army Distinguished Service Cross for his heroism at Chartres and Lèves on August 16.

Twentieth Corps fought a successful five-day battle for Chartres from August 15 to August 19, 1944. General de Gaulle visited Chartres to celebrate its liberation on August 19 before taking Rambouillet in preparation for entering Paris. Among the notables to meet him in the square in front of the cathedral was Silvia Monfort.

Twentieth Corps went on to seize a bridgehead seventeen miles east, over the Aunay River, thirteen miles beyond Chartres, and reached the Seine at Melun. To the north, the Seventh Armored Division established various bridgeheads over the Seine, including at Mantes-Gassicourt.

On August 18, the *Stars and Stripes* daily US Armed Forces newspaper reported that General Patton's Third Army troops had neared Paris the night before, after capturing Chartres, Orléans, and Dreux—three capital cities on the main road into the French capital. The German high command reported heavy fighting about twenty-five miles from Paris, on the main Chartres-to-Paris road. The American advance broke through on a sixty-mile front between Orléans and Dreux in what Berlin termed "and all-out drive for Paris" by strong tank and motorized-artillery formations.

A UPI report from Chartres said French Resistance forces fought the Germans in the streets before the American entry and deserved a "lion's share" of the credit for capture of the city. Roger Joly, who had been in combat during the war himself, wrote in his book *La libération de Chartres* (The liberation of Chartres), based on archival research and witness interviews, that

> [t]he liberation of Chartres was essentially the work of the people of Chartres themselves.
>
> The Americans received the order to safeguard this symbolic city, with her cathedral, which Maurice Clavel, then head of the Resistance in Eure-et-Loir, and his partner, Sylvia Montfort, dreamed of liberating.
>
> From 15 to 19 August, the Twentieth US Army Corps fought against German units in often extremely violent combat. Simultaneously, at the cost of severe losses, the local resistance and the Resistance fighters repelled the occupiers outside the city. . . .
>
> The symbolic value remains intact: how and why men of all ages decided one day to risk their lives to liberate the city where, on 17 June 1940, Jean Moulin engaged, alone, in the first battle of the Resistance.

PART IV
POSTWAR

CHAPTER TWENTY-FOUR

Light Returns to Its Shrine: Fongrenon and Chartres, Winter 1944–1945 to November 1950

EARLY ON A WEDNESDAY MORNING AT FONGRENON, NINE MONTHS after the liberation of Chartres, the light of dawn reached down the ventilation shaft and seeped through cracks in the wall of the tiny wooden shack in which that night's security guard had been finishing his overnight shift. Soon after, the guard would learn from the arriving quarry workmen that the German generals in Berlin had finally surrendered and the war in Europe had ended. The guards would no longer need to worry that Nazi informers or Vichy collaborators might denounce them to the Germans or that Gestapo thugs or detectives might pound on or force open the door of the quarry and discover the anti-German cartoon and slogans Frenchmen had scribbled on the walls inside. All of that was over. But the guards continued to worry about other things. Mr. Block, the chief guard, would ask whether Historic Monuments or the National Museums would fund the guards' pay of 1,683 francs per month for keeping watch over the crates and whether the payments would continue as long as security was needed—and indeed whether the government would have the cash to pay it.

They did not suspect that all over Europe, Nazi officers and sympathizers were still scrambling to loot private and public art collections and hide them in salt mines or isolated castles in Austria, Italy, France, Switzerland,

and elsewhere and that teams of Allied monuments officers were chasing those conspirators to recover the treasures before they could slip into the black markets' oblivion. They also probably didn't know that Nazi war criminals were fleeing under false identities through France on fishing and cargo vessels with murky itineraries to unknown ports, where they would assume new identities in South America and elsewhere.

Within weeks, citizens of Chartres and authorities in Paris clamored for Jean Trouvelot to mobilize his Historic Monuments staff to seal the cathedral from moisture by returning the windows and reinstalling them and thereby enabling both Chartres citizens and other French and foreign visitors to again experience their unique light. But before the windows could be moved, work was needed at Fongrenon and Chartres, and along the route between them.

During the war, only a couple of projectiles had hit the cathedral, but the violence of nearby explosions had damaged sections of the vitrex window coverings, particularly along the cathedral's western facade, and had broken, bent, or ripped out iron window frameworks.

Monuments Service contractors had partially repaired the frameworks by makeshift means, and where they could gain access to frameworks as support, they had replaced the vitrex, but now missing and damaged iron armatures would have to be replaced for the windows to be reinstalled.

Restoration work on some of the windows stored in the cathedral's inner crypt by two specialist glassworkers in the space in the basement of the old bishop's palace had continued during the occupation. They had removed one crate at a time from the cathedral's inner crypt across the courtyard, and in each case they had replaced it before taking out another, but not all of the crates concealed in the inner crypt had been accessible. In 1940, in the workers' haste to return the crates from Berchères-les-Pierres to Chartres, they had been unable to pack them in with any logical order, and because the priests had disguised and fenced off the inner crypt "to avoid indiscretions"—as Trouvelot had described their motivations—the glassworkers during the war had finally reached a point at which they had to refrain from further work because they could no longer replace the crates even one at a time in such a manner without attracting attention.

Because of missing windows and destroyed vitrex coverings, the cathedral had been open to the elements. Photos taken during the winter of 1944 and 1945 showed that snow had accumulated around the floors and had covered woodwork, wooden chairs, and the altar, and in winter priests had been unable to celebrate services or other ceremonies, except in the north side aisle of the crypt. Some reported experiencing this problem during the previous winter as well. By mid-1945, moisture had damaged the building, furniture, and organs.

In late August 1945, three months after the German surrender, Trouvelot wrote to René Capitant, who had been installed as the new minister of national education in the provisional government, requesting resources, including trucks, fuel, and men, to repatriate the windows from Fongrenon.

As of late August 1945, around one-third of the windows had been restored, despite the scarcity of materials such as tin and lead, as well as coal, gas, and electricity to heat the soldering irons. Another third of the windows had been largely restored with the exception of those in the crates not accessible in storage at Chartres or hidden at Fongrenon. The last third of the windows comprised stained glass that had yet to be completely restored: the rose windows, the bays of the west facade, and the independent bays of the Chapel of Saint Piatus of Tournai that adjoined the choir.

No sooner had Trouvelot sent his letter than Raoul Doutry, the new minister of reconstruction, toured the cathedral and agreed that the windows should be returned and the building sealed. Jean Chadel, who had become prefect of Eure-et-Loir, assured Trouvelot he would assist in obtaining the necessary fuel, and his secretary-general and Jean Maunoury (again architect of the Historic Monuments Commission) worked to arrange transportation. Trouvelot also discussed preparations for these operations with Jean Verrier, inspector general of historic monuments, who had been active in safeguarding and repatriating artworks.

Doutry and Jean Chadel pledged assistance to obtain five thousand liters of fuel for nine trucks to travel empty to the Dordogne from their home companies in Eure-et-Loir, either in convoy or individually, to pick up the sixty-five tons of window-loaded crates and transport them back from Fongrenon to the cathedral. The Fine Arts Administration also undertook to help arrange for a small truck to be in La Tour-Blanche to shuttle the crates down from the quarry to the highway where the crates could be loaded on the large trucks. Trouvelot engaged master glassmaker Françoise Lorin to begin restoring the windows situated in forty of the crates that had remained at the cathedral. Françoise was the son of Charles Lorin, who had participated in the 1918 removal and later reinstallation of the Chartres windows, as well as in the 1939 removal and concealment of the windows.

Meanwhile, architect Froidevaux again inspected the crates at Fongrenon quarry and found that the seventy were too dilapidated from moisture to make the trip to Chartres. Trouvelot arranged for seventy replacement crates to be manufactured and shipped by truck to Fongrenon.

In October, Trouvelot completed his estimate for all remaining work that could be accomplished prior to return of the stained glass, consisting of repair of metalwork, procurement and assembly of scaffolding, repair of window openings, and replacement of about fifty-three hundred square feet of restored stained glass, all of which would permit full closure of two chapels of the ambulatory, a number of high bays of the nave, and various isolated bays.

Late in October, Trouvelot received word from the departmental dispatcher of Road Transport that only until December 1, 1945, could the Fine Arts Administration have access to nine trucks from trucking companies surrounding Chartres, ranging in size from five to fifteen tons each, which would collectively be capable of transporting the sixty-five tons of window-carrying crates and would have reserved for it five thousand liters of fuel, but the truckers would be required to provide insurance in the amount of one million francs for each five tons of stained glass.

The directorate at the Fine Arts Administration would make 500,000 francs available to the prefecture, of which 350,000 francs would cover the transportation and fuel and 150,000 francs would cover labor and other costs. Inspector General Jean Verrier worked with Trouvelot to prepare for the operation. Froidevaux recommended, and Trouvelot agreed, that on-site assistance at La Tour-Blanche should be arranged, but the Fine Arts Administration had only fifteen days to give definitive instructions and carry out the operation, after which the service would no longer have the transportation at its disposal.

On the last day of October at Chartres, some local children found some incendiary pellets left by the Germans and had some fun throwing these at the wooden containers holding the windows from the Church of Saint-Pierre, and a fire broke out in the chapel of the crypt, and these windows were destroyed. Two other items in the crypt also burned in the blaze: lapidary vestiges of the cathedral's rood screen and a fourteenth-century statue of the Virgin Mary from the tympanum of the open door of the cathedral's Chapel of Saint Piatus of Tournai.

By the start of winter, of the total amount of glass included in Trouvelot's October estimate, approximately six thousand square feet had been reinstalled.

By mid-November, the Fine Arts Administration had instructed the Fongrenon depot's guards to permit removal of the crates. Eight trucks departed to the Dordogne in a pair of convoys in time to arrive on November 25. They were furnished by truckers from Dreux, Nogent-le-Rotrou, Chartres, Charray, Courville, and Gallardon. Glassworker François Lorin left his Chartres workshop with members of his team to travel to Fongrenon to handle the stained glass in the quarry under supervision of Froidevaux, with plans to return with the convoy of trucks. The larger trucks were unable to maneuver all the way to the quarry.

For the loading, unloading, and handling, the service requested that contractors be limited to companies who had worked for Historic Monuments because the service was familiar with their personnel and such companies were familiar with careful handling of artworks. A company that had been previously engaged by the Historic Monuments Service provided a team of men in the Dordogne to haul the crates by cart from the three rooms in which the crates had been concealed deep inside the quarry out to its west doorway and the small truck to shuttle them down the three hundred-foot incline to the road on which the convoy of trucks and other workers waited. From the back of the quarry, a pickup truck loaded the crates and shuttled them to the trucks waiting on the main road near Fongrenon Manor.

The Fine Arts Administration had difficulty arranging food and overnight lodging for the twenty to thirty workers and drivers in the countryside along the convoy's route in the town of La Tour-Blanche. Everywhere people were refusing to house and feed workers, because people had hardly enough food for their own needs. At the site, the loading of crates took two days, and police officers watched over the work during a two-day loading process and accompanied the convoy back to Chartres. The convoy was equipped with fire extinguishers. It left La Tour-Blanche on the twenty-seventh for the two-day return trip to Chartres, the first pair of convoys of trucks, framed by police vehicles, carried most of the sixty-five tons of stained glass to be returned to the cathedral, excluding the windows contained in the seventy damaged crates.

On the morning of November 28, the convoy of trucks delivered the crates to the cathedral, and the crates entered through the Royal Portal doors—first opened for Henry IV in 1594 on the occasion of his coronation and since then opened only on rare occasions. Buntings hung in front of the steps of the forecourt. Workmen placed the crates containing the upper windows in the attics and those for the lower windows in the crypt.

The seventy replacement crates finally arrived at Fongrenon two weeks later, and the windows from the damaged crates were transferred by Lorin's men. The second and last convoy left Périgord on December 15, and by the end of the day all the crates had been stored in the crypts of the cathedral.

By the end of December, Trouvelot submitted another estimate, this time for replacement of sixty-four hundred square feet of fully restored stained glass, which could only be replaced following the repair of the iron frameworks and some secondary repairs. It included the five hundred square feet that had already been newly replaced in addition to five hundred square feet previously replaced.

Once the funds for those items were approved, Trouvelot had hoped to carry out the immediate replacement of all of the windows that by then had been restored, consisting of, approximately, 11,840 square feet. This would complete the reinstallation of the first third of the windows.

For the second third of the windows, the partially restored stained glass, Trouvelot estimated that roughly three-fourths required work that could be done fairly quickly, but the remainder would require more time. He estimated the cost of that work to be 2.5 million francs.

For the final third of the windows—comprising stained glass that had not been restored since the nineteenth century and would require the repair of its leadwork and require large scaffoldings—Trouvelot estimated the cost to be four to five million francs. He also estimated that by November 1947 two-thirds, perhaps more, of the windows would be reinstalled.

Trouvelot estimated that if workers commenced work right away, they should be able to complete all glazing of the upper part of the choir before the onset of winter and could close many of the bays, always beginning with the work that could be completed quickly on the partly restored or easy-to-restore bays—the importance being to close the largest amount of surface area as quickly as possible. But even into the spring of 1946, Trouvelot was unable to obtain official approvals to permit payment for the work.

In March, a snowstorm of exceptional power swept over the region, with snow penetrating the cathedral and requiring architect Maunoury to order a crew to shovel it out.

Given these conditions, still with no official approvals for payment having arrived by late August, Trouvelot took the initiative on August 28, even before receiving final authorization, to appoint Lorin, along with glassmakers from the Gaudin workshop, to carry out the restoration work under Trouvelot's supervision, with work to commence immediately after the holidays, and to perform window restoration work in parallel with window reinstallation.

Trouvelot had reported to his superiors that the glassmaker workshop company had been required to make considerable cash advances of their own, becoming obliged to obtain loans and post collateral to pay their staff, while their lenders had become more and more demanding, refusing to make any more uncollateralized advances. To avoid a slowdown or stoppage of work, he implored his superiors and finally succeeded in having them open a line of credit to be made available to the glassmakers to limit their need to post additional security and further immobilize the companies' financial resources. Official approvals and payment finally came. On-site workshops were assembled and staffed, scaffolding was erected, and the teams of glassmakers went to work.

By October 1948, all of the stained glass had been restored and reinstalled, consisting of 7,595 panels. This work was done by the Lorin and Gaudin workshops under the supervision of architect Trouvelot. The final panel of the final window to be reinstalled was the Annunciation panel (panel 1) of the Incarnation Window (Delaporte's window number 2), which is the center lancet window beneath the western glass rose window.

In the 2007 words of scholar Baritaud, the cathedral, with the reinstallation of that panel—as if to embody the building's twelfth- and thirteenth-century glass heritage—did "once again become the cathedral of light, powerful and colorful, transmitting its true message of beauty and spirituality."

Gene Currivan had written from Chartres in the *New York Times* ten days after Griffith's death, describing his visit to the cathedral with two other reporters, as workmen in the building ended their day of repairs by lighting candles:

CHARTRES CATHEDRAL

Architecture, statuary, stained glass expressed the unity of the human spirit. The workmen on this Cathedral, after the long day, "lighted candles on the carts around the church, over which they kept watch, singing hymns and songs."

If we cannot now re-create the feeling of that age, at least we can look back reverently to "the Court of the Queen of Heaven," as Henry Adams wrote, and be glad that this monument to piety and art has not been ruined by Hitler's Yahoos.

Currivan was not able to witness the windows, as they had not yet been reinstalled. Now they finally had been.

Captain Walter Hancock, another of the Monuments Men—who visited the cathedral the same week as had Currivan and the demolitions expert, Stewart Leonard—is reported to have said about the cathedral after standing inside it, "One could stand within the enclosure and see in a new, overhead light the figures of the kings and queens of Judah and the Christ of the Apocalypse. For a moment, the cathedral seemed both a monument to the Allied triumph and a structure out of time, beyond the war, something that would stand forever, even when the world was gone."

The windows' repatriation and reinstallation had spanned thirty-seven months since Trouvelot's August 1945 letter seeking authorization from the Fine Arts Administration, but the story did not end with the reinstallation. Criticism would arise two years later concerning the administration's placement of seven of the 7,595 panels. Two years later, Carlier published criticisms in his April–June 1950 issue of *Les pierres de France*, complaining about the placement of five of the panels during the reinstallation. A few months later, *Le Monde* published an article echoing Carlier's criticisms. Trouvelot promptly reported to the Fine Arts Administration with his explanation of seven alleged errors raised by Carlier and others and of the corrective action he and his staff had already taken.

In a report of August 5, 1950, Jean Maunoury, the architect of historic monuments for Chartres, reported to the director of architecture of the Fine Arts Administration refuting some of the allegations made by *Le Monde* and replying to Carlier's allegations repeated in the newspaper. Maunoury informed the director of the corrections made and to be made still and fired back a refutation. A month later, Trouvelot filed a report with the director in which he placed the matter in perspective and praised the work done:

> I thought it may be of some use to provide a brief retelling of the history of the removal of the stained glass windows, given that we have read on a number of different occasions various articles containing gross errors, repeated either by complaisance or by ignorance. . . .

NOTE: The reinstallation of the stained glass was carried out by Mr. Lorin, glassworker of Chartres who, with significant dedication by himself and his team made, in particularly difficult conditions, a section of the removal, oversaw the transportation, the restoration work and the reinstallation. Despite their care, the mistakes indicated above have occurred, mistakes that may have been made during the re-placement in the midst of scaffoldings that covered up sections of the windows and made it difficult to take a view of the entirety. Mr. Lorin was the first to recognize and rectify these mistakes. He and his extremely conscientious workers, who love their art, have taken great pains to avoid making mistakes in the Cathedral of Chartres which they have a particularly strong affection for.

Epilogue—Chartres and the United States of America: Spring 1944–1995

Four months after Griff's death, at a ceremony at Fort Hamilton in New York, the US Army post nearest Nell's Brooklyn home, an Army officer pinned the Distinguished Service Cross onto her coat, representing his posthumous award—the second highest award for valor, next to the Medal of Honor—while she stood in a line facing the audience with other family members. The DSC was awarded for Griff's "extraordinary heroism in connection with military operations against an armed enemy." The Army also posthumously awarded him the Purple Heart, the Legion of Merit, and the Silver Star.

Nell and little Alice, and the other members of Griff's family, had been left with many questions about his death. Those who knew Griffith, and most members of his family, attributed the highest of motives and conscious public purposes to Griff's inspection of the cathedral and to his valor in leading the push through Lèves. Some were incensed by any suggestion that Griff's motives could have been anything but the finest. Alice Griffith Irving, Griff's daughter—his only living descendant, aged thirteen when he died—told me seventy years later, "His main mission that fateful day was to investigate the delay of the Seventh Armored Division for their mission to clear the advancement to Paris. He . . . no doubt was appalled that our own forces were on the verge of destroying the cathedral. He was the kind of man who would take charge of a volatile situation. The same attitude led to his death later in the day. He was doing a job someone else should have been doing and was doing poorly."

Another close relative, retired Army lieutenant general Thomas N. Griffin Jr., Griff's nephew—eleven years old when his Uncle Griff was killed—told me in 2013 that, having studied all the facts he could find,

275

including US Army archives, he is certain that there was no actual order to attack the cathedral; in fact, there were orders to the contrary. But he is also sure that there were young soldiers from the Seventh Armored Division who were new to combat and likely would have wanted to destroy the cathedral towers if they thought they were being used by the Germans to spot artillery and that General Eisenhower's order concerning protection of monuments was well known. He also believes that although Griff was on the back of an armored vehicle when he was killed, Griff would not have been leading a column in such a vehicle.

Certain members of Colonel Griffith's Texas-originated nuclear family—Griff's great-nephews, David Coffey and his brother, Kevin Coffey, grandsons of Griff's sister Dorothea Humphrey, the older of Griff's two sisters—revealed that there was perhaps another side to Colonel Griffith's character. David Coffey, a professor of military history, wrote to me in 2014. "From an early age," he said,

> I was attracted to the whole idea of [Colonel Griffith]. He became something of a hero to me. But as I grew older and became an academic historian, I came to wonder if there might be a bit of hagiography involved. I say this only because my main sources of information were his adoring sisters Dorothea (my grandmother) and Harrison [Griffith's sister Tiny]. There was a fierce bond among those Griffith siblings. . . .
>
> I have questions about the story. Certainly, some things don't make a lot of sense. Why would an essential, high-ranking staff officer take such action? What prompted him to grab an M1 and jump on a tank, knowing he was an easy target? He was no doubt destined for higher rank and responsibility. These are questions I can't answer. . . .
>
> Clearly, there were some issues in Colonel Griffith's own family that resulted in separation and divorce. My brother and I have speculated that Colonel Griffith may have been depressed, even reckless as a result. But this doesn't seem to jibe with his career arch or his performance, which from what I do know was well regarded.

Kevin Coffey, David's brother, who later corresponded with me from Scotland, maintains that he is the person of his generation who has showed the most interest in Griff, having talked with Dorothea about Griff, and to a lesser extent with Griff's brothers and sister. Kevin had also met Eugene Schulz and spoken and corresponded with him about Colonel Griffith, including about the different perception of the colonel held by Kevin's side of the family. Kevin wrote:

> One thing that was always clear from my grandmother . . . is that the main reason for not only the split in his marriage to Alice's mother but also for the subsequent cool relations between Griff's family and Alice and family was . . . that her parents might have been less than thrilled and she too might have wondered what she had done [in marrying Griff] once the heady period of infatuation was over. I must stress that this was my grandmother's perception and it might be unfair to the other side. But certain other factors and testimonies over the years lead me to believe it's probably fairly accurate.

Kevin reported that one of Griff's brothers, Lawrence, used to refer to the colonel's death as "Webb's suicide" (Colonel Griffith's siblings called him Web or Webb). Kevin described Colonel Griffith as "pretty taciturn," and he went on to say,

> [Griffith] was a pretty quiet and reserved man. Kind but commanding. The Griffiths were tough people. . . . They were self-sufficient, capable, strong-willed people with a fierce sense of duty and loyalty—to family, to country, to community and friends. They did what needed to be done. There was sometimes a ruthless streak, which surfaced most noticeably in the second born, Lawrence, who was an independent oil man and who was very hard to warm to, but it was present to some extent in all of them. . . .
>
> But I seem to recall that my Aunt Jane (my mother's surviving sister, born the same year the colonel was killed) [said] that the 2nd marriage was no more successful than the first . . . in relation

to the "suicide" claim, I seem to recall a hint that perhaps the Colonel was unhappy in his personal life—couldn't get it right. . . .

It's easy when one reads the account given by Foree, which my grandmother and uncles Lawrence and Philip all believed was accurate, to understand why Lawrence referred to Web's death as suicide.

Griffith's in-law families, both eastern, can be seen in a light somewhat different from his Texas-originated nuclear family. Griff's first wife, Alice, married four more times.

Griff's own family knew him longer and in a sense more intimately. They adored Griff throughout his life, but they knew a private side of him, not necessarily the big bulldog, driving, fighting military training expert who had so much punch that at times he had to be held back.

In 1961, seventeen years after Griffith's death, local leaders in Lèves unveiled an engraved chest-high marble plaque on the wall of the building on the side of the street where Griff had been found dead. The plaque reads, "Ici fut tué le 16 aôut 1944 le Colonel Américain Welburn" (Here was killed on August 16, 1944, the American Colonel Welburn).

Based probably on Griffith's dog tags, someone had mistaken his first name for his last and misspelled it (reading "Griffith, Welborn B. Jr." as "Colonel Welburn"). Since 1961, on every August 16, the town's residents have gathered and placed flowers at the memorial, but Griffith's true identity had remained a mystery to the townsfolk.

Bertrand Papillon—witness as a teenager in 1944 to some of the events surrounding Griffith's death and still a resident of Lèves—had become an amateur historian and had founded a single-room museum in Lèves with memorabilia from the world wars. For years, he had known of the marble plaque that bore the name "Colonel Welburn" but had been unable to learn more about the colonel. Papillon had for years conducted research concerning the liberation of Lèves and had written to governmental and military agencies, both in France and in the United States, seeking information concerning the colonel, without success. He enlisted the help of Marianne Pradoura, an American living in Chartres married to a Frenchman, to translate Papillon's letters into

English. With a stroke of luck, he contacted a diligent archivist at the US Army Personnel Records Center in Saint Louis who consulted an Army history volume using the colonel's unusual first name, Welborn, and found that a Colonel Welborn Barton Griffith had been killed in Lèves on August 16, 1944.

With more help from Mrs. Pradoura, he placed an "In Search Of . . ." ad in the April 1995 *Retired Officers Association* magazine.

Nell Griffith, then eighty-three, and General Griffin both read the magazine. By mid-March, letters and phone calls to Lèves had finally led to the family learning what happened to Colonel Griffith, and the people of Lèves finally learned that the American who had been killed liberating their town had also been the man credited with saving the cathedral.

Chartres and Lèves officials invited Alice and General Griffin and their families to be honored in three ceremonies in Chartres and Lèves on the August 16, 1995, anniversary of Griffith's death. At the cathedral, by special invitation, they passed in procession through the Royal Portal and then heard the "Star Spangled Banner" performed on the cathedral's organ for only the second time in history. Canon Legaux welcomed the guests with a speech, expressing regret that Nell had been too frail to attend, and thanking Mrs. Pradoura and Mr. Papillon for their assistance. He paid homage to all soldiers of the liberation, including those of the Resistance, and said,

> May this moment of shared friendship be not only a moment of remembrance but also an appeal so that no matter where we are or who we might be, we will become artisans of peace in the mutual respect of our differences. . . .
>
> A phrase from Andre Malraux seems to me to be particularly appropriate for the ceremonies today. He wrote: "The only tomb worthy of a hero is in the hearts of the living."

What lessons emerge from the story of the Chartres windows, and Griffith and the cathedral?

One is that we cannot let our differences divide us, because they will, if left unchecked. When people of good will work together and agree to tolerate, listen to, and compromise with each other, humankind can accomplish great things and save the world—or at least a small slice of it.

Griff brings to mind one of Shakespeare's unsung characters, the servant in *King Lear*, one of Cornwall's minions who was long accustomed to doing Cornwall's bidding but who objects to Cornwall's torture of Gloucester and speaks up, compelled to stop what he is witnessing. In response, Cornwall runs the servant through with his sword, killing him.

Griff's situation is different, of course, but we feel Griff's loss no less. Scholar Stephen Greenblatt explains, "Shakespeare did not believe that the common people could be counted upon as a bulwark against tyranny. . . . In *King Lear*'s nameless servant, however, he created a figure who serves as the very essence of popular resistance to tyrants. That man refuses to remain silent and watch. It costs him his life, but he stands up for human decency. Though he is a very minor figure with only a handful of lines, he is one of Shakespeare's great heroes."

Griff, too, was not of the elite military class. He was of the common people. Yet he spoke up and gained perhaps an uncanny sense of inner strength that almost catapulted him into action—leading the way for the armored column in a manner that took him out of his element and cost him his life. That he stumbled in that process, by perhaps needlessly exposing himself to danger, does not require that we honor him less.

A person may be remembered, may leave a mark or a message, not only by what he writes but also by other art he creates or by his actions. Colonel Griffith will be remembered for his actions.

Griffith's story is one of loss and sacrifice, but also, if Griffith consciously acted to save the cathedral, his sacrifice is akin to the stories of miracles, blessings, healings, birth, death, and resurrection reflected in Chartres' very windows for nine hundred years.

AFTERWORD: AUTHOR'S NOTE

THIS IS A WORK OF NONFICTION. MY SOURCES HAVE BEEN NOTED IN THE text, notes, and bibliography. I have considered the correctness and reliability of various sources and compared them to each other and have drawn inferences based on the entirety of what I have uncovered and application of my common sense. In certain segments, I have told the story as I believe it happened. In some contexts, I have reasoned from historical context and included details that I believe would have been present, including, in a few instances, adopting names for characters who are known to have existed and for whom I deemed selecting a name necessary in order to communicate the story with reasonable efficiency, avoiding qualification that would have detracted from my ability to communicate what happened. That is, as Professor Mazzeo has written, the "details are, in all cases, based on the scaffolding of known facts, but where there are gaps in the scaffolding—and some gaps are significant—I have made the leap of inference based on my best judgment and larger knowledge of the period and the people about whom I am writing" (Mazzeo, *Irena's Children*, 267).

I have also, in isolated cases, offered a description of what I believe were certain characters' own ideas or concerns or sensations, and I reframed or created some limited dialogue. In each such case, this again is based on my extrapolation from the "factual scaffolding," as Mazzeo would put it, and my sense of the speaking character based on my research, including witnesses' recollections. For any readers who care to evaluate the record on their own, I can be reached through the publisher.

ACKNOWLEDGMENTS

In my research for this book, the Griffith family members were kind, generous, and helpful, beginning with the colonel's daughter, Alice Irving, and her husband, Frederick Irving (US Army, ret.), and including offspring of the colonel's siblings and in-laws—Kevin Coffey, David Coffey, Dick Griffith, Jane Henegar, and Thomas N. Griffin (US Army, ret.). In addition, Gary Hendrix, husband of a deceased niece of the colonel, provided immeasurable help to me by assembling items collected from the family and selecting from voluminous correspondence by Virginia Harrison (Tiny) DeKay, a priceless resource. I am grateful to the family for sharing with me their memories, impressions, photos, and documents. I also owe gratitude to Eugene Schulz for relating to me his World War II experiences, including from his time working for the colonel, and for producing his memoir.

I also thank Alice Irving for acquainting me with Bertrand Papillon and thank Thomas Griffin for introducing me to Marianne Pradoura. I thank Mr. Papillon for generously guiding me and my wife through his museum, Lèves, and the cathedral. And I am grateful to Mrs. Pradoura for producing her translation of the diary of Father Douin and for sharing with me the remarkable story of discovery of the diary.

For her excellent research assistance and translation work, I am grateful to Crystal Bennes, who is also a talented stained-glass artist.

All translations from the original French of quoted writings of Achille Carlier, Jean Zay, Jean Moulin, and Jean Trouvelot (except for the Trouvelot *Passive Defense Report*) are by Crystal Bennes. Translations of excerpts from Theirry Baritaud's *La Depose* brochure are by Noelle Britte. All other translations from the original French are by me, for which I employed open-source tools (and in addition, for translation of the Trouvelot *Passive Defense Report*, French transcription assistance of Eva Morath), and for any errors in all such translations I assume sole responsibility.

I am deeply grateful to Mike Magnuson for his mentoring and editorial consulting that improved most pages of this manuscript, and I thank Scott Korb, Sanjiv Bhattacharya, and Debra Gwartney—together with Mike and members of the faculty of the Pacific University MFA faculty—for their guidance.

My thanks also to Timothy K. Clark and Luke Norczyk for reading my manuscript and sharing their insightful comments.

I also thank Michael Clement, Patrick Cointepoix, and Thierry Baritaud for generously furnishing photographs.

Time and again, people who did not know me generously answered my questions and introduced me to other resources. They included writers Bill Neal, Elizabeth Karlsgodt, Mary Clooney-Robinson, Michael J. Klug, Claudine Lautier, and engineer/writer Thierry Baritaud. The staffs of the following institutions also graciously aided me: in Paris, the Médiathèque d'accueil et de recherche des archives nationales, Médiathèque Charenton, and Médiathèque de l'architecture et du patrimoine; in Chartres, Archives départmentales de la Eure-et-Loir, International Stained-Glass Centre, and Diocese of Chartres. In the United States, I sought information from the United States Military Academy at West Point; US National Archives and Records Administration; Twentieth Corps Association; Cushing Memorial Library; Archives of Texas A&M University; Corps of Cadets Center at Texas A&M University; Firestone Library of Princeton University; Salt Lake City Public Library; Library of Congress; Monuments Men Foundation; *Goldsboro News-Argus*, North Carolina; and in Quanah, Texas: Hardeman County Historical Museums, Thompson Sawyer Public Library, and *Quanah Tribune-Chief*.

My deepest gratitude goes to my wife, Elizabeth Russell Pollak, lost to cancer in 2019, to whom I dedicate this book. I cherish her, and we miss her more than words can express. She lived and breathed this project alongside me from the beginning. Without her steady support—giving me space and sustaining inspiration—this book would not have emerged.

I endeavor to stand, of course, on the shoulders of the thousands of writers and scholars who have devoted energy, passion, time, and effort to studying and writing about Chartres Cathedral. The concept of dwarfs standing on the shoulders of giants has been traced to Bernard of Chartres in the twelfth century and repeated often. A 1989 bibliography of publications concerning the cathedral consumes nine hundred pages: Jan van der Meulen, Deborah Cole, and Rüdiger Hoyer, *Chartres: Sources and Literary Interpretation; A Critical Bibliography* (Boston: G. K. Hall, 1989).

NOTES ON SOURCES

NOTES TO PREFACE

ix   "More than three thousand years": Susannah Cullinane, Hamdi Alkhshali, and Mohammed Tawfeeq, "Tracking a Trail of Historical Obliteration: ISIS Trumpets Destruction of Nimrud," CNN, April 13, 2015, http://www.cnn.com/2015/03/09/world/iraq-isis-heritage/.

x   "He had spent his life preserving antiquities": Frederik Pleitgen, "Saddest Job in the World? The Race to Save Syria's History from Obliteration," CNN, August 20, 2015, https://www.cnn.com/2015/08/19/middleeast/syria-antiquities-damascus/index.html.

x   "Syrian official": Syria's director of the General Department of Antiquities and Museums, Maamoun Abdulkarim, quoted in Pleitgen, "Saddest Job in the World."

x   "Refusing to pledge allegiance to ISIS": Don Melvin, Ralph Ellis, and Salma Abdelaziz, "Group: ISIS Beheads Expert Who Refused to Reveal Location of Valuable Antiquities," CNN, updated August 20, 2015, http://www.cnn .com/2015/08/18/middleeast/isis-executes-antiquities-expert/.

x   "Looting architectural sites": Melvin, Ellis, and Abdelaziz, "ISIS Beheads Expert"; Cullinane, Alkhshali, and Tawfeeq, "Tracking a Trail," quoting Stuart W. Manning, director of the Cornell Institute of Archaeology and Material Studies and chair of the Department of Classics at Cornell University.

x   "Violation of history": Elise Blackwell, *Hunger* (New York: Little, Brown, 2003), 135.

x   "Lectures about great cathedrals": William R. Cook, *The Cathedral*, DVD lecture series (Chantilly, VA: Teaching Company, 2010).

xi   "Multiple blog references": For example, Steven Payne, "Top Comments: The American Solider Who Saved Chartres Cathedral," *Daily Kos*, December 20, 2014, http://www.dailykos.com/story/2014/12/20/1350669/-Top-Comments -The-American-GI-who-saved-Chartres-Cathedral. This is one example of many similar blog posts. Another, with links to more, is by Dennis Aubrey, "The Monuments Man of Chartres," *American Friends of Chartres*, accessed March 28, 2019, http://www.friendsofchartres.org/aboutchartres/colonelwelborngriffin/.

xii   "Common source": His citation reads as follows:

> The President of the United States of America, authorized by Act of Congress, July 9, 1918, takes pride in presenting the Distinguished

Service Cross (Posthumously) to Colonel Welborn Barton Griffith, Jr. (ASN: 0-16194), United States Army, for extraordinary heroism in connection with military operations against an armed enemy while serving as Operations Officer (G-3) with Headquarters, XX Corps, in action against enemy forces on 16 August 1944 at Chartres and Lèves, France. On 16 August 1944, Colonel Griffith entered the city of Chartres, France, in order to check the actual locations and dispositions of units of the 7th Armored Division which was occupying the city. Upon observing fire being directed at the cathedral in the center of the city, with utter disregard for his own safety, Colonel Griffith, accompanied by an enlisted man, searched the cathedral and finding that there were no enemy troops within, signaled for cessation of fire. Continuing his inspection of outlying positions north of the city, he suddenly encountered about fifteen of the enemy. He fired several shots at them, then proceeded to the nearest outpost of our forces at which point a tank was located. Arming himself with an M1 rifle and again with complete disregard for his own safety, Colonel Griffith climbed upon the tank directing it to the enemy forces he had located. During the advance of the tank he was exposed to intense enemy machine-gun, rifle, and rocket-launcher fire and it was during this action, in the vicinity of Lèves, France, that he was killed.

General Orders: Headquarters, Third US Army, General Orders No. 75 (October 21, 1944).

xiv   "Making him a saint": Tilar Mazzeo, *Irena's Children* (New York: Gallery Books, 2016), xii.

xv   "Methods for protection of monuments": André F. Noblecourt, *The Protection of Cultural Property in the Event of Armed Conflict*, Museums and Monuments VIII, trans. from original French text of August 1956 (Paris: United Nations Educational, Scientific and Cultural Organization, 1958), text available online at https://unesdoc.unesco.org/ark:/48223/pf0000071205, 130; Elizabeth Karlsgodt, *Defending National Treasures: French Art and Heritage under Vichy* (Palo Alto: Stanford University Press, 2011), 102–18.

xvi   "Professor Peter Sahlins": John Hickey, "Notre Dame Fire like the Burning of the Library of Alexandria, Historian Says," *Berkeley News*, University of California, Berkeley, April 15, 2019, https://news.berkeley.edu/2019/04/15/notre-dame-fire-a-loss-to-the-french-that-americans-cant-completely-visualize/.

NOTES TO PROLOGUE

xvii   "Crown jewel was its cathedral": Reims Cathedral's naves were the length of a football stadium. It was France's equivalent of Westminster Abbey, site of coronations of kings, royal weddings, and funerals since the Middle Ages, built in the twelfth century on the site of the basilica where Clovis I was baptized by Saint Remi, bishop of Reims, in 496, which in turn had been built on the site of Roman baths.

xviii   "He knew then what it meant": Maurice Landrieux, *The Cathedral of Reims: The Story of a German Crime*, trans. Ernest E. Williams (London: Kegan Paul, Trench, Trubner & Co., 1920), 11.

xviii   "German officers couldn't believe": Landrieux, *Cathedral of Reims*, 12. His phrasing, quoting Abbé Andrieux's diary from two days later.

xix   "Prussians claimed . . . the shelling was a mistake": Landrieux, *Cathedral of Reims*, 13. Two Prussian officers had set out for Reims but hadn't returned, so the Prussian commander assumed they had been taken prisoner and so ordered the batteries to make the city suffer the consequences. The two officers had never even set foot in Reims. The bombardment (182 shells) killed 60 and injured another 140.

xix   "Abbé Rémi Thinot": Landrieux would later write—in his 1920 book—a memorial footnote dedicated to Thinot, praising his dedication to the cathedral, his "ardent nature," his almost "foolhardy courage," and his contribution as photographer of a third of the many photos in the book. Thinot joined the French Army in January 1915 and was killed while performing his duty as chaplain, meriting a military citation, which read, "Having gone into the trenches at the moment of an attack to perform his ministerial functions, he was there mortally wounded whilst going to the succor of soldiers buried under the débris of a mine explosion, and while exhorting the men to do their duty." Landrieux, *Cathedral of Reims*, 4, n. 1.

xix   "Violent gust of air": Landrieux, *Cathedral of Reims*, 17.

xix   "Hurt to see their Joan of Arc": Landrieux, *Cathedral of Reims*, 21.

xx   "Electricity in the air": Landrieux, *Cathedral of Reims*, 22; Landrieux's phrasing.

xx   "Proclamation that the hostages would be hung": Landrieux, *Cathedral of Reims*, 23; the phrasing is that of the proclamation.

xx   "French troops entered the city": Relieved to see them go, most townspeople had feared they would have been next to be ordered to "host" German officers. Word circulated that a German staff colonel had said on Friday evening to his French host, "Tomorrow you will hear a violent cannonade. You will probably have the moral satisfaction of seeing your own troops back; but behind Reims, on the heights, we shall stand firm, and we shall not loosen our grip upon you." Landrieux, *Cathedral of Reims*, 24.

xx   "Red Cross flag": On the seventeenth, Abbé Andrieux brought a third Red Cross flag that eventually weathered all storms, ensuring that at all times two flags were visible on the cathedral, which continued to float on the ruins, long after the ensuing fire. Landrieux, *Cathedral of Reims*, 27.

xx   "Pity for the coming disaster": Landrieux later learned that the French had decided that if the Germans had wished to make the cathedral a shelter for German wounded, why not make those wounded a safeguard for the cathedral, since an army does not fire on its own wounded? Or, "at any rate, one had not seen it done yet." Landrieux, *Cathedral of Reims*, 25.

xxi   "Only a chaplain": Abbé Prullage, curate at Stadholm, in Westphalia.

xxi   "Shell crashed through . . . archbishop's palace": Landrieux, *Cathedral of Reims*, 28.

xxi   "Five German officers among the wounded": "There was no room for mistake [*sic*]," Landrieux concluded, "and the wounded German officers—there were five of them—were under no illusion" about their fellow German units: "they were aiming at the cathedral!" Landrieux, *Cathedral of Reims*, 29.

xxi   "Shells . . . fell throughout the town":

> One's ears followed the direction of the shells. One could feel them com-ing—sneaking, menacing; then suddenly bursting quite close, or maybe passing with an angry whistle over our heads, to carry destruction a little farther away. With a grip of the heart we marked the places where they fell. We recorded the wound without having seen the blow: a falling wall, a roof broken in, like a soft crust beneath a furious, invisible shock; then a jet of smoke, black, thick, heavy, which spurted upwards, enormous and powerful, as from the crater of a volcano, the noise of the explosion reaching us a long time afterwards.

Landrieux, *Cathedral of Reims*, 30.

xxii   "Soldiers in their red uniform trousers": Associated Press, "Conditions in Vienna Reported as Normal," *Dallas Morning News*, November 23, 1914, 7.

xxii   "Killing their own soldiers": The major was a Dr. Pflümacker. Landrieux, *Cathedral of Reims*, 32.

xxii   "Stone chunks littered": Landrieux, *Cathedral of Reims*, 34.

xxiii   "The a cappella lament": Landrieux wrote, "One had the impression of a hostile power, tenacious, stubborn, insistent, in a merciless struggle to overthrow the temple. The shells bit into the stone, broke down the walls, battered in the roofs, made havoc with statues, pinnacles, bell turrets, and counterforts. But the bruises were not deep enough, nor the wounds wide enough, the mass of the structure was not broken; the cannon had not succeeded in that. The monstrous howitzers had not arrived. The noble mutilated building still stood erect, more majestic than ever under the tempest." Landrieux, *Cathedral of Reims*, 38.

xxiii   "Stained-glass rose window burst": Landrieux described the breaking of the rose window:

> Soon we heard a hard cracking noise: half of the Great Rose broke, and a thick smoke entered through the breach. And just at this moment a ray of sunlight, the only one we had seen during this day of fog and rain, filtered softly through the gaping wound, slowly traveled along the nave to the sanctuary, caressed the altar, remained there a moment, and then disappeared.
>
> Man's effort proves powerless: we are defeated.
>
> The arches are still trembling beneath the shells.
>
> With a terrifying rumble, and the sound of breaking and crashing, the scaffolding fell on the Parvis, and fire flakes flutter in eddies under the roofs.

Landrieux, *Cathedral of Reims*, 40.

xxiv "Cast the straw out": Landrieux emerged believing that but for the straw in such quantities in the naves, the fire may not have caused so much damage. In the end, a spark from a shell was all that was needed to cause the huge blaze. Landrieux, *Cathedral of Reims*, 39.

xxiv "Streamlets of lead": Landrieux, *Cathedral of Reims*, 42.

xxiv "The sparks pricked on their faces": Landrieux, *Cathedral of Reims*, 42.

xxv "Four distinct fires": Landrieux, *Cathedral of Reims*, 42.

xxv "Wretched man, what are you going to do?" Landrieux, *Cathedral of Reims*, 44.

xxvi "The captain ran to the factory": But the next day at the cathedral, the fire's debris still smoking, Landrieux found three more prisoners, burned alive on the spot. He saw "their limbs convulsed with pain and on their faces the fixed expression of a supreme vision of fear and anguish." Landrieux, *Cathedral of Reims*, 47.

xxvi "A symbol of hope": "A silent furnace, without flames or smoke, was glowing; and this furnace, its contours clearly outlined by the nave and the transept, formed, stretched over the city, an immense fiery cross, the Corps of Redemption: disaster, spread out before the face of Heaven, moulded itself in to the symbol of hope." Landrieaux, *Cathedral of Reims*, 53, n. 2, quoting the commandant, who continued, "The spectacle was grant and terrifying. [No] spectacles have moved me to such grief as this enormous fiery cross, in a flaming aureole—cross of martyrdom and of hope, which, invisible from below, offered itself on that evening alone to Heaven."

xxvi "Celestial ambassadors": Malcolm Miller, *Chartres Cathedral*, 2nd rev. ed. (New York: Riverside Books, 1997), 93.

xxvii "Landrieux and Thinot carried on": Within a year and a half, Landrieux was ordained bishop of Dijon. For another decade he continued to publish religious writings and books, including, in 1920, *Cathedral of Reims*, containing scores of photographs of the Reims bombardment, many by Abbé Rémi Thinot. Thinot entered the French Army in January 1915. Despite his exemption, he served as military chaplain to a French infantry corps. Landrieux praised Thinot for his "ardent nature, his almost foolhardy courage, his apostolic zeal [that] predestined him for this mission." Landrieux, *Cathedral of Reims*, 4.

Thinot was killed March 16 by a bullet in the head at Gueux in the Battle of the Marne, trying to save men buried under debris of a mine explosion. Landrieux, *Cathedral of Reims*, 4, n. 1.

xxvii "Total war": The attack became a benchmark for propaganda. But it caused no change in the international norm governing protection of cultural monuments. That norm remained only a nonbinding principle. It traced back to the Brussels Conference of 1874, which had followed the Franco-Prussian War, in which the warring sides had accused each other of illegal acts. But there were no rules for settling claims. That conference proposed, "The commander of a besieging army, when bombarding a fortified town, must take all measures in his power to spare, as far as possible, churches and buildings for artistic, scientific, and charitable purposes." The Hague Conventions on Land Warfare in 1899 and 1907 codified the Brussels Conference principle into international law, adding only that protected buildings are to be saved only if "they are not being used at the time for military purposes" with "distinctive and visible signs" that are "notified to the enemy beforehand." It remained the governing rule, unmodified until after World War II. But these rules should not even have been applicable to Reims in 1914, because it was not a "fortified town." The French had declared to the Germans that Reims was an open town.

xxvii "857 days": Landrieux, *Cathedral of Reims*, 52.

xxvii "Historic Monuments Department began taking defensive measures": After partisans during the French Revolution vandalized and destroyed widely, the French created an institutional framework to preserve historic monuments. That framework evolved over the next century when the French state and its units acquired many historic structures, including cathedrals. In 1830, the French Department of Historic Monuments was founded to safeguard and maintain them under the Ministry of Education and Fine Arts, to be overseen by a Historic Monuments Commission (Commission des monuments historiques), its members including archeologists, an inspector general, architects, politicians, scholars, and members of the Council of State (Conseil d'État).

In 1887, the first Law for the Protection of Historical Monuments and Creation of Chief Architects of Historic Monuments was adopted, creating a framework for direct government intervention, setting up a body of chief architects competent in restoration. Churches, however, were regulated by the Ministry of Religious Affairs. But by 1905, the French, having separated church from state, abolished the Ministry of Religious Affairs and reassigned diocesan architects who had worked on cathedrals to work instead under the chief architects for the Department of Historic Monuments. This drive to protect French monuments took a further leap in 1913 when the 1887 act was replaced with a new, stronger law for the protection of historic monuments, which gave the state power to preempt the owner of a classified historic monument and proceed with restoration work. The Department of Historic Monuments could exercise those powers to preserve France's historic monuments. The new powers of the department would prove critical for later protection of stained glass windows at Reims, Chartres, and elsewhere throughout France.

xxvii "Most stained-glass windows had by then been destroyed": Landrieux wrote,

> If only it could have removed our thirteenth-century glass also! The most ancient windows, those in the apse, at least the three in the middle, are only slightly touched. For others, behind the transept, two on each side, are riddled with holes; the last are in shreds.
>
> Of the high windows in the nave, whose coloring of reds, purples, and intense blues is so amazingly warm and vigorous, which burnish the rays of the midday sun, only one, one of twenty, is intact. . . .
>
> As for that marvel, a Great Rose of the Entrance, that dazzling mosaic of flowers, where shine in glory around Our Lady triumphant all the fires of the rainbow, it is broken through the middle, half of it remains. . . .
>
> The illuminated gallery of the triforium, of a more severe tone, which formed a kind of modulated foundation of light for the rose win-

dow has, with it, suffered the effects of the fire; the four bays in the right have flown into pieces; it has suffered, in addition from the fall of stones. Though one or two bays on the left still preserve some panels entire, the others only retain some beautiful fragments hanging by a thread from the ironwork.

One only of the two roses in the transept, that at the northern cross-bar, belongs to the thirteenth century; it is very badly damaged—less, however, than the other, which had been altogether destroyed by a storm and restored in the Sixteenth century. . . .

In the great modern window above the sacristies, one counts several holes. The sombre windows of a blue (perhaps too monotonous) tone in the Chapel of the Blessed Sacrament, and those of a sweet pearly tint in the Sacred Heart Chapel, were seriously spattered by the fall of a shell in the street, by the apse, and the pressure of air, forcing the glass away from the lead, has left an empty silhouette of some of the figures.

Landrieux, *Cathedral of Reims*, 122–23.

An unnamed British reporter, whose work was published in a Dallas newspaper, wrote in 1919,

When, close to a year ago, the German shells crashed down on the Cathedral of Rheims, whatever other damage they may not have done, they certainly robbed the world of a masterpiece of ancient art alike unique and irreplaceable. For the chief glory of Rheims Cathedral, one that haunts the memory even more than the soaring lines and mounting spires of its magnificent fabric, was the solemn beauty and vivid, glowing tints of its noble interior, turned by the light streaming through a myriad storied panea to a veritable dream in chiaroscuro and color. Just so, through those very panea the light had streamed for close to seven centuries, and the quaint medieval figures of saint and angel had watched serenely the crowning of monarch after monarch of ancient France, had frowned, one might almost think, on the English usurper and smiled benignly on the heroic Maid whose mission here reached its culmination. Few things, in fact, bring home to us the very soul of the Middle Ages, with all its mystery and longing and romance, more vividly than do these masterpieces of the stained-glass designer's art.

"The Romance of Stained Glass: Masterpieces of Ancient Art, and Irreplaceable, Destroyed by the War," *Dallas Morning News*, April 2, 1919, 4.

xxviii "Further work on proactive preservation . . . was subordinated to more pressing matters": In 1915, the bombardment continued at Reims, one hundred shells hitting the cathedral that year and the next. Early that year, the cathedral's architect and the Department of Historic Monuments took steps to protect against further damage, erecting a protective structure around the sculpture-laden doorways of the roofless cathedral's western facade. Sandbags rested in a thirty-foot V-shaped frame at the west door. Its timbers formed two layers: the lower, head-high, of bags end-to-end; the other, twenty-five feet of horizontal bags, like bricks of a Roman wall. The structure represented Reims's shout of victory for surviving and was safe enough for Cardinal Lucon, the archbishop, to traverse. It would be another year before masonry protections would be placed elsewhere in the building around other valuable statues and work would commence to collect fallen pieces of carvings and sculpture for future restoration. Once the war ended, the Historic Monuments service would restore the cathedral over a period of forty years.

NOTES TO CHAPTER 1

3   "EU–funded project": Little did I realize that I was witnessing another story unfolding—which could and may be the subject of another book: the restoration of the cathedral's walls and windows in the twenty-first century, which is becoming a controversial battle of its own between forces wanting to preserve and restore the cathedral to its bright condition as in the Middle Ages and those opposing, wanting to leave it in its current dark condition. And it's a metaphor for the fact that even this nine-hundred-year-old edifice is itself the focus of an ongoing saga, which may very well continue for another millennium or more.

5   "Hilltop with subterranean grottoes": A well almost one hundred feet deep stands under the cathedral. It is believed to have been used by druids for divination. They studied the water after stirring it with an oak rod.

5   "Four thousand sculptures": The sculptures are arrayed in nine sculpted portals, three on each of the three facades, which display a portion of the collection, giving a striking educational overview of religious history. Scholars say we know nothing of the individuals who carved the sculptures, including friezes of scenes from the Bible, grotesques of demons, and portraits of saints. A surge in cathedral building that began around 1100 created a demand for architects, craftsmen, and masons. Bands of masons formed into guilds and moved across Europe, taking work where they could find it. At the time, serfs were tied to the land they farmed, so the masons became known as *freemasons*. They infused new ideas into the cathedrals, from alchemy and tones in music to theological and philosophical notions of harmony.

5   "Precious relics": They include the Sancta Camisa of Mary (a piece of Middle Eastern cloth, the tunic or chemise worn by Mary, either on the day of the Annunciation or on the night of the Nativity, depending on the version), which was donated by the grandson of Charlemagne. They also include the head of Mary's mother, Anne, donated by Blanche of Castile.

5   "Groundbreaking innovations": The four major innovations follow:

1. Side doors in its transept allowed pilgrims to view the relics without disturbing the Mass in progress.
2. Special features were created to display an array of windows that project light in a new way, by means of a three-part elevation, which starts with its low nave arcade. Above that is its new medium-level triforium, and above that is its

high clerestory (with its upper oculus windows and lower lancet windows). By removing the lofts that often surrounded the side naves of previous churches, the nave was directly illuminated, allowing light from the aisle windows to reach the center of the nave. Émile Mâle, art historian, wrote that a Gothic building can be regarded as the shrine to that set of stained glass it accommodates.

3. New four-part pointed-ribbed groin vaults allowed for higher vault (more room for stained-glass windows), more than forty-five feet high.

4. And flying buttresses also allowed more room for stained glass—and light, as an expression of the divine.

6   "How to 'read' a window": Leo J. O'Donovan, "The Voice of Chartres: Malcolm Miller Illumines the Gothic Jewel," *America*, December 22, 2008, https://www.americamagazine.org/issue/681/article/voice-chartres, quoting Malcolm Miller. Mr. Miller is an English iconographer whose life's work since the 1950s has been to teach and conduct tours of the cathedral.

6   "Glass ... uneven surface and impurities ... play a vital role": The blue of panes in Chartres Cathedral is said to have been obtained by grinding down sapphires, and the deep red by mixing in pure gold. Victoria Finlay, "My Lifelong Quest for Color," *Iris*, November 2, 2014, http://blogs.getty.edu/iris/my-lifelong-quest-for-color/.

"The tonal beauty of the older windows is in part due to the very imperfections of this technique. The unequal thickness of the panes, the inclusion of little air bubbles and grains of sand create sparkling refractions of light." Alfons Lieven Dierick, *The Stained Glass at Chartres* (Berne: Hallway Ltd., 1960), 6.

Little is known about who produced the windows. The windows were contributed by various donors, including forty-three by many of the guilds at the time, including bakers, money-changers, vintners, winesellers, innkeepers, apothecaries, haberdashers, farriers, wheelwrights, fishmongers, carpenters, shoemakers, fur merchants, and butchers, images of whom appear in some of the windows. Miller, *Chartres Cathedral*, 14–15. Others were donated by dignitaries, such as Blanche of Castille; Louis de Bourbon, Count of Vendôme; Count Thibault VI of Chartres; and Pierre Mauclerc, Count of Dreux. Miller, *Chartres Cathedral*, 49, 50, 71, 90.

6   "Light at Chartres has special significance": Joan Gould, "Seeing the Light in Chartres," *New York Times*, December 18, 1988, https://www.nytimes.com/1988/12/18/travel/seeing-the-light-in-chartres.html.

Notes to Chapter 2

9   "War ... already affecting Texas ranchers and ... farmers": Russian supplies of grain had been cut off, and the United States—with a price guaranty—was urging farmers to plant wheat, which transformed wheat into a global commodity and would stimulate a sharp increase in the acreage of wheat harvested nationwide, a tenth of it from Texas.

10   "Quanah in 1909": Life in Quanah, Texas, had been difficult, even for an eight-year-old, but challenges had been cushioned by support among neighbors. Settlers

had come with high hopes, bringing families in prairie schooners piled with house-hold goods, but many had failed in drudgery and disease, victims of drought.

Bill Neal, grandson of settlers, described their solidarity: "Unity was a domi-nant beat. . . . Settlers, though a crusty, individualistic lot, were thrown together in this melting pot, and they overlooked individual differences in the common goals of survival and conquering the frontier. Hardships only cemented this spirit of unity. Being a neighbor meant much more than simply living next door, and the latch string was always open." W. O. Neal, *The Last Frontier: The Story of Hardeman County* (Quanah, TX: Quanah Tribune-Chief, 1966; Medicine Mound, Texas: Downtown Medicine Mound Preservation Group, 2015), vi.

NOTES TO CHAPTER 3

17 "Camille Enlart": Jean-Marc Hofman, "Camille Enlart s'en va-t-en guerre: Le musée de Sculpture comparée pendant la Première Guerre mondiale," *In Situ* 23 (2014), http://insitu.revues.org/10894. For a dozen years Camille Enlart had been director of the comparative sculpture museum (later the Musée national des mon-uments français—or the National Museum of French Monuments). After the war, Enlart would write, "The war made our patriotism more conscious, and the jealous fury of our enemies, by striving upon the works of art, rendered them dearer to those whom the artistic glories of France left indifferent."

17 "Albert Thomas": A thirty-seven-year-old politician and diplomat, Albert Thomas had spent seven months organizing munitions factories and increasing production in factories aggressively as subminister of artillery and munitions under the minis-ter of war and became undersecretary of state for artillery and munitions.

18 "One journal . . . fall of a bundle": "Workers were installing crates of explosive material on a truck when one of them fell, causing all the machinery in the vicinity to explode." "L'explosion de la rue de Tolbiac," *Journal des débats politiques et lit-téraires*, October 22, 1915, https://gallica.bnf.fr/ark:/12148/bpt6k4858090/f3.item .r=explosion%20rue%20de%20tolbiac.

18 "Another newspaper reported . . . a truck . . . passing over a gutter": Testifying to the "stigmata" of the event. "L'explosion de la rue de Tolbiac," *Journal des débats politiques et littéraires*, October 22, 1915, https://gallica.bnf.fr/ark:/12148/bpt6k4858090/f3.item. r=explosion%20rue%20de%20tolbiac. It reported that there "is nothing left" and continued, "Not a wall, not a pillar standing, nothing but burned debris, wrecks of all kinds, twisted pieces of metal, beams and half-burned boards, reduced glass in crumbs, plaster, rags, and everywhere spots of blood. In the whole neighborhood, there is not a house that has not suffered the violence of the explosion: all the windows of the shop-keepers, all windowpanes, were broken, the shutters ripped off. The floor is littered with pieces of glass and seems riddled with grape shot, debris iron, and cast iron." A church suffered all of its stained-glass windows broken. An old movie theater nearby was transformed into a morgue. Forty-five people died; sixty more were injured.

18 "Newspaper reported that the president . . . moved to tears": "L'explosion de la rue de Tolbiac," *Journal des débats politiques et littéraires*.

19 "State refused to recognize its responsibility": Ségolène Cuerq, "4 mars 1916, 9h25," *Saint-Denis et la guerre de 14*, City of Saint-Denis website, municipal archives, Feb-

ruary 25, 2016, http://archives1418.ville-saint-denis.fr/explosion-fort-double-cou
ronne/. Thereafter, a petition by neighbors of the fort against the state failed when
the state was found not responsible for maintaining a deposit of ammunition in
the unexploded part of the fort. Text archived at "Arret Regnault Desroziers," Rep-
ertoire de Jurisprudence II, accessed February 19, 2018, cached at http://archive
.wikiwix.com/cache/?url=http%3A%2F%2Fwww.lexinter.net%2FJPTXT2%2Far
ret_regnault_desroziers.htm.

20   "Archeological Society of Eure-et-Loir": The ASEL, as it is known, is a secular
nonpolitical body founded in 1856 and accredited by France's Ministry of National
Education, which controlled historic monuments. The society continues today with
a mission to study and disseminate local and national history and heritage of the
department of Eure-et-Loir, which includes Chartres.

20   "Father Yves Delaporte": He was then preparing what would become a leading
book published in 1926 depicting the stained-glass windows of Chartres Cathedral.
Yves Delaporte and Étienne Houvet, *Le vitraux de la cathédrale de Chartres: Histoire
et descriptions*, 4 vols. (Chartres: É. Houvet, 1926).

21   "Firemen from Paris and two glassworkers . . . attempt a salvage operation": Pneu
Michelin, *Reims and the Battles for Its Possession*, Illustrated Michelin Guides to the
Battle-Fields (1914–1918) (Clermont-Ferrand: Michelin & Cie, 1919), 32.

21   "February 22, 1918": This meeting of the Historic Monuments Commission was
attended by, among others, M. Bernier, M. Berr de Turique, and M. Paul Boeswillwald; fifteen commission members were also present at the May 10 meeting, along
with nonmembers Gabriel Ruprich-Robert and Pierre Paquet (in 1920 Paquet
would go on to become inspector general). "22 février 1918," minutes of the French
Historic Monuments Commission (Commission des monuments historiques),
archived at École nationale des Chartres (website), accessed February 18, 2018,
http://elec.enc.sorbonne.fr/monumentshistoriques/Annees/1918.html.

22   "Big Bertha cannon": It was powerful enough to reach Paris from the border
between Picardy and Paris, seventy-five miles away. With it, the Germans' aim was
to show the French in Paris that they were as vulnerable as people at the front. Big
Bertha shot 350 times, killing 250 Parisians and wounding another 620. The worst
of it hit on March 29, 1918. A single shot hit the roof of the sixteenth- and seventeenth-century Church of Saint-Gervais-et-Saint-Protais in Paris, collapsing it on
the congregation during Good Friday services, killing eighty-eight and wounding
another sixty-eight.

22   "Carlier . . . felt indignation": Achille Carlier, "Des mesures preventives qui permettraient d'assurer le sauvetace des vitraux de la Cathédrale de Chartres en cas
d'attaque brusquee: Danger que fait courir au monument le voisinage immédiat
d'un camp d'aviation militaire. Matérial de dépose et préparation d'équipes
(400,000 francs at 350 hommes) permettant la descente simultanée et rapide de
toutes les verrières dès l'instant de l'alerte. Etude remise à la Direction des Beaux-
Arts en Juin 1935" [Preventive measures to ensure the rescue of the stained-glass
windows of the cathedral of Chartres in the event of a sudden attack: Danger posed
by the monument in the immediate vicinity of a military aviation camp. Equipment
for the laying and preparation of teams (400,000 francs at 350 men) allowing the

simultaneous and rapid descent of all glass-works from the moment of the alert. Study submitted to the Direction des Beaux-Arts in June 1935], *Les pierres de France* 7 (June 3, 1935): 1–26 [in reprint] (hereafter Carlier, "Study"), 18–20.

23   "Explosion ... blew out numerous windows at the Basilica of Saint-Denis": The basilica windows damaged by the explosion of La Courneuve were windows of the basilica's choir that had not been removed and were among the oldest stained glass in the world, deep blue in color, which had proved to be irreproducible using current scientific methods. Three stained-glass windows were spared. Jean Baert, "1918 Catastrophe de la Courneuve," *Aux carrefour de l'histoire*, no. 46 (October 1961), text available online at https://e-nautia.com/jnono.masselot/disk/Histoire%20 11/1918%20Catastrophe%20de%20la%20Courneuve.pdf. The cardinal of Paris visited La Courneuve after the explosion and deplored the loss of the windows at Saint-Denis and also at the churches of Bourget, de Stains, and de Bobigny, likewise damaged by the explosions. "Visite de Son Eminence le cardinal de Paris à La Courneuve," *La semaine religieuse (Paris)*, March 23, 1918, 353–54.

    Irony suffused the tragedy at La Courneuve. The town had become a place of passage and shelter for many refugees coming from France's regions torn apart by the war. The town had developed the function of hosting and treating wounded, including in a factory where munitions had been produced. The disaster made the front page of many French newspapers and attracted worldwide press coverage.

23   "Spring offensive": Although the German Army still occupied much French territory, the war developments that precipitated the May 10 meeting may have been Germany's launching of its second spring offensive (Ludendorff Offensive), the Battle of the Lys (in the British sector of Armentières), and the subsequent appointment of General Ferdinand Foch as commander in chief of Allied forces on the Western Front. And although the United States had declared war on Germany on April 6 of the prior year, 1917, it would not be until June 21, 1918, that a significant American troop force of fourteen thousand was deployed in France.

24   "Paul-Louis Boeswillwald": Then seventy-four years old, Boeswillwald had been preceded on the Historic Monuments Commission by his father, Émile. Collectively, the two served on that commission and in the Historic Monuments Service for most of the first hundred years of the organizations' existence. Father and son are credited with leaving their mark on both.

24   "Émile Brunet": He was president of the Société des Antiquaires de France—the Society of Antiquaries of France—and a member of other learned societies, who would go on to be a recipient of prestigious awards and a noted amateur photographer.

24   "Proximity ... of the Lucé artillery factory": The members discussed the proposal, recounting that over the past seven months the ministry, the prefecture of Eure-et-Loir, and the Ministry of Armaments had debated the extent of the risks posed by the Lucé factory. They had also heard from the prefect and from the mayor of Chartres, who reported being shocked by the explosion at La Courneuve and its impact on windows at Saint-Denis and who had pressed the minister of armaments to move the factory. They reported that the minister had considered the request but refused—although he did order that the quantity of explosives stored at the Lucé

factory be reduced by three quarters and imposed greater security measures and more careful monitoring.

24 "Étienne Houvet": The resulting collection of the photographs would be published in 1926 by Houvet and Canon Delaporte as the first major collection of such images for the cathedral. Delaporte and Houvet, *Les vitraux*.

24 "Three master-glassmaker workshops": The work excluded the cathedral's several forty-foot-diameter rose windows, probably because their removal would have been too difficult or time-consuming.

25 "Membership ... again met": A Canon François argued in the meeting that the removal project should continue, if for no other reason because of the danger posed by the large stocks of munitions surrounding the Lucé factory. During the meeting it was also noted that the ministry overseeing the Historic Monuments Service had mandated that color photographs from all angles be taken and all precautions taken to ensure perfect conservation and that measures should be employed to ensure that the windows not end up being taken to Germany or to America.

In the meeting Canon Delaporte said he would in a subsequent meeting point out various errors and transpositions that had been committed at various times in the past in the course of repairs made to certain of the stained-glass windows and the steps he proposed to take to ensure that in the reinstallation of the windows such errors would be corrected and similar transpositions not happen again. The canon would then guide the work of the glassmakers at the appropriate times. He also proposed that certain clear glass panels that had been inserted in the past would now be replaced to the extent possible with new panels based on drawings previously made of the stained-glass panels that such clear glass had replaced. The drawings had been completed previously by Gaignières.

Professor Mayeux of the École des Beaux-Arts and Mr. Hausoulier, member of the institute, also attended the July 25 meeting.

26 "On August 30, the commission convened": The meeting was attended by ten members, eight of whom had also attended the May 10 meeting. Among them were Charles Louis Génuys and Paul-Frantz Marcou. Génuys, then sixty-five years old, had been a diocesan architect and then, for two decades, chief architect of historic monuments of the Marne, Ardenne, and the dome of Les Invalides; for five years he had been an inspector general of historic monuments, and he was also professor-lecturer at the Trocadéro. Marcou, then fifty-eight, an inspector of historic monuments, had written a report in 1917 on difficulties presented when intervening to protect art close to the front; this report led to the creation of an interdepartmental commission and protection service for artworks. Both Génuys and Marcou had been present for the March 2 inspection at the Trocadéro. Non-members Pierre Paquet and Gabriel Ruprich-Robert attended, together with Lucien Sallez, then fifty years old, who had also been a chief architect under the prior diocesan regime and would later become inspector general of historic monuments.

26 "They continued the removal work": It is unclear where the removed windows were stored.

27 "Conceptual framework to identify": In some cases, as important as the substantive story told by the windows' images was determining who had donated and who had

created certain of the windows. For example, guilds of bakers, farriers, and carpenters had joined to donate certain windows that feature images of them performing their trades. That information has led to research regarding the origins of the cathedral and its various components, construction, and financing.

27 "Cathedral would protect itself": An example was a small periodical aimed at pilgrims who visited the cathedral, called *La Voix de Notre-Dame de Chartres*. Its message, and that of its editors and followers, was essentially that the only way to help the devotees of Chartres Cathedral persevere in the face of the incomprehensible horrors of war was to "retreat to an inner world of warm devotion and merit." There was "little point," they argued, "to reveling in the glories of the cathedral, so intelligently and brilliantly crafted, or the historical traditions of a people who were—both cathedral and people—in danger of destruction." Joseph F. Byrnes, "Perspectives of 'La Voix de Notre-Dame de Chartres' on the Pilgrimage at Chartres during the XIXth and XXth Centuries: A Profile in Social History," *Marian Library Studies* 10, no. 12 (1978): 159–206, https://ecommons.udayton.edu/cgi/viewcontent.cgi?article=1082&context=ml_studies.

27 "Would those changes hold for the next war?": Military air activities near the cathedral temporarily subsided. The military aviation school closed in favor of other schools at Avord, Istres, and Étampes. But the field was soon devoted to the fleet of military bombing aircraft and expanded, to be known as Air Base 122, on flatter terrain only two and a quarter miles from the cathedral.

27 "It overly reassured those who opposed so-called passive defense": Byrnes, "Perspectives," 199–201.

28 "A handful of young men . . . would go on to play vital roles": René Planchenault, Ernest Herpe, and Lucien Prieur each served during the war.

Planchenault served for forty-five years in the service of French historic monuments in various capacities, first elevated from archivist to inspector of historic monuments in 1930 and then inspector general of the Historical Monuments Service in 1945. In World War II, he had left civil administration to join the Monument Service, designing in 1932 the mobilization plan implemented at the outbreak of the war for removing artworks from the museums of France to safekeeping sites in the countryside, and also stained-glass windows from churches. During World War I, at age fifteen, Planchenault had served in a cavalry regiment and later as a decorated officer in the artillery, which caused him to become deaf, an encumbrance throughout the remainder of his career.

Herpe served in the military during World War I and would go on to serve as chief architect for the Historical Monuments Service (1920–1956) and inspector general of historic monuments in 1941. During the Chartres stained-glass-window project, Herpe was a principal in the Historical Monuments Service and had to deal with Achille Carlier, who would become his nemesis.

And Lucien Edward Louis Prieur was in active service as a captain in World War I, serving from 1912 to 1918. He served in the interwar years as chief architect of historic monuments and then again in the second war as chief of the Historical Monuments Service to France's wartime Grand Quartier Général (GCG) from

September 1939 to July 1940, and in 1947 he became deputy to the inspector general of historic monuments.

Notes to Chapter 4

29   "Sydney Good": He was John Good's oldest son.

29   "Watched Sydney's casket lowered": Griff had known Josephine, John's second wife, as Sydney's stepmother, and the only mother Sydney had really known, but she had also died when Sydney had been seventeen and Griff eleven. Griff perhaps thought of Josephine as his own second mother, and his view of Sydney's casket descending into the ground likely planted in Griff's mind his earliest impression of the cost of human loss in war. Griff knew that Sydney—having been killed by the flu in camp—had never really made it into the war. On Griff's return ride to Dallas, he likely thought about that; maybe it contributed to his choice of a military career.

And Griff learned something else from the Good family: By the time Sydney had died, John had remarried—his third wife, Rosa—a sister of John's first and second wives, so Griff saw that when John had lost his first wife, John had found and married a second, and that even after losing the second, John had found and married a third. Griff saw that a personal loss—even deaths of successive wives—need not mean the end for a man. There could be other wives. This is the way men could sometimes get by. It may not be with a sister-in-law, or even two, but there could be someone else out there for a man to find, and often was.

30   "Harvest work": Griff learned that back in Quanah his mother advocated requiring school children and their mothers to pick cotton in the fields on Saturdays from October to December.

30   "Influenza pandemic": Sydney's death in El Paso had been one of the early ones. The pandemic spread in waves for seventeen weeks, from September 1918 through January, and killed twenty to forty million people worldwide, with the highest death rates among young, healthy adults, in rural areas and cities, and among soldiers, killing more solders than did battles in the war. By late October, in El Paso nearly five thousand cases had been reported, with four hundred dead. By October 4, there were seven hundred cases at Camp Logan near Houston, and in thirty-five counties, and by October 25 reports exceeded twenty-six thousand cases and five hundred deaths, and then a week later more than one hundred thousand cases and two thousand deaths were reported in the state's urban centers alone.

30   "Liberty Loan parade": In those years, Griff's father, Welborn Sr., was also active in Quanah's own campaign to sell Liberty Bonds for the war effort.

31   "Orville (F. O. Jr.)": He studied electrical engineering at Texas A&M and would be a junior if and when Griff were to enroll and with the other students from North Texas was one of sixteen members of its Panhandle Club, along with cousin L. H. Griffith.

31   "Griff found time for football": With his height, when Griff looked downfield—even crouched in a three-point stance, wearing cleats, his number twenty-five uniform, and soft leather helmet—he was able to look over opposing linemen and backfielders.

31   "Griff's demeanor": Perhaps it had been Griff's experiencing the work and dedication of his father, mother, uncles, and cousins that had led him to distill dignity from their

workaday accomplishments, despite their drudgery, or perhaps it had been his time away from his family—attending school and earning his keep—that had done it.

This Dallas time in Griff's life was one of getting himself under way, setting his life in motion, launching his young adulthood—on his own terms. He had a foundation to develop a fairly good sense of who he was and from where he had come. At age nine, he had met more than one hundred Griffith and Smith relatives at a June long-weekend family reunion in Salado, the town south of Temple where Welborn had grown up. The group had included ten of his father's brothers and sisters, and their families, some of whom had traveled several hundred miles to attend. On that trip, with his family, Griff had also visited his mother's parents and aunts and uncles in Temple. While growing up in Quanah, Griff had also learned about Quanah Parker, leader of the Comanches by the end of the forty-year Comanche Wars, who had been respected by whites and Indians alike for his bravery, integrity, and willingness to change.

Griff knew of his own Welsh ancestors who had lived in New York, including Alonzo Griffith, his grandfather, who had traveled overland to Texas as surveyor for Stephen Austin's second colony "to better their lot," his aunt Tiny would later say. Alonzo had then fought in the Civil War and, after the war, was known to have walked back to Texas from Tennessee; he had eventually settled in Salado and had been a founder of its Grange chapter. And Griff was aware and proud of his father's business and civic leadership in Quanah. Also, on Griff's mother's side of the family, he knew there had been military leaders like Captain Smith, his maternal grandfather, and—several generations back—on this maternal side, there had been also Ham White—a notorious Texas and Oklahoma bank and stage robber who had been famous as almost a Robin Hood.

But now it was time for Griff to determine who he was to be, and, whatever the outcome, he wanted to earn it himself—by dint of his own wits and strength—and he wanted to do something big, something ambitious, and something consequential.

33   "Calls for a good scrap and furnishes a thrill": The "good scrap" and "thrill" foretold in this quotation would become rich with irony.

34   "Welborn sold the store:" In September back in Quanah, another recently arrived businessman teamed up with Tom Mitchell to offer to buy Welborn Sr.'s Piggly Wiggly. Welborn named his price, and they snapped it up so quickly he said it made his head swim.

35   "Griff and Alice's daughter was . . . named . . . Alice": That Griff's wife Alice bore the same first name as her mother and daughter, both also named Alice, and that Major Torrey's middle name, Houston, was the same as that of his material grandfather, Colonel Daniel Houston, were indicative of the role that tradition and proper order must have played in the life of the Torreys. Griff's name, Welborn Barton Griffith, was the same as his father's, but the names Welborn and Barton were not family names; Welborn Barton had been the name of Griff's grandparents' family doctor—also their close friend—who had delivered their children in Salado in the second half of the nineteenth century, including his father, Welborn. Griff's grandparents had chosen the name out of gratitude to honor the doctor, a gesture

that Welborn repeated during his lifetime in naming his horses and dogs after his lifelong friends, John R. Good and his wife Rosa.

35   "Military-defense planning in case of Japanese attack": There were two plans for the Thirty-First Infantry's employment. One plan employed the regiment north of Fort Stotsenburg to counter landings at Lingayen Gulf, and the other plan employed the regiment to defend beaches along Legazpi Bay, south of Manila. Thirty-First Infantry Regiment Association, "Chapter 5: Manila Again, 1932–1941," Association website, 2014, http://www.31stinfantry.org/wp-content/uploads/2014/01/Chapter-5.pdf, page 8 (also available as chapter 4 in B. McCaffrey, *The 31st Infantry Regiment: A History of "America's Foreign Legion" in Peace and War*, afterword by S. Townsend [Jefferson, NC: McFarland, 2018]).

37   "After almost two years … defense planning": The readiness of the Thirty-First Infantry for combat eventually diminished. It started with two officers and about seventy men, but after subtracting cooks, clerks, supply personnel, orderlies, guards, and those on leave, sick call, or in confinement, company strength was around twenty men for training. Thirty-First Infantry Regiment Association, "Chapter 5: Manila Again, 1932–1941," 3.

NOTES TO CHAPTER 5

39   "Émile Brunet, chief architect": He was also architect-in-chief for the restoration of the Soissons Cathedral from 1915 to 1919 and demonstrated his knowledge in that project. Carl F. Barnes, "The Gothic Architectural Engravings in the Cathedral of Soissons," *Speculum* 47, no.1 (January 1972): 60–64.

39   "Repaired or restored the windows through the centuries": Cathedral records list the year of origin of each of the 176 windows and the year or years in which the work on each was performed, including the names of artisans who did restoration work. See, for example, Mediathèque Charenton (Paris), 81 28 17.

39   "Losing the original artists' iconographic intention": For example, see discussion in Clark Maines, "The Charlemagne Window at Chartres Cathedral: New Considerations on Test and Image," *Speculum* 52, no. 4 (October 1977): 804–805.

40   "This iconographic debate … would not be settled": And the debate has continued. One scholar concluded in 1977 that Delaporte's new sequence was deficient compared to the "original" order in place before the 1918 removal and resequencing of the panels: "In the arrangement of the panels today, the three narratives represented in the Charlemagne Window are only additively linked and are inadequately related. In contrast, the original order of the panels expresses an iconologically complete statement. It offers a more complex iconography and, at the same time, a more integral comprehensive meaning, fusing two legends into a new iconographic statement about the nature of Charlemagne's sin in relation to the Spanish crusade and subtly integrating a third legend, in the Jerusalem crusade, into the total statement of Christian victory." Maines, "The Charlemagne Window," 823.

40   "Eugène Emmanuel Viollet-le-Duc": One of the most famous French architects of the nineteenth century, Eugène Emmanuel Viollet-le-Duc was known to the general public for his restorations of medieval buildings, initially commissioned by Prosper Mérimée, and later became professor of art history and aesthetics at

the École des Beaux-Arts before his death in 1870. He spent 1845–1864 restoring Notre-Dame de Paris. When he'd finished, in the words of one commentator, "all signs of previous alterations by royalty and clergy, of destruction by mobs, revolutions, and former misguided repairs and restorations, as well as the decay of six centuries, had been removed. Criticism of his work at Notre-Dame and at other sites has ranged from virulent condemnation to hesitant praise." Daniel D. Reiff, "Viollet le Duc and Historic Restoration: The West Portals of Notre-Dame," *Journal of the Society of Architectural History* 30, no. 1 (1971): 17–30.

The same commentator concluded that "the restorations of Viollet-le-Duc [the author Reiff presents the name as 'Viollet le Duc'] saved literally dozens of churches from destruction, both by decay and barbaric amateur 'restoration.' Because it was part of the Romantic movement, he carried the restoration further in some places than a purely historical approach would sanction; but from his theories, and the specific example of his restoration of the portals of Notre-Dame, we can unquestionably put far greater faith in his work than many have previously allowed." Ibid., 30.

Carlier would not have agreed. In 1945, Carlier wrote that "Voillet-le-Duc is one of the greatest criminals in history." Achille Carlier, *Les anciens monuments dans la civilisation nouvelle* (Paris: 55 Rue de Varenne, 1945), 2:469; quoted in Louis Réau, "Viollet-le-Duc et le problème de la restauration de monuments," *Le cahiers techniques de l'art* 3 (1956): 29.

41   "Carlier had grown incensed": Carlier wrote:

> It was in February 1918, the memory of the place, as that of the people, has remained with me down to the smallest of details, and I still feel the indignation of my fifteen years given the inadequacy of protection available to shelter the gates of Notre-Dame de Paris, when every night an air raid could cause the most terrible of disasters. On Thursdays and Sundays, at Parvis, the high school I attended, where I observed that the construction of sandbags had hardly advanced, I could not understand why so urgent and grave a work was conducted with such slowness and negligence. One group started with the Saint-Anne gate; then, as little progress was made, they undertook to work simultaneously at the door of Judgment. Leading the operation was an old man in a white coat and black hat who, like his companions, moved incredibly slowly. It took so much time to get, lift, and put into position a single earth bag. And when five o'clock struck, everyone went away, conscious of having done far more work than [the result] was worth. "Gothas" [German heavy bombers] might come, but in the evening, the workers would not lift a single bag after 5 p.m. Nearby, a woman endlessly repeated that "it would be better to build hospitals than to take care of masterpieces." The atmosphere was not one conscious of undertaking a great mission, nor one of enthusiasm.

The "Gothas" were kind enough to respect Notre-Dame de Paris. And how much time they had generously been given to riddle the portals with bullets, during the interminable ascent of sandbags. Moreover, when everything was all over, one was astonished to find that, with the exception of the small bas-reliefs of the base and gates, the workers had stopped after protecting almost precisely all of the modern elements, leaving uncovered all the ancient elements, which are, it is true, the most finely wrought.

Achille Carlier, "Des mesures préventives qui permettraient d'assuerer le sauvetage des Vitraux de la Cathérale de Chartres enc as d'attaque brusquée, Complément No. 1" [Preventive measures to ensure the rescue of the stained-glass windows of the cathedral of Chartres in the event of a sudden attack], *Les pierres de France* 7 (January 31, 1936): 48 [in reprint], Mediathèque Charenton (Paris), 81 28 17 (hereafter Carlier, "Supplement No. 1").

41   "Ardent supporter of the preservation of French medieval monuments": Tassos C. Papacostas, "Gothic in the East: Western Architecture in Byzantine Lands," in *A Companion to Medieval Art: Romanesque and Gothic in Northern Europe*, ed. Conrad Rudolph (Hoboken, NJ: Wiley-Blackwell, 2009), 518–19.

41   "Articles . . . defended the vision . . . championed by John Ruskin": Achille Carlier, just like Camille Enlart, was a student at the French School in Rome and subscribed fully to Enlart's views. He won the First Grand Prize of Rome and French Artists Medal of Honor. Papacostas, "Gothic in the East," 518–19.

       Reims Cathedral, a symbol of the destruction of World War I, underwent stylistic changes through successive repairs, finally completed in 1937, eliminating features that architects for the repairs identified as misdeeds. Karlsgodt, *Defending National Treasures*, 103–104.

41   "Extolled the value of creative freedom": Carlier's publication, *Les pierres de France* (the stones of France), was likely named after John Ruskin's *Stones of Venice* (New York: Farrar, Strauss and Giroux, 1960), a three-volume treatise on Venetian art and architecture first published by Ruskin between 1851 and 1853. In *The Stones of Venice*, Ruskin examines Venetian architecture in detail, including over eighty churches, and discusses architecture of Venice's Byzantine, Gothic, and Renaissance periods, Venice's original buildings in Ruskin's day then suffering from neglect and decay. The book has also been described as a social polemic, chronicling the fall of Venice from its peak through the Renaissance to what Ruskin viewed as Venice's modern condition of political impotence and social frivolity.

41   "Carlier militantly defended medieval art": Nothing appears to have been published concerning the family or individual bearing of Achille Carlier.

42   "Fervor and foresight": Perhaps his uniquely French character of passion and patriotism drove them to adopt extreme measures that resulted in the windows' being removed in time to avoid war damage.

42   "Supplementary Inventory of Historic Monuments": Prescribed by the law of December 31, 1913, the mandated inventory was to list buildings that, although not deserving immediate classification as historic monuments, nevertheless presented an archaeological interest historical enough to make conservation appro-

priate. It was an enormous task, which began with René Planchenault preparing a questionnaire to be circulated to architects and local correspondents in the various departments throughout France, soliciting them to submit proposals for certain buildings in their departments to be considered for inclusion in the Supplementary Register, with Planchenault to check and control them. If they were accepted by the Commission of Historical Monuments, whose powers superseded his, Planchenault would oversee the drafting of ministerial decisions.

Over seven years, Planchenault generated and processed twelve thousand files and assembled the inventory list of more than seven thousand records, which gave the Fine Arts Administration the means to intervene to safeguard even monuments owned by individuals rather than the state. André Lepeyre, "René Planchenault (1897–1976)," in *Bibliothèque de l'école des Chartres*, vol. 135, bk. 2, ed. Société de l'École des Chartres, 415–21 (Paris: Libraire Droz, 1977) (text available online at https://www.persee.fr/doc/bec_0373-6237_1977_num_135_2_460023?q=René+Planchenault+(1897–1976). See also T. Imbert, "Nécrologie: René Planchenault," *Les monuments historiques de la France*, no. 1 (1977): 64 (text available online at http://www.mediatheque-patrimoine.culture.gouv.fr/pdf/inventaires/0080-035.pdf).

42 "National plan of 'mobilization'": "If, at the beginning of the hostilities in 1939, the windows of our churches and objects have been sheltered, it is thanks to the work undertaken by competent teams working according to standards established by René Planchenault. This action, which has been too much ignored, saved from the disaster an important part of the national heritage, which had been endangered in the zones of combat or bombardment." Imbert, "Nécrologie."

42 "Consequences of bomb explosions": Karlsgodt, *Defending National Treasures*, 104.

42 "No specific measures were adopted": Julia S. Torrie, *"For Their Own Good": Civilian Evacuations in Germany and France, 1939–45* (New York: Berghahn Books, 2010), 25.

42 "Germany reintegrated the Saarland": Torrie, *"For Their Own Good"*, 25.

42 "Enacting a passive-defense organization": Torrie, *"For Their Own Good"*, 25.

43 "Encouraged construction of shelters": Torrie, *"For Their Own Good"*, 25.

43 *"Les pierres de France"*: He styled it the *Journal of the Society for the Respect and Protection of French Historical Monuments* and named himself its director. This was probably the same as the Society for the Protection of Ancient Buildings, which was established in 1877 at William Morris's initiative in reaction to destructive restoration. In its 1877 manifesto, which contained guidelines for proper conservation and decried restoration and copying, which destroyed the monument's authenticity, Morris and his adherents pleaded for "preservation" in the place of "restoration." Andrea Yount, "William Morris and the Society for the Preservation of Ancient Buildings: Nineteenth and Twentieth Century Historic Preservation in Europe," PhD dissertation, Western Michigan University, 2005, pp. 2–3, available online at https://pdfs.semanticscholar.org/f9d2/f23f2080276b6e9ac934b1dc983cf7f791f3.pdf. Eugene Kalčič, "Eugène Emmanuel Viollet-le-Duc and Monument Protection: A Case Study," *Urbani ozziv* 25, no. 2 (2014): 130–42, http://urbani-izziv.uirs.si/Portals/uizziv/papers/urbani-izziv-en-2014-25-02-005.pdf.

44 *"L'Écho de Paris* joined"*: René Johannet, "Des expériences vont ê'tre tentées pour protéger les vitraux de Chartres," *L'Écho de Paris*, March 10, 1936, 1–2, available online at https://gallica.bnf.fr/ark:/12148/bpt6k8158395/f1.item.

44 "Nationalization of the railroads": By the 1930s, road competition had begun to take its toll on the railways, and the rail network needed pruning. The narrow gauge lines suffered most severely from road competition; many thousands of miles of narrow gauge lines closed during the 1930s. Many private railway-operating companies faced financial difficulties. That the rail companies only operated on leases paved the way for the nationalization of the French rail lines under the socialist government of the 1930s, which in 1937 nationalized the railway system and formed the Société Nationale des Chemins de fer Francais (SNCF). "Our History: Two Centuries of History; Retrace the History of Rail in France," SNCF website, accessed September 6, 2019. https://www.sncf.com/en/group/history/two-centuries-history.

44 "The rail depot, together with the air base": The Lucé munitions plant that had been a worry during World War I had either been eliminated or moved. It appears to have no longer been a subject of discussion.

46 "Twenty-eight-page article": Carlier, "Study," 3.

46 "One of the most precious works of art to be created by Humanity": Carlier, "Study," 3; emphasis in original.

47 "New kind of scaffolding": He also had produced sample metal cases that looked like primitive sheet-metal precursors to the Samsonite suitcases of the 1950s, but also hinged to be foldable, and each was reinforced with several interior metal rods as crossbars.

48 "He refuted many of the criticisms": He discussed the dangers to the cathedral posed by the nearby military airbase and arguments why it should be moved at least a dozen miles away from the city, and certainly not expanded in place. If the airbase were not moved, he wrote, a plan should be implemented to remove the windows from the cathedral within two hours following any signal of enemy attack. He further discussed the need for financing to pay for the work, the need to create specialized scaffolding and store it in place at the cathedral for immediate availability in case of attack, the need to fabricate crates of a sufficient nonflammable material and in sufficient quantity, also to be stored in place on-site, for storage of removed windows, and the need for a temporary lighting system to be installed. He provided a description of the window-removal tests to be conducted at the cathedral, using the new rapid-assembly scaffolding, to be performed on real cathedral stained-glass windows; he specified that the test windows selected would be windows installed only thirty years before, which were not ancient treasures. He also provided commentary on how the teams should be selected and trained to conduct the work, the role of on-site architects during the work, and the need for collaboration with the military. Carlier, "Supplement No. 1," 30–54.

48 "Replacing their cement anchors with malleable material": Each stained-glass window consisted of a set of separate detachable panels, each with at least one horizontal edge. Each panel contained one or more images, composed of colored

or painted glass, joined together with soldered lead grooved strips, called *cames*. Many windows contained up to several dozen panels. Each window was secured by a traditional saddle-bar system, used to keep each stained-glass panel from sagging in the wind and collapsing.

The system was composed of an assembly with two key features: The first was a set of long thin metal horizontal strips or straps (each, a *feuillard*) (2) on the outside of the window that clamped the window against a long, thicker, horizontal metal saddle bar, called a *barlock* (*barlotière*) (1). The strap was held in place by a row of U-shaped cleats (each, a *panneton*) (3) welded laterally along the barlock in intervals of less than a meter, resting along the horizontal edge between adjoining panels (and serving as a base on which the upper panel rests). The strap was held in place by a row of keys (each, a *clavette*) (4), each inserted into its own cleat. The second feature of the system is a series of thin metal rods (round or rectangular) (each, a *vergette*) (6) welded horizontally to the outside of the window in the center portion of each panel, spaced between the strap that ran along the panel's lower edge and the strap that ran along the panel's upper edge. Each tie is attached by a row of lead ties (each, an *attache*) (5), welded to the rectangular frame on the edges of the window and to the cames of the panel wherever they intersect the rod, all on the outside surface of the window. Each rod is sealed in the masonry of the bay jamb holding the window. In the figure below, the inside is to the left, and the outside is to the right.

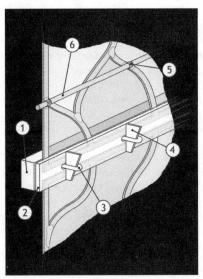

Diagram of metal anchors for stained-glass windows. Illustration by Christophe Miss.
SOURCE: "FERRONNERIE," PRISME ATELIER DE VITRAIL (WEBSITE), NOVEMBER 2011, HTTP://WWW.PRISME-ATELIER-VITRAIL.COM/2010/11/.

The cathedral windows were secured in a manner that Carlier believed rendered their removal more time-consuming and dangerous than necessary. He believed that the unsealing of the masonry around each rod or pin would be time-consuming and dangerous, risking breakage of the border pieces of the valuable glass panels. He recommended removing the sealing from each rod in advance and instead supporting the rod with a forked bracket or by flattening the rod and trapping it beneath support bars. He also proposed placing an insulator on the reverse side of the saddle bar to avoid any unnecessary adhesion of caulking, while ensuring that only necessary putty remained.

If these preparations—which he predicted would take weeks—were made to all of the windows in advance, Carlier argued, the window could later be removed quickly. He therefore proposed that these advance changes be carried out as preventive measures. He also noted that confessionals and various items of furniture had been attached to the walls of the cathedral that would impede the window-removal work. He proposed that sealants or other means of attachment be removed in advance such that the items be placed on rolling platforms to be moveable at the time when urgent work on the windows would begin.

49 "Annihilate in an instant the incomparable windows": Anne Fouqueray, "Pour la protection des verrières de Chartres," *Le Journal*, February 17, 1936, 7, text available online at https://gallica.bnf.fr/ark:/12148/bpt6k7651100w/f7.item.r=Chartres.

49 "Plying pressure on the military to relocate": She named two of the organization's eminent vice presidents, the Marquise de Maillé and Raymond Escholier, curator of the Petit Palais. She also reported that Louis Léglise, president of the Chamber of the French Glass Masters, attested to Carlier's competence and that the organization called Safeguarding French Art approved of Carlier's project.

49 "Short-term loans alone prevented France from defaulting": Stephen Schuker, "France and the Remilitarization of the Rhineland, 1936," in *The Origins of the Second World War*, ed. Patrick Finney (London: Arnold Press, 1997), 238.

49 "Newspapers called for the League of Nations to use sanctions": James T. Emmerson, *The Rhineland Crisis 7, March 1936: A Study in Multilateral Diplomacy* (Ames: Iowa State University Press, 1977), 116.

49 "French forces . . . would be at the disposal of the League of Nations": Ralph A. C. Parker, "The First Capitulation: France and the Rhineland Crisis of 1936," *World Politics* 8, no. 3 (April 1956): 358.

49 "France . . . could easily reoccupy": Correlli Barnett, *The Collapse of British Power* (Hampshire, UK: Pan Macmillan, 2002), 336.

50 "On March 9, Carlier arrived": Mr. Battais, the guardian, opened the cathedral. Raymond Gilbert, the mayor of Chartres, had exempted the project from donation fees. Carlier and his truck driver, with the bell ringer, Mr. Normand, unloaded the scaffolding into the transept.

50 "Install a metal sheet in the keystone": Jean Maunoury, the cathedral's architect, arrived to assist. Maunoury would become integral in the planning of the projects at Chartres until he was mobilized on the eve of the attack.

50 "Another pulley . . . for a rope . . . through a small trapdoor": Before the tests, the cathedral architect and the Fine Arts Administration agreed to install a trapdoor for such a purpose, possibly to be duplicated at other locations if proven valuable.

50 "A special committee . . . to rescue Chartres' stained glass": Mellot replied that because he was a father of six, he would not be mobilized and said, "A team? I will make it my business." Carlier also met with a Henri Alexandre to ask about assembling teams. Alexandre replied, "Looking for volunteers? Look no further; myself and my son are here when you are ready." Achille Carlier, "Des mesures preventives qui permettraient d'assuerer le sauvetage des Vitraux de la Catherale de Chartres enc as d'attaque brusquee, Complement No. 2" [Preventive measures to ensure the rescue of the stained-glass windows of the cathedral of Chartres in the event of a sudden attack], *Les pierres de France* 7 (April 29, 1936): 85 [in reprint], Mediatheque Charenton (Paris), 81 28 17 (hereafter Carlier, "Supplement No. 2").

Within days, Mellot, Alexandre, and the newly created committee concerning itself with saving Chartres' stained glass assembled a team of nine Chartres volunteers, consisting of a Mr. Bouchet, André Chédeville, Jan Damoiseau, Mr. Godard, Mr. Laillet (one of the leaders of the Chartres stained-glass-rescue committee), Yves Mellot, and Messrs. Moisy, Sevestre, and Soumeilhan. Ibid., 38.

The upper-window scaffolding was paid for by SFA. The lower-window scaffolding was paid for by Carlier himself.

50 "Sent Carlier a written commitment of further support": On behalf of the committee dedicated to the rescue of Chartres' stained glass, Mr. Lailett said that (1) upon acceptance of the scaffolding, the committee would constitute a team to be trained to assemble it, and (2) upon delivery of the scaffolding, the team would be ready, (3) seek a location in Chartres where a stained-glass window might be set up to train teams of volunteers, (4) assign each team its own window, with which the team would become familiar in terms of location, approach challenges, value, and composition, (5) open a subscription to raise funds for the project, including for construction of a stained-glass window for training and independent night lighting, and, when raised, would pay these funds to the Fine Arts Administration on the sole condition that the administration allow for the rescue of a new window, and (6) form a committee of patronage composed of preeminent residents of Chartres. Carlier reported soon after that the patronage committee had been formed and "includes all of the most important notables of the city." Carlier, "Supplement No. 2," 87–88.

50 "Seven-by-twenty-seven-foot upper windows": Approximate dimensions are twenty-six feet, seven inches, by seven feet, two inches. See Delaporte and Houvet, *Les vitraux*, for comprehensive descriptions of the windows.

51 "Telescoping crane on wheels": Supplied by French supplier Fauchex, it was a precursor to the modern "cherry picker."

51 "Tests had revealed new risks": During the tests, one of the senior-most of the observing officials of the Fine Arts Administration, when questioned as to what the signal would be for action, replied, "The question is solely a matter for the Fine Arts Administration, and the city does not need to worry about it; the administrator of Fine Arts will send specialists from Paris." Carlier, "Supplement No. 2," 91.

51 "Order twenty such scaffolds": The twenty would consist of six for the nave, four for the transept, nine for the choir, and one to be placed at the disposal of the local society, for use with its proposed volunteers.

52 "The committee . . . set . . . resolutions . . . endorsing Carlier's resolve": The Chartres stained-glass-rescue committee would also arrange for Canon Delaporte to give a series of lectures to volunteers concerning the history and art of the stained-glass windows to enhance their education and promised to begin the training as soon as the Fine Arts Administration had adopted a scaffolding system. Meanwhile, the Chartres committee would open a subscription for funds to pay the expenses of the Fine Arts Administration to obtain the scaffolding. Letter from the committee to save Chartres' stained glass, to the director general of the Fine Arts Administration, April 17, 1936, Mediathèque Charenton (Paris), 81 28 17.

52 "Supplement No. 2": The document further argued the need to relocate the air base, described in detail the two test scaffoldings and the tests conducted at the cathedral, clarified his relinquishing of rights concerning the newly invented scaffolding, offered pros and cons for the telescopic crane–supported platforms, theorized on how to organize and train volunteers, provided the rationalization for selection of the particular windows on which the tests were run, introduced the committee dedicated to safeguarding the Chartres stained-glass windows, and speculated as to what signal the Fine Arts Administration would give to summon the volunteers. Carlier, "Supplement No. 2."

52 "It would be criminal to resign oneself to the loss": Carlier, "Supplement No. 2," 88.

53 "May have gotten under the skin of the Fine Arts Administration's staff": Carlier's "Supplement No. 2" ("Complément No. 2") published his letters to the director general of the Fine Arts Administration that accompanied his "Study" and "Supplement No. 1," and he complained in it that he had not received a reply from the administration to his letter of March 30. He also included in the document a number of complaints about administrative delay and self-serving remarks about his financial independence and the good faith of the citizens of Chartres engaged in the campaign to save the windows.

53 "WHAT WILL BE THE SIGNAL . . . ?": Mediathèque Charenton (Paris), 81 28 17, 91 [in reprint]. Emphasis in original.

54 "They had already been moving forward with the project": What Carlier seems to have failed to appreciate is that the Fine Arts Administration had responsibilities broader than only the saving of Chartres Cathedral and its windows. Other cathedrals in northern and eastern France faced risks as well. Some, such as those in Metz, Amiens, and Paris, were closer than Chartres to the likely path of invading German armies. Also, it would have been natural for the Fine Arts Administration to be frustrated by Carlier's public, detailed disclosure of the issues, weaknesses, and concerns in the planning effort to save the treasured windows. In time of impending war, the administration's staff likely viewed that disclosure as unnecessary and unwise.

NOTES TO CHAPTER 6

58 "Police state": Three years before, in 1932, Japanese forces had attacked Shanghai on the pretext of Chinese resistance in Manchuria, resulting in a brief undeclared

war that ended in a truce. Soon the Japanese had installed a puppet state in Manchuria. And a year later, Japanese forces had occupied part of Inner Mongolia, invaded North China, and captured the city of Shan-haik-wan. Following a truce under which a large area was demilitarized, Chinese troops withdrew first, followed by a pullout of Japanese troops.

65   "Selecting Griff as an observer": A 1988 report of the Center for Military History on the program lists Griff—but only mentioned his service through July 1935 in Japan and China, not his service in the Philippines. Griff was one of the two thousand West Point graduates (between 1802 and 1975) who had been selected for the military observer role.

Historically, their intelligence gathering had focused primarily on the Prussians, until 1919. The report reached two conclusions: that the observers were chosen for their individual talent and ability, professional competence, and intellectual brightness, and that peacetime—as opposed to wartime—observations by observers had had the greatest impact on the US Army as an institution. Thomas S. Grodecki, "Military Observers, 1815–1975," unclassified final report by the Center of Military History, 1–3, 17, 193, March 16, 1988, http://www.dtic.mil/dtic/tr/fulltext/u2/a194175.pdf.

NOTES TO CHAPTER 7

69   "Public pressure to act as Germany rearmed": By early 1936, Hitler had been führer for over a year and had earlier engineered adoption of the Nuremberg Laws. The United States had adopted the Neutrality Acts, which, among other things, boycotted arms sales to belligerent nations. Italy had invaded Ethiopia, and in Britain there were both a new prime minister and a new monarch.

69   "Georges Huisman ... had ... been leading the Fine Arts Administration": The choice to appoint Georges Huisman director general of the Fine Arts Administration would have been made by Aimé Berthod, Prime Minister Daladier's minister of national education, but Huisman was apparently recommended by Jean Zay, who was an influential senator during Daladier's government.

70   "Cannes Film Festival": Georges Huisman, then forty-seven, was a proponent of modern art. He would carry out Jean Zay's idea to create the Cannes Film Festival, first conceived by Zay in 1938. Due to the onset of World War II, the festival's intended 1939 inauguration was postponed until 1946, with Huisman its jury president.

In June 1940, Huisman, with his wife and son, boarded the ocean liner SS *Massilia* from Bordeaux, along with twenty-seven deputies, senators, and senior officials, including Jean Zay, bound for Casablanca on June 21, 1940, with the intention of forming a resistance government in North Africa.

70   "Jean Verrier": Then forty-nine, Jean Verrier had worked on, among other things, methods of presenting the fifteenth-century Bayeux Tapestry; as a classmate of René Planchenault, he also worked on classification of objects. Verrier would later become instrumental in the postwar restoration of much of France's stained glass.

70   "Pierre Paquet": He was then sixty-one. Paquet restored buildings, including Paris's historic private Hôtel de Cluny, built by the Abbot of Cluny in 1330 and rebuilt in 1510, and Sainte-Chapelle and Brittany's Mount Saint-Michel.

70   "Eugéne Rattier": He was then seventy-two.

70   "Auguste Labouret": Georges Huisman handmarked the memo for copies to be circulated to several persons, which suggests that they'd attended the meeting: Eugéne Rattier, Pierre Paquet, Émile Brunet, and Jean Verrier.

71   "Special crates": Carlier had insisted that the Reims Cathedral disaster should have taught that all possible steps should be taken to prevent flammable material from being introduced to the site. By November 4, the Fine Arts Administration had received a proposal from a vendor, Marcillet & Point, for one thousand cases to be made of English poplar, a choice of material that would later prove a bad one, exposing the windows to a near miss: Five years after removal and being put into safekeeping, seventy of those wood cases would suffer water damage and rot while in storage in the rooms of the quarry. Their windows would have to be removed and new cases constructed and then repacked, exposing the windows in nearly a seventh of those crates transported from the cathedral to protect them from breakage and water damage.

71   "Need for an on-site generator": Nevertheless, the Fine Arts Administration found a gas-powered generator on a trolley to provide independent light at the cathedral. From the report of Pierre Paquet, May 23, 1936, Mediathèque Charenton (Paris), 81 28 9.

The Fine Arts Administration also scheduled on-site tests of telescoping cranes of various sizes and directed its staff to place orders with private ventures for scaffolding and other project materials. Right after the tests, the Fine Arts Administration ordered six telescoping platforms capable of reaching a height of forty-two feet—one of which could extend as high as eighty-two feet—and informed the committee for the preservation of stained glass and the French Army that the Chartres committee might use Carlier's scaffolding for training volunteers at the old church in Chartres known as the Collégiale Saint-André, to be arranged by Maunoury.

At the end of May, from his offices at the Fine Arts Administration, Director General Georges Huisman communicated with Madame la Marquise de Maillé about a fundraiser to be held by the Saving French Art group, to raise money to aid in the purchase of the scaffolding.

71   "Léon Blum": He was the first Socialist and first Jew to hold the office of French prime minister, and he formed a thirty-five-member governing council, the Council of the Popular Front Government, with the Socialists holding the majority of seats, Radicals holding over one-third, and Socialist-Republicans two seats.

71   "Jean Zay": Then thirty-two, Zay had been born in Orléans. His father—whose Jewish parents moved from Alsace to France in 1871—edited a daily radical newspaper. Zay's mother, from a Protestant family in the Beauce region surrounding Chartres, taught primary school. Zay attended secondary school in Poitiers and

then became a journalist, director of a radical-socialist newspaper, and a barrister in Orléans. He married Madeleine Dreux in 1932 and with her had two daughters. He joined the Radical Party at age twenty-one and became the youngest member of the National Assembly at twenty-seven.

71   "Blum had chosen Zay . . . because of his youth": Blum wrote, "I think it takes a young person to [lead] the National Education, and that's why I'm sending you." Jean Zay, *Souvenirs et solitude* (Paris: Rene Julliard, 1946), 242.

For six months prior to the election, Zay had served as undersecretary of state for the presidency of the council under Albert Saurat, Blum's predecessor as prime minister, and had taken charge of the reform of the state and preparations for the election. In light of Blum's victory, Zay had influence in Blum's divided cabinet. A number of the ministers, including Jean Zay, were opposed to Blum's policy of nonintervention. Marcel Ruby, *La vie et l'œuvre de Jean Zay* (Paris: L'Impremerie Bereskiak, 1969), 330.

Under Blum, France collaborated with Britain and twenty-five other countries to formalize an agreement against sending any munitions or volunteer soldiers to Spain.

72   "Energetic and positive nature": Emmanuel Berl and Jean Nohain, "Fonds Jean Zay (1904–2004): Introduction," Archives Nationales (French National Archives) website, accessed September 16, 2018, https://www.siv.archives-nationales.culture.gouv. fr/siv/rechercheconsultation/consultation/ir/consultationIR.action?udId=&full Text=&consIr=&formCaller=&details=false&irId=FRAN_IR_028000&gotoAr chivesNums=false&frontIr=&optionFullText=&auSeinIR=trueeeftab720; see also Emmanuel Berl and Jean Nohain, interview of Jean Zay, February 10, 1937, in Archives Nationales (French National Archives), 667 AP 56, file no. 2.

72   "Modern principles of planning and logistics": Zay soon became known as France's great reforming minister of national education. He believed public schools were the workshop for shaping citizens. He modernized France's education system and brought socially and economically disadvantaged students into the schools, increased the years of mandatory schooling to fourteen from twelve, limited class sizes, harmonized syllabi, created library buses to promote reading in working-class and immigrant neighborhoods, and launched experimental classes. And he adopted a rule forbidding the wearing of religious symbols or clothing in the schools and also made physical education mandatory, his team building hundreds of swimming pools, soccer fields, and bicycle tracks across France.

Outside the field of education, Zay unified national theaters, created museums for modern art and folkcraft, promoted copyright protection, and promoted creation of the Cannes Film Festival as a counterpoint to Venice's, which had been dominated by Mussolini and Hitler. He also supported creation of the French National Centre for Scientific Research.

72   "Wartime prison diary": Benjamin Ivry, "What He Contributed, What He Endured," *Forward*, June 28, 2011, https://forward.com/culture/139254/what-he -contributed-what-he-endured/.

72   "Captain Alfred Dreyfus": Zay, *Souvenirs et solitude*, quoting Anatole France's description of Major Georges Picquart.

73   "Soldiers . . . for removal and crating": Letter from Defense Minister, July 4, 1936. Mediathèque Charenton (Paris), 81 28 17.

73   "Coordinated effort to incorporate a national 'passive' civil defense": Karlsgodt, *Defending National Treasures*, 68.

73   "Lists of art objects": Led by Henri Verne, director of France's national museums, the administration developed a system of labeling the relative importance of pieces using colored stickers: red meaning top-priority works, blue for second tier, and yellow and black for works judged not to require evacuation, which would instead be protected on-site. Karlsgodt, *Defending National Treasures*, 68.

74   "Forced the professionals to listen": Carlier employed confrontation as his primary method for convincing others. Fourteen years later, in the context of a later dispute with Carlier over issues involving a handful of alleged errors in positioning of stained-glass windows reinstalled in the cathedral after World War II, Jean Maunoury would look back to refer to the "vehemence" of Carlier's 1926 critiques of the Fine Arts Administration and described Carlier as having "failed" in his "contest" with the administration.

       Ernest Herpe, a chief architect of historic monuments since 1920, served as a principal in the Fine Arts Administration later during the Chartres stained-glass window project. In 1939, when Herpe led a major cleaning of the facade of Notre-Dame de Paris, Carlier "went apoplectic," according to one author who referred to Herpe as Carlier's "enemy." Two years later, Herpe would be appointed inspector general of historic monuments.

74–75 "National legal framework for the passive-defense program": Karlsgodt, *Defending National Treasures*, 68.

75   "Blum stepped down": Anti-Semites hated Léon Blum. He would twice later return as prime minister of France, first for two months in March 1938, long enough to ship heavy artillery and other much-needed military equipment to the Spanish Republicans. But he was unable to establish a stable ministry. Then, in April 1938, his Socialist government fell, and he was removed from office. His second return lasted two months, starting in December 1946. As such, he was a perennial object of particular hatred from anti-Semitic elements.

75   "A kind of heritage-triage system": So characterized by Elizabeth Karlsgodt, *Defending National Treasures*, 104. Zay designated four categories—each assigned a color—into which monuments or artworks were to be categorized according to their importance, and he ordered the staff to procure personnel necessary for execution of the orders.

75   "Departments from which artworks were . . . withdrawn and . . . directed": Jean Zay, "Instruction sur la protection en cas de guerre des monuments et oeuvres d'art dans les départements de l'intérieur," August 12, 1937, AMN R1 4, Archives des museés nationaux, Paris, 3–4. The instructions focused on protection of portals and sculptured elements against explosions of projectiles, withdrawal of all removable objects, starting with stained-glass windows, construction of ramparts, and strengthening defense against fire.

       Zay ordered dispersal of art objects to locations outside urban areas into sites where they could be protected against fire, humidity, and theft. And he ordered the Historical Monuments Service to classify monuments and art objects into four categories of priority, proportionate to their importance: first, monuments or artworks of exceptional importance, for which protective arrangements must be made in peacetime; second, those that were to be protected automatically upon mobilization; third, those for which protection would be carried out immediately on issuance of orders; and fourth, those impossible to withdraw, which must be protected in place.

75   "Better to pursue measures . . . useless rather than . . . be taken by surprise": Zay, "Instruction sur la protection," 4.

76   "Indemnity payments": Karlsgodt, *Defending National Treasures*, 70.

77   "Captain Lucien Edward Louis Prieur": He was forty-seven, married with three children, and from Boulogne-Billancourt. He'd been employed since 1926—and during the interwar years—as a chief architect of historic monuments in Bordeaux. He'd studied language science and then architecture at the Paris School of Fine Arts.

77   "Ernest Herpe": He was fifty-two. Some of the staff were young and would later build careers in architecture, protection of historic monuments, and theater.

       Jeanne Laurent, then thirty-six, was a behind-the-scenes administrator in the stained-glass-window-removal project who would later brief the Historic Monuments Commission for authorizations and to report on progress. She was the daughter of a Bretton farmer, educated at the School of Chartres (where she met politicians, intellectuals, and theater personalities). She was trained as an archivist paleographer and had joined the Ministry of National Education in 1930 and then the Fine Arts Administration.

       She would go on to play a role in the French policy of decentralization and democratization of culture under the Fourth Republic. She has been described as "one of those rare women of the high administration who were determined to turn into concrete actions an idealistic project mocked by many." She succeeded in institutionalizing the concept of theatrical decentralization, putting in place ways to support artistic creation—whether financial, material, or intellectual. In so doing, the arts were made more accessible to all classes of French society, whereas previously they had been perceived by many to be reserved for bourgeois elites. This is why many theater directors in the French capital liked to criticize her. As early as 1952, she was forced onto the sidelines, assigned to a new position unconnected with her previous work. Naomie Retailleau, "Jeanne Laurent: Une Bretonne à la conquête de la culture," Unidivers: Le webzine culturel de Breton, April 26, 2017, https://www.unidivers.fr/jeanne-laurent-politique-culture-bretagne/.

77   "Project managers": They created an inventory of the windows mapped out on architectural drawings in multiple copies that were to be placed in multiple locations for access and security. To ensure that cases of suitable size and shape would be prepared and stationed nearby to hold the stained-glass windows for transport and storage—and to ensure that workmen would be able to eventually restore each window and return each individual panel to its rightful position—the Fine Arts Administration cataloged each of the cathedral's bays and its respective windows, as well as its respective iron framework, or armatures.

With that work, they created a floor plan showing the location and identifying number of each window, indicating its type (stained or clear; scalloped, beveled, or straight) and category, its respective date of creation over the last nine hundred years, name of donor (group or prominent person), the years in which repair work had been done and by whom, where relevant, and, for each window, which category of the four types of protective crate should be used to store and transport it. The plan formed a comprehensive record of each of the 41 high bays with its respective high windows and the aisles with their 38 low windows, aggregating 174 windows in all, containing over 7,700 glass panels, representing over thirty thousand square feet of stained glass.

77   "Contractors responded with bid proposals": A private firm named the Office Commercial des Bois sent a proposal to Jean Trouvelot dated May 19, 1938, to supply wooden crates of poplar in four sizes at a stated cost per crate, to be delivered to the cathedral or other location in Chartres. The proposal excluded panels of Celotex, which it noted would be expensive. The proposal stated that a separate proposal for such panels would be provided in a subsequent step with an additional charge per square meter to be specified. Letter Marcillet & Pont to the Fine Arts Administration, November 4, 1936.

77   "Equipment and supplies . . . would not fit in . . . attic": Materials stored at or near the cathedral prior to September 1938 were listed in a report of Chief Architect Jean Trouvelot, dated October 19, 1939.

78   "Building Q": The building, dating from the thirteenth century, had been used as an extension of the cathedral to store tithes and other payments of rent on the church's land, typically in the form of food, storing grain on the ground floor and in a vaulted underground chamber, wine in the cellars, and wheat, spelt, oats, and other flours on higher floors. It also contained a prison and an oven. Today it and adjoining buildings house the International Stained-Glass Centre and stained-glass museum.

78   "Distributed fire extinguishers": One report indicates that the 1938 operations ended up securing the sand and bags that actually were needed the following year; without that rehearsal, the military would have absorbed them all. Service des monuments historiques, n.d., Médiathèque d'accueil et de recherche des archives nationales, Paris, F21 3981, document 19.

78   "Mathieu & Marçais": Letter with proposal from Enterprise Mathieu & Marçais, to the Fine Arts Administration, for the full project, with lists of personnel and equipment, September 9, 1938.

79   "Celotex": A brand of board made of cane fiber, used for insulation or as a vapor barrier, siding, or layer under a roof, a trademark of Celotex Limited.

79   "Director of passive defense": Richard J. Overy, *The Bombing War: Europe, 1939–1945* (London: Allen Lane/Penguin, 2013), 562.

80   "*Le Journal*": Anne Fouqueray, "Le plan de protection des vitraux de Chartres sera-t-il appliqué?" *Le Journal*, September 19, 1938, 7, text available online at https://gallica.bnf.fr/ark:/12148/bpt6k76324332/f7.item.r=Chartres.

80   "Two solutions": Jean Trouvelot's team described the dilemma in a later report to the Minister of National Education: the first of two alternatives would be to

remove the windows quickly "in difficult conditions," hoping to get them out of harm's way to save the maximum number as quickly as possible in case of a quick attack, even though many of the windows were still installed with hard putty, caulked with flashing cement or gypsum cement, and attached to the stone window frames by deep holes in adjoining travertine stone and even though the glass of most of the windows was brittle and many were curved in shape, making packing them in crates a delicate operation.

The second alternative would be to mount all available scaffolding and hoists, moving all packaging cases to be ready in place near their designated windows but deferring actual dismounting of the windows in order to first remove the windows' flashings in situ and secure them with pins to make them ready for the rapid and easy removal of the greatest number of windows possible. Jean Trouvelot, "Passive Defense Works Executed at the Cathedral of Chartres [September 1938 until 24 August 1939]," 20–25, report dated February 22, 1940, to the Minister of National Education, appended to a report to the same minister, dated October 19, 1939, Archives départmentales de la Eure-et-Loir [4 NC Art. 83] (hereafter Trouvelot, "Passive Defense Report").

80   "Time for a decision": The British and French representatives in Prague presented the Anglo-French proposal to allow the Sudetenland to be annexed, and their ambassadors informed Czechoslovakia's president that his country would have to accept that plan or face Germany alone, following which the Czech government resigned, Jan Syrový became prime minister, and his government mobilized its military. France ordered partial mobilization of its military. In Berlin, Hitler made a speech threatening Czechoslovakia with war, and the French government was ready to announce that France would not enter a war purely over Czechoslovakia.

Notes to Chapter 8

82   "The visit afforded . . . opportunities for talks": Griff and his father would have discussed things Griff had mentioned in letters from the Philippines, such as Griff's pondering whether it was still worth it to him to stay in the military, continuing to train, rather than do something else, such as join his father and brothers in the business, or perhaps head east to be nearer to his daughter and maybe start a career in business. Griff would have also told his dad about his adventures in Shanghai, Manila, and Japan.

82   "He also loved dogs": In Quanah, where Welborn Sr. had enjoyed hunting wolves, he owned wolfhounds, which he kept at the Good Ranch. He loved horses and always had his own, which he rode daily as long as he was able. In Temple, he rode his horse to work and back and to home and back for lunch. When the livery stables all closed, he built his own "stable" on a lot near the store. When he could no longer ride his last horse, he boarded it at a farm until its death. All his horses were called John in honor of his friend, John R. Good.

83   "Parkinson's disease": Welborn had enjoyed swimming and had often gone with Lula to a large pool near Temple. He swam only on his back, with his long, thick feet sticking out of the water. Lula swam well but in "puppy" fashion. They talked to each other during their swims, unless others spoke to them. Many other swimmers greeted them,

but their daughters ignored them. Welborn was devoted to has grandchildren, with infinite patience in answering his granddaughters' questions, which usually began, "Why is . . . ?" In the years when he could no longer speak well enough to be easily understood, his granddaughter Dorothea said she enjoyed a companionship with him in which words were unnecessary.

83   "Daughter of a major": In the face of that risk, he would have had to contemplate leaving the Army. He went on long walks with his daughter and would vent his frustrations with the Army, generated by lack of funding and scarcity of opportunities for promotion. But he probably did not relish going back to Temple, and certainly not to Quanah to run grocery stores. Instead, he probably considered going into some other business, likely on the East Coast, where Tiny and his uncle Harrison were living.

In my interview with Griff's daughter in 2015, she told me that her mother, Alice, had turned out to be spoiled, sheltered by her snobbish parents who had always looked down on Griff and his family. Alice damaged the lives of a series of husbands, Griff being only the first. She would have five husbands in total. Her second would be killed in the war, and the next two marriages she would end in divorce, as she had her first. She was survived by her fifth husband.

83–84 "Emory Land . . . a recently retired vice admiral": He would soon oversee design and construction of the more than four thousand Liberty ships and Victory ships that would fly the US flag during World War II. Emory Scott Land, *Winning the War with Ships: Land, Sea and Air—Mostly Land* (New York: R. M. McBride, 1958).

85   "Count's assignment": They sought clarification from the War Department in Washington regarding the meaning (and implications for their social and economic status) of an unexpected change that had been made in Count's title—his original title of naval attaché having been changed without explanation to *assistant to* the naval attaché.

85   "Drive from Paris to Chartres": Along the way, their route having been delayed by a bicycle road race, they'd stopped for a memorable lunch, which she described as follows: "For approximately sixty cents each, we had the following: hors d'oeuvres of several varieties, ham with a delicious sauce, mushrooms creamed in a wine sauce and served on bread which had been soaked in grease (delicious), partridge broiled and served with minute shoestring potatoes and wonderful watercress; a perfect green salad with a French dressing, as only the French can make; fresh wild strawberries with sourcreme ice cream—wonderful!—and wine!" Letter from Tiny, September 19, 1939, 3.

87   "A year of instruction": "There was a facetious saying at one time in the army that the student body was made up of 'aides, adjutants, and asses.' If this in fact was a basis of selection, results have more than justified its worth." Orville Z. Tyler Jr., *The History of Forth Leavenworth, 1937–1951* (Fort Leavenworth, KS: Command and General Staff College, 1951), available online at https://apps.dtic.mil/dtic/tr/fulltext/u2/a437831.pdf, 4.

By statute, a "qualified" recommendation on graduation from the college was a requirement for being added to the general staff corps.

88 "A status and a conviction that they were important": The school picked up and delivered the students' baggage, directed each to quarters marked with his name, made and ready, and issued his equipment quickly. Students were fed in a large, polished dining room at ten-man tables and were provided transportation when walking was not desirable. Overall, the atmosphere made each student feel that the post and the school existed only to facilitate his primary mission—to graduate as a trained commander and general staff officer—and that he was the school's only reason for being.

88 "That sense of accomplishment and of fitting": And that sense appears to have been somehow mirrored in Griff's thoughts about his family. From Leavenworth, he wrote a letter to little Alice in which he told her of his Welsh ancestry. And he must have felt close to his family—or at least to his sister Tiny. Sometime soon after she left for Europe, he sent her copies of pictures he had taken at her send-off and also sent her a camera, for which she thanked him.

Griff displayed his pride in December, when he participated as one of six groomsmen for Captain Douglas Valentine, a Leavenworth classmate, at Valentine's wedding in Appleton, Wisconsin, attended by six hundred, in which all six groomsmen—in full ceremonial uniform, with swords—formed an arch of sabers under which the bride and groom and wedding party marched out to the two-hundred-person reception.

89 "Amiens Cathedral": Tiny called it a gem and wrote that it was considered the purest Gothic church in France, built at the same time as Chartres Cathedral and Notre-Dame de Paris, but that most of Amiens' original glass windows had been destroyed and replaced, "so their beauty is very commonplace by comparison with Chartres, but nonetheless beautiful to me. . . . I can't imagine the love, work, and awe of God that went into the building of such a magnificent structure. . . . Back in the cathedral . . . I slipped away [from the guide] and just sat and looked at the beautiful perspective of the interior as a whole." Letter from Tiny, spring 1939.

Notes to Chapter 9

92 "Plans to take over the lead": Mastorakis, a twenty-seven-year-old from Paris, had been trained in historic-buildings architecture.

92 "Sunday, September 25": On that day, Tiny had attended the cathedral's last Mass to be held for months.

92 "Jean Chadel": During World War II, he would become a recognized Resistance figure and at the time of liberation of Chartres would become prefect of Eure-et-Loire.

93 "Cherry pickers": This apparatus, designed for a different use by Mr. Faucheux, the eponymous founder of his Chartres construction firm, consists of a platform on which two men can stand. A system of telescopic tubes controlled by a motor makes it possible to raise this platform, either vertically or following on at variable angles, up to a height that can reach, depending on the apparatus, a maximum of nine, fifteen, or twenty-four meters, which has not yet been exceeded. When the machine, which is moved by means of a tractor, has arrived at the desired location, it takes only five minutes to get the platform to the desired level, which can then be raised and lowered in tiny increments. The prices, depending on the height at which

the device allows access, varied from 10,500 francs (for twelve meters) to 11,750 (for fifteen meters), 13,500 (for eighteen meters), and 21,500 (for twenty-four meters). This is to say that this device would be three to five times more expensive than one of the scaffoldings proposed.

Each unit, designed to be pulled by a truck and maneuvered by a team of men, was built on a metal platform about four feet square, with two automobile tires on an axle near its front, one right, the other left, holding the platform a foot and a half above the floor. Two small, six-inch swivel wheels supported the rear end, attached to vertical shafts that permitted 360-degree motion. A vertical triangular steel frame was affixed to the base platform by means of a swivel, having attached to it a tall steel telescopic shaft, some eight to ten inches in diameter at the base and six to eight inches in diameter at the top. The shaft was attached to the triangular frame together with adjustable supporting cables so as to be capable of being raised and lowered into various angles, as well as being extendable in length.

Three sizes of the device were on hand, varying from thirty-two to eighty feet in height. Also attached to the base of the shaft at its rear was a large steel box into which varying quantities of counterweights were placed. The top of the shaft had affixed to it a horizontal platform, two to four feet in size, surrounded by a waist-high, fencelike rectangular guardrail forming a basket in which a worker could stand, albeit on its somewhat-tilted floor. The base was fitted with adjusting cranks and hand-powered cable winches. At each corner of the square base, adjustable-height vertical stabilizer shafts were attached, which would be set firmly on the floor to level and stabilize the unit before a worker climbed into the basket to be raised to a high level to perform the work.

93 "Charles Lorin and eight of his men": They included Messrs. Bourgeot, Delange, Menry, and Tournel, plus one other, together with two employees of Mr. Leglise.

95 "The second of the two window-removal alternatives": They determined that it would be futile to think that the windows could be removed in a few hours without major risk. As summarized by Jean Trouvelot,

> After action of this kind, little would be likely to remain of the ancient stained-glass windows, and serious restoration work would be required. It would be preferable in this case that the removal of the stained glass [be carried out in a reasonable manner].
>
> We believe that by making improvements in organization and equipment, the task could be simplified. [These may include [an] increase in the number of scaffolds, training and organization of volunteers, requisition of specialists, modification in the fashion of fixing the stained glass . . .]

Note that the bracketed text above indicates illegible handwriting whose meaning the translator approximated. From Trouvelot, "Passive Defense Report."

95 "Longer than . . . would have dared to hope": The period of extreme worry would not start even for another year. The period of the "Phony War" would last from September 3, 1939, to May 10, 1940.

95 "Thousands of window panels": Each window panel was about fifteen to forty inches in size.

95 "*Feuillards*": The strips (*feuillards*) of the ambulatory windows were modified as they were progressively restored and the fittings were repaired, consolidated, and sealed. The flashings and hardened putty of many of the windows that had been installed thirteen years before in 1925, composed of hydraulic lime and cement that had ensured perfect seal, were removed and replaced with new flashings with less lime and "lean" sands (soft putty and soft flashings), permitting easier and faster removal.

The saddle bars and strips were restored, consolidated, and sealed to preserve them in place. In general, the type of frame selected needed to be capable of supporting stained glass weighing approximately four pounds per square foot and configured with mullions, allowing subdivision of larger areas into panels of approximately fourteen linear perimeter feet. In addition to the overall structural requirements, the frames or sash had to include a glazing rebate that measured three-eighths of an inch to a half inch wide by three-eighths of an inch to a half inch deep and allowed the panels of stained glass to engage into the frame or sash a minimum of one-quarter inch. An allowance of three thirty-seconds to one-eighth of an inch between the stained glass panel and the frame was typical.

95 "Preparatory work on . . . other parts": Jean Trouvelot continued in early 1939 to solicit bids for further work on the cathedral using the scaffolding that remained in place. On February 1, 1939, he received a proposal from Entrepose to supply equipment for scaffolding for use in the high nave and apse of the choir and for repairing a layer of paint using the scaffolding furnished for the windows of the high nave. Archives départementales de la Eure-et-Loir, 4T NC Art. 83, 4T NC Art. 84. The Fine Arts Administration sought additional financing to accomplish this and other work.

95 "Extraordinary service": In his report to the HMC following the portion of the project between September 1938 and early September 1939, Jean Trouvelot wrote,

> We must pay tribute and express our gratitude to all those who helped us in this difficult task: to Mr. Chadel, secretary-general of the prefecture, to Mr. Gilbert, mayor of Chartres, to Bishop Harscouët, Bishop of Chartres, and to the cathedral curate who facilitated the accomplishment of our mission. To Mr. Grand, president of the volunteers of Chartres, who placed himself entirely at our disposition and who spared no effort, recruiting staff and facilitating the regulation of immediate expenditures. To the businesses of Chartres, heads of business and industry, to the volunteers of Chartres, a Mr. Germain, colleague of Mr. Maunoury, to the glassmakers/painters, to all the workers, to the military, all of whom were intelligently devoted and are above all praise. All have an enormous amount of good will and have worked hard to overcome any difficulties.
>
> Personally we extend our thanks to our two colleagues Louis Linzeler and Michael Mastorakis, who lead the maneuver under our direction and who worked diligently all the time they were on-site,

smoothing out difficulties, providing guidance, leading the work, educating team leaders, managing the work. It was they who, under our direction, prepared and realised the coordination of the Passive Defence works, both at our offices in Paris and on-site. We extend to them our particular thanks and our profound gratitude.

With what we have, despite the lack of resources and funds, all involved did their utmost considering the circumstances in which the work was performed.

Trouvelot, "Passive Defense Works," 25.

96 "National petition": The petition was signed by a number of prominent Frenchmen: the poets Paul Claudel and Paul Valéry; Raoul Dautry, managing director of railway fees; Léon Bérard, senator; René Johannet, writer; editorialists Paul-Emile Cadilhac (*L'Illustration*), André Pironneau (the *Times*), and Albert Mousset (*Journal des débats*); Louis Marin, former minister; and several members of the French Academy. The petition read in part,

> At 580 meters from the cathedral was gradually established an important base for military aviation. In case of war, the immediate attack of this base by the opponent would have the effect of annihilating the set of [glassworks] absolutely unique, universally famous, and that is one of the biggest titles of glory of France. This loss, consumed in an instant, would be forever irreparable. History has pilloried the Turks, who had installed a powder magazine in the Parthenon. The Chartres aviation camp is a monstrosity of the same order. The same state of weakness would be inflicted on us indelibly . . . if the disaster occurred. . . . Our country [is] threatened with a definitive and total loss . . . The honor of France, to whom . . . this deposit [is entrusted] [requires that we must account to] future French, as well as to the whole of Humanity.

The matter was debated in the senate, pressed by Leon Bérard, senator and academician. It was opposed by Jean Valadier, senator of Eure-et-Loir, concerned about the impact of closing the base on the local economy and employment, calling Bérard "a maniac obsessed by an incoercible fear." Minister of the Air Guy La Chambre claimed that the air base was not a target for the enemy but, on the contrary, a guarantee of security for the area. Carlier gave a radio interview to press his petition and campaign, which was unsuccessful. "Worry of the French Chartrains and 'Intellectuals,'" *Cathédrale Notre-Dame de Chartres* (website), accessed February 19, 2018, http://www.cathedrale-chartres.org/fichiers/hebdo-cathedrale/hebdo-2014/414-hebdo-280714-030814.pdf.

NOTES TO CHAPTER 10

97 "War production into high gear": Nicole D. Risser, *France Under Fire: German Invasion, Civilian Flight, and Family Survival during World War II* (Cambridge: Cambridge University Press, 2012), 31.

97 "Peace dissolved into war": Czechoslovakia split into two parts when its German-leaning Slovak portion left behind its remaining Czech portion, which the Germans occupied in violation of the Munich Agreement. Hitler soon demanded the return of Poland's Danzig, and the French and British stepped in to guarantee Polish independence.

97 "Four hundred thousand exiles": Risser, *France Under Fire*, 30.

98 "He had taken charge": He rejoined the military in September 1939 as chief of the military's Monuments Service to the GQG. S.v. "Grand Quartier Général (1939–1940)," Wikipedia, last edited January 5, 2019, https://en.wikipedia.org/wiki/Grand_Quartier_Général_(1939–1940).

98 "Train almost a quarter of the workers on-site": Karlsgodt, *Defending National Treasures*, 105.

98 "Zay launched both evacuations": It is not clear what event, precisely, triggered his action. It was likely the rapidly escalating tension between Germany and Poland during the second and third weeks of August 1938. The French and British had been trying to convince the Polish to permit the Soviets to enter Poland in the event of a German invasion, but as late as August 20, the Poles continued to refuse, and the French and British negotiations for a military treaty with the Soviets turned sour on the twenty-first.

99 "Windows ... with rigid flashings": Removal of windows sealed with hard cement took six times longer to remove than windows sealed with soft putty. Their old, hard cement made it difficult to remove their glass panels from the masonry without breaking many of them. Most of such remaining windows likely consisted of windows that, while of stained glass or in some cases of clear glass, were of relatively recent vintage, installed in modern times, most likely the eighteenth and nineteenth centuries.

In the 1938 work, priority would have been given to the majority of the windows that dated back to the Middle Ages—those most worthy of saving in case of an early attack. To extend such work now to the newer windows, some of the artisans began training workers to remove hard cement and to loosen them from the jambs.

99 "Positioning the scaffolding": Stained-glass windows consist of an arrangement of individual panels, each depicting a scene, such as a biblical or allegorical or historical scene, all grouped into a geometric design. Between the panels within the window is a heavier geometric iron framework that holds the panels together, each in a unique shape, with all pieces joined together to form a graphic image. The individual pieces of glass had been pieced together by inserting their edges into flexible lead "cames" consisting of back-to-back grooves, and held in place by soft putty pushed into the cames to hold the panel together. The putty was made from a mixture of powdered chalk, linseed oil, and clear spirits, to accelerate the drying process. The putty had a firm viscous consistency and set slowly.

The many panels of a window are held together by a framework or armature, constructed of iron, fashioned into a pattern of circles or quatrefoils and other shapes with room in between them for a series of background panels. As the windows were removed, the heavy iron framework that held the panels was left in place, and substituted coverings were inserted into the framework to provide a substitute temporary seal of the building from the elements. Two materials were used: One was a particleboard known as vitrex. The other was the earliest form of clear Plexiglas, intended to permit light to enter the building. On the lowest levels of such substitute windows, scenes were painted, to be viewed by parishioners and visitors, in a crude effort to at least remind them of the withdrawn stained-glass windows.

The larger stained-glass windows of the cathedral contained as many as thirty or forty panels. On the outer edges of the windows—such as the tall, narrow, arched shape of a lancet window—there often appears a narrow band of edging up to several inches wide, sometimes shaped in a scalloped pattern. In the cathedral, most edging like this consisted of stained glass, but quite a few consisted of clear glass; this edging tended to be fashioned of thin, brittle glass that was susceptible to breaking. During the 1918 removal of the stained-glass windows, many such edging pieces had been broken, and so the teams were determined to use extra caution to minimize damage during the 1939 removal.

Each stained-glass window also contained two additional types of supports, called *saddle bars*. Those were horizontal metal bars whose ends were inserted into the masonry on either side of the window to give it structural support. The saddle bars are of two types. One type is used in pairs and is positioned within horizontal slots formed by the upper edge of one panel and the horizontal lower edge of the panel above it, with one horizontal bar placed on the outside of the window and the other on the inside. The outer bar had welded onto it small cleats that formed keyholes; the inner bar contained slots that fit over such cleats and are attached by means of keys or *clavettes*. The cleats fit between the lower and upper panel of glass and the saddle bars are wide enough to hold the lower and upper panels in place and are secured in place by means of the keys inserted into the cleats.

A second type of saddle bar is used on one side of the window only. It has metal ties called *vergettes* that are welded onto it, soldered directly to only the cames of the window wherever they intersect with the saddle bar.

In addition to the cement holding each piece of glass into the cames of its panel, a window carries cement, which serves as "flashing" around its outer edges to seal the window into the window jamb.

100   "Assumption Window": A lancet-shaped window thirty-two feet tall and more than six feet wide, with a pair of two-foot curved-glass border panels whose continuations surround the edge of the window, forming a border about four inches wide. Its border panels join at the top to form the apex of the window's pointed arch. The background appearing in those panels is an intricate pattern of small, multicolored glass pieces depicting flowers symmetrically intertwined around green and yellow vines. The scenes it depicts include shoemakers—who donated the window—shown using various tools, as well as scenes from the life of Mary, including her death, funeral, Assumption, and Coronation.

100   "Removal of a stained-glass window": It is essentially a six-step process:

1. First, the scaffold is moved into position, and the designated storage crate (or pre-determined size and shape) to contain the window is hoisted up to the work platform to be available to hold the pieces of the window as soon as they are removed.
2. Second, in the case of ancient windows, as a precaution, a drawing or cartoon is made, in duplicate, of the complete window and of each of its panels, usually by means of a rubbing (such drawings numbered according to a master plan and then one copy of such drawing to be kept in a file and the other to be inserted into the crate in which the window is to be transported and stored).
3. Third, to remove the panels, each key is removed to release the saddle bars between panels, and for those saddle bars attached with vergettes, each vergette is unsoldered and detached.
4. Fourth, the putty around the edges of the panel is removed to separate it from its cames, and in the case of panels whose edges are positioned at the outer edges of the window, the flashing that constitutes the seal between the edge of the window and the window jamb must be freed or broken.
5. Fifth, each panel is disassembled into individual pieces of glass, and each such piece is individually wrapped and inserted into its own compartment inside its designated storage crate.
6. Sixth, the crate is lowered down to the floor to be sealed, labeled, and transported, and the workers then move to a lower platform on the scaffold to be in position to remove the next lower level of panels.

101   "Chapel of Notre-Dame-Sous-Terre": From there, the gallery's fifty rows of moveable wooden chairs—which had for years been arranged four-abreast along each wall, with a five-foot-wide walkway running from one end of the crypt to the other—would have been cleared and moved elsewhere.

101   "Life of the Virgin Mary Window": It was also a lancet, created in the early thirteenth century, the same size at the Assumption Window. It consisted of twenty-five picture panels and almost twice that many smaller panels that depict hundreds of small arches constructed of thin, curved, red-glass strips forming larger rounded arches with a background in multiple shades of dark blue. The window narrates Mary's life in twenty-four scenes, starting with Mary's parents and including the Annunciation, the Nativity, the Massacre of the Innocents, the Flight into Egypt, and others.

101   "Charlemagne Window": It was one of the largest class of lancet windows, also made in the thirteenth century, and consisted of twenty-two picture-scenes—about the travels and exploits of Charlemagne, including his journey to Jerusalem—and a larger number of intricate background panels.

103   "Exodus of artworks": Starting that day and for the next eight weeks, the Fine Arts Administration, working with the defense ministry, dispatched trucks loaded with more than two thousand cases and fifteen hundred additional objects, making more than 230 trips from national museums, including from Paris, Versailles, Saint-Germaine, and others, to storage depots—mostly rural châteaus—a hundred sites in fifty-five French administrative departments.

     The Louvre alone evacuated a thousand cases or more of Greek, Roman, Asian, and Egyptian artifacts and antiquities and 268 cases of paintings and hundreds of drawings, engravings, sculptures, and other artworks. On each trip, at least one museum staff member and one or two guards rode along, with museum personal inventorying the items both on departure and arrival of each convoy. Museum staff outfitted the buildings with firefighting equipment and notified local firefighters of the deposits and from then on conducted periodic inspections. Karlsgodt, *Defending National Treasures*, 74–75.

103 "Daylight in the aisles . . . washing out the colors": "To all who come there its architecture, sculptures, and windows present an unforgettable image of light, strength, and repose, symbolic of the Faith of the Middle Ages." Dierrick, *Stained Glass at Chartres*, 3.

104 "Then he visited Chartres Cathedral": The same day, the French government placed the railways under military control. The following day, Britain and France delivered their final warnings to Hitler to withdraw from Poland. And the British and French proclaimed that the Germans had mobilized toward Poland.

104 "Through the wide windows, a brutal light": Zay, *Souvenirs et solitude*, 307.

105 "Plexiglas": A registered trademark of Evonik Industries AG.

106 "Three large protective structures": The new structures were 6–9 feet deep at the base, 30 feet high, and 45–150 feet in length. In all, they employed, among other things, 67,000 sandbags and more than 17,000 linear feet of the tubing, 3,100 feet of cable, and 650 feet of vitrex.

106 "The only mishap": Jean Trouvelot wrote in his October 19 report to the Fine Arts Administration, "We note that the restoration of certain windows is long overdue, particularly the rose windows, and above all we are pleased to express our recognition of the contractors, glass painters, workers, and volunteers who have all worked with dedication, intelligence, and initiative that is beyond praise. The mobilized, despite their desire to see their families before setting off, worked until the last moment." Arch. Eure-et-Loir 4 T NC86.

106 "Over 193,000 square feet of stained glass": Karlsgodt, *Defending National Treasures*, 105.

106 "On September 13, Jean Zay resigned": Marcel Ruby, *La vie et l'œuvre de Jean Zay* (Paris: Éditions Corsaire, 1994), 415. See also "Jean Zay (1904–1944)," *Musée Protestant*, accessed October 28, 2019, https://www.museeprotestant.org/en/notice/jean-zay-1904-1944-2/.

107 "Chartres' windows rested in the crypt": In mid-November, Mauritius Jusselin, curator of antiquities and art objects of Eure-et-Loir, prepared a detailed list of all of the crates: from the Church of Saint-Pierre de Dreux (2 cases), Saint-Pierre Chartres (123 cases), Saint Aignan de Chartres (9 cases), and Notre-Dame de Chartres (923 cases). Thierry Baritaud, *La depose des vitraux de la cathedrale de Chartres* (Chartres: Centre International du Vitrail, 2015), 4.

Notes to Chapter 11

111 "Lend-Lease Act": Selig Adler, *The Isolationist Impulse: Its Twentieth Century Reaction* (Santa Barbara: Greenwood/Praeger: 1957, 1974), 282.

112 "The Germans took them by surprise": Max Hastings, in an article for the *Washington Post*, summarized the relevant question and answered it:

How was it, then, that the US Army found it enormously difficult, indeed often impossible, to defeat Germans encountered on anything like even terms?

First, there was the extraordinary failure of the Western Allies in 1944–'45 to provide their ground forces with adequate weapons. By that phase of the war, American and British technology had created a host of miracles: superb combat aircraft, antisubmarine-warfare equipment, radar, the amphibious DUKW, the proximity fuse, and the jeep. Through Ultra, the greatest cipher-breaking operation of all time, the Allies possessed extraordinary knowledge of the German order of battle, deployments, and often—though not in the Battle of the Bulge—German intentions.

Yet amid all this, in northwest Europe the Allied leaders invited their ground troops to fight the Wehrmacht with equipment inferior in every category save artillery and transport. German machine guns, mortars, machine pistols, antitank weapons, and armored personnel carriers were all superior to those of Britain and America. Above all, Germany possessed better tanks. The Sherman, which dominated the Allied campaign, was a superbly reliable piece of machinery. But it was fatally flawed by lack of an adequate gun to penetrate the Tiger and Panther and by poor battlefield survivability in the face of German tank guns.

These shortcomings were well understood in Washington and London before the 1944 campaign began. But the chiefs of staff expressed their confidence that Allied numerical superiority was so great that some qualitative inferiority was acceptable. This confidence was a fatal delusion....

One of the greatest American achievements of the war was the expansion of a tiny prewar peacetime force of 190,000 into an army of more than eight million men. Yet an inevitable consequence of this transformation was a chronic shortage of high-quality, trained career leaders. In all America's wars, her allies have agreed that the able West Pointer has no superior. The problem, in World War II, was that there were nowhere near enough of these to lead an army of eight million men.

Max Hastings, "Their Wehrmacht Was Better than Our Army," *Washington Post*, May 5, 1985, https://www.washingtonpost.com/archive/opinions/1985/05/05/their -wehrmacht-was-better-than-our-army/0b2cfe73-68f4-4bc3-a62d-7626f6382dbd/.

113 "Tank destroyers would ... perform an important function": "In the offensive against tanks, TDs relied on mobility and heavy firepower to offset the disadvantage of their light protective armor. They operated on the offensive in conjunction with heavy armor and were utilized to supplement the speed and firepower of the slower but more heavy armored vehicles. They were particularly adapted to this role when soggy terrain would not support the weighty tank. The TD vehicle, with less ground pressure, could maneuver through friendly units, outmaneuvering hostile armor as well, using this capability to attain an advantageous position, accomplish its fire mission, and move to the flank or rear for another strike." John A.

Nagl, "Tank Destroyers in WWII: Flawed Doctrine, Unmatched Bravery," *Armor* (January–February 1991): 26–31, https://www.tankdestroyer.net/images/stories/ArticlePDFs/Armor_Mag_Article_TDs_in_WWII.pdf.

113 "Salem Academy": At Nell's college graduation, she had been called upon to read a research paper about George Washington that she had written.

114 "Americans shifted their attitude": Nicholas John Cull, *Selling War: The British Propaganda Campaign against American "Neutrality" in World War II* (Oxford: Oxford University Press, 1996), 185, 241.

114 "The Army reorganized the Leavenworth school": Tyler, *History of Fort Leavenworth*, 11–22.

114 "Changing its basic course . . . to ten weeks": The ten-week course was for general staff officers. For reservists, it developed a separate three-month course. Tyler, *History of Fort Leavenworth*, 11.

115 "Armored Force Subsection": Tyler, *History of Fort Leavenworth*, 11–22.

116 "Family life close to his work": In what could be a reflection of that enjoyment with Nell at Leavenworth, Griff wrote a handwritten note to little Alice for her keepsake. He told her of his Welsh origins and included a copy of the Griffith family crest and explained to her that its earliest version was Gruffyedd, a combination of the two welsh words—*Griff* and *Flyd*, meaning strong and faith—and that his earliest ancestor, named Rhys ap Tudur, a Welsh nobleman who died in 1412, was a member of the Tudor family of Penmynydd who held positions of power under Richard II of England.

Griff may have been driven by something more: years passing by quickly in relation to the pace of his own accomplishments, taking note that the training and experience he had gathered since starting out as an infantry officer at Benning had cost him a decade. If he were to stay in the military, how much longer would he have to wait to find his way into the thick of some action?

117 "Camp Young in the California desert": The US Army had created Camp Young in the desert to prepare for the Africa campaign, and General Patton activated the camp, twenty miles east of Indio, California, in April 1942, but he left in late July to help prepare for the invasion of North Africa. Camp Young would become the Army's largest military post, by area. It started with ten thousand square miles and would nearly triple in size by mid-1943. The size made possible combined operations using aircraft and live-fire exercises employing all types of arms and moving men away from camp conveniences into harsh environments to temper them for the discomforts and hazards of combat over extended time.

117 "Each tent contained cots surrounding a stove": Eugene G. Schulz, *The Ghost in General Patton's Third Army: The Memoirs of Eugene G. Schulz during His Service in the United States Army in World War II* (Bloomington, IN: Xlibris, 2012), 11–13.

118 "Lifetime of honorable dealings": Humphrey wrote in part,

In these days when honor among nations has become a lost virtue, I think any citation, in the realm of honor, no matter how local, should not go unspoken.

I have in mind a man to whom honor was not a creed but a habit.

Honorable dealing was the basis of his business and professional life. Cheating, a penny either one way or the other, was unthinkable.

Honor extended farther than business transactions, however. It extended to thinking and believing. It extended to all human relationships.

It was a virtue that never was compromised. It almost was a way of life.

In involved straight thinking and straight talking. Where the chips fell was only incidental.

Honorable dealing, to this man, involved no dodges, no subterfuge, no saying-one-thing-while-thinking-another, because honor, truth, and straightforwardness went hand in hand. . . .

I never heard him mention honor. It wasn't something to be talked. But you knew what he felt about men in places of responsibility who lacked it.

It belonged in business, in public life, in community dealings, in private life. The world needs more men with that ideal.

Through a long life, W. B. Griffith contributed that, more than anybody else, to his community. And although I have had the honor to be his son-in-law, I could have said these things just as freely, if not more freely, if I hadn't been.

Walter R. Humphrey, "The Home Towner," *Temple Daily Telegram*, September 8, 1942.

118   "The normal pattern": The training—in the toughest desert conditions with infantry, artillery, tanks, and aircraft—included forced marches day and night, firearms disassembly and reassembly, hand grenades and explosives, chemical weapons, communications linkage and cabling, art and application of camouflage, bridge building, and attack-destroy-and-move-on battle tactics.

119   "Griff's corps would be relocating to Fort Campbell": The corps was then still called the Fourth Armored Corps.

NOTES TO CHAPTER 12

123   "Full of picture books, with pages of colored glass": Philip Ball, *Universe of Stone: A Biography of Chartres Cathedral* (New York: Harper, 2008), 233–34.

123   "A metaphor for the divine": Transillumination, "Metaphor for the Divine: Brian Clarke on Stained Glass," YouTube video, 3:52, November 13, 2010, https://www.youtube.com/watch?v=VYaS0NfLODQ.

123   "Stained-glass windows changed the light": One observer—writing of the difference between literary fiction and genre fiction—points to stained glass as a metaphor, noting the way a stained-glass window "changes what's on the other side, and the way you change perspective to see what's out there . . . a huge part of the experience." Katherine Locke, "Stained Glass Windows: Reflecting on a Writing Excuses Podcast Episode," *Katherine Locke* (blog), January 31, 2017, https://www.katherinelockebooks.com/blog/2017/01/31/stained-glass-windows-reflecting-on-a-writing-excuses-podcast-episode.

123 "'Something improper' about this untransformed light": Ball, *Universe of Stone,* 234. In addition, back in August when Minister Zay visited the cathedral while the windows were being removed, he noticed the brightness of the light resulting from removal. He would write in his diary years later, "through the wide windows, a brutal light, no longer filtered by the stained-glass windows, entered the cathedral, blazed in the innermost corners of the apse, beamed down upon the defenseless altars. It seems that the sanctuary had been violated, left to the forces of nature." Zay, *Souvenirs et solitude,* 307.

124 "A grandiose building": The new palace was intended as an official showcase for 1930s creativity. Forty sculptors, twenty painters, and an artisan metalworker collaborated on its inside and exterior. Four years later, Adolf Hitler would be photographed in front of the palace during his tour of Paris. It would also be the site at which the United Nations General Assembly adopted the Universal Declaration of Human Rights in 1948, and it served as the initial headquarters of NATO while its new headquarters was being built.

The meeting was held at the palace for reasons not entirely clear—likely because of the large number of attendees and because of its celebratory nature—but the location did not work out well. The minutes indicate that the acoustics were poor and there was no projection equipment to display the many photographs taken during the removal of the windows from various sites, which instead were passed during the meeting by hand from attendee to attendee. Minutes of the meeting of the Historic Monuments Commission, February 23, 1940. Jean-Daniel Pariset, ed., "23 février 1940," *Procès-verbaux de la Commission des monuments historiques, de 1848 à 1950, conservés à la Médiathèque de l'architecture et du patrimoine (Charenton-le-Pont)* (Paris: Médiathèque de l'architecture et du patrimoine, 2014), http://elec.enc.sorbonne.fr/monumentshistoriques/Annees/1940.html#93215. The minutes from 1848 to 1950 are preserved in the Médiathèque de l'architecture et du patrimoine (Charenton-le-Pont, Paris).

125 "Pivotal impact on the discovery of looted works of art": Robert M. Edsel, *The Monuments Men: Allied Heroes, Nazi Thieves and the Greatest Treasure Hunt in History* (New York: Center Street Hachette Book Group, 2009), xviii. See also Lynn H. Nicholas, *The Rape of Europa: The Fate of Europe's Treasures in the Third Reich and the Second World War* (New York: Vintage, 1995). Valland was then forty-five.

125 "Jaujard ... would be appointed ... director general": Jacques Jaujard was then forty-five, and was later appointed to other significant positions. During the war he would also manage to successfully remove artworks from the Louvre and place them in Provence—against the orders of the Vichy government.

126 "Führermuseum": Edsel, *Monuments Men,* 24.

127 "Stones are masterfully carved and fitted": Ball, *Universe of Stone,* 197.

128 "They would have known": Those present at the meetings of the Historic Monuments Commission during both wars included the following, present at both the February 23 meeting and one or more of the meetings relating to Chartres during World War I: Louis Bonnier (1856–1946), architect of the city of Paris and director of architectural services and walks and plantations of the city of Paris; Pierre Pacquet (1875–1959), diocesan architect from Cambrai and Bordeaux from 1901

and from Blois from 1904, inspector general of historic monuments from 1920; and Gabriel E. M. Ruprich-Robert (1859–1953) (son of Victor Ruprich-Robert), chief architect for historic monuments in France's departments of Puy-de-Dôme, Eure-et-Loir, and Eure.

129 "Moulin was unique in his dedication": Charles Pomaret, minister of the interior for a time, who in 1940 served for a short time in the first Pétain cabinet, wrote years later of being told by former minister of the interior Albert Sarraut "that Moulin was not only the youngest prefect in France but also one of the two best." "He was distinguished 'by his calm lucidity, and his shining humanity, which impressed all who came into contact with him.'" Alan Clinton, *Jean Moulin, 1899–1943: The French Resistance and the Republic* (New York: Palgrave, 2002), 79.

129 "Hérault": In 1917, Moulin's father had found him a position in the office of the prefect there, where he worked off and on through law school and until early 1922, when he was appointed prefect of Savoie. Four years later, Jacquier would become secretary general to the prefect of Hérault, and even later, in 1937, he would become prefect of the Dordogne. This commonality of experience in Montpellier between prefectural officials Moulin and Jacquier—and the friendship between architects Jean Trouvelot and Froidevaux—probably played a role in Laurent's team being able to target and qualify a haven for the Chartres windows, and then for Moulin to be able to quickly arrange for inspection and qualification of the site and to work out the legal and financial details with Jacquier to secure the site.

129 "First air-raid sirens sounded on May 10": Risser, *France Under Fire*, 86.

129 "Parisian suburbanites reported hearing cannon fire": Risser, *France Under Fire*, 86.

129 "Belgian refugees swarmed into France": It may just have been the growing pressure from these May events that forced the Fine Arts Administration to find a storage location. Amid countrywide panic and uncertainty as to what parts of France would be occupied, the administration likely concentrated its search for locations far to the southwest but away from the Atlantic coast.

Frightened refugees, including French and even foreign men intent on joining the Resistance fighters outside the city, could even have taken refuge in the crypt, among the one thousand wooden crates that had been strapped and nailed in place—accompanied by smells of food scraps and cries of children crammed into the tight space—as written by novelist Johanna Skibsrud. Johanna Skibsrud, *Quartet for the End of Time: A Novel* (New York: W. W. Norton, 2014), 365–66. If word of refugees living among the crates had reached Jean Moulin in his office at the prefecture, pressures on Moulin and his staff to find a safe site for the windows would have ratcheted to a new peak.

130 "Yves-Marie Froidevaux": He would later go on to hold similar positions in three other departments and would become inspector general of historic monuments and would be a professor at the National School of Fine Arts and at the School of Chaillot (Center for Higher Studies in the History and Preservation of Ancient Monuments—CESHCMA—in Paris).

130 "Town of La Tour-Blanche": It is in the region of New Aquitaine in the department of the Dordogne, the borough of Perigueux, the canton of Ribérac. According to the General Inventory of Cultural Heritage (Inventaire général

du patrimoine culturel), the castle is the historic former home of Achards and Dejean de Jovelle and later became the property of Joussain. "Inventaire général du patrimoine culturel," Ministère de la Culture (website), archived on December 10, 1026, at http://archive.wikiwix.com/cache/?url=http%3A%2F%2Fwww.culture .gouv.fr%2Fpublic%2Fmistral%2Fmerimee_fr%3FACTION%3DCHER CHER%26FIELD_1%3DREF%26VALUE_1%3DIA24000861. At the time, the mayor of Cerles was François Mazières, serving from May 1935 to May 1953.

130 "Listed in the General Inventory of Cultural Heritage": It is known as the Mérimée database. It contains information from the Historical Monuments Service and the General Inventory of Cultural Heritage and is named after the writer Prosper Mérimée, first chairman of the Historic Monuments Commission and also inspector general of historic monuments.

131 "On June 3 . . . German bombers attacked the Chartres airfield": Peter Scott Janes and Keith Janes, "Rudolf Ptacek," *Conscript Heroes*, http://www.conscript-heroes .com/Art01-Rudolph-Ptacek-960.html, accessed June 2, 2018.

Notes to Chapter 13

133 "Operation Paula": The German codename given for the World War II Luftwaffe offensive operation to destroy the remaining units of the French air force in 1940. Eleven hundred aircraft were part of the operation, which was launched June 3. Ron Mackay, *Heinkel He 111*, Crowood Aviation Series (Marlborough: Crowood Press, 2003), 10; Christopher Chant, *The Encyclopedia of Codenames of World War II* (London: Routledge and Kegan Paul, 1987), 10, 62.

133 "Second bombing raid": Janes and Janes, "Rudolf Ptacek."

134 "Journalists reported": "German Bombers Hit Paris," United Press International, June 3, 1940 (text available online at https://www.upi.com/Archives/1940/06/03/ German-bombers-hit-Paris/4413583280132/).

134 "Attacked twenty-eight railways": Edward Hooton, *Luftwaffe at War: Blitzkrieg in the West* (London: Chervron/Ian Allan, 2007), 84.

135 "Foreigners and displaced persons": Presumably Jean Chadel would have offered some payment and food to the workers, as had been offered back in August and September.

135 "Roger Grand": Identity not confirmed. According to notes linked in the minutes of the Historic Monuments Commission of February 24, 1940, this refers possibly to Roger Grand (1874–1962), historian and French politician, a student of the National School of Chartres (archivist paleographer) who began his career as an archivist in the Department of Archives of Cantal, where he provided the impetus to create the society of Haute-Auvergne, and then became professor of history of law at the School of Chartres, while continuing to pursue farming. He presided over the National Union of Agricultural Unions and served as senator of Morbhian from 1927 to 1933. Pariset, "23 février 1940."

135 "Line up more volunteers": He would also have made calls to Mastorakis to corral ropes and dollies and pushcarts and more men to be on hand when needed throughout the day at both the cathedral and the rail spur. In addition, he would have made calls and sent telegrams to Jacquier and Herpé to wrangle trucks to

meet the two trains in the Dordogne and haul crates into the trucks, vans to be available at the road closest to Fongrenon to shuttle the crates off the trains onto trucks (to get them closer to the quarry), and smaller vans to shuttle the crates up the dirt road to Fongrenon. He also would have made calls to scrounge men to haul the crates onto handcarts and then up into the quarry and made still more calls to line up armed guards to watch over the crates around the clock in the quarry for the coming weeks and months, and maybe years, as long as the crates would have to remain sequestered.

135   "Work for Air Minister Pierre Cot": During the latter portion of that time, from mid-1937 to April 1939, Jean Moulin ran a program called Aviation Populaire, intended to democratize aeronautical skill and enthusiasm and popularize aviation.

135   "Official residence": Clinton, *Jean Moulin*, 70.

137   "Looking for a way out of the war": Risser, *France Under Fire*, 92–93.

139   "115–140 men": There would have been three dozen men in two shifts, totaling seventy-two men, plus another dozen men to handle the carts, plus three men in each truck (another twenty to forty-five). There would also have been men on each boxcar, a minimum of nine in all.

144   "At dusk, the locomotive pulled out": Baritaud, *La depose*, 5.

145   "No way for a locomotive to get through": Jean Trouvelot, Report to the Minister of National Education, March 11, 1946, Mediathèque Charenton (Paris), 81 28 16; Thierry Baritaud, "The Light of Chartres in the Périgordian Dark," *Nontron-naises Chronicles, Journal of the Historical and Archaeological Society of Périgord*, no. 23 (2007): 48.

146   "An explosion . . . destroyed all nearby railcars": Sources conflict as to the time gap between the departure of the second train and the German attack that exploded the rail cars. According to a report from Jean Trouvelot to the minister of national education, dated March 11, 1946, "Some hours later, the carriages that had contained the cases exploded." But according to Baritaud's 2001 report, "As for Berchères-les-Pierres station, it was bombed four days after the departure of the two trains that carried the stained-glass windows." Baritaud, "The Light of Chartres," 48.

NOTES TO CHAPTER 14

151   "Crypt of Saint Lubin": Saint Lubin—or Leobinus—had been a peasant child who, by studying, rose to become a sixth-century bishop of Chartres. He was considered by the winemakers to be their patron saint. They and the innkeepers donated the window called the Life of Leobinus (number 63), in the north aisle of the nave, in which the wine theme appears, illustrating various aspects of the cultivation of wine.

151   "Emerged from the crypt holding the Camisa": Ball, *Universe of Stone*, 8–9, 20–21.

152   "Whereabouts of the windows must remain a secret": Maurice Jusselin, "Eure-et-Loir Objets mobiliers: Etat des objets d art replies et des depots dans le depart-ment," Report of Les Conservateurs des Antiquités et Objets d'Arts, Les Con-servateur des Antiquités et Objets d'Arts, Chartres, May 23, 1943, Mediathèque Charenton (Paris), 80 3 63, pp. 2–4.

152   "Pressure-tested veteran trainman": Perhaps he was even a veteran of World War I who also had lived through the difficult years suffered by the French rail industry

during the interwar period that had resulted in the 1938 nationalization of the French railroads. Such a veteran operator, likely hating the Boche, if he'd heard about this opportunity to pilot the train containing the windows, would have felt compelled to volunteer to join the mission.

153 "Who were the men recruited to unload": Today we don't know for sure, even though five months later a group of the night watchmen would inscribe their names for posterity on one of the interior walls of the quarry.

153 "Avoid scrutiny of German warplanes": In view of damage to the rail network around Paris, the locomotive would be needed back in Chartres. The engineer likely sought to make the run back to Chartres under cover of darkness.

154 "Fongrenon . . . within . . . Cercles": The castle was built in the seventeenth century. It had first been the home of a family by the name of Achards, an ancient Anglo-Saxon family name. The Dejean de Joelle family then acquired it, after which the Joussain family acquired it.

155 "Finally rested at Fongrenon": On the wall of Room 3, where the first hundred crates were stored, one of the men carved into the wall a horizontal line and an arrow pointing to it with the words *1st reduced*, to mark the position of the first deposit.

156 "Secrecy and security": And the creation of the Vichy zone likely required a change of the guarding personnel. Only persons authorized could cross the demarcation line, and then only at official crossing points on presentation of an identity card and a pass delivered by German authorities responsible for the area's civil and military administration, accompanied by a full set of documents including certificate of domestication, identity photograph, and reason for crossing, granted only in cases of urgent need (such as funerals, close relatives' serious illness, or births, and only after complying with a series of procedures and bureaucratic delays). For persons living within ten miles of the line, exceptions were possible upon demonstration of need. But for those guarding the windows, surely the risk of breaching secrecy would have been substantial. So anyone living west of the line would have had to have been replaced with someone living east of the line. General Secretariat for the French Ministry of Defence, "The Demarcation Line," Remembrance and Citizenship series, no. 7, accessed July 7, 2018, http://www.civs.gouv.fr/images/pdf/documents_utiles/documents_dhis toire/the_demarcation_line.pdf.

156 "Evacuation of government officials": Risser, *France Under Fire*, 91.

156 "Ordered punishment of prefects": Risser, *France Under Fire*, 92.

156 "Spare Paris from destruction": Risser, *France Under Fire*, 92. After the war, in his memoirs Reynaud bitterly revealed that General Weygand and Marshall Pétain had never intended to mount a military defense of Paris.

156 "Slow-moving columns of refugees": Within a few days, the wealthier districts of the city were nearly deserted, and the population of the working-class districts dropped by more than 70 percent. Alfred Fierro, *Histoire et dictionnaire de Paris* (Paris: R. Laffront, 1996), 236.

156 "High-ranking military officers and civil servants in retreat": Clinton, *Jean Moulin*, 83–84.

157 "First prefect du Tille had found at his post": Clinton, *Jean Moulin*, 84–85.

157 "Promised to provide meals to refugees": During the afternoon, refugees passing through reported that German troops had entered Paris. Jean Moulin went to Dreux to inspect the latest damage. He drove with Mayor Vilette and Subprefect Ressuer. They saw the destruction of many new buildings. Moulin wrote, "Nobody said a word, but each of us had the same thought: So. It is over." Clinton, *Jean Moulin*, 85.

158 "Refugees . . . pouring into the cathedral's crypt, seeking shelter": Clinton, *Jean Moulin*, 87.

159 "Moulin . . . wearing a scarf": Clinton, *Jean Moulin*, 91–92.

159 "Moulin was removed from office by the Vichy government": Pierre Assouline, "Beneath the Scarf of Jean Moulin," trans. Ruth Larson, *South Central Review* 25, no. 2 (Summer 2008): 9.

159 "Those in charge of the library could not refuse": Ironically, they would even later celebrate the return of the books and manuscripts by staging an exhibition of them at the library in March 1942. But the items would no longer be protected from bombs.

Notes to Chapter 15

163 "G-3's primary responsibility": United States Army, Twentieth Corps, *The XX Corps: Its History and Service in World War II* (Halsted, KS: W.E.B.S., 1984), 79, 90.

163 "Setup of the G-3 office": Massa's job, as cartographer, would have been to plot on acetate-covered war maps with grease pencils all information revealing movements of each unit of the force as soon as they were received from the field, including name and number, location, strength, and vector.

165 "Fort Slocum": There the men would be housed for a few days to a week for equipment to be loaded and supplies assembled. Most enlisted men would get a one-day pass for last-minute R&R in the city. Only after their return to the fort would they receive orders to pack up and ship out the same evening. Launches would take them to a converted passenger steamer in the East River. They and others—sixteen thousand men in all—would be loaded to sail across the Atlantic to an unknown destination.

Notes to Chapter 17

181 "Chief keeper of Château de Pierrefonds": Fifty-five miles northeast of Paris, Château de Pierrefonds was erected in the late fourteenth century by Duke Louis of Orléans but had fallen into ruins by the seventeenth century, until Napoleon III commissioned architect Eugène Viollet-le-Duc to rebuild it. The architect applied his designs to create the ideal château, such as would have existed in the Middle Ages.

181 "Seven watchmen:" The watchmen were Jules Pillot, Alexis Moreau, M. M. Aupy, and Messrs. Charlelia, Deport, and Etourneau.

182 "Detailed inventories of the French collections": The Kunstschutz, the German cultural conservation program, which in 1940 had been reconstituted as a branch of the Nazi occupation government, was headed by Count Wolff-Metternich, a former German professor of architecture. The number of depots totaled fifty-eight and was eventually reduced to forty-one. Ten depots were maintained for national museums and thirty-one for provincial museums, not including others created for

items such as the glass from historic monuments. Karlsgodt, *Defending National Treasures*, 309, and appendixes A, B, and C.

182 "Germans knew of the existence": Baritaud, "The Light of Chartres," 48.

182 "Certain elements of the German regime": Edsel, *Monuments Men*, 127; Karlsgodt, *Defending National Treasures*, 39–41.

182 "It may have been only a matter of time": Stained-glass windows may not have been a priority among Hitler's parameters of artistic taste, but such windows were the subject of German looting, including those of Strasbourg Cathedral and other locations.

182 "Certain Vichy figures as collaborators and others as resisters": Karlsgodt, *Defending National Treasures*, 264–65.

183 "Drawings were discovered by Baritaud in 2001": Baritaud, "The Light of Chartres," 48.

184 "Appears to have been the work of the American planes": Hans van der Hoeven, *Lost Memory: Libraries and Archives Destroyed in the Twentieth Century* (Paris: United Nations Educational, Scientific and Cultural Organization, 1996), 14.

184 "Leaves of parchment fused together": In early 1948, departmental archivist Maurice Jusselin and Canon Yves Delaporte would begin work to identify the manuscripts. Beginning in the 1950s, some manuscripts would be studied by specialists who would continue identifying texts and putting the fragments in order. In later years, some of the manuscripts would be restored using transportable noninvasive multispectral imaging and volumetric-screening equipment developed to study the surface of planets, furnished by the University of Rochester's Lazarus Project. "Chartres," *The Lazarus Project*, accessed February 27, 2019, http://www.lazarus projectimaging.com/previous-projects/chartres/.

185 "The British Special Operations Executive had parachuted Moulin back into France": Jean Moulin's report to de Gaulle of the May 27 meeting, at 48 Rue du Four on the left bank of the Seine, "described the extraordinary difficulties that had been overcome to hold the meeting at all. The statements agreed to at the meeting clearly showed the hand of Moulin himself, carefully balancing a clear republican stance with attention to the sensitivities of the Resistance chiefs." Clinton, *Jean Moulin*, 174. According to historian Alan Clinton, "It is sometimes said that the CNR was more important for what it was than for what it did. Nevertheless, its establishment has generally been considered in retrospect as the cardinal wartime event in the continuity of the French state and its Republic and the crowning achievement of Jean Moulin." Ibid., 151.

186 "He could convince others": Jean Zay suffered a similar fate only weeks after D-Day. He had resigned as minister in 1939 to join the French Army, and he had served as a second lieutenant attached to the French Fourth Army headquarters. He had been given leave to attend the last session of the French Parliament, held in Bordeaux in June 1940. With many other politicians, in June 1940 he had boarded the vessel SS *Massilia* in Bordeaux, bound for Casablanca to join in forming a resistance government in North Africa. But he was arrested in August 1940 for desertion and returned to France, where he was held at the military prison.

Zay was convicted of desertion by a military tribunal in October 1940 and sentenced to deportation for life, the sentence later commuted to internment in France. But he was allowed to communicate with friends and family. In June 1944, he was removed from the prison by three members of the Milice paramilitary group, purportedly so he could be transferred to another French prison in Melun, but they murdered him in a wood near an abandoned quarry. After the war, Zay's conviction would be posthumously annulled by an appeals court. His body was found in 1946 under a pile of stones. Eventually, the surviving Milice militiaman would be convicted of Zay's murder. In 2014, Zay would be recognized at the Panthéon in Paris as a leading figure in the Resistance.

NOTES TO CHAPTER 18

188 "V-mail": The Smithsonian describes V-mail as follows: "V, or Victory mail, was a valuable tool for the military during World War II. The process, which originated in England, was the microfilming of specially designed letter sheets. Instead of using valuable cargo space to ship whole letters overseas, microfilmed copies were sent in their stead and then 'blown up' at an overseas destination before being delivered to military personnel." "V-mail," Smithsonian National Postal Museum (website), accessed February 28, 2019, https://postalmuseum.si.edu/exhibits/past/the-art-of -cards-and-letters/mail-call/v-mail.html.

189 "Grif": Letters about Colonel Griffith to his brother Philip from military colleagues, as well as letters from his sister Tiny, refer to him as "Griff," and those few of his relatives who did not still call him Web seem to have preferred to call him Griff with two Fs (e.g., Gary Hendrix, husband of Griff's deceased niece, who is meticulous in such matters). Although Griff's own writings that spell his name with one F are very persuasive as to his preferred spelling, that does not square with how virtually all of the others spelled it. Also, V-mail required extreme condensation. See photo of the document at https://www.dropbox.com/s/zkstchcwshb8bk0/ DSC07284.jpg?dl=0.

193 "A sobering experience for me": Schulz, *The Ghost*, 102.

195 "Monte Cassino": In November and December 1943, American forces fought in Italy to overcome German Berhardt/Reinhard defenses, which were situated in a bulge pushing the Allies back from their key objective, which was the German Gustav defenses. An informal border called the Gustav line ran inland from the Tyrrhenian coast northeast across Italy to the Adriatic coast near Ortona. The Berhardt/Reinhard demarcation was intended by the Germans only to delay the Allies from reaching the Gustav line and, behind it, the Hitler line. Those two lines together were the main German winter defenses across Italy. The battle was a historically gruesome one. The Fifth US Army sustained sixteen thousand casualties, and the Italian town of San Pietro was completely destroyed.

By late December, the Fifth Army paused to regroup before its planned assault of the Gustav-line defenses, including the Abbey of Monte Cassino, dating from the eighth century and further back to pagan times. Greg Bradsher and Sylvia Maylor, "General Dwight D. Eisenhower and the Protection of Cultural

Property," *Text Message*, website of the US National Archives, February 10, 2014, http://text-message.blogs.archives.gov/2014/02/10/general-dwight-d-eisenhower -and-the-protection-of-cultural-property/.

In January 1944, the Fifth Army attacked Cassino and was thrown back. In March, five hundred bombers lay waste to it, but the follow-up Allied attack failed. Not until May did a massive allied ground attack finally reach the summit of Monte Cassino and seize what was left of the abbey.

195 "Shortly we will be fighting our way across the Continent": Dwight D. Eisenhower, General, US Army, Commander in Chief, from the Allied Forces Headquarters, letter order to all commanders of Allied forces, subject: Historical Monuments, December 29, 1943 (copy of letter archived at https://text-message .blogs.archives.gov/2014/02/10/general-dwight-d-eisenhower-and-the-protec tion-of-cultural-property/).

196 "It is a responsibility of higher commanders to determine": Dwight D. Eisenhower, General, US Army, Commander in Chief, from the Allied Forces Headquarters, letter order to all commanders of Allied forces, subject: Historical Monuments, December 29, 1943 (copy of letter archived at https://text-message .blogs.archives.gov/2014/02/10/general-dwight-d-eisenhower-and-the-protec tion-of-cultural-property/).

Notes to Chapter 19

199 "Sweetheart: My new fountain pen has disappeared": Griffith's handwritten letter of July 19, 1944 to Nell; emphasis in original. Ellipses indicate indecipherable words. Presentation of the word *Pinka* is based on the author's reading of the similar word appearing in another of Griffith's handwritten letters, but this word may actually be a nickname such as "Pinka" or "Punka."

201 "Walker was venerated by his subordinates": Walker's grandfathers, both paternal and maternal, had been officers in the Confederate Army. A 1912 graduate of West Point, Walker had fought in World War I as executive officer of an infantry brigade in France commanded by George C. Marshall. He taught at the Command and General Staff College at Fort Leavenworth, as did Griffith, and also at West Point. After World War II, he led the Fifth Army and then the Eight Army in its occupation of Japan and later in Korea, where he was killed in a military traffic accident during the Korean War. Russett Vance Eastman and the US Army, "The Campaigns of Normandy and Northern France, 1 August–31 August 1944," in *History of the XX Corps Artillery, 21 October 1943–9 May 1945* (Miesbach, Germany: Buchdruckerei W. F. Mayr, 1946), 90.

202 "His praise of legendary General Canham": Canham was already a sergeant when he took a course in the Army's first preparatory school to allow soldiers from the ranks to attend the academy at West Point. He was chosen and graduated from West Point in 1926, a year after Griffith. He was decorated for his valor as a colonel on Omaha Beach and the fighting that followed to take Saint-Lô. His actions on and after D-Day were legendary:

Canham's regiment landed on the Dog Green sector of Omaha Beach along with one company of Army Rangers. Shortly after hitting the beach, Canham was shot through the wrist[;] refusing evacuation, he moved his men off Omaha and inland. Sergeant Bob Slaughter (D Company, 116th) remembers Canham screaming at soldiers to move off the beach and go kill Germans. Slaughter remembers him yelling at one lieutenant hiding in a pillbox from a German mortar barrage, "Get your ass out of there and show some leadership!" Don McCarthy (Headquarters Company, 116th) remembers seeing Canham walking upright along the beach in the face of enemy fire[:] "I got the hell out of there and moved forward. I was more afraid of Colonel Canham than I was of the Germans."

For his actions on Omaha Beach, and the fighting to take-Saint Lô, Canham received the Distinguished Service Cross. "Canham, Charles D. W., MG," *Army: Together We Served* (website), accessed April 27, 2019, https://army.togeth erweserved.com/army/servlet/tws.webapp.WebApp?cmd=ShadowBoxProfile& type=Person&ID=259605.

His DSC citation reads in part:

Canham landed on the beach shortly after the assault wave of troops had landed. At the time, the enemy fire was at its heaviest and had completely arrested the attack. Though wounded shortly after landing, Colonel Canham, with utter disregard for his own safety, continued to expose himself to the enemy fire in his efforts to reorganize the men. His personal bravery and determination so inspired and heartened the men that they were able to break through the enemy positions. Colonel Canham's outstanding leadership, gallantry, and zealous devotion to duty exemplify the highest traditions of the military forces of the United States.

"Charles Draper William Canham," *The Hall of Valor Project*, accessed April 21, 2019, https://valor.militarytimes.com/hero/21949.

According to the Arlington National Cemetery website,

In 1942, he took command of the 116th Infantry Regiment, 29th Infantry Division[,] before it sailed for England. This regiment and the 16th Infantry Regiment, 1st Infantry Division[,] were chosen as the first to land at Omaha beach. Shortly after hitting the beach, Canham was shot thru the wrist[;] refusing evacuation, he moved his men off Omaha and moved inland. For his actions on Omaha Beach and the fighting to take St. Lo he received the Distinguished Service Cross and was promoted to Brigadier General and took over command as the Assistant Division Commander of the 8th Infantry Division. It was [in] this capacity that he took in the name of his 8th Division troopers in the surrender of Brest.

Upon entrance to the German command headquarters of General
Ramcke, commander of the German 2nd Parachute Division, Canham
was asked for his credentials[;] without hesitation he turned to the [dirty
and tired American] [GIs] accompanying him [whom he had brought to
witness the surrender] and said, "These are my credentials." The account
of this event which was reported in the New York Times saw in this
spontaneous statement of a combat leader the greatest tribute ever paid
to the real power of the American Army, [the individual soldier].

Michael Robert Patterson, "Charles Draper William Canham," *Arlington National
Cemetery Website*, updated January 27, 2006, http://www.arlingtoncemetery.net/
cdwcanhan.htm.

203 "Bailey bridge": The Bailey was a revolutionary engineering invention named for
Donald Bailey, civil engineer in the British War Office. The bridge was designed
to be easily transportable in a standard truck. Forty men using simple tools could
erect the bridge in ten-foot steel sections in three to four hours. Each bridge section consisted of only seventeen parts and could span a gap of up to 240 feet. With
additional supports, consisting of another nine parts, the bridge could be expanded
to almost any distance.

204 "Seventy-five thousand enemy troops ... could still be encircled": Martin Blu-
menson, Chapter 28, "Drive to the Seine," in *US Army in World War II: European
Theater of Operations; Breakout and Pursuit* (Washington, DC: Office of the Chief of
Military History, 1961) (text available online at http://www.ibiblio.org/hyperwar/
USA/USA-E-Breakout/USA-E-Breakout-28.html).

205 "Madame Clavel, deputy commander of the FFI battalion": The British SOE and
American OSS infiltrated agents into France to provide tactical advice and spe-
cialist skills like radio operation and demolition. In June, shortly after the invasion,
Eisenhower had placed two hundred thousand Resistance fighters under command
of General Marie-Pierre Kœnig and the French high command had decreed the
FFI subject to French military law.

As regions were liberated, the FFI organized into light infantry units to serve
as additional manpower to regular Free French Forces. The FFI units manned less
active areas of the front lines, allowing regular French army units to mass in decisive
areas. They sabotaged railway lines, seized or destroyed bridges, cut German supply
lines, and provided intelligence to the Allies.

Many FFI units included former French soldiers. They wore civilian clothing
and an FFI armband. General Patton would eventually declare that the rapid
advance of his army through France would have been impossible without FFI
fighting aid, and Alexander Patch, another three-star American general, is said to
have estimated that from the time of the Mediterranean landings until September
1944, FFI forces gave help equivalent to that of four military divisions.

206 "Pseudonym Sinclair": In 1939, age sixteen, she had met Maurice Clavel, who
directed the Resistance network in Eure-et-Loir. She participated in the liberation
of Nogent-le-Rotrou and of Chartres in 1944. Once the war ended, she was one

of the notables who welcomed General de Gaulle on the square in front of the Chartres Cathedral. She and Clavel married after the war. She was decorated with the Croix de Guerre by General de Gaulle and with the Bronze Star by General Patton.

206 "A load of bazooka ammunition": Eastman and the US Army, "The Campaigns of Normandy," 79, 83.

206 "Three additional operations": In one, they liberated Vernon, about one hundred miles north of the CP. Town residents, with only a few weapons, took in over 130 pilots parachuted in the area and gathered and transmitted information. On August 18, they tried to blow up the bridge with about fifteen pounds of plastic explosives. It wasn't enough to make the damaged bridge fall, but it did trigger street fights between Resistance fighters and German soldiers, and on August 19, forty French fighters managed to take three German tanks and two trucks. The German troops retreated to Vernonnet to occupy the right bank of the river. Vernon's own fighters would hold the town alone for a week, until British soldiers arrived.

In another operation, they carried out a series of disruptions in the Oise region, north of Paris surrounding Bouvais, coordinated by British SOE and American OSS teams. The FFI confront German units in combat, but, as concluded in a later military report, "like termites they caused the whole German edifice to crumble." Steven J. Zaloga, *Liberation of Paris 1944: Patton's Race for the Seine*, Campaign, 194 (Oxford: Osprey, 2008), 29. They impeded German combat transit and by harassment helped to demoralize and speed the German evacuation. For Patton's Third Army, the FFI provided reconnaissance and intelligence. The FFI were deeply appreciated by US units for their service. Ibid., 30.

In yet another operation, they worked with a Jedburgh team, named "Alec," that had parachuted into Loir-et-Cher on August 10 and operated in the Fréteval forest near Vierzon, a city about a hundred miles south, that served as a railway and road communication hub in the Cher department of the central Loire Valley, about two hours from Paris. The Resistance team protected more than 130 Allied airmen who had evaded capture and worked their way to a camp in the forest, from which the American Third Army liberated them. Jean de Blommaert was parachuted into France and made his way to Paris to start arrangements for the camp. A British officer, Airey Neave of MI9 (the British Military Intelligence Section 9), was in overall control of the operation. The first evaders were brought from Paris on May 20, 1944.

In the clandestine Operation Jedburgh, around three hundred British SOE, US OSS, Free French Forces, and Dutch and Belgian personnel dropped by parachute into occupied France and elsewhere for sabotage and guerrilla warfare and to lead the Resistance forces against the Germans. Eisenhower ensured that the French would lead the Jedburgh teams in France. The parachuting teams consisted of three men: a commander, an executive officer, and a noncommissioned radio operator, one of whom was British or American and the other French, with a radio operator from anywhere. They carried weapons, sabotage equipment, and a Type B Mark II radio, more commonly referred to as the B2 or "Jed Set." They wore military uniforms and were equipped with medical supplies, food such as K and C ration packs, sleeping bags, field glasses, and maps on silk like their radio ciphers.

209 "Griffith, as senior operations officer": The G-3 covered infantry, armor, artillery, cavalry, antiaircraft units, and the G-3 Air Corps (air reconnaissance and tactical fighter-bomber air support). Twentieth Corps, being a "corps" of two or more divisions, then consisted of the Seventh Armored Division, the Fifth Infantry Divisions, and Corps Artillery Units, each varying from ten thousand to eighteen thousand troops. From time to time during operations, Twentieth Corps expanded with newly assigned divisions and shrank due to reassignments of divisions. Over the course of the war, it included as many as twenty-one separate divisions. Eastman and the US Army, "The Campaigns of Normandy," 89.

209 "Construe the tactical plan into step-by-step objectives": Eastman and the US Army, "The Campaigns of Normandy," 90.

209 "Griffith . . . attaching himself . . . to Allison's Twenty-Third": This according to a study later conducted by Roger Joly, himself a Resistance fighter, who based his research on archives and interviews with Resistance-fighter witnesses.

210 "All members of . . . Corps staff followed this practice": Eastman and the US Army, "The Campaigns of Normandy," 83.

210 "Third Battle of Ypres": Vejas Gabriel Liulevicius, "The Great Battles of Attrition," part 1, lecture 9, in *World War I: The Great War*, The Great Courses, Guidebook, outline part V.B 3–6 (Chantilly, VA: Teaching Company, 2006), 3–6.

211 "Griffith and Dugan drove through": An area that years later would be designated the Regional Natural Park of the Perche (Parc naturel régional du Perche).

211 "American first lieutenant, James O. Gomer": Frédéric Hallouin, "Histoire passion," *Courville sur Eure*, no. 39 (April 2012): 26–27, http://www.courville-sur-eure .fr/uploadji/Courville%20info-N39.pdf, English translation available online at http://www.7tharmddiv.org/courville-gomer.htm. Gomer's platoon was in the Twenty-Third Armored Infantry Battalion, to which Griff had attached himself to observe closely the upcoming battle at Chartres.

211 "Three explosions": Early the following morning, the first American soldiers to arrive had examined the destruction of the bridge of the Rue d'Illiers. A few Courville citizens had welcomed them from across the river. With the help of an English-speaking refugee, they had shown the soldiers that one of the sidewalks of the bridge remained intact, permitting them to cross on foot. The soldiers had radioed engineers who had arrived and had gone to work immediately with a bulldozer to remove felled trees and one or two truckloads of soil to quickly arrange passage for vehicles. The soldiers had heard a suspicious noise at a destroyed house opposite the entrance to a school near the center of town. They had immediately begun shooting, but no Germans had been found. The city center had then filled with American troops and their equipment. The troops had distributed cigarettes, candy, chocolate, and chewing gum—which the French had not seen over the four years of occupation—together with instant coffee, a convenience previously unknown to the French. Soon the cafes had become full, with toasts and jubilation celebrating arrival of the Americans.

211 "A respected and capable strategist": Schulz, *The Ghost*, 165.

Notes to Chapter 20

214 "Three thousand German troops": William M. Roseboro Jr., After Action Report from Headquarters Combat Command "B," Seventh Armored Division, Battle Report, September 3, 1944, New York: APO 257, 2, available for download at https://509thgeronimo.org/campaigns/documents/CbtCmdBAug44toJun45.doc.

214 "Two hundred to three hundred men per twenty-four-hour period": Roseboro, After Action Report, 2.

215 "Cathedral's western facade": The cathedral is oriented from west to east, as are all Gothic cathedrals, with the altar at the east end and the transom intersecting in a north-south direction, such that if viewed from the air, it would appear as a cross.

218 "Like a giant owl with wings high": Today we have only a single record to establish that Griffith visited the cathedral that first time on August 15, a matter that draws its significance from events that would follow the next day. A letter from Mel Stark to Colonel Griffith's younger brother Philip, written decades later, confirms that Stark and Colonel Griffith did enter and investigate the cathedral a first time on August 15 as the battle for Chartres was unfolding. Stark's letter was in response to Philip's own investigation into the life of his brother; his interest was piqued by an apparently contradictory account of events at the cathedral that appeared in *Reader's Digest* in 1965: Gordon Gaskill, "The Day We Saved Chartres Cathedral," *Reader's Digest* (August 1965): 102–107.

218 "Germans beat up the mayor": Albert Love, *The Fifth Division in the ETO: Iceland, Ireland, England, France, Germany, Luxembourg, Czechoslovakia, Austria* (Atlanta: Fifth Division Historical Section, 1945), 76.

219 "Daybreak . . . after a long night": Through a remarkable turn of events, Father Douin's diary would find its way into the hands of Colonel Griffith's daughter, Alice Griffith Irving.

220 "Adept at translating the flow of information": Schulz, *The Ghost*, 151–55.

220 "The corps' standing order remained in place": Leslie Allison, After Action Report, Month of August 1944: Seventh Armored Division, Twenty-Third Armored Infantry Battalion: Battle at Chartres, August 15–18, 1944, APO #257, C/o Postmaster US Army 1944 (text available for download from https://webcache.googleuser content.com/search?q=cache:avj1PjJp7p0J:https://www.7tharmddiv.org/docrep/ N-23-AAR.doc+&cd=1&hl=en&ct=clnk&gl=us&client=safari); United States Army, "31st Tank Bn Records of Action of Night of 15–16 August 1944: Relating to the Tank Buried at Chartres," US Army After Action Report, compiled by Wesley Johnston at *U. S. 7th Armored Division Association* (website), 2008 (text available online at https://webcache.googleusercontent.com/search?q=cache:OHZqbAH CVRwJ:https://www.7tharmddiv.org/docrep/images/Places-Maps-Photos/ France/Chartres%2520Area/31%2520Tank%2520Records%252015-16%2520 August%25201944.doc+&cd=1&hl=en&ct=clnk&gl=us&client=safari); interview with General Thomas Griffin (US Army Ret.), 2018.

221 "No reason to fire on the cathedral": Letter from Melville I. Stark to Philip Griffith, Colonel Griffith's brother, 1970, 1.

221 "Appointed Griffith . . . first-line director of . . . operations": Éric Santin, *Derniers combats: 1944, Eure-et-Loir; ordres et comptes rendu de batailles*, 2nd edited ed. (Paris: Santin, 2009), 3–5.

221 "God be with you": Schulz, *The Ghost*, 160.

221 "Griffith . . . hopped into his jeep": Schulz, *The Ghost*, 160.

222 "Sources are in conflict": One source, Eugene Schulz, would later write in his memoir that "the order to destroy the cathedral was given because it was suspected that the Germans were using the twin towers as observation posts." Schulz, *The Ghost*, 160. But in a 2014 interview Schulz conceded that he had never seen any such order in writing or heard any confirmation that any such order was actually issued or who might have issued it. Thomas N. Griffin, a retired US Army general and nephew of Griffith, told me in a 2018 interview that he had personally researched whether any such order had been issued and found no evidence that one had been. Yet he had no doubt that in those particular circumstances some hot-headed officer might well have told his troops to fire on the cathedral out of fear that the Germans were using its towers.

222 "Griffith's job was foremost": Schulz, *The Ghost*, 151–52.

NOTES TO CHAPTER 21

226 "Griff didn't like what he saw": Kenneth Foree, "They Nearly Stopped the War to Bury Texan," *Dallas Morning News*, August 25, 1945. Foree, a veteran reporter, conducted a one-year investigation into Griffith's actions at Chartres before publishing his article.

228 "Wasn't an art buff": Foree, "They Nearly Stopped the War."

230 "Couldn't tell whether they'd understood": Schulz, *The Ghost*, 159–65, 316–23.

231 "His panic": Paul Douin, *The Diary of Father Paul Douin (August 12 through August 23, 1944)*, transcr. Agnes Douin, trans. Marianne Pradoura, reporting events jointly experienced on August 16 by seventy-year-old Father Drouin and forty-year-old Father Maurice Cassegrain.

NOTES TO CHAPTER 22

238 "Restrained his pistol arm": Gene Currivan, "Troops Spare Chartres Cathedral in Routing Out German Snipers: Use Only Small Arms to Prevent Damage to Famous Edifice—Patrols Have Field Day in Rounding Up Collaborators," *New York Times*, August 16, 1944.

239 "Ambulance drove them off": Joseph Driscoll, "Chartres Cathedral Nazi Snipers' Nest," *New York Tribune*, August 16, 1944, 1, 3.

239 "Lives of these men had been known": Currivan, "Troops Spare Chartres Cathedral."

239 "Characters with swords and stern faces": Currivan, "Troops Spare Chartres Cathedral."

241 "Griff . . . lost his temper": Captain Carl K. Mattocks, infantry, Seventh Armored Division, the man who led the attack on Lèves, when it finally got under way, described the division as "green" in a letter to Philip Griffith, Colonel Griffith's

brother, dated January 1, 2001. Mattocks went on to say that he understood General Walker's sending Griff to "provide impetus to a 'green' division," noting, however, that the small armored divisions were manned with considerably less infantry than a full infantry division. Mattocks believed that more infantry personnel might have contributed to a different outcome for Griffith.

This would be only one of many instances in which General Walker would not be happy with the pace of the Seventh Armored Division operations. Also, difficulties with Major General Silvester's accomplishments as a commander would not end there. Silvester had been a US National Guard officer, not a West Pointer, and had been only temporarily made a major general. Less than six months after the incident at Chartres, in January 1945, Silvester would be reverted back to his permanent rank of colonel and relieved of his command of the Seventh Armored Division, as a result of that division having been badly mauled by the Germans near Venlo in November 1944.

During the Battle of the Bulge, the Seventh Armored Division (then part of the Ninth Army) would come under the control of British Field Marshal Bernard Montgomery's Twenty-First Army Group. Montgomery would become displeased with Silvester's performance as well and would engineer Silvester's replacement, which would be carried out by General Omar Bradley, the Twelfth Army Group Commander. At the time of Silvester's replacement, the Seventh would be holding an extended front and be on loan to the British Second Army. Silvester would be removed from his command shortly afterward at the time the division was to revert to control by the American Ninth Army. Other members of the division command would also be released in the shakeup. A 1946 inquiry requested by Silvester would vindicate General Bradley.

241 "Griffith took charge himself": Mel Stark, who worked as a young lieutenant colonel with Griffith for more than two years, said in a letter to Griffith's brother Philip two decades later that when Griffith took leadership in Chartres, he was doing the battalion commander's job and the division commander's job, in getting them moving again, and that Griffith "had no use whatever with . . . incompetent people." The Seventh Armored Division was under the command of a general who, Stark said, was "the poorest general I have ever known." For that division, he said, the fight at Chartres was its first; "the cathedral fell into its sector of the City, and the soldiers were trigger-happy and poorly[] led, or both." Stark continued,

> I can remember Griff's weaknesses as well as his great strengths, because these made the whole man. That hair-trigger temper he frequently displayed came my way only once, and he was right. He was extremely patient with people who wanted to learn and who wanted to do—he had no use whatsoever with lazy people. And if he drove people, he drove himself more, and in setting this example I always considered he was leading, not driving. Never in my life have I known a more dedicated man; this [led] to his death, which I have always considered should never [have] occurred when and how it did. . . . The armored unit Griff was leading when killed had "frozen." . . . The Division

346

Commander was relieved and reduced, but that's little compensation for some of the effects of his failures.

Letter from Colonel Mel Stark, dated April 7, 1970, to Philip L. Griffith, brother of Colonel Griffith. Two additional sources referred to Lieutenant Colonel Samuel L. Irwin as one of the weakest of commanders. Interviews with Colonel Fredrick F. Irving, US Army (ret.), in January 2015, and with Lieutenant General Thomas Griffin, US Army (ret.) March 2018.

241 "The column would need enough men and equipment": This would not be the end of the matter for Lieutenant Colonel Samuel L. Irwin. He would in fact be reassigned by the corps five days later on August 21 to the Eighth Armored Group until transfer to Second Armored Division on November 20, 1944. On August 21, Lieutenant Colonel Edwin Keeler replaced Irwin as battalion commander of the Thirty-Eighth, but Keeler would be wounded three weeks later by artillery near Point-du-Jour, France.

241 "They likely checked both routes": The Boulevard Jean Jaurès, east of the hill, followed alongside the east bank of the Eure River and intersected a road that ran east for two miles to the airfield. The Boulevard Charles Péguy, on the left, paralleled the railroad tracks and also met the Boulevard Jan Juarès, at the north end of the hill and then led into a junction called Place Drouaise, a busy village commercial and residential district. From there, the main two-lane paved road northward, the Rue du Bourgneuf, headed parallel to the Eure River for a distance of a mile and a half into the village of Lèves.

242 "Griff grabbed Dugan's carbine": Letter from William L. Dugan to Philip Griffith, August 17, 1966.

242 "I'm going with you": Foree, "They Nearly Stopped the War."

242 "Griff may . . . have stood on a tow hitch," Santin, *Derniers combats*, 3–5. Santin described it as an armored truck, but all other sources, including the Army DSC citation, called it a tank. Captain Carl K. Mattocks, who called it a light tank, was likely in the best position to know, since he led the attack on Lèves. One element of his unit cleared out the center of the village, while another deployed on the south edge of the village to attack to the east toward the airport. A later report of an investigation by the Army Headquarters in Washington, as of 1966, identified two other witnesses besides Dugan and Cullen. They were David W. Washburn of Bells, Texas, and Carbin O. Maynard, of Baxter, Tennessee, both now deceased.

242 "The M5—about the size of . . . a minivan": On the tank he was likely more exposed than back at the cathedral when he had circled its perimeter before inspecting the inside of the building. At the cathedral he'd had good reason to think there had been Germans looking down on him. But on the tank, although he didn't suspect Germans would be lying in wait by the side of the road, he should have.

244 "The two-lane street narrowed": The building was known to locals as the windmill of Sainte Josépha.

245 "Once the shooting erupted": Letter from Dorothea Griffith to Tiny, Lawrence, and Philip Griffith, dated August 1961, quoting from Dorothea's conversation with a Dr. Barre, who had been sergeant major of the G-1 Section of Twentieth Corps

during the battle for Chartres and knew Griffith well and had great respect for him. Barre, in G-1 Section, handled the details of preparation of Griff's body for burial.

246   "Griff's left hand still held his carbine": Foree, "They Nearly Stopped the War."

247   "They brought chairs": Citation, US Army Headquarters, Fort Jay, awarding Distinguished Service Cross, addressed to Mrs. Welborn B. Griffith Jr., Brooklyn, New York, November 1944, "for extraordinary heroism in connection with military operations against an armed enemy while serving as Operations Officer (G-3) with Headquarters, XX Corps, in action against enemy forces on 16 August 1944 at Chartres and Lèves, France."

247   "Lost to history": Robert E. Cullen, memorandum to Adjutant General (Awards and Decorations Branch), Washington, D.C., on behalf of Commanding General, September 15, 1944.

NOTES TO CHAPTER 23

250   "Father Launay": Santin, *Derniers combats*, 3–5.

250   "Father Douin": Douin, *Diary*, 9.

250   "A handful of American news correspondents": Currivan, "Troops Spare Chartres Cathedral"; Gene Currivan, "Chartres Tower Hit by Nazi Shell; But Cathedral as a Whole Is Virtually Intact—Statuary, Glass in Safekeeping," *New York Times*, August 25, 1944 (wired August 17; delayed), 3, https://www.nytimes.com/1944/08/25/archives/chartres-tower-hit-by-nazi-shell-but-cathedral-as-a-whole-is.html.

      The reporting events were jointly experienced by Currivan and fellow reporters Joseph Driscoll of the *Herald Tribune* and David McNicholl of the Australian Consolidated Press. See Joseph Driscoll's account in Driscoll, "Chartres Cathedral." Veteran war correspondent Gaskill, almost twenty years after the events of August 16, 1944, wrote a narrative describing his experience of that 1944 day in Chartres with companions and war correspondents Clark Lee and Bob Reuben, both deceased by the time of the publication. Gaskill, "The Day We Saved Chartres Cathedral."

250   "No serious structural damage": Currivan, "Troops Spare Chartres Cathedral."

250   "Attractive to the German snipers": Currivan, "Troops Spare Chartres Cathedral."

251   "Father Guédou": Jean Guédou (1914–1986).

251   "Mr. Tuvache managed to survive": Ellipses in Father Douin's original.

252   "Morning's casualty list": Casualty report, August 17, 1944, obtained from Alice Griffith Irving.

      The corps also lost another senior officer, Major Alfred J. Scott, III, in Chartres. He was one of the original corps liaison officers. He was killed with his driver while delivering dispatches to other units. Eastman and the US Army, "The Campaigns of Normandy," 79, 83.

253   "Half dozen snipers": Driscoll, "Chartres Cathedral."

253   "Climbing, crawling, and stooping": Gene Currivan, "Chartres Tower Hit."

253   "The Germans weren't giving up": The Thirty-Eighth Armored Infantry Battalion started with an attack on Chartres on August 18 but was held up by friendly artillery fire. The attack continued on the next day, and the battalion met the Twenty-Third Armored Infantry Battalion in the town. One platoon of C Company was captured by enemy forces but eventually—after the intervening Ger-

man surrender—was called upon to guard the German prisoners. United States Army, After Action Report of the Thirty-Eighth Armored Infantry Division, Seventh Armored Division, August 1944, pp. 2–3 (text available for download at "7th Armored Division: 38th Armored Infantry Battalion: 38 AIB After Action Reports," at https://www.7tharmddiv.org/docrep/#4408).

254 "Many FFI complained": Roger Joly, *La Libération de Chartres: Récits et témoignages rassemblés et commentés* (Paris: Le Cherche Midi Ed, 1994), 131–32.

255 "Griffith gave everything he had": Foree, "They Nearly Stopped the War."

255 "Gaskill's evoked a somewhat different scene": Gaskill, "The Day We Saved Chartres Cathedral."

258 "The magazine's editors stood by their story": In their letter back to Philip, the editors wrote, on October 18, 1965,

> Your letter didn't come as a surprise to the Researcher who did the pre-publication check of "The Day We Saved Chartres Cathedral" while she was working in our Paris office. [She wrote:] "I heard at least half a dozen stories from American and Frenchmen alike about how they had saved Chartres Cathedral—and no doubt, that all may have. The important thing is of course, that they did."
>
> There were about six days, during the third week of August 1944 when the general confusion created by the advance of General Patton's Third US Army (Twentieth Corps), and the retreat of the Germans, Chartres' spires were doubtless suspected, by at least a dozen different groups of American soldiers and French maquis, of harboring German snipers. Each time some wanted to fire first and check later and no doubt some insisted on checking first, volunteering to climb the spires themselves, thus saving Chartres. In the chaos of war different people contribute to saving the same thing, but not all get heard about—though this in no way diminishes their valor.
>
> We published Gordon Gaskill's story—after checking it—because it was the one sent to us and we are glad to have had an opportunity to discuss it with you.
>
> —The Editors

258 "Both . . . accounts . . . could have occurred": Letter from Major General J. C. Lambert, adjutant general, to Count DeKay, April 7, 1966.

259 "Gaskill's story seems . . . outweighed": Gaskill's story, which appeared in the general-interest publication *Reader's Digest*, not in a historical or military journal, let alone a peer-reviewed one, was nonetheless defended by the editors of that publication when questioned by Griffith's relatives after it appeared. Alice Griffith Irving noted in a March 2015 e-mail to me that she doubted that Gaskill had a personal relationship with Eisenhower that would have enabled him to pull rank on the trigger-happy lieutenant, and during her many visits to Chartres and Lèves since the war in which she met with relevant locals no one ever mentioned a crowd

in the square protesting any firing or any ringing of the bell in the tower, and no druggist or hotel proprietor ever came forward. As of the time of those visits, she said, all the witnesses would not have died.

260 "Taper answered": Edsel, *Monuments Men*, 105–108.

261 "His record was always superior": Letter dated August 18, 1944, from General Walton H. Walker to Nell Griffith.

261 "In November 1944": He was also awarded the American Silver Star and later the French Croix de Guerre, the Legion of Honor, the Legion of Merit, and the Purple Heart.

262 "The liberation of Chartres was . . . the work of the people": Joly, *La Libération*, 137.

NOTES TO CHAPTER 24

266 "Ripped out iron window frameworks": Jean Trouvelot, report to the Minister of National Education, March 11, 1946, Mediathèque Charenton (Paris), 81 28 16.

267 "Open to the elements": Jean Trouvelot, report to the Minister of National Education, March 11, 1946, Mediathèque Charenton (Paris), 81 28 16.

267 "René Capitant": A leftist professor, René Capitant had also participated in formation of the Resistance movement Combat in the Clermont-Ferrand area but early in the war had fled to Algeria, where he taught as a law professor at the University of Algiers.

267 "Jean Verrier": Verrier had tangled with the Nazis and the Kunstschutz during the war, and in spring 1944 he had worked to safeguard the Bayeux Tapestry from Allied bombing by moving it to Paris and then to another safe location. Carola Hicks, *The Bayeux Tapestry: The Life Story of a Masterpiece* (New York: Random House, 2011), 215, 235, 262.

268 "Seventy were too dilapidated": Froidevaux, chief architect of historic monuments from 1939 to 1983, did not yet know that he would be appointed project manager of Chartres Cathedral twenty-nine years later. In 1953, he was appointed assistant to the General Inspectorate of Historical Monuments and, in 1974, inspector general of historic monuments. In 1981, he prepared a major study on the conservation of the Chartres windows. Yves-Marie Froidevaux, "La cathédrale Notre-Dame de Chartres," *Monuments historiques de la France* 23, no. 1 (1977): 65–72; Yves-Marie Froidevaux, *Techniques de l'architecture ancienne: Construction et Restauration*, 4th ed. (Liège: Pierre Mardaga, 2001); and Yves Marie Froidevaux, "La travaux de restauration de la crypte," *Notre-Dame de Chartres*, no. 29, December, 1976, 4.

272 "Annunciation panel": Panel 1, located as the bottom-corner panel on the south edge of the center lancet window. Malcolm Miller describes it as follows: "In this first panel, the angel Gabriel, with two fingers raised in salutation and carrying a herald's scepter like Mercury, announces to Mary, 'Behold, thou shalt conceive in thy womb and bring forth a son and shalt call his name Jesus.' Mary has risen from her seat, and her gesture expresses surprise." Miller, *Chartres Cathedral*, 32.

272 "Incarnation Window": Baritaud, "The Light of Chartres," 48. The West Rose celebrates Christ's Second Coming as judge and is placed above the three twelfth-century lancet windows that narrate Christ's first coming. Malcolm Miller wrote

that they face west "so that the sun sets upon the evening of time." Miller, *Chartres Cathedral*, 88.

272   "The cathedral of light": Baritaud, "The Light of Chartres," 48.

273   "Something that would stand forever": Footnote in original omitted from this quotation. Edsel, *Monuments Men*, xvii, quoting Captain Walker Hancock, US First Army, who was forty-three when he had the experience in Chartres Cathedral. Born in Saint Louis, Missouri, Hancock was a renowned sculptor who had won the prestigious Prix de Rome before the war and designed the Army Air Medal in 1942.

273   "Carlier published criticisms": Carlier, "Study."

273   "*Le Monde*": Albert Mousset, "Les vitraux de Chartres: Ont-ils été replacés à l'envers?" *Le Monde*, August 2, 1950, https://www.lemonde.fr/archives/article/1950/08/02/les-vitraux-de-chartres-ont-ils-ete-replaces-a-l-envers_2057258_1819218.html.

273   "Trouvelot . . . explanation": Jean Trouvelot, report to the director of architecture, Office of Architecture, Minister of National Education, September 11, 1950.

273   "Maunoury . . . refuting": Trouvelot wrote:

> The reinstallation of these 7,595 panels has given rise to criticism of seven of them.
>
> There was, in effect, an error in the replacement of three panels:
>
>   a. High choir window, thuribuler angel, the panel of the hands of the angel placed upside down. This panel has just been put back in place.
>
>   b. Chapel of the Martyrs in the ambulatory (Saint-Chéron), two panels were inverted. These panels have just been put back in place.
>
> By contrast in the north side aisle, the window of Saint-Eustache, two panels have changed position in the reinstallation in order to correspond with a more-logical presentation of the scenes (nothing proves that these panels, removed many times over the centuries, were, before 1939, in their original order).
>
> In the north ambulatory, Saint-Julien l'Hospitalier, one has criticised the installation of two square panels of the corner border of the frame at the bottom of the bay. These panels, around 0.20 × 0.20, are in place.
>
> Concerning the reinstallation of the panel depicting a dove in the rose of the northern transept cross, we draw attention to the four doves of that rose, positioned side-by-side in its foils. These windows were executed in the fourteenth century. The same cartoon was used to make the two doves in the center, which were then reversed for symmetry. Another cartoon was used to make the two doves in profile, and these two panels, made using the same cartoon, were not then reversed as they should have been. As a result, in order to obtain the symmetry, it was originally necessary to complete one of these panels with the painted side facing the exterior, a troublesome orientation for the conservator of

stained glass—who must reposition the painting toward the interior of the building. In fact, the painting that creates the design is delicate; the firing process somewhat incorporates it into the glass, but in the long run the atmospheric conditions will eat away at the paint and ultimately erase it. We have judged it preferable to reinstall the panel in view of what is best from a conservation standpoint.

In the Middle Ages and especially in the fourteenth century, one often used the same cartoon for many different characters and was content to modify various attributes or colorations. We also come across errors or inversions that were more or less rectified at the time of placement. In general, it is the overall effect that counts, and one must analyse the monument very closely to identify all of the various anomalies dating from the time of construction.

Jean Trouvelot, report to the Director of Architecture, Office of Architecture, Minister of National Education, September 11, 1950, Mediathèque Charenton (Paris), 81 28 16, pp. 2–3.

273 "I thought it may be of some use": Trouvelot, report to the Director of Architecture, 2–3.

Notes to Epilogue

275 "Other family members": Among them, standing in the center of the line, was Griff's first wife, Alice Torrey. Alice would marry a third husband a year later, also an Army colonel, in November 1945.

275 "DSC": General Orders: Headquarters, Third US Army, General Orders No. 75 (October 21, 1944).

275 "Silver Star": The citation, which had been issued prior to the DSC, bestowed this prior award (posthumously) "for conspicuous gallantry and intrepidity against the enemy during World War II. Colonel Griffith's gallant actions and dedicated devotion to duty, without regard for his own life, were in keeping with the highest traditions of military service and reflect great credit upon himself, his unit, and the United States Army." General Orders: Headquarters, Twentieth Corps, General Orders No. 24 and later revoked by No. 41 (October 24, 1944), inasmuch as the DSC was awarded for the same action pursuant to General Orders No. 75.

275 "Some were incensed by any suggestion": Sergeant Major Barre, for example, who had served in the G-1 Section (Personnel) of the corps at the time of Griff's death, had known all about the efforts General Walker had expended to get Griffith reassigned from Leavenworth to the corps. Barre was incensed at the idea, intimated by Foree's 1945 *Dallas Morning News* article, that Griffith's actions at Lèves might have been foolhardy. Griffith "was . . . aggressive but cautious and . . . he would never have done anything foolish," Barre said. Dr. Barre, quoted in a 1961 letter from Griffith's sister Dorothea to her sister, Tiny, and her brothers, Philip and Lawrence.

Dugan, who had been with Griffith on the sixteenth, both at the cathedral and on the road to Lèves, wrote in a 1966 letter to Griff's brother Philip that

Dugan found Griffith "to be one of the gamest men I ever saw [*sic*] he had more guts then [*sic*] most men and was not afraid of anything, and he would not send his men where he would not go himself and treated me the finest [*sic*] . . . as far as the cathedral it happened the way the citation read [*sic*]. I was there when it happened." Letter from Dugan to Philip Griffith, received by the latter in 1966.

Cullen, who had been with Griff on the sixteenth "from the moment we left Corps Hqrs until a few minutes before his death," said he had "read the magazine article in which the writer [Gaskill] told of doing exactly what 'Grif' did. When I finished reading it I told my wife that the writer was [not being truthful] and explained to her what had actually happened on the August day in 1944 in Chartres. It does not seem to me even remotely possible that the reporter who wrote the article could have done what he claims."

Mel Stark, who was also with Griff at the cathedral and at the Thirty-Eighth's assembly area on the sixteenth, wrote to Philip Griffith in 1970:

> I feel compelled to say . . . that here was a tremendous person. Had Griff lived I believe he could have worn many stars, rising to the tops of his profession in only a few more years, and in the zone where the competition was extremely tough. He was a great American, just naturally, and epitomized a breed which if not gone, is disappearing far too rapidly for the good of our nation. He is gone a long time, but I'm sure he is well remembered; I, and most of the people who were close to him, know how he encircled our lives, and frequently under the kind of conditions we prefer to forget.

Letter from Melville I. Stark to Philip Griffith, April 7, 1970.

275 "His main mission that fateful day": Letter from Alice Griffith Irving to the author, dated December 2014, confirmed by interview with the author in Jacksonville, Florida, on January 12, 2015.

276 "Would not have been leading a column in such a vehicle": Also, Kevin Coffey pointed out to me that there remains a discrepancy between Mr. Schulz's account—"partly, he [Schulz] admitted, based not on his direct knowledge but from his later correspondence with my great uncle's family—and the impression my uncle's descendants also have, is that there was an actual formal order to destroy the cathedral and that Colonel Griffith's actions led to the rescinding of that order. However the account on my side of the family . . . is less dramatic. In the account I grew up with, there was not a direct order . . . but rather the Colonel simply came across indiscriminate firing directed at the cathedral." E-mail from Kevin Coffey, December 16, 2014.

Although others have either asserted or implied that the Germans had spotters in the towers to guide artillery and that an American order was issued to shell the cathedral based on unconfirmed suspicion that it was being occupied by the Germans and that Griffith gained permission to voluntarily cross enemy lines, no evidence has been found to support those assertions.

277 "Pretty taciturn": E-mail from Kevin Coffey, December 14, 2014.

277 "A . . . quiet and reserved man": E-mail from Kevin Coffey, December 17, 2014.

278 "Married four more times": Her final marriage, to George Graham Hume, lasted until her death, as Alice Torrey Hume.

279 "*Retired Officers Association* magazine": Today the Military Officers Association of America, as it is now known, can be found online at http://www.moaa.org.

279 "The American . . . killed liberating their town . . . had also been . . . credited with saving the cathedral": In addition, perhaps certain Catholics may believe that because August 15 was the Solemnity of the Assumption, the most logical explanation for Griffith's presence at the cathedral that day and the next may have been that the Virgin Mary, keeping watch over and safeguarding the cathedral, had directed him to go there.

280 "One of Shakespeare's unsung characters": Stephen Greenblatt, *Tyrant: Shakespeare on Politics* (New York: W. W. Norton, 2018), 144–45.

280 "He stands up for human decency . . . one of Shakespeare's great heroes": Greenblatt, *Tyrant*, 144–45.

Bibliography

Adams, Henry. *Mont-Saint-Michel and Chartres*. New York: Gallery Books, 1985.

Adler, Selig. *The Isolationist Impulse: Its Twentieth Century Reaction*. Santa Barbara: Greenwood/Praeger: 1957, 1974.

Allison, Leslie. After Action Report, Month of August 1944: Seventh Armored Division, Twenty-Third Armored Infantry Battalion: Battle at Chartres. August 15–18, 1944. APO #257, C/o Postmaster US Army 1944. Text available for download from https://webcache.googleusercontent.com/search?q=cache:avj1PjJp7p0J:https://www.7tharmddiv.org/docrep/N-23-AAR.doc+&cd=1&hl=en&ct=clnk&gl=us&client=safari.

Army: Together We Served (website). "Canham, Charles D. W., MG." Accessed April 27, 2019. https://army.togetherweserved.com/army/servlet/tws.webapp.WebApp?cmd=ShadowBoxProfile&type=Person&ID=259605.

Associated Press. "Conditions in Vienna Reported as Normal." *Dallas Morning News*, November 23, 1914, 7.

Assouline, Pierre. "Beneath the Scarf of Jean Moulin." Translated by Ruth Larson. *South Central Review* 25, no. 2 (Summer 2008): 1–21.

Aubrey, Dennis. "The Monuments Man of Chartres." *American Friends of Chartres*, accessed March 28, 2019. http://www.friendsofchartres.org/aboutchartres/colonelwelborngriffin/.

Baert, Jean. "1918 Catastrophe de la courneuve." *Aux carrefour de l'histoire*, no. 46 (October 1961). Text available online at https://e-nautia.com/jnono.masselot/disk/Histoire%2011/1918%20Catastrophe%20de%20la%20Courneuve.pdf.

Ball, Philip. *Universe of Stone: A Biography of Chartres Cathedral*. New York: Harper, 2008.

Baritaud, Thierry. *La depose des vitraux de la cathedrale de Chartres*. Chartres: Centre International du Vitrail, 2015.

———. "The Light of Chartres in the Périgordian Dark." *Nontronnaises Chronicles, Journal of the Historical and Archaeological Society of Périgord*, no. 23 (2007): 45–50.

Barker, Eugene C. "Austin, Stephen Fuller (1793–1836)." *Handbook of Texas Online*. Accessed January 25, 2015. https://tshaonline.org/handbook/online/articles/fau14.

Barnes, Carl F. "The Gothic Architectural Engravings in the Cathedral of Soissons." *Speculum* 47, no.1 (January 1972): 60–64.

Barnett, Correlli. *The Collapse of British Power*. Hampshire, UK: Pan Macmillan, 2002.

Berl, Emmanuel, and Jean Nohain. "Fonds Jean Zay (1904–2004): Introduction." Archives Nationales (French National Archives) website. Accessed September 16, 2018.

https://www.siv.archives-nationales.culture.gouv.fr/siv/rechercheconsultation/
consultation/ir/consultationIR.action?udId=&fullText=&consIr=&formCaller=&-
details=false&irId=FRAN_IR_028000&gotoArchivesNums=false&frontIr=&op
tionFullText=&auSeinIR=trueeftab720.

Berl, Emmanuel, and Jean Nohain. Interview of Jean Zay, February 10, 1937. Archives
Nationales (French National Archives). 667 AP 56, file no. 2.

Blackwell, Elise. *Hunger*. New York: Little, Brown, 2003.

Blumenson, Martin. Chapter 28, "Drive to the Seine." In *US Army in World War II: European Theater of Operations; Breakout and Pursuit*. Washington, DC: Office of the
Chief of Military History, 1961. Text available online at http://www.ibiblio.org/
hyperwar/USA/USA-E-Breakout/USA-E-Breakout-28.html.

Bradsher, Greg, and Sylvia Maylor. "General Dwight D. Eisenhower and the Protection
of Cultural Property." *Text Message*, website of the US National Archives. February
10, 2014. http://text-message.blogs.archives.gov/2014/02/10/general-dwight-d
-eisenhower-and-the-protection-of-cultural-property/.

Britton, Charles C. *The Quanah Route: A Texas Short Line Railroad*. Fort Collins, CO:
Joed Books, 1990.

Burckhardt, Titus. *Chartres and the Birth of the Cathedral*. Bloomington, IN: World Wis-
dom Books, 1996. In English, translated from the German by William Stoddart.
Originally published as *Chartres und die Geburt der Kathedrale* (Olten, Switzerland:
Urs Graf Verlas, 1962).

Byrnes, Joseph F. "Perspectives of 'La Voix de Notre-Dame de Chartres' on the Pilgrimage at Chartres during the XIXth and XXth Centuries: A Profile in Social History."
Marian Library Studies 10, no. 12 (1978): 159–206. https://ecommons.udayton
.edu/cgi/viewcontent.cgi?article=1082&context=ml_studies.

Carlier, Achille. "Des mesures preventives qui permettraient d'assurer le sauvetace
des vitraux de la Cathédrale de Chartres en cas d'attaque brusquee: Danger que
fait courir au monument le voisinage immédiat d'un camp d'aviation militaire.
Matérial de dépose et préparation d'équipes (400,000 francs at 350 hommes)
permettant la descente simultanée et rapide de toutes les verrières dès l'instant
de l'alerte. Etude remise à la Direction des Beaux-Arts en Juin 1935" [Preventive
measures to ensure the rescue of the stained-glass windows of the cathedral of
Chartres in the event of a sudden attack: Danger posed by the monument in the
immediate vicinity of a military aviation camp. Equipment for the laying and
preparation of teams (400,000 francs at 350 men) allowing the simultaneous and
rapid descent of all glass-works from the moment of the alert. Study submitted
to the Direction des Beaux-Arts in June 1935]. *Les pierres de France* 7 (June 3,
1935): 1–26 [in reprint]. (Carlier, "Study")

———. "Des mesures préventives qui permettraient d'assuerer le sauvetage des Vitraux
de la Cathérale de Chartres enc as d'attaque bruquée, Complément No. 1" [Pre-
ventive measures to ensure the rescue of the stained-glass windows of the cathedral
of Chartres in the event of a sudden attack]. *Les pierres de France* 7 (January 31,
1936): 30–54 [in reprint]. Mediathèque Charenton (Paris) 81 28 17. (Carlier,
"Supplement No. 1")

———. "Des mesures préventives qui permettraient d'assuerer le sauvetage des Vitraux de la Cathérale de Chartres enc as d'attaque bruquée, Complément No. 2" [Preventive measures to ensure the rescue of the stained-glass windows of the cathedral of Chartres in the event of a sudden attack]. *Les pierres de France* 7 (April 29, 1936): 58–92 [in reprint]. Mediathèque Charenton (Paris), 81 28 17. (Carlier, "Supplement No. 2")

———. "Le drame des vitraux de Chartres pendant la Guerre" [The drama of the stained glass windows of Chartres during the War]." *Les pierres de France* 13 (April–June 1950): 30–34 (update to issue of April 29, 1936). Mediathèque Charenton (Paris), 81 28 16.

———. *Les anciens monuments dans la civilisation nouvelle* (Paris: 55 Rue de Vareene, 1945).

Cathédrale Notre-Dame de Chartres (website). "Worry of the French Chartrains and 'Intellectuals.'" Accessed February 19, 2018. http://www.cathedrale-chartres.org/fichiers/hebdo-cathedrale/hebdo-2014/414-hebdo-280714-030814.pdf.

Chant, Christopher. *The Encyclopedia of Codenames of World War II*. London: Routledge and Kegan Paul, 1987.

Clinton, Alan. *Jean Moulin, 1899–1943: The French Resistance and the Republic*. New York: Palgrave, 2002.

Coffey, David. *Soldier Princess: The Life and Legend of Agnes Salm-Salm in North America, 1861–1867*. College Station: Texas A&M University Press, 2002.

Cook, William R. *The Cathedral*. DVD lecture series. Chantilly, VA: Teaching Company, 2010.

Cooney, Mary Kathryn. "May the Hatchet and the Hammer Never Damage It!" The Fate of the Cathedral of Chartres during the French Revolution." *Catholic Historical Review* 92. no. 2 (2006): 193–214.

Cowley, F. E. After Action Reports of the Seventh Armored Division's Division Artillery: Transcribed from Original Documents in Box 15609 (Seventh Armored Division 607-ART-0.1 to 607-ART-0.3) of Record Group 407 (Adjutant General's Office) by Beverly Kent and Rudd Wilmsen. September 1, 1944–October 1, 1945. Text available for download at https://www.7tharmddiv.org/docrep/N-7AD-Arty-AAR.doc.

Cuerq, Ségolène. "4 mars 1916, 9h25." *Saint-Denis et la guerre de 14*. City of Saint-Denis website, municipal archives. February 25, 2016. http://archives1418.ville-saint-denis.fr/explosion-fort-double-couronne/.

Cull, Nicholas John. *Selling War: The British Propaganda Campaign against American "Neutrality" in World War II*. Oxford: Oxford University Press, 1996.

Cullinane, Susannah, Hamdi Alkhshali, and Mohammed Tawfeeq. "Tracking a Trail of Historical Obliteration: ISIS Trumpets Destruction of Nimrud." CNN, April 13, 2015. http://www.cnn.com/2015/03/09/world/iraq-isis-heritage/.

Currivan, Gene. "Troops Spare Chartres Cathedral in Routing Out German Snipers: Use Only Small Arms to Prevent Damage to Famous Edifice—Patrols Have Field Day in Rounding Up Collaborators." *New York Times*, August 16, 1944.

———. "Chartres Tower Hit by Nazi Shell; But Cathedral as a Whole Is Virtually Intact—Statuary, Glass in Safekeeping." *New York Times*, August 25, 1944 (wired

August 17; delayed), 3. https://www.nytimes.com/1944/08/25/archives/chartres
-tower-hit-by-nazi-shell-but-cathedral-as-a-whole-is.html.

Dallas Morning News. "The Romance of Stained Glass: Masterpieces of Ancient Art, and Irreplaceable, Destroyed by the War." April 2, 1919, 4.

Delaporte, Yves, and Étienne Houvet. *Le vitraux de la cathédrale de Chartres: Histoire et descriptions*, 4 vols. Chartres: É. Houvet, 1926.

Dierick, Alfons Lieven. *The Stained Glass at Chartres*. Berne: Hallway Ltd., 1960.

Driscoll, Joseph. "Chartres Cathedral Nazi Snipers' Nest." *New York Herald Tribune*, August 16, 1944, 1, 3.

Dugan, Mark. *Knight of the Road: The Life of Highwayman Ham White*. Athens: Swallow Press/Ohio University Press, 1990.

Eastman, Russett Vance, and the US Army. "The Campaigns of Normandy and Northern France, 1 August–31 August 1944." In *History of the XX Corps Artillery, 21 October 1943–9 May 1945*, 11–18. Miesbach, Germany: Buchdruckerei W. F. Mayr, 1946.

École nationale des Chartres (website). "22 février 1918." Minutes of the French Commission des monuments historiques. Accessed February 18, 2018. http://elec.enc.sorbonne.fr/monumentshistoriques/Annees/1918.html.

Edsel, Robert M. *The Monuments Men: Allied Heroes, Nazi Thieves and the Greatest Treasure Hunt in History*. New York: Center Street Hachette Book Group, 2009.

———. *Saving Italy: The Race to Rescue a Nation's Treasures from the Nazis*. New York: W. W. Norton, 2014.

Egan, Timothy. *The Worst Hard Time: The Untold Story of Those Who Survived the Great American Dust Bowl*. New York: Houghton Mifflin, 2006.

Emmerson, James T. *The Rhineland Crisis 7, March 1936: A Study in Multilateral Diplomacy*. Ames: Iowa State University Press, 1977.

Fierro, Alfred. *Histoire et dictionnaire de Paris*. Paris: R. Laffront, 1996.

Finlay, Victoria. "My Lifelong Quest for Color." *Iris*, November 2, 2014. http://blogs.getty.edu/iris/my-lifelong-quest-for-color/.

Foree, Kenneth. "They Nearly Stopped the War to Bury Texan." *Dallas Morning News*, August 25, 1945.

Fouqueray, Anne. "Pour la protection des verrières de Chartres." *Le Journal*, February 17, 1936, 7. Text available online at . https://gallica.bnf.fr/ark:/12148/bpt6k7651100w/f7.item.r=Chartres.

———. "Le plan de protection des vitraux de Chartres sera-t-il appliqué?" *Le Journal*, September 19, 1938, 7. Text available online at https://gallica.bnf.fr/ark:/12148/bpt6k76324332/f7.item.r=Chartres.

Froidevaux, Yves-Marie. "La cathédrale Notre-Dame de Chartres." *Monuments historiques de la France* 23, no. 1 (1977): 65–72.

———. *Techniques de l'architecture ancienne: Construction et Restauration*, 4th ed. Liège: Pierre Mardaga, 2001.

———. "La travaux de restauration de la crypte." *Notre-Dame de Chartres*, no. 29, December, 1976, 4.

Gaskill, Gordon. "The Day We Saved Chartres Cathedral." *Reader's Digest* (August 1965): 102–107.

General Secretariat for the French Ministry of Defence. "The Demarcation Line." Remembrance and Citizenship series, no. 7. Accessed July 7, 2018. http://www.civs.gouv.fr/images/pdf/documents_utiles/documents_dhistoire/the_demarcation_line.pdf.

Gould, Joan. "Seeing the Light in Chartres." *New York Times*, December 18, 1988, https://www.nytimes.com/1988/12/18/travel/seeing-the-light-in-chartres.html.

Greenblatt, Stephen. *Tyrant: Shakespeare on Politics*. New York: W. W. Norton, 2018.

Grodecki, Thomas S. "Military Observers, 1815–1975." Unclassified final report by the Center of Military History, 1–3, 17, 193. March 16, 1988. http://www.dtic.mil/dtic/tr/fulltext/u2/a194175.pdf.

Gwynne, S. C. *Empire of the Summer Moon: Quanah Parker and the Rise and Fall of the Comanches, the Most Powerful Indian Tribe in American History*. New York: Scribner, 2010.

Hallouin, Frédéric. "Histoire passion." *Courville sur Eure*, no. 39 (April 2012): 26–27, http://www.courville-sur-eure.fr/uploadji/Courville%20info-N39.pdf. English translation available online at http://www.7tharmddiv.org/courville-gomer.htm.

Hastings, Max. "Their Wehrmacht Was Better than Our Army." *Washington Post*, May 5, 1985. https://www.washingtonpost.com/archive/opinions/1985/05/05/their-wehrmacht-was-better-than-our-army/0b2cfe73-68f4-4bc3-a62d-7626f6382dbd/.

Hickey, John. "Notre Dame Fire like the Burning of the Library of Alexandria, Historian Says." *Berkeley News*, University of California, Berkeley. April 15, 2019. https://news.berkeley.edu/2019/04/15/notre-dame-fire-a-loss-to-the-french-that-americans-cant-completely-visualize/.

Hicks, Carola. *The Bayeux Tapestry: The Life Story of a Masterpiece*. New York: Random House, 2011.

Hofman, Jean-Marc. "Camille Enlart s'en va-t-en guerre. Le musée de Sculpture comparée pendant la Première Guerre mondiale." *In Situ* 23 (2014). http://insitu.revues.org/10894.

Hofsommer, Donovan L. *The Quanah Route: A History of the Quanah, Acme & Pacific Railway*. College Station: Texas A&M University Press, 1991.

Hogan, D. W. H., Jr. *A Command Post at War: First Army Headquarters in Europe, 1943–45*. Washington, DC: Center for Military History, 2000.

Hooton, Edward. *Luftwaffe at War: Blitzkrieg in the West*. London: Chervron/Ian Allan, 2007.

Humphrey, Walter R. "The Home Towner." *Temple Daily Telegram*, September 8, 1942.

Imbert, T. "Nécrologie: René Planchenault." *Les monuments historiques de la France*, no. 1 (1977): 64. Text available online at http://www.mediatheque-patrimoine.culture.gouv.fr/pdf/inventaires/0080-035.pdf.

Ivry, Benjamin. "What He Contributed, What He Endured." *Forward*, June 28, 2011. https://forward.com/culture/139254/what-he-contributed-what-he-endured/.

Janes, Peter Scott, and Keith Janes. "Rudolf Ptacek." *Conscript Heroes*. Accessed June 2, 2018. http://www.conscript-heroes.com/Art01-Rudolph-Ptacek-960.html.

Johannet, René. "Des expériences vont ê'tre tentées pour protéger les vitraux de Chartres." *L'Écho de Paris*, March 10, 1936, 1–2. Available online at https://gallica.bnf.fr/ark:/12148/bpt6k8158395/f1.item.

Joly, Roger. *La Libération de Chartres: Récits et témoignages rassemblés et commentés*. Paris: Le Cherche Midi Ed., 1994.

Journal des débats politiques et littéraires. "L'explosion de la rue de Tolbiac." October 22, 1915. https://gallica.bnf.fr/ark:/12148/bpt6k4858090/f3.item.r=explosion%20 rue%20de%20tolbiac.

Jusselin, Maurice. "Eure-et-Loir Objets mobiliers: Etat des objets d art replies et des depots dans le department." Report of Les Conservateurs des Antiquités et Objets d'Arts. Les Conservateur des Antiquités et Objets d'Arts. Chartres, May 23, 1943. Mediathèque Charenton (Paris), 80 3 63, pp. 2–4.

Kalčič, Eugene. "Eugène Emmanuel Viollet-le-Duc and Monument Protection: A Case Study." *Urbani ozziv* 25, no. 2 (2014): 130–42. http://urbani-izziv.uirs.si/Portals/ uizziv/papers/urbani-izziv-en-2014-25-02-005.pdf.

Karlsgodt, Elizabeth. *Defending National Treasures: French Art and Heritage under Vichy*. Palo Alto: Stanford University Press, 2011.

Katzenellenbogen, Adolf. *The Sculptural Programs of Chartres Cathedral: Christ, Mary, Ecclesia*. Baltimore: Johns Hopkins University Press, 1959.

Kuranda, Kathryn M., Christine Heidenrich, Dean A. Doerrfeld, Rebecca Gatewood, Kirsten Peeler, Katherine E. Grandine, Heather McMahon, and Benjamin Riggle. *Army Ammunition Production during the Cold War (1946–1989)*. Aberdeen Proving Ground, MD: US Army Environmental Command, 2009. https://aec.army.mil/ application/files/1614/9505/0982/ammo-storage02.pdf.

Lambourne, Nicola. *War Damage in Western Europe: The Destruction of Historic Monuments during the Second World War*. Edinburgh: Edinburgh University Press, 2001.

Land, Emory Scott. *Winning the War with Ships: Land, Sea and Air—Mostly Land*. New York: R. M. McBride, 1958.

Landrieux, Maurice. *The Cathedral of Reims: The Story of a German Crime*. Translated by Ernest E. Williams. London: Kegan Paul, Trench, Trubner & Co., 1920.

La semaine religieuse (Paris). "Visite de Son Eminence le cardinal de Paris à La Courneuve." March 23, 1918, 353–54.

Lautier, Claudine. "Les vitraux de la cathédrale, les ateliers de peintres-verriers de la cathédrale au xiiie siècle." Chartres et sa cathédrale. *Archéologia*, no. 5 (June 1994): 46–55.

Lazarus Project, The. "Chartres." Accessed February 27, 2019. http://www.lazarusproject imaging.com/previous-projects/chartres/.

Lepeyre, André. "René Planchenault (1897–1976)." In *Bibliothèque de l'école des Chartres*, vol. 135, bk. 2, edited by Société de l'École des Chartres, 415–21. Paris: Libraire Droz, 1977. Text available online at https://www.persee.fr/doc/bec_0373 -6237_1977_num_135_2_460023?q=René+Planchenault+(1897–1976).

Liulevicius, Vejas Gabriel. "The Great Battles of Attrition." Part 1, lecture 9, in *World War I: The Great War*. The Great Courses. Guidebook. Outline part V.B 3–6. Chantilly, VA: Teaching Company, 2006.

Locke, Katherine. "Stained Glass Windows: Reflecting on a Writing Excuses Podcast Episode." *Katherine Locke* (blog). January 31, 2017. https://www.katherinelock ebooks.com/blog/2017/01/31/stained-glass-windows-reflecting-on-a-writing-ex cuses-podcast-episode.

Love, Albert. *The Fifth Division in the ETO: Iceland, Ireland, England, France, Germany, Luxembourg, Czechoslovakia, Austria.* Atlanta: Fifth Division Historical Section, 1945.

Mackay, Ron. *Heinkel He 111.* Crowood Aviation Series. Marlborough: Crowood Press, 2003.

Maines, Clark. "The Charlemagne Window at Chartres Cathedral: New Considerations on Test and Image." *Speculum* 52, no. 4 (October 1977): 801–23.

Mazzeo, Tilar. *Irena's Children.* New York: Gallery Books, 2016.

McCaffrey, B. *The 31st Infantry Regiment: A History of "America's Foreign Legion" in Peace and War.* Afterword by S. Townsend. Jefferson, NC: McFarland, 2018.

Melvin, Don, Ralph Ellis, and Salma Abdelaziz. "Group: ISIS Beheads Expert Who Refused to Reveal Location of Valuable Antiquities." CNN, updated August 20, 2015. http://www.cnn.com/2015/08/18/middleeast/isis-executes-antiquities-expert/.

Miller, Malcolm. *Chartres Cathedral,* 2nd rev. ed. New York: Riverside Books, 1997.

Ministère de la Culture (website). "Inventaire général du patrimoine culturel." Archived on December 10, 1026. http://archive.wikiwix.com/cache/?url=http%3A%2F%2F www.culture.gouv.fr%2Fpublic%2Fmistral%2Fmerimee_fr%3FACTION%3 DCHERCHER%26FIELD_1%3DREF%26VALUE_1%3DIA24000861.

Mousset, Albert. "Les vitraux de Chartres: Ont-ils été replacés à l'envers?" *Le Monde,* August 2, 1950. https://www.lemonde.fr/archives/article/1950/08/02/les-vitraux -de-chartres-ont-ils-ete-replaces-a-l-envers_2057258_1819218.html.

Musée Protestant. "Jean Zay (1904–1944)." Accessed October 28, 2019. https://www .museeprotestant.org/en/notice/jean-zay-1904-1944-2/.

Nagl, John A. "Tank Destroyers in WWII: Flawed Doctrine, Unmatched Bravery." *Armor* (January–February 1991): 26–31. https://www.tankdestroyer.net/images/stories/ ArticlePDFs/Armor_Mag_Article_TDs_in_WWII.pdf.

Neal, W. O. *The Last Frontier: The Story of Hardeman County.* Quanah, TX: Quanah Tribune-Chief, 1966; Medicine Mound, Texas: Downtown Medicine Mound Preservation Group, 2015.

Nicholas, Lynn H. *The Rape of Europa: The Fate of Europe's Treasures in the Third Reich and the Second World War.* New York: Vintage, 1995.

Noblecourt, André F. *The Protection of Cultural Property in the Event of Armed Conflict.* Museums and Monuments VIII. Translated from the author's original French text of August 1956. Paris: United Nations Educational, Scientific and Cultural Organization, 1958. Text available online at https://unesdoc.unesco.org/ark:/48223/ pf0000071205.

O'Donovan, Leo J. "The Voice of Chartres: Malcolm Miller Illumines the Gothic Jewel." *America,* December 22, 2008. https://www.americamagazine.org/issue/681/article/ voice-chartres.

Overy, Richard J. *The Bombing War: Europe, 1939–1945.* London: Allen Lane/Penguin, 2013.

Papacostas, Tassos C. "Gothic in the East: Western Architecture in Byzantine Lands." In *A Companion to Medieval Art: Romanesque and Gothic in Northern Europe,* edited by Conrad Rudolph, 510–30. Hoboken, NJ: Wiley-Blackwell, 2009.

Pariset, Jean-Daniel, ed. "23 février 1940." *Procès-verbaux de la Commission des monuments historiques, de 1848 à 1950, conservés à la Médiathèque de l'architecture et du patrimoine*

(Charenton-le-Pont). Paris: Médiathèque de l'architecture et du patrimoine, 2014. http://elec.enc.sorbonne.fr/monumentshistoriques/Annees/1940.html#93215.

Parker, Ralph A. C. "The First Capitulation: France and the Rhineland Crisis of 1936." *World Politics* 8, no. 3 (April 1956): 355–73.

Patterson, Michael Robert. "Charles Draper William Canham." *Arlington National Cemetery Website*. Updated January 27, 2006. http://www.arlingtoncemetery.net/cdwcanham.htm.

Payne, Steven. "Top Comments: The American Solider Who Saved Chartres Cathedral." *Daily Kos*, December 20, 2014. http://www.dailykos.com/story/2014/12/20/1350669/-Top-Comments-The-American-GI-who-saved-Chartres-Cathedral.

Pleitgen, Frederik. "Saddest Job in the World? The Race to Save Syria's History from Obliteration." CNN, August 20, 2015. https://www.cnn.com/2015/08/19/middleeast/syria-antiquities-damascus/index.html.

Pneu Michelin. *Reims and the Battles for Its Possession*. Illustrated Michelin Guides to the Battle-Fields (1914–1918). Clermont-Ferrand: Michelin & Cie, 1919.

Pogue, Forrest C. *The Supreme Command*. Washington, DC: Government Printing Office, 1996.

Polidor, Amberly. "Chartres Cathedral: The Land and Its People." *Sacred Land Film Project*. March 1, 2004. http://sacredland.org/chartres-cathedral/.

Potter, Charles, ed. *The Resistance, 1940*. Baton Rouge: Louisiana State University Press, 2016.

Prisme Atelier de Vitrail. "Ferronnerie." November 2011. http://www.prisme-atelier-vitrail.com/2010/11/.

Réau, Louis. "Viollet-le-Duc et le problème de la restauration de monuments." *Le cahiers techniques de l'art* 3 (1956): 29.

Reiff, Daniel D. "Viollet le Duc and Historic Restoration: The West Portals of Notre-Dame." *Journal of the Society of Architectural History* 30, no. 1 (1971): 17–30.

Ressler, Stephen. *Understanding the World's Greatest Structures: Science and Innovation from Antiquity to Modernity*. The Great Courses DVD lecture series. Chantilly, VA: Teaching Company, 2010.

———. *Understanding Greek and Roman Technology: From Catapult to the Pantheon*. The Great Courses DVD lecture series. Chantilly, VA: Teaching Company, 2010.

Retailleau, Naomie. "Jeanne Laurent: Une Bretonne à la conquête de la culture." *Unidivers: Le webzine culturel de Breton*. April 26, 2017. https://www.unidivers.fr/jeanne-laurent-politique-culture-bretagne/.

Risser, Nicole D. *France Under Fire: German Invasion, Civilian Flight, and Family Survival during World War II*. Cambridge: Cambridge University Press, 2012.

Roseboro, William M., Jr. After Action Report from Headquarters Combat Command "B," Seventh Armored Division. Battle Report. September 3, 1944. New York: APO 257. Available for download at https://509thgeronimo.org/campaigns/documents/CbtCmdBAug44toJun45.doc.

Ruby, Marcel. *La vie et l'œuvre de Jean Zay*. Paris: Éditions Corsaire, 1994.

———. *La vie et l'œuvre de Jean Zay*. Paris: L'Impremerie Bereskiak, 1969.

Ruskin, John. *The Stones of Venice.* New York: Farrar, Strauss and Giroux, 1960.

Santin, Éric. *Derniers combats: 1944, Eure-et-Loir; ordres et comptes rendu de batailles,* 2nd edited ed. Paris: Santin, 2009.

Schuker, Stephen. "France and the Remilitarization of the Rhineland, 1936." In *The Origins of the Second World War,* ed. Patrick Finney, 206–21. London: Arnold Press, 1997.

Schulz, Eugene G. *The Ghost in General Patton's Third Army: The Memoirs of Eugene G. Schulz during His Service in the United States Army in World War II.* Bloomington, IN: Xlibris, 2012.

Skibsrud, Johanna. *Quartet for the End of Time: A Novel.* New York: W. W. Norton, 2014.

Smithsonian National Postal Museum (website). "V-mail." Accessed February 28, 2019. https://postalmuseum.si.edu/exhibits/past/the-art-of-cards-and-letters/mail-call/v-mail.html.

SNCF. "Our History: Two Centuries of History; Retrace the History of Rail in France." Company website. Accessed September 6, 2019. https://www.sncf.com/en/group/history/two-centuries-history.

Société archéologique d'Eure-et-Loir. "Séance du 4 octobre 1917," p. 442; "Séance du 26 avril 1917," p. 476; and "Séance du 25 juillet 1917," p. 478. In *Procès-verbaux de la Société archéolgique d'Eure-et-Loir,* vol. 13. Chartres: Impr. Garnier. Text available online ("Les vitraux de la Cathédral et l'usine de guerre de Lucé") at https://gallica.bnf.fr/ark:/12148/bpt6k54160730/f474.item.r=Les%20vitraux%20de%20la%20Cathedral%20et%20l'usine%20de%20guerre%20de%20Luce.

Stocks, Ernest J. After Action Reports of 736th Field Artillery Battalion: Battalion Activities during August 1944; APO 403. September 3, 1944. Text available online at http://freepages.rootsweb.com/~ebgschol/military/aareports/1.1944_sept.html.

Thirty-First Infantry Regiment Association. "Chapter 5: Manila Again, 1932–1941." Association website. 2014. http://www.31stinfantry.org/wp-content/uploads/2014/01/Chapter-5.pdf. Also available as chapter 4 in *The 31st Infantry Regiment: A History of "America's Foreign Legion" in Peace and War* (Jefferson, NC: McFarland, 2018).

Tole, Eva Kay Wallace. *Quanah Centennial, 1884–1984.* [Quanah, TX]: [City of Quanah], 1984.

Torrie, Julia S. *"For Their Own Good": Civilian Evacuations in Germany and France, 1939–45.* New York: Berghahn Books, 2010.

Transillumination. "Metaphor for the Divine: Brian Clarke on Stained Glass." YouTube video, 3:52. November 13, 2010. https://www.youtube.com/watch?v=VYaS0NfLODQ.

Turnbo, Charles A. *Salado, Texas: College Frontier Town.* Salado, TX: Yardley Publishing, 2007.

Tyler, Orville Z., Jr. *The History of Fort Leavenworth, 1937–1951.* Fort Leavenworth, KS: The Command and General Staff College, 1951. Available online at https://apps.dtic.mil/dtic/tr/fulltext/u2/a437831.pdf.

United Press International. "German Bombers Hit Paris." June 3, 1940. Text available online at https://www.upi.com/Archives/1940/06/03/German-bombers-hit-Paris/4413583280132/.

United States Army. After Action Report of the Thirty-Eighth Armored Infantry Division, Seventh Armored Division, August 1944, pp. 2–3. Text available for download at "7th Armored Division: 38th Armored Infantry Battallion: 38 AIB After Action Reports," at https://www.7tharmddiv.org/docrep/#4408.

———. "31st Tank Bn Records of Action of Night of 15–16 August 1944: Relating to the Tank Buried at Chartres." US Army After Action Report. Compiled by Wesley Johnston at *U. S. 7th Armored Division Association* (website). 2008. Text available online at https://webcache.googleusercontent.com/search?q=cache:OHZqb AHCVRwJ:https://www.7tharmddiv.org/docrep/images/Places-Maps-Photos/ France/Chartres%2520Area/31%2520Tank%2520Records%252015-16%2520Au gust%25201944.doc+&cd=1&hl=en&ct=clnk&gl=us&client=safari.

United States Army, Twentieth Corps. *The XX Corps: Its History and Service in World War II.* Halsted, KS: W.E.B.S., 1984.

United States Department of Health and Human Services. "Texas." *The Great Pandemic: The United States in 1918–1919.* Archived at https://cybercemetery.unt .edu/archive/allcollections/20090305003317/http://vietnamese.pandemicflu.gov/ pandemicflu/envi/24/_1918_pandemicflu_gov/your_state/texas.htm.

United States Military Academy. *The Howitzer, 1922.* Yearbook of the United States Corps of Cadets. West Point, NY: Corps of Cadets of the United States Military, 1922. Available online at http://cdm16919.contentdm.oclc.org/cdm/compound object/collection/howitzers/id/15221/rec/21.

———. *The Howitzer, 1923.* Yearbook of the United States Corps of Cadets. West Point, NY: Corps of Cadets of the United States Military, 1923. Available online at http://cdm16919.contentdm.oclc.org/cdm/compoundobject/collection/howitzers/ id/16151/rec/22.

———. *The Howitzer, 1924.* Yearbook of the United States Corps of Cadets. West Point, NY: Corps of Cadets of the United States Military, 1924. Available online at http://cdm16919.contentdm.oclc.org/cdm/compoundobject/collection/howitzers/ id/16713/rec/23.

———. *The Howitzer, 1925.* Yearbook of the United States Corps of Cadets. West Point, NY: Corps of Cadets of the United States Military, 1925. Available online at http://cdm16919.contentdm.oclc.org/cdm/compoundobject/collection/howitzers/ id/21024/rec/24.

University of Michigan Center for the History of Medicine. "Dallas, Texas." *Influenza Encyclopedia: The American Influenza Epidemic of 1918–1919; A Digital Encyclopedia., Dallas, Tx.* Accessed April 28, 2019, http://www.influenzaarchive.org/cities/ city-dallas.html#.

van der Hoeven, Hans. *Lost Memory: Libraries and Archives Destroyed in the Twentieth Century.* Paris: United Nations Educational, Scientific and Cultural Organization, 1996.

van der Meulen, Jan, Deborah Cole, and Rüdiger Hoyer. *Chartres: Sources and Literary Interpretation; A Critical Bibliography.* Boston: G. K. Hall, 1989.

Vickers, Salley. *The Cleaner of Chartres.* New York: Penguin Group, 2012.

Wikipedia. S.v. "Grand Quartier Général (1939–1940)." Last edited January 5, 2019. https://en.wikipedia.org/wiki/Grand_Quartier_Général_(1939–1940).

Wilson, George W. *Mischief, Mayhem and Miscreants: From the Quanah Tribune-Chief, Sept. 29, 1898, to May 18, 1899, and June 13, 1907, to May 27, 1909.* Manuel, TX: G. W. Wilson, 2012.

Winieska, Françoise. *Août 1944: La libération de Rambouillet, France: Missions de reconnaissance américaines à Rambouillet & ses proches environs en août 1944.* Rambouillet: SHARY, 1999.

Zaloga, Steven J. *Liberation of Paris 1944: Patton's Race for the Seine.* Campaign, 194. Oxford: Osprey, 2008.

Zay, Jean. *Souvenirs et solitude.* Paris: Rene Julliard, 1946.

———. "Instruction sur la protection en cas de guerre des monuments et oeuvres d'art dans les départments de l'intérieur." August 12, 1937, AMN R1 4, 3–4. Archives des museés nationaux, Paris.

Archives

Eure-et-Loir (Archives départmentales de la Eure-et-Loir):
  4T NC Art. 83
  4T NC Art. 84
Médiatheque Charenton-le-Pont (Mediathèque Charenton [Paris]):
  80 11 17—Biographical information on Captain Lucien Prieur
  80 3 53; 80 3 54; 80 3 55; 80 3 57; 80 3 59; 80 3 60; 80 3 61; 80 3 62; 80 3 63; 80 3 65—Historic monuments during the two world wars
  0081 028 009; 0081 028 010; 0081 028 011; 0081 028 0012; 0081 028 016; 0081 028 017—Restoration works in Eure-et-Loir
Médiathèque d'accueil et de recherche des archives nationales, Paris; Médiathèque d'accueil et de recherche des archives nationales, Paris.
Médiathèque de l'architecture et du pationce, Paris; Médiathèque de l'architecture et du patrimoine, Paris.
US National Archives, II, College Park, Maryland.

Newspapers

Amarillo Globe
Appleton Post Crescent
Benton Journal
Brooklyn Daily Eagle
Chicago Daily News
Chicago Daily Tribune
Dallas Morning News
Fort Worth Star-Telegram
Goldsboro N.C. News-Argus
Kansas City Star
New York Times

Oshkosh Northwestern
Quanah Times
Quanah Tribune-Chief
San Antonio Light
Stars & Stripes (Daily Newspaper of the US Armed Forces in the European Theatre of Operations)
Temple Daily Telegraph

Unpublished

Avril, Yves. Mayor of Chartres. Speech delivered at Chartres City Hall, August 16, 1996.

Douin, Paul. *The Diary of Father Paul Douin (August 12 through August 23, 1944)*. Transcribed by Agnes Douin, and translated by Marianne Pradoura.

French Military, Citations for Criox de Guerre avec Palm, and Legion of Merit.

Legaux, Cannon. Speech delivered at Chartres Cathedral, August 16, 1996.

Schulz, Eugene G. *The Colonel Griffith Story: Hero of Chartres Cathedral*. Milwaukee: (Unpublished), 2014.

Trouvelot, Jean. "Passive Defense Works Executed at the Cathedral of Chartres [September 1938 until 24 August 1939]," 20–25. Report dated February 22, 1940, to the Minister of National Education, appended to a report to the same minister, dated October 19, 1939. Archives départmentales de la Eure-et-Loir [4 NC Art. 83]. (Trouvelot, "Passive Defense Report")

———. Report to the Minister of National Education. March 11, 1946. Mediathèque Charenton (Paris), 81 28 16.

———. Report to the Director of Architecture, Office of Architecture, Minister of National Education, September 11, 1950, Mediathèque Charenton (Paris), 81 28 16.

US Army, Citations for Distinguished Service Cross, Silver Star, Legion of Honor, Purple Heart.

Yount, Andrea. "William Morris and the Society for the Preservation of Ancient Buildings: Nineteenth and Twentieth Century Historic Preservation in Europe." PhD dissertation, Western Michigan University, 2005. Text available online at https://pdfs.semanticscholar.org/f9d2/f23f2080276b6e9ac934b1dc983cf7f791f3.pdf.

Interviews and Direct Correspondence

Coffey, David, PhD
Coffey, Kevin
Griffin, Thomas N. (US Army, Ret.)
Griffith, Richard
Hendrix, Gary
Henegar, Jane
Irving, Alice (January 2015)
Papillon, Bertrand (May 2015)
Pradoura, Marianne
Schulz, Eugene G. (October 2014)

INDIRECT CORRESPONDENCE
Collier, General William A.
Cullen, Robert B.
DeKay, Virginia Harrison Griffith
Dugan, William L.
Foree, Kenneth
Griffith, Philip
Griffith, Colonel Welborn B., Jr.
Mattocks, Captain Carl K.
Spahr, Colonel D. D.
Stark, Colonel Melville I.
Reader's Digest, Editors of
US Army Command
Walker, General Walton H.

Index

215–16; Chartres and, 254; at
Chartres and Lèves, 226, 238–39;
French Army and, 341; informer
execution and, 238–39; Monfort
and, 205–6; in Normandy, 205–7;
Third Army and, 206–7
Foree, Kenneth, 258–59; *Dallas Morning
News* and, 254–55
Fort Campbell, 119
Fortitude South, 193–94
Fort Leavenworth school, 87–88, 89,
90, 113; G-2 at, 114–15; G-3 at,
114–15, 117, 119
Fort Slocum, 165, 167, 180, 336
Fouqueray, Anne, 309; Carlier and, 80;
Chartres and, 48–49; *Le Journal*
and, 70, 80
Fourth Armored Corps, 118, 162, 164
Fourth Armored Division, 161–62, 188
France, 39, 137, 296; air-raid sirens in,
129; Basilica of Saint-Denis in, 19,
21, 23, 75, 298; Battle of Amiens
and, 25; Big Bertha cannon and,
22, 297; cultural heritage in, 40;
D-Day in, xii, 194, 200, 339–40;
Fine Arts Administration in,
21; franc value in, 49; German
occupation in, 155–56, 158–59;
grenade factory explosions in,
17–19; growing German threat
and, 42–43; Griffith, T., in, 85–87,
89, 112; High Commission on
Civil Defense in the Ministry
of the Interior in, 42–43; June
bombing raids in, 133–34; La
Courneuve grenade factory
explosion in, 23, 75, 298; national
funerals in, 19; passive-defense
program in, 27–28, 42–43, 69,
74–75, 79, 126; reconstruction in,
40; Second Battle of the Marne
in, 25; War Powers Act and, 79;
wartime preservation planning in,
42. *See also* Historic Monuments

Commission; refugees and
displaced persons, World War II
French Army: FFI and, 341; in Reims,
xx–xxi; Senegalese members of, 158;
Thinot in, 289, 291; in World War
I, xx–xxi, 9; Zay and, 106, 337
French Forces of the Interior. *See* Forces
françaises de l'intérieur
French Revolution, xiv
Froidevaux, Yves-Marie, 130, 350;
Fongrenon and, 268, 269
FUSAG. *See* First US Army Group

G-2 Military Intelligence Department,
222; at Fort Leavenworth school,
114–15; in Marlborough, 189; in
Normandy, 202, 208–9
G-3 Military Operations Department,
343; in Chartres, 209, 221, 222,
223; at Fort Leavenworth school,
114–15, 117, 119; in Normandy,
202, 205, 209; responsibilities of,
162–63; Stark and, 163
Gaskill, Gordon: Chartres Cathedral and,
255–58; Eisenhower and, 257, 349;
Griffith, P., and, 258, 349; Irving on,
349–50; in *Reader's Digest*, 255–58,
349, 353
Gaudin, Jean: Paris studio of, 26, 99;
workshop, 271, 272
Génuys, Charles Louis, 299
German prisoners, in Chartres, 254
German troops: in Chartres, 214, 217,
218–19, 220–21, 223, 249–51,
252–54, 261; in Chartres and
Lèves, 242, 245, 247; clearing the
church at Chartres and, 225–26,
234; Reims and, xviii–xix, xxi–xxiii,
xxvi–xxviii; snipers and, 216, 217,
218, 220, 226, 227, 233, 235, 238,
249–51, 252–53, 349
Germany, 129; Angers and, 203; Austria
and, 78, 81; Battle of the Falaise
Pocket and, 204; Czechoslovakia

SAVING THE LIGHT AT CHARTRES

327; window anchors and, 48,
307–8; window coverings after,
122–23, 140, 266; workers for, 99,
103–4, 105; Zay and, xv, 98, 104–5.
See also transportation, for Chartres
Cathedral window relocation
window restoration, 3–4, 267; in Chartres
Cathedral crypt, 157–58; criticism
for reinstallation, 273; Lorin, F.,
and, 268, 271, 274; Trouvelot
on, 273–74, 351–52; window
frameworks and, 266; in World War
I, 26–27, 39–40; in World War II,
270–72, 273
window storage: crypt and, 101, 107;
excavation spaces for, 45; location
identification, 13, 76, 127–28;
moisture and, 266, 267. *See also*
Château de Fongrenon
World War I: aircraft in, 26, 41; Battle of
the Lys in, 298; French Army in,
xx–xxi, 9; grenade factory in, 17–19,
23, 298; Griffith, Jr. and, 13–14;
historic monuments and, xv, 17;
Historic Monuments Commission
in, x, xxvii, 21, 24, 26, 297; Historic
Monuments Department in, xxvii,
293, 294; Planchenault in, 300;
Prieur in, 300; Third Battle of Ypres
and, 210. *See also* Reims; window
removal, World War I

World War II, 312; Battle of Guadalcanal,
118, 161; Battle of the Bulge, 328,
346; military technology in, 112,
127; Munich Agreement and, 71,
94, 97; North Africa in, 70, 119,
161, 312, 329, 337; Operation
Jedburgh, 342–43; Roosevelt and,
111–12; tank destroyers in, 112,
113, 328. *See also specific topics*
Wyoming, 82–83

Yoshida (secret police), 58–61, 62–63
The Youth's Companion (magazine): British
Boy Scouts in, 13–14; Reims in, 13

Zay, Jean: Blum and, 71, 314; Cannes
Film Festival and, 70, 312; Chartres
Cathedral window removal and,
xv, 98, 104–5; death of, 106–7,
338; Dreyfus and, 72; education
system and, 314; evacuation orders
for historic monuments by, 97, 98,
103, 324; family of, 313–14; in
French Army, 106, 337; Historical
Monuments Service and, 315–16;
Ministry of National Education
and Fine Arts and, 70, 75; in North
Africa, 312, 337; from Orléans,
71, 313; passion of, 72; politics
of, 71–72; in prison, 72–73, 106,
337–38; Resistance and, 72

384

About the Author

Victor A. Pollak has practiced as a business lawyer since 1976 with law firms in Chicago and Salt Lake City before turning to writing. He holds a BA from Antioch College, a JD Cum Laude from Loyola University of Chicago School of Law, and an MFA in writing from Pacific University. He divides his time between Tucson and Salt Lake City.